Mathematical Models of Attitude Change
Volume 1
CHANGE IN SINGLE ATTITUDES AND COGNITIVE STRUCTURE

HUMAN COMMUNICATION RESEARCH SERIES

PETER R. MONGE, Editor

Mathematical Models of Attitude Change
Volume 1
CHANGE IN SINGLE ATTITUDES AND COGNITIVE STRUCTURE

John E. Hunter
Department of Psychology
Michigan State University
East Lansing, Michigan

Jeffrey E. Danes
Department of Marketing
Virginia Polytechnic Institute and
State University
Blacksburg, Virginia

Stanley H. Cohen
Department of Psychology
West Virginia University
Morgantown, West Virginia

1984

ACADEMIC PRESS, INC.
(Harcourt Brace Jovanovich, Publishers)

Orlando   San Diego   New York   London
Toronto   Montreal   Sydney   Tokyo

ACADEMIC PRESS, INC.
Orlando, Florida 32887

United Kingdom Edition published by
ACADEMIC PRESS, INC. (LONDON) LTD.
24/28 Oval Road, London NW1 7DX

Library of Congress Cataloging in Publication Data

Hunter, John E. (John Edward), Date
    Mathematical models of attitude change.

    (Human communication research series)
    Bibliography: v. 1, p.
    Includes index.
    Contents: v. 1. Change in single attitudes and
cognitive structure.
    1. Attitude change--Mathematical models. 2. Social
groups--Mathematical models. 3. Sociometry--Mathematical
models. 4. Cognition--Mathematical models. I. Danes,
Jeffrey E. II. Cohen, Stanley H. (Stanley Hymie),
Date. III. Title. IV. Series.
HM291.H84 1984   303.3'8   84-3044
ISBN 0-12-361901-7 (v. 1 : alk. paper)

To our families . . .

Ronda, Tanya, and Lance Hunter
Kathy, Nathan, Eric, and Mark Danes
Judy, Adam, and Joshua Cohen

Contents

II. ATTITUDE CHANGE STUDIES

10. Attitude and Source Change in a Simulated Social Network

11. Change in Political Party and Issue Attitudes

12. Belief Change and Accumulated Information

13. Cognitive Inconsistency and Change in Purchase Intention

III.   RELATIONS BETWEEN ATTITUDES

Preface

This volume presents a detailed and comprehensive treatment of mathematical models of attitude change. Previous work in attitude change has been devoted to verbal discussions of attitude change theories. This volume translates verbal theory to families of mathematical attitude change models. The mathematical models presented in this volume address three areas: (1) existing verbal attitude change theories which are translated into families of mathematical models; (2) attitude change theories that have been previously quantified are critiqued, and alternative mathematical models are given; and (3) new theory and corresponding mathematical models are offered.

This volume also addresses a somewhat neglected area of attitude change theory: models of source change—change in the attitude toward the source of information. For nearly every attitude change model discussed, corresponding models for change in attitude toward the source of information are also given. This volume therefore explicitly considers two types of attitude change: attitude toward the object of the message (or what is ordinarily termed attitude change) and attitude toward the source of the message (or what we have termed source change). In Part I, mathematical models of attitude change are derived from the following theories:

Reinforcement theory
Information processing theory
Social judgment theory
Balance theory
Congruity theory
Cognitive dissonance theory
Cognitive consistency theory

Part II presents empirical work designed to test selected mathematical models of attitude change. Chapter 10 compares the predictions made by the following models: reinforcement, information processing, social judgment, balance, congruity, and dissonance. The results of this experiment support the information processing paradigm. Chapter 11 uses panel data obtained from survey research to compare the predictions made by reinforcement, congruity, and information processing theory. This study also supports the information processing paradigm. Chapter 12 deals with an attitude-related variable: belief and belief change. The results of two experiments designed to test four information processing models of belief change are discussed in Chapter 12. The model that gave the best fit to the data assumes that belief change is proportional to the amount of change advocated and inversely proportional to the amount of information a person has accumulated on the topic prior to the reception of a message. Chapter 13 deals with change in behavioral intentions rather than attitude change. This chapter reports on two studies that compare models derived from cognitive consistency theory with models derived from information processing theory. Once again the information processing models gave the best fit to the data.

Part III moves from the consideration of how single attitudes change to a systematic study of how many, but related, attitudes change. Related attitudes can be pictured as forming a hierarchical structure. Specific and concrete attitudinal objects may be viewed as subordinate to more general, abstract attitude objects. For example, one's attitude toward the war in Iran is an attitude on a specific topic and is less abstract than one's attitude toward war in general. In this case, one would expect attitudes toward war in general to have an influence on attitudes toward specific wars.

Chapter 14 discusses a general theory for change in hierarchically organized attitudes and is followed by a presentation of research designed to test different hierarchical models which is reported in Chapter 15. The attitude–behavior controversy is addressed from a hierarchical perspective and is reported in Chapter 16. Chapter 17 develops models of change in hierarchically organized attitudes using alternative theories of attitude change.

The development and use of communication and attitude change models is indeed pervasive. Communication and attitude change are topics of concern in a variety of disciplines: administration, advertising, business, communication, consumer behavior, decision sciences, education, journalism, management, marketing science, political science, psychology, sociology, and speech. By their very nature these topics have been and will probably remain multidisciplinary areas of study, and the work presented here reflects that fact. The topical areas in this volme include psychology, sociology, communication, political science, and marketing science.

This volume was written for advanced undergraduate and graduate students whose training requires a comprehensive and rigorous treatment of attitude change. Its approach is eclectic; that is, we attempted to include all major theories of attitude change as well as other approaches to the study of communication, cognition, and change. Most of these theories, however, have not been previously quantified. The work presented in this volume is devoted primarily to deriving mathematical models from the major (and minor) premises of the major theories of attitude change. That is, each theory is represented by a family of models that are common in major premises but differ in minor premises. A working knowledge of algebra and sequences and familiarity with calculus and matrix algebra are the only mathematical tools required. In nearly all cases, the theories and models are verbally described before translation to equations.

We wish to give special thanks to those who made contributions to selected chapters in this volume: T. Daniel Coggin (Chapter 11), Ralph L. Levine (Chapter 14), O. Karl Mann (Chapter 13), M. Scott Poole (Chapters 15 and 16), Scott E. Sayers (Chapter 14), and Joseph Woelfel (Chapter 12).

For their continual support and encouragement, we also express our gratitude to friends, colleagues, and staff (far too numerous to mention by name) at our respective institutions: the Department of Psychology at Michigan State University, the Department of Marketing at Virginia Polytechnic Institute and State University, and the Department of Psychology at West Virginia University. In particular, we give special thanks to Janice Blevins of Virginia Polytechnic Institute and State University for her help with typing various drafts of this book. Our appreciation is also extended to Ginger Wagner and Cathy Gorman (Major Illustrators) and to Vincent Scott (Graphic Arts Supervisor) of the Graphics Learning Resource Center at Virginia Polytechnic Institute and State University, Blacksburg, Virginia. Last but not least, we wish to express sincere appreciation to Peter R. Monge for his advice and counsel and to the staff at Academic Press whose expenditures of time and effort on behalf of this book have been exemplary, and with whom it has been a joy to work.

CHAPTER 1

Introduction

This book is devoted to the development of mathematical models of attitude change and group processes. The book uses contemporary theory for the development of the mathematical models. We present the core of each theory in a way that renders a direct comparison and contrast among each of the theories. Narrative presentations of most of the theories presented in this book are available in the classic works of Insko (1967) and Kiesler *et al.* (1969). A more recent review of contemporary and classic theories of attitude change is given by Petty and Cacioppo (1981).

The connecting thread among all models is *communication*. All of the mathematical models developed in this book contain most of the major components of the communication process: source, message, receiver, and effects. Channels of communication are not explicitly considered. Our major area of emphasis is the change produced by the message, that is, changes in attitude toward an object, attitude toward the source of the message, beliefs about the object, and behavioral intentions.

SOME IMPORTANT DEFINITIONS

Contemporary theories of attitude change have been plagued by a proliferation of incompatible definitions of the term attitude (see Fishbein and Ajzen, 1975). The term "attitude" has been used for emotional states, behavioral

1

dispositions, beliefs, opinions, and perceived social distances. We view *attitude* as an affective, evaluative, or emotional response to some object. Attitudinal objects may be ideas, places, things, or persons. For example, "Kathy" may be the object, and "I love Kathy" may be the attitudinal response. All of the group dynamics models presented in Volume 2 of this work are derived from selected models of attitude change. Thus, this work serves the important function of connecting two heretofore seemingly separate areas of study: attitude change and group dynamics.

For all models of attitude change, *messages* play the central role in stimulating change, and there are two major types of messages: external and internal. *External messages* are those transmitted from a source (speaker, medium, or advertiser) to a receiver (listener or consumer). For external messages, there are two subtypes: explicit and probe. For the *explicit message*, the source attempts to define (or redefine) the affective response to the object. When a source tells a receiver that "Jerry Brown (object) was a good governor (affect)," the source has presented an explicit message. For the *probe message*, the source may not attempt to define (or redefine) the attitudinal object. An example probe message is "What do you think of Jerry Brown?" In this case, the attitudinal response to the message is the same as the attitudinal response to the object of the message. *Internal messages* are those transmitted within the mind of an individual receiver; they occur when a person merely "thinks" about an attitudinal object or sets of attitudinal objects. In all cases, the attitudinal message is viewed in terms of its affective, evaluative, or emotional meaning.

The term message is often used in an ambiguous way. Unless otherwise stated, we use message to describe a singular, unitary phrase describing an object, such as "war is hell." However, a paragraph describing the horrors of war is also often refered to as a "message." In our terminology, such a paragraph would be defined as consisting of multiple, compound, or sequential messages. Chapter 3 in this volume presents information processing models to deal with processing many messages on the same topic.

Much of the past work in attitude theory has ignored *source change*, that is, change in the attitude toward the source of information. This book considers both attitude and source change; for every basic attitude change model discussed, source change models are also given. As discussed in Volume 2 of this work, both source change and attitude change play an important role in the development of theories for group dynamics.

This study also considers one other important approach to communication, cognition, and change: the work of William J. McGuire and Robert S. Wyer, which treats beliefs and behavioral intentions as subjective probabilities. In the area of "cognitive organization and change," we develop several mathematical models for change in belief and change in behavioral intention.

Belief has often been used in ambiguous ways. It has been used as a statement, acceptance or rejection of a statement, and partial acceptance or rejection. For example, the statement "Jerry Brown will run for President" reflects a particular belief. However, not all who consider this statement will agree with it. If one agrees, then one "believes the statement is true." If one disagrees with the statement, then one "believes the statement is false." Of course, complete acceptance or rejection are not the only two possible outcomes, for there could be partial acceptance, that is, partial belief. If a person half accepts and half rejects, then the person is "uncertain," that is, not sure if the statement is true or false. Uncertainties in belief are captured using subjective probabilites. The connection between subjective probability and belief is given by the degree to which a person accepts a statement. If there is complete agreement, then the subjective probability is 1.0; if there is complete disagreement, then the subjective probability is .00; if there is half agreement, then the subjective probability is .50. Belief is viewed as a continuous variable. Many authors [see Fishbein & Ajzen (1975)] break down statements into "objects" and "attributes" and speak of the association between them. For the statement given above, "Jerry Brown" is the object and "will run for President" is the attribute. According to Fishbein and Ajzen (1975), if a person thinks that a given statement is "true" then there is a perceived perfect association between the object and attribute. If a person thinks that a given statement is false, then there is no perceived association between the object and attribute.

Behavioral *intentions* are also treated as subjective probabilities; they are derived from statements such as "Next spring I will buy an American car." For belief change, *messages* are viewed as sets of symbols that associate (or disassociate) an object with (from) an attribute. For attitude change, the message "Jerry Brown was a great governor" is viewed in terms of the affect it conveys. However, for belief change, the same message may also be viewed in terms of the belief value it communicates. Occasionally, the term *component message* is used to emphasize the fact that only one object and one attribute are contained in the message. Like beliefs, messages are seen as continua, ranging from "true" to "false."

The last part of Volume 1 considers models of attitude change for many rather than just a single attitude. Related attitudes can be pictured as forming a hierarchical structure; that is, specific and concrete attitudinal objects may be viewed as subordinate to more general, abstract attitude objects. For example, one's attitude toward the war in Iran is an attitude on a specific topic and is less abstract than one's attitude toward war in general. Since war in general encompasses all wars regardless of their geographic location, one would therefore expect attitudes toward war in general to have an influence on attitudes toward specific wars. The mathematical models presented in the last part of Volume 1 consider how attitudes change when they are part of a general-to-specific hierarchy.

BACKGROUND AND CONTEXT

The first part of this volume quantifies six major theories of attitude change: reinforcement, information processing, social judgement, balance, congruity, and dissonance theory. The last chapter in Part I, considers a newer approach to the study of communication, cognitive organization, and change: theories of cognitive consistency. This last chapter does not deal with attitude, as defined above; but rather, it considers cognitive organization and change based on the relations between beliefs and beliefs and behavioral intentions.

The six major attitude theories fall into the following categories. First, there are the theories that attempt to predict attitude change on the basis of the content of the message, and there are two categories. "Reinforcement theories" assume that a message with positive affect will induce positive attitude change and a message with negative affect will induce negative attitude change. The theories that assume the impact of a message is a function of the difference between the message and the receiver's attitude will be called "information processing theories." Information processing theories include Carl I. Hovland's work on proportional change (the linear discrepancy hypothesis), Muzafer Sherif's work on social judgement, and Leon Festinger's work on cognitive dissonance. A third category of theory is the work labeled "affective consistency," and the two major theories that fall within this domain are Fritz Heider's and Theodore Newcomb's balance theory and Charles Osgood's and Percy Tannenbaum's congruity theory. Finally, there is the work by William J. McGuire and Robert S. Wyer, which we categorized as cognitive consistency theory. The last chapter of Part I, however, shows that cognitive consistency can be derived from information processing principles; thus, cognitive consistency theory can also be classified with those theories listed under information processing.

Each of the above theories has a number of major and minor postulates. The major postulates constitute the substantive core of the theory, and they are used to create the "basic" model for each theory. However, to test the theory in varying contexts, additional assumptions must be added to the theory to generate specific predictions. These minor assumptions may or may not be made; and therefore it is the minor assumptions that are the primary causes of ambiguities within any single theory. The presence of models that differ only by minor assumptions result in theories that are represented by a family of mathematical models, rather than one single model.

The attitude change theories presented in Part I require initial assumptions to be explicitly stated. For example, a given theory may assert that change is monotone increasing (or decreasing). However, it is known that there are an infinite number of monotonic functions. Thus, the first model is derived using a simple linear function. If other monotone functions give substantially the same results, no other examples are presented. On the other hand, if there are gross qualitative differences between alternative versions, then a further selection of examples is presented.

The context for building the attitude change models in Part I was carefully selected to maximize the comparability among the models representing different theories. The context selected is called *passive communication*; in this context, the receiver simply receives messages from a source about an object. The initial attitude toward the object may be positive or negative, the initial attitude toward the source may be positive or negative, and the message may be one of endorsement or castigation. The receiver is asked only to listen to (or read) the message and is not encouraged to respond in active ways such as role play or openly commit himself to a position that might be contrary to that taken by his peers or reference groups. The passive communication paradigm has been used by congruity, balance, and other affective consistency theorists. Brown (1962) has noted cognitive dissonance may also be considered in this framework. Moreover, the passive communication paradigm was the traditional paradigm for the early work in information processing [Anderson (1959), Hovland *et al.* (1953)] and in communication [Katz and Lazersfled (1955), Sherif *et al.* (1965)]. By and large, the majority of the empirical work on attitude change has employed the passive communication paradigm.

Within the paradigm of passive communication, a static analysis of the attitude change situation reveals five basic elements: a *source* who delivers a *message* to a *receiver* about some *object* through some *channel*. At any moment in time, it is assumed that one can use an affective or evaluative scale to measure

1. the *attitude* of the receiver toward the object,
2. the affective or evaluative content of the *message*, and
3. the receiver's affect toward the *source*.

Messages and attitudes toward the object and source are dynamic, that is, they may change over time. For the most part, the analysis will be restricted to two discrete points in time: immediately prior to and subsequent to message presentation. If n denotes the time prior to message presentation and $n + 1$ denotes the time after message presentation, then the situation is described by:

a_n = the attitude of the receiver toward the object at time n

s_n = the attitude of the receiver toward the source at time n

m_n = the affective value of the message at time n

The term *attitude change* is reserved for the change in the receiver's attitude toward the object. The term *source change* is reserved for the change in his attitude toward the source. Both attitude and source change may be expressed as

$$\Delta a = a_{n+1} - a_n \qquad \text{and} \qquad \Delta s = s_{n+1} - s_n$$

Both attitude and source change are modeled as functions of m, a, and s, and that is

$$\Delta a = f(a, s, m) \qquad \text{and} \qquad \Delta s = g(a, s, m)$$

The passive communication paradigm used for Part I of this volume has several advantages, simplicity is one; but the most important is that all models of attitude and source change are found as functions of a, s, and m. Thus, all represented theories may be easily compared and contrasted.

This volume is organized so that once Part I is completed, the reader can move to any section. The last two parts are relatively independent of each other. Part II contains empirical studies that compare selected models against one another. Part III develops models of change for attitudes embedded in a hierarchical system.

Volume 2 extends selected attitude change models to group processes and develops mathematical models of group communication and group dynamics.

THE PASSIVE COMMUNICATION CONTEXT

The next seven chapters develop theories of attitude and source change in the passive communication context, that is, in settings where the receiver is simply asked to listen to (or read) a message (or set of messages) describing some attitudinal object.

Whenever a theory contains a basic model, the basic model is presented first and is followed by technical modifications. The modifications of the basic model are given as a table and a discussion. The reader may choose to first read the basic models and then move to more detailed elaborations of each model. Not all chapters contain basic models.

The eighth and last chapter in Part I (Chapter 9) is devoted to belief rather than attitude change. This chapter presents cognitive consistency theory and shows that this theory must have a much more narrow application than has been previously assumed. Finally, it is shown that the essential parts of cognitive consistency theory can be derived from information processing principles.

CHAPTER 2

Reinforcement Theory

The models to be presented in this chapter are those that assume that agreement strengthens an attitude whereas disagreement weakens it. This basic theory is implicit in much of the analysis of the attitude change process. To illustrate this, the assumption will be cast in the language of three groups: learning theorists, mass communication theorists, and extreme socialization theorists.

To a learning theorist an attitude is the receiver's covert evaluative response to an object. If the source agrees with the receiver, he is rewarding that response. If the source disagrees with the receiver, he is punishing that response. This conception of attitudes and attitude change has been argued by such theorists as Doob (1947) and Miller and Dollard (1941).

To mass communication theorists such as Katz and Lazarfeld (1955) or Klapper (1949), an attitude is a position held by the subject on some social or political issue. If the receiver is exposed to a message that agrees with his position, then his attitude is "bolstered" and his position becomes more entrenched. If the receiver is exposed to a message that disagrees with his position, then his attitude is "shaken" and his loyalties waver. Thus a mass communication theorist measures the strength of an attitude by the receiver's resistance to a persuasive message. If a single message has only a limited impact, then the more polar the receiver's attitude, the greater the number of messages it will take to shift the receiver's attitude to neutral. Thus the mass communication theorist's "resistance to a persuasive message" is precisely equivalent to the learning theorist's "resistance to extinction."

To an extreme socialization theorist such as Bandura (1962) or Bronfenbrenner (1976), an attitude is a set of verbal statements that the subject acquires by imitating other people. Here there are two distinct theories. The first is a passive imitation theory. If the receiver is passively watching the source without considering the consequences of his own future actions, then a message that agrees with his position increases the probability of imitation by strengthening the memory trace of the corresponding act. A message that disagrees with the receiver's position interferes with his later recall. The second is an active imitation theory. If the receiver actively considers the consequences of imitating or not imitating the source, then he implicitly assumes (and anticipates) that if he imitates the source, the source will be pleased, whereas if he does not imitate the source, the source will be displeased. The extent to which the receiver will internalize the actions of the source is the extent to which the source serves as a positive model for the receiver's imitation. Both imitation theories have the same mathematical implication: the attitude is strengthened by agreement and weakened by disagreement.

BASIC REINFORCEMENT MODEL

The basic theory of reinforcement postulates that the message issued by the source either reinforces or punishes the listener's attitudinal response. This process can be formulated in two tables. The first generates the basic equation for attitude change and the second generates the basic equation for source change. The other models in this chapter are derived by making variations in these equations that stem from specialized technical assumptions that differentiate one reinforcement model from another.

Table 2.1 characterizes the attitude change process: reinforcement strengthens the attitude whereas punishment weakens it. One crucial fact brought out by this table is that strengthening a positive attitude means that attitude change is positive whereas strengthening a negative attitude means that attitude change is negative. Thus a positive message has a positive impact on a positive attitude and a negative message has a negative impact on a negative attitude. On the other hand, a positive message punishes a negative attitude which weakens that attitude. To weaken a negative attitude is to cause a change that is algebraically positive. Thus the algebraic sign of the impact of a positive message is positive for either a positive or a negative attitude, though for different reasons. A similar statement applies to the negative sign of the weakening of a positive attitude by a negative message. From this it follows that the algebraic sign of attitude change is predicted by reinforcement theory

TABLE 2.1

REINFORCEMENT THEORY: ATTITUDE CHANGE

Attitude toward object a	Message value m	Reinforcement process	Attitude change Δa
+	+	Strengthen positive object attitude	+
+	−	Punish positive object attitude	−
−	+	Punish negative object attitude	+
−	−	Strengthen negative object attitude	−

to be the same as the algebraic sign of the message value, that is,

$$\text{sign}(\Delta a) = \text{sign}(m)$$

The simplest equation with this property is

$$\Delta a = \alpha m, \qquad \alpha > 0 \qquad (2.1)$$

Reinforcement theory argues that all receivers react in the same direction to the message. A positive message will create positive change in all receivers; that is, after the message each receiver will be more favorable or less unfavorable toward the object as a consequence of the message. A negative message will cause all receivers to shift in the direction of a more negative attitude toward the object; receivers will either be more unfavorable or less favorable toward the object.

The amount of change is assumed to be a function of the strength of the message. This in turn is assumed to be a function of its affective value.

Like most workers in the area, reinforcement theorists have focused on the impact of the message on the receiver's attitude toward the object, that is, attitude change. Past theorists have given less attention to the possibility of change in the receiver's attitude toward the source, which we will call "source change." Thus the analysis below is based less on past theoretical work and more on the general body of reinforcement theory itself. As before, we can differentiate three categories of reinforcement theorists: those who view attitude change as a special case of stimulus–response learning, those who view it as a species of imitation, and the mass media communication theorists. Despite the differences in terminology, reinforcement theorists all draw the same basic distinctions that ultimately produce the same qualitative theory of source change. In all cases, source change will depend on whether the source is rewarding or punishing the receiver's attitudinal response.

Table 2.2 characterizes source change. The basic principle is that, if the source reinforces the receiver, then there is an immediate positive emotional

TABLE 2.2

Listener's attitude a	Source message m	Reinforcement condition	Reaction to source	Source change Δs
+	+	Reward	Pleasure	+
+	−	Punish	Pain	−
−	+	Punish	Pain	−
−	−	Reward	Pleasure	+

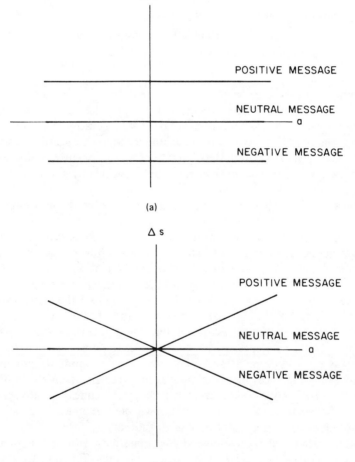

(a)

(b)

Fig. 2.1. Basic reinforcement model for (a) attitude change and (b) source change.

reaction that results in positive change toward the source. If the source punishes the listener, then there is an immediate negative reaction that causes negative source change. In Table 2.2 we see that the algebraic sign of source change is always the same as the algebraic sign of the product of the listener's object attitude and the source message value, that is,

$$\text{sign}(\Delta s) = \text{sign}(am)$$

The simplest equation with this property is

$$\Delta s = \beta ma \tag{2.2}$$

This completes our derivation of the basic reinforcement model:

$$\Delta a = \alpha m \quad \text{and} \quad \Delta s = \beta ma \tag{2.3}$$

The graphs for these models are given in Fig. 2.1.

The remainder of this chapter presents various theoretical and technical alternative models consistent with reinforcement theory. We shall first present the attitude change models and then the source change models. A summary of the variations in reinforcement theory is given in Tables 2.3 and 2.4.

THEORETICAL AND TECHNICAL ALTERNATIVES

Fishbein's Attitude Theory

Fishbein (1961, 1965, 1967) and Fishbein and Ajzen (1975) assume that an object can be viewed as a bundle of attributes. The receiver's attitude toward the object is then derived from his evaluations of the attributes. Following Rosenberg (1956) and others, Fishbein used the following model for combining values across attributes:

$$A = \sum_{j=1}^{n} b_j a_j \tag{2.4}$$

where A is the attitude toward the object, a_j the value of the jth attribute, and b_j the subjective probability that the object has the jth attribute.

Fishbein's basic model is not a model of change but a static model that relates the receiver's attitude to the evaluative beliefs that pertain to the object. In our notation, Fishbein's model is

$$a = \sum_i b_i m_i \tag{2.5}$$

where b_i is the subjective probability that the belief is true and m_i the emotional value of the belief, that is, the message value of the belief statement. A dynamic model of attitude change must be derived from this static model by asserting

TABLE 2.3

REINFORCEMENT ATTITUDE CHANGE: SUMMARY

Model	Assumptions
Basic reinforcement: constant change $\Delta a = \alpha m, \alpha > 0$	Constant change. All receivers are equally affected by messages. Positive messages produce positive change; negative messages produce negative change.
Fishbein's impression formation $a_n = \omega \sum_{i=1}^{n} m_i$ $\omega = w b_0 (1 - b_0)$	Receiver forms new beliefs about an object. Sequential messages, that is, sequential attribute descriptions, are presented; each message describes the object using a different attribute. For simplicity, each message is assumed to have equal weight w and equal initial belief b_0 such as $b_0 = .50$, that is, an uncertain object-attribute association.
Fishbein's repetition $\Delta a = \alpha m$ $\alpha = w b_i (1 - b_i)$	Same as basic reinforcement model except α is not a fixed constant but varies from person to person and attribute to attribute.
Polarity $\Delta a = \alpha m / 1 + a^2$	Same as basic model except extreme attitudes are more resistant to change.
Absolute bounds $\Delta a = \begin{cases} \alpha m(M - a) & \text{if} \quad m = + \\ \alpha m(M + a) & \text{if} \quad m = - \end{cases}$	Same as constant change except upper (M) and lower (L) attitude values are assumed. Symmetric model is assumed, that is, $L = -M$
Probability bounds $\Delta a = \begin{cases} \alpha m(1 - a) & \text{if} \quad m = + \\ \beta m a & \text{if} \quad m = - \end{cases}$	Same as absolute bounded model except nonsymmetric model is assumed. Attitude is treated as the probability that a receiver will make a positive statement about the object. This model is similar to the Bush–Mosteller linear operator model (1955).
Absolute bounds with polarity $\Delta a = \alpha m(M^2 - a^2)$	Same as absolute bounded model, except polarity effect is assumed
Probability bounded with polarity $\Delta a = \alpha m a(1 - a)$	Same as probability bounded model, except polarity effect is assumed.

TABLE 2.3 (cont.)

Model	*Assumptions*
Reinforcement vs. punishment $\Delta a = \begin{cases} \alpha(1 - a) \text{ if } a = \text{pro} > \frac{1}{2}; m > 0 \\ (\alpha - \gamma)(1 - a) \text{ if } a = \text{con} < \frac{1}{2}; m > 0 \\ -\beta a \text{ if } a = \text{con} < \frac{1}{2}; m < 0 \\ -(\beta - \delta)a \text{ if } a = \text{pro} > \frac{1}{2}; m < 0 \end{cases}$	Agreement acts as reward; disagreement as punishment. Attitude is probability of receiver making a positive (pro) statement about object. The parameters $(\alpha - \gamma)$ and $\beta - \delta$ are punishing parameters.
Two-factor theory: pro and con $\Delta a = (2\alpha - \gamma)m$	It is assumed that receivers have two response tendencies, pro and con; messages act on both tendencies.
Two-factor theory: nonsymmetric $\Delta a = \dfrac{(\alpha + \beta)a}{(\alpha + \beta)a + 1 - \beta}(1 - a)$	Nonsymmetric two-factor hypothesis with attitude as a probability of response.
Two factor theory: symmetric $\Delta a = \dfrac{2\alpha a}{2\alpha a + 1 - \alpha}(1 - a)$	Same as above, except reward and punishment are symmetric; $\beta = \alpha$ and both β and α are small.
Basic model with extinction $\Delta a = \alpha m - \varepsilon a$	The magnitude of attitude change is weakened by reactive inhibition, that is, the amount of "effort" or "fatigue" produced during the response. This model follows from Hull (1943). The parameter ε measures the strength of reactive inhibition.
Basic model with source credibility $\Delta a = \text{credibility } \alpha m$	Sources of high credibility produce greater attitude change than those with low credibility.
Unbounded attitude toward source Credibility $= e^{\sigma s}/1 + e^{\sigma s}$	Logistic ogive. Credibility is a symmetric function of the receiver's attitude toward the source s. Credibility ranges from zero when $s = -\infty$ and one when $s = +\infty$. σ is a scaling parameter corresponding to the derivative of the ogive at $s = 0$.
Bounded attitude toward source Credibility $= (s + M)/2M$	Attitudes toward source are assumed to have upper and lower bounds. Credibility is zero at the lower bound $-M$ and one at the upper bound $+M$.
Attitude toward source as probability Credibility $= s$	Attitude toward source is treated as probability of receiver making a positive statement about the source.

TABLE 2.4

S<small>MALL</small> R<small>EINFORCEMENT</small> S<small>OURCE</small> C<small>HANGE</small> M<small>ODELS</small>: S<small>UMMARY</small>

Model	Assumptions
Basic	
$\Delta s = \beta am$	Source change is positive when source agrees with receiver and negative when they disagree. Source change has no limits and is a monotone function of the product am.
Asymptotic	
$\Delta s = \dfrac{\beta}{[1 + (am)^2]^{1/2}} am$	Same as above except source change levels off for large agreement or disagreement.
Polarity effects	
$\Delta s = \dfrac{\beta}{1 + s^2} am$	Source change as defined by basic model is modified to account for potential difficulty in modifying established attitudes toward the source.
Polarity and asymptotic effect	
$\Delta s = \dfrac{\beta}{1 + s^2} \dfrac{am}{[1 + (am)^2]^{1/2}}$	Basic model modified by both polarity and asymptotic effect.
Absolute limits	
$\Delta s = \beta am(M^2 - s^2)$	Attitudes toward source have upper (M) and lower (L) bounds; $L = -M$. Polarity effect is implicitly assumed.
$\Delta s = \beta(a - \tfrac{1}{2})ms(1 - s)$	Both attitude toward source and attitude toward object are defined as the probability of receiver making positive statements about source or object.

change in one of the components. Fishbein has presented no mathematical model for such processes.

In principle, Fishbein's model would predict change from either of two kinds of messages: a message that changes a subjective probability b_i or a message that changes an affective value m_i. However, in practice there are very few messages that seek to change the affective value implied by a belief. Furthermore, Lutz (1975) found that it is much more difficult to write messages that will change the affective meaning of beliefs than it is to write messages that will change subjective probabilities. In the following derivations we assume that all messages are arguments for or against beliefs. Our convention is to break down passages and utterances into a succession of component messages that apply to single beliefs. This means that a basic model of change would consider one attribute or evaluative belief at a time. Thus the basic model is a model of belief change. Because Fishbein is a reinforcement theorist, he would assume that an argument in favor of the belief will increase the subjective probability whereas an argument against the belief will decrease the subjective probability. This suggests the model

$$\Delta b = w$$

where the sign of w is given by the direction of the argument and the magnitude of w depends on the strength of the argument, that is, the weight w is a message value for the subjective probability. However, subjective probability is bounded above by 1 and below by 0 and hence the model must be nonlinear:

$$\Delta b = wb(1 - b) \tag{2.6}$$

The impact of such an argument on attitude depends on the value of the ith attribute. That is,

$$\Delta a = \sum \Delta(b_i m_i) = m_i \Delta b_i = m_i w b_i (1 - b_i) \tag{2.7}$$

Fishbein's Impression-Formation Model

According to Fishbein and Ajzen (1975), there should be two phases to attribute development: an impression-formation phase in which the receiver is being introduced to new beliefs about the object and a following period in which messages are devoted to changing existing beliefs. In this section we shall derive Fishbein's additive impression formation model by assuming that we are considering the first messages about an object and that each message pertains to a different attribute. For simplicity we assume that the attributes are numbered in the order in which they are introduced. The messages will be assumed to assert the presence of the attribute in question. Thus the messages assert attribute 1, attribute 2, and so on. The corresponding attribute values are thus m_1, m_2, and so on. For simplicity we also assume that each message has the same weight, though this is easily modified.

As each attribute is asserted for the first time, the subjective probability increases from some baseline value such as $b = .50$ suitable for objects of its type. For example, if the object is a person, then the baseline probability for friendly would be high whereas the baseline probability for hideous would be low. Thus the initial increase in probability is

$$\Delta b = wb_0(1 - b_0) \tag{2.8}$$

For simplicity we ignore the differences in baseline across attributes. If the argument weights are all equal and if the baselines are all equal, then the probability increase is constant across attributes and can be denoted by a parameter. Let us use ω for that parameter and define it as

$$\omega = wb_0(1 - b_0) \qquad (2.9)$$

The attitude change produced by the nth message is then given by

$$\Delta a = \sum m_i \Delta b_i = m_n \Delta b_n = m_n \omega = \omega m_n \qquad (2.10)$$

This formula for attitude change differs from the basic reinforcement model only in using the parameter ω in place of α. The succession of attitude values observed would be

$$
\begin{aligned}
a_1 &= \omega m_1 \\
a_2 &= \omega m_1 + \omega m_2 \\
a_3 &= \omega m_1 + \omega m_2 + \omega m_3 \\
&\ \ \vdots
\end{aligned}
\qquad (2.11)
$$

that is, each message adds the amount ωm_n to the preceding attitude value. This is the reason it is called an "additive" model. The general formula for the nth attitude value is

$$a_n = \sum_{i=1}^{n} \omega m_i = \omega \sum_{i=1}^{n} m_i \qquad (2.12)$$

that is, the attitude toward the object is simply proportional to the sum of the message values heard to that point.

This additive model from reinforcement theory is in sharp contrast to the nonadditive model derived from information processing theory (discussed in Chapter 3). This point was made at some length in the raging argument between Fishbein (Fishbein and Ajzen, 1975) and Anderson (1971) in regard to impression formation.

Fishbein's Repetition Model

The general attitude change equation for Fishbein is

$$\Delta a = \alpha m$$

where m is the m_i for the attribute in the message and

$$\alpha = wb_i(1 - b_i) \qquad (2.13)$$

This is the same as the basic reinforcement model except that the value of α is not a fixed constant but varies with attribute and person depending on how many messages the receiver has had on that attribute. In particular, this model predicts that repetitions will have a diminishing impact. Once the subjective probability has reached one on a given dimension, further repetition will have no effect at all.

We now consider further modifications of the basic reinforcement model.

Polarity and Attitude Change

If the assumption that all individuals change by the same amount seems unreasonable, one might well ask which receivers would be least affected. Several studies [Cantril (1944), Cantril (1946), Hutchinson (1949), Riland (1959), and Weksel and Hennes (1965)] have reported evidence that individuals with more polarized or extreme attitudes feel more intensely about the object. If receivers who feel more intensely are more resistant to the message, then attitude change will be inversely related to attitude polarity (the absolute magnitude of the attitude irrespective of sign). Attitude change is still proportional to message strength, but the message has rapidly diminishing impact on receivers with extreme attitudes. One model with this property is

$$\Delta a = \alpha m/(1 + a^2) \tag{2.14}$$

The graph of the polarity model is presented in Fig. 2.2b.

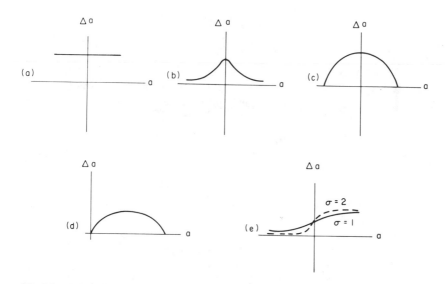

Fig. 2.2. Reinforcement models of attitude change as a function of attitude toward the object: (a) constant change (basic model), (b) constant change with polarity, (c) bounded with agreement–disagreement symmetry, (d) attitude as a probability, and (e) constant change with reward–punishment asymmetry.

Models with Absolute Bounds

The reinforcement models above have the property that, if a positive level of source credibility is maintained, then a sequence of messages that all have the same message value will drive the attitude to plus infinity if the messages are positive and minus infinity if the messages are negative. Thus these reinforcement models do not predict absolute limits on attitudes. However, the assumption of an absolute upper bound M is not logically inconsistent with reinforcement theory. Hence its existence or nonexistence can be treated as an ad hoc technical assumption. Mathematically this is fairly straight-forward. Let $\Delta a = f(a)$ be a model such that a increases without bound. To revise this equation so that it is zero at $a = M$ while leaving the sign of the equation unchanged for $a < M$, we multiply it by the factor $M - a$. Finally, to avoid a model that oscillates about the value M, we multiply by a constant α that is less than $1/f(a)$ near M. Thus, for example, the model

$$\Delta a = \alpha(m/M)(M - a) \quad \text{if} \quad m = + \tag{2.15}$$

would yield an asymptotic increase to M. In similar fashion we could impose a lower bound L on the attitudes produced by a negative message by multiplying through by the factor $a - L$ and a suitable small constant α. That is, if

$$\Delta a = f(a) \quad \text{for} \quad m < 0$$

produces a decrease without bound, then

$$\Delta a = f(a)\alpha(L - a) = \alpha f(a)(-L + a) \tag{2.16}$$

will yield an asymptotic decrease to L.

In particular, if the lower bound is the negative of the upper bound, that is $L = -M$, then a symmetric linear reinforcement model without polarity would be given by

$$\Delta a = \begin{cases} \alpha m(M - a) & \text{if} \quad m = + \tag{2.17} \\ \alpha m(M + a) & \text{if} \quad m = - \tag{2.18} \end{cases}$$

The most common bounded reinforcement models occur when the value of the attitude is assumed to be the probability that the subject will make a positive statement about the object. A nonsymmetric linear model without polarity, with α and β restricted to $0 \leq \alpha, \beta \leq 1$, would be

$$\Delta a = \begin{cases} \alpha m(1 - a) & \text{if} \quad m = + \tag{2.19} \\ \beta ma & \text{if} \quad m = - \tag{2.20} \end{cases}$$

The asymmetry here reflects the fact that an attitude is not a bipolar quantity in this model. In mathematical learning theory, the above model is known as a "Bush–Mosteller linear operator model" (1955). A linear operator model is a linear equation with probabilities as variables. This model was assumed by Cervin and Henderson (1961) in their model of dyadic interaction and by Rainio (1962) in his more general theory. It is a special case of the model proposed by Abelson (1967) for dyadic interaction that will be discussed below.

If the assumption of absolute upper and lower bounds is made in conjunction with the assumption of polarity effects, then a simpler and more unified approach is available. To impose both an upper bound M and a lower bound L, we can multiply an equation by both factors $M - a$ and $a - L$ or by the quadratic term $(M - a)(a - L)$. It is worth noting that this multiplication implicitly generates polarity effects without further modification. The resulting simplification is evident in the fact that a reinforcement model with upper bound M, lower bound -M, and polarity effects is given for both positive and negative messages by the single equation

$$\Delta a = \alpha m(M^2 - a^2) \tag{2.21}$$

which is shown in Fig. 2.2c. If a is the probability of a positive statement, then the corresponding model is

$$\Delta a = \alpha m a(1 - a) \tag{2.22}$$

which is shown in Fig. 2.2d.

Reinforcement versus Punishment

Abelson (1967) developed a model of attitude change derived from reinforcement theory in which attitude is viewed as the probability of a person making a positive statement about some object. He argued that messages that agree with the attitude strengthen (reward) the attitude and messages that disagree (punish) weaken the attitude. Abelson (1967) also argued that a person has two response tendencies—a tendency to endorse (pro) the object and a tendency to reject (con) the object—and that a message may act on both tendencies. If the message endorses the object, the receiver's tendency to agree is rewarded and the receiver's tendency to disagree is punished.

Agreement–Disagreement Asymmetry

As noted above, Abelson (1967) viewed attitude as a probability of a person making a positive response about some object. If p is the tendency to make positive comments and n is the tendency to make negative comments, attitude is given as

$$a = p/(p + n)$$

Further, Abelson (1967) provided for asymmetry of pro and cons statements but did not provide for the intensity of the message, that is, positive messages are $+$ and negative messages are $-$. As such, his model would be

$$\Delta a = \begin{cases} \alpha(1-a) & \text{if} \quad a = \text{pro} > \tfrac{1}{2} \quad \text{and} \quad m = + \\ (\alpha - \gamma)(1-a) & \text{if} \quad a = \text{con} < \tfrac{1}{2} \quad \text{and} \quad m = + \\ -\beta a & \text{if} \quad a = \text{con} < \tfrac{1}{2} \quad \text{and} \quad m = - \\ -(\beta - \delta)a & \text{if} \quad a = \text{pro} > \tfrac{1}{2} \quad \text{and} \quad m = - \end{cases} \qquad (2.23)$$

where γ and δ are positive parameters that measure the extent to which punishment is weaker than reward, that is, $\alpha - \gamma$ and $\beta - \delta$ are punishing parameters.

We now wish to generalize Ableson's distinction in a way that is compatible with the reinforcement models that assume the bipolar attitudes discussed earlier. To do this we assume that a model given without this assumption represents the maximum amount of attitude change. To the extent there is disagreement the change will be in the same direction but of smaller magnitude. Thus we assume that agreement enters the attitude change equation as a multiplier. Next we assume that, for a fixed message, the more polar the receiver's attitude, the greater the resulting agreement or disagreement. Similarly for attitudes of constant value—the greater the polarity of the message, the greater the resulting agreement or disagreement. These last two assumptions allow the product am to be a measure of the quantitative agreement or disagreement between source and receiver. The actual multiplicative factor that will enter the equation will then be a positive function of the product that increases from zero at perfect (i.e., infinite) disagreement to one at perfect (i.e., infinite) agreement. That is, the multiplier will be an ogival (S-shaped) function. One ogive that is a symmetric function of agreement is

$$\text{multiplier} = e^{\sigma am}/(1 + e^{\sigma am}) \qquad (2.24)$$

where σ is a positive constant that is large to the extent that reward and punishment are asymmetric.

Thus, using this multiplier, the asymmetry of agreement and disagreement or reward and punishment becomes a technical assumption that may be added to any of the models in this section. For the simple reinforcement model without polarity effects or limits, the resulting model is shown in Fig. 2.2e. The others behave similarly.

Two-Factor Theory

Abelson's (1967) discussion suggests a new model that he did not develop. As noted earlier, he assumed that the receiver has two response tendencies: a pro tendency and a con tendency. Any message should then act on *both* tendencies.

Thus a positive message would agree with the positive tendency and disagree with the negative tendency. If p denotes the positive tendency and n the negative, we might model this by

$$\Delta p = \alpha m \qquad \text{if} \quad m = + \qquad (2.25)$$
$$\Delta n = -(\alpha - \gamma)m \qquad \text{if} \quad m = + \qquad (2.26)$$

We might then define the bipolar attitude as the difference between these tendencies (Atkinson and Birch, 1970), that is, $a = p - n$. We then have

$$\Delta a = \alpha m - \left(-(\alpha - \gamma)\right)m = (2\alpha - \gamma)m \qquad (2.27)$$

which is the same as the model without two tendencies, that is, there is no agreement–disagreement asymmetry. If the message is negative, we have

$$\Delta p = (\alpha - \gamma)m \qquad \text{if} \quad m = - \qquad (2.28)$$
$$\Delta n = -\alpha m \qquad \text{if} \quad m = - \qquad (2.29)$$

and hence

$$\Delta a = \left(\alpha - \gamma - (-\alpha)\right)m = (2\alpha - \gamma)m \qquad \text{if} \quad m = - \qquad (2.30)$$

which is the same as Eq. (2.27). Again there is no asymmetry. Thus Abelson's distinction between the impact of reward and punishment need not lead to an agreement–disagreement asymmetry.

Of course the development above is not Abelson's model. Abelson assumed that attitude was the probability of a positive response, that is,

$$a = p/(p + n) = \text{old } a \qquad (2.31)$$

Furthermore, if the attitudes are approximately to satisfy linear operator equations, then the response strengths cannot satisfy the simple additive laws in Eqs. (2.27) and (2.30). Instead the equations must be linear, say,

$$\Delta p = \alpha p \qquad \text{if} \quad m = + \qquad (2.32)$$
$$\Delta n = -\beta n \qquad \text{if} \quad m = + \qquad (2.33)$$

where α and β are positive constants. In this case, we have

$$\Delta a = \text{new } a - \text{old } a = \frac{(1 + \alpha)p}{(1 + \alpha)p + (1 - \beta)n} - \frac{p}{p + n}$$
$$= \frac{(\alpha + \beta)a}{(\alpha + \beta)a + 1 - \beta}(1 - a)$$
$$= \theta(1 - a), \qquad (2.34)$$

where the fact that θ is not constant opens the possibility that there might be agreement–disagreement asymmetries. Now if reward and punishment are exactly *symmetric* (the relative increase in the positive tendency equals the relative decrease in the negative tendency), then $1 - \beta = 1/(1 + \alpha)$. If α is small, then this equation means that we have $\beta \cong \alpha$. If punishment is equivalent to reward then for small α and β, $\beta = \alpha$ and

$$\Delta a = \frac{2\alpha a}{2\alpha a + 1 - \alpha}(1 - a) \qquad \text{if} \quad \beta = \alpha \tag{2.35}$$

or

$$\theta = \frac{2\alpha a}{2\alpha a + 1 - \alpha} \qquad \text{if} \quad \beta = \alpha, \quad \text{and both are small} \tag{2.36}$$

The fact that θ is always higher when a is pro than when a is con means that there is an observed agreement–disagreement asymmetry even though we assumed no reward–punishment difference!

We now consider reinforcement with extinction.

Reinforcement with Extinction

The model to be presented below assumes that extinction is an independent process. This model is not derived from contemporary learning theory; it is directly contrary to it. All current theorists that we have examined assume that the experimental finding of extinction is a special case of acquisition processes. That is, the decline in the frequency of a response is produced either by the reinforcement of an alternative response or by the counterconditioning effects of punishment. Furthermore, we shall note evidence from the attitude change literature that appears to contradict the extinction model.

Why do we present a theory that seems to have no empirical support? There are several reasons, the most important of which is that the extinction model is the only reinforcement model that leads to reasonable predictions in later theoretical developments. That is, we shall later extend theories of attitude change to three areas: models of cognitive structure, models of group discussion, and models of dynamic sociometry. In each of these contexts, the basic reinforcement model makes bizarre predictions. However, the extinction model with a strong extinction parameter makes predictions that are consistent with the data.

A second reason is that some authors have assumed that the linear discrepancy model of information processing theory (presented in the next chapter) is consistent with reinforcement theory. We shall show conditions under which the extinction model matches the linear discrepancy model, but we shall note that this occurs only under conditions that appear to be inconsistent with other evidence.

Pavlov (1927) assumed that the extinction and acquisition of conditioned responses are independent processes. The model presented here is derived from Hull's (1943) theoretical explanation of the Pavlovian position. Hull assumed that there is effort associated with the production of a response. This effort produces "reactive inhibition" that temporarily reduces the strength of the response. Rapid repetition of the response without reinforcement causes a cumulation of reactive inhibition that is observed as "fatigue," a lowering of the response rate. With time, the reactive inhibition dissipates and the response shows "spontaneous remission" or "reminiscence." However, Hull believed that not all of the inhibitory effect was subject to dissipation when the response ceased. A portion of the inhibition produced by response production is registered in "conditioned inhibition" that produces a smaller but permanent reduction in response strength. If there is no further reinforcement of the response, then the cumulative effect of conditioned inhibition is to reduce the response strength to zero and hence produce the extinction of the response.

Consider now the impact of a "probe" message such as "How do you feel about Russia?" This message will elicit an attitudinal response but provide no reinforcement for it. Thus, according to Hull's theory, there will be a change in the response strength produced by conditioned inhibition. This change will be a weakening of the response strength. The simplest model for this effect is

$$\Delta a = -\varepsilon a \tag{2.37}$$

where ε is a positive parameter. A succession of such probe messages would produce the sequence

$$a_n = (1 - \varepsilon)^n a_0 \tag{2.38}$$

which is exponential decay to zero. That is, a succession of probe messages would produce the extinction of the emotional response.

If the emotional response is elicited by a message, then there are two change processes: the reinforcement of the message and the conditioned inhibition of response production. The reinforcement effect would be given by models such as those above whereas the conditioned inhibition is modeled by the extinction equation. The simplest model with conditioned inhibition is

$$\Delta a = \alpha m - \varepsilon a \tag{2.39}$$

This model contradicts the fundamental assumption of all other reinforcement models: a positive message need not always have a positive effect and a negative message need not always have a negative effect. The effect of the message depends on the receiver's current attitude. For a positive message, the attitude change is positive only if

$$m > \varepsilon a/\alpha \tag{2.40}$$

Let us name the ratio of ε to α by the letter ρ, that is, let ρ be defined by

$$\rho = \varepsilon/\alpha \qquad (2.41)$$

Then we note that a positive message will have a positive effect only if $m > \rho a$. If the attitude is negative, this will pose no problem. But if the attitude is positive, then the message will have a positive effect only if the strength of the message is greater than ρa. That is, a weak positive message might actually produce negative change. How weak the positive message must be to produce negative change depends on two things: the size of the ratio ρ and the strength of the positive attitude a. If the extinction parameter ε is small relative to the message parameter α, then the ratio ρ is small and the product ρa will be small. That is, if the extinction parameter is small in comparison to the message parameter, then there is little difference between the extinction model and the basic reinforcement model. However, for the reinforcement model to make reasonable predictions about cognitive structure and group dynamics (Volume II), the extinction parameter must be at least as large as the message parameter. If so, then the ratio ρ must be greater than or equal to one. The positive message will then produce a positive effect only if the message is stronger than the attitude of the receiver. This is a stark departure from the basic reinforcement model.

The basic reinforcement model predicts that a long string of positive messages will drive the receiver's attitude to an ever more positive value. Every positive message further increases the receiver's resistance to counter-persuasion. This is not true for the extinction model. A long string of positive messages with message value m will produce an attitude that levels off at an asymptotic value a^* given by

$$a^* = \alpha m/\varepsilon = m/\rho \qquad (2.42)$$

If the extinction parameter is much smaller than the message parameter, then the reciprocal of ρ is much larger than one and the asymptotic value of the attitude is much larger than the value of the single message. That is, weak messages can have a large cumulative effect as predicted by the conventional reinforcement theories. However, if the extinction parameter is greater than or equal to the message parameter, then the asymptotic value of the attitude is less than or equal to the single message value. Again this is a stark departure from the writings of the reinforcement theorists.

We shall not review the evidence that caused the learning theorists to reject the Hullian model of extinction. Most of this evidence can be found in contemporary treatments of the interference theory of forgetting (Deese and Hulse, 1967). However, we shall review the evidence from the attitude literature that appears directly to contradict the extinction model. This contradictory literature stems from experiments by Zajonc (1968) and others on the effects of "mere exposure."

Zajonc simply presented certain stimuli to subjects again and again without reinforcement. This is an experimental extinction paradigm. Thus the extinction model would predict that attitudes would decay exponentially to zero. Zajonc found just the opposite. Attitudes to the initially positive stimuli became slightly more positive after the series of exposures. That is, the Zajonc experiment suggests that emotional responses do not extinguish as predicted by the extinction model. On the contrary, the Zajonc findings suggest that emotional responses are to a very small extent self-reinforcing. The Zajonc (1968) findings have been supported in several other studies.[†] Another stream of research by Tesser and associates also shows that emotional responses are self-reinforcing [Tesser (1976, 1978) Tesser and Cowan (1975), Tesser and Dann Heiser (1978), and Tesser and Leone (1977)]. Tesser's (1978) work on thinking and attitude change has shown that attitude change occurs by simply allowing a person to think about attitudinal objects; the longer the thinking time, the larger the change.

For the special case where the extinction parameter is exactly equal to the message parameter, the extinction model takes on a special form. That is, if $\varepsilon = \alpha$, then

$$\Delta a = \alpha m - \varepsilon a = \alpha m - \alpha a = \alpha(m - a) \qquad (2.43)$$

which is known as the linear discrepancy equation [Hovland and Pitzker (1975), Anderson and Hovland (1957)]. We shall derive this same equation in Chapter 3 from the basic assumptions of information processing theory. However, information processing theory predicts that a probe message has the effect of delivering a message with value $m = a$. Thus the effect of a probe message predicted by information processing theory is

$$\Delta a = \alpha(m - a) = \alpha(a - a) = 0 \qquad (2.44)$$

that is, information processing theory predicts no change in the Zajonc experiment. This is much closer to the actual findings of very small increases than is the extinction model prediction of exponential decay to 0.

We now consider source credibility within the context of reinforcement theory.

[†] Brickman, et al. (1972), Burgess and Sales (1971), Harrison (1968), Harrison and Crandall (1972), Janisse (1970), Matlin (1970, 1971), Messmer (1979), Perlman and Oskamp (1971), Seagert and Jellison (1970), Stang (1974a, 1974b), Suefeld, et al. (1971), Tucker and Ware (1970), and Zajonc and Rajecki (1969)].

SOURCE CREDIBILITY

The major premise of the reinforcement models (with or without a polarity factor) involves message strength. Weak messages yield less attitude change, strong messages exert more influence. However, most reinforcement theorists would also argue strongly for a second component to message impact: the receiver's attitude toward the source. For a learning theorist both the receiver's positive emotional response to agreement and his negative emotional response to disagreement will be much stronger if the receiver likes the source than if he dislikes the source, and the stronger the emotion, the greater the reinforcement value of the message. The mass communication theorists would assume that the impact of a message would be a function of how much influence the source has over the receiver. In particular, the personal influence of a source would be much greater if the receiver likes him than if the receiver dislikes him. The socialization theorist would predict that the receiver is much more likely to imitate a positive role model than a negative role model, particularly if the receiver engages in the active contemplation of the consequences.

In the attitude change literature the source component is referred to as the effect of source credibility that reflects the observation that the receiver reports change in his attitude if he "believes" the source. This terminology will be incorporated throughout the book, although it is not appropriate to some theorists.

The functional form of the credibility effect is determined by the following statements. The full impact of the message is only realized from a perfectly credible source. If the source is not perfectly credible, the impact would be less. If the source is perfectly incredible, the impact will be zero. Because "impact" means absolute change, source credibility must be a multiplicative effect. That is,

$$\Delta a = \text{source credibility} \cdot \text{message strength} \qquad (2.45)$$

For the reinforcement theorists, source credibility is a symmetric function of the receiver's attitude toward the source, going from zero when $s = -\infty$ to one when $s = +\infty$. One such function is the logistic ogive

$$\text{source credibility} = e^{\sigma s}/(1 + e^{\sigma s}) \qquad (2.46)$$

If this assumption is combined with the multiplicative law, the basic model becomes

$$\Delta a = e^{\sigma s}\alpha m/(1 + e^{\sigma s}) \qquad (2.47)$$

The graph of Δa on a with s parameterized is presented in Fig. 2.3a. Attitude change increases which message strength and credibility. For the same message, credible sources are more persuasive than incredible sources.

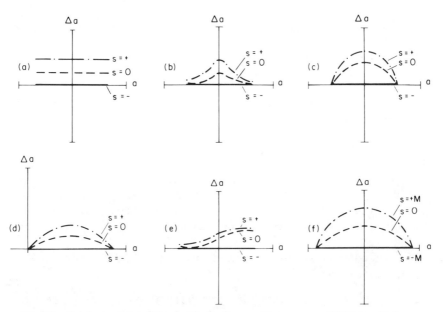

Fig. 2.3. Reinforcement models of attitude change with a source credibility multiplier as a function of attitude toward the object: (a) constant change (ogival multiplier), (b) constant change with polarity (ogival multiplier), (c) bounded and agreement–disagreement symmetry (ogival multiplier), (d) attitude as a probability (ogival multiplier), (e) constant change with reward punishment asymmetry (ogival multiplier), and (f) bounded bipolar attitude (linear multiplier).

If individuals with extreme attitudes are more resistant to change, then a constant change with polarity and source effect would be

$$\Delta a = \frac{e^{\sigma s}}{1 + e^{\sigma s}} \frac{\alpha m}{1 + a^2} \tag{2.48}$$

This model is graphed in Fig. 2.3b as a function of a and s. For source credibility fixed, the model makes predictions identical to Eq. (2.4), the constant change with polarity model.

The other models are shown in Fig. 2.3 c–e.

The logistic formula in Eq. (2.46) above was chosen because it is one of the simplest mathematical formulas for mapping a bipolar infinite attitude continuum into finite source credibilities. However, if the receiver's attitude toward the source is bounded, then much simpler formulas are possible. In fact, if there is to be a perfectly credible and perfectly incredible source in the bounded models, then the logistic function must be discarded. If we want the source credibility to be zero at the absolute lower bound of $-M$ and one at the absolute upper bound of $+M$, then the linear source credibility function

would be
$$\text{source credibility} = (s + M)/2M \qquad (2.49)$$

If the attitude toward the source is a probability, the equation is even simpler;
$$\text{source credibility} = s \qquad (2.50)$$

The formula for the bounded bipolar model of attitude change with linear source credibility is
$$\Delta a = \alpha(s + M)(M^2 - a^2), \qquad \alpha = m/2M \qquad (2.51)$$

This model is shown in Fig. 2.3f.

There is a long history of empirical support for the source credibility effect. The classic studies of prestige suggestion were reviewed in Tannenbaum (1953) and Hovland (1954). An excellent review of more recent work is found in McGuire (1969). However we shall argue in Chapter 10 that these findings may be spurious.

We now consider models of source change within the context of reinforcement theory.

REINFORCEMENT THEORY: SOURCE CHANGE

Asymptotic Reinforcement Effects

The basic model for source change given earlier assumed that source change is positive if the source agrees with the receiver ($am = +$) and negative if he disagrees ($am = -$). If the emotional reaction produced by the message is an increasing function of the intensity of the message and the intensity of the attitude, then source change will be a monotone function of the product am,
$$\Delta s = \beta am.$$

The basic model assumes that emotional reaction, or source change, has no upper limit; however, if source change levels off for large agreement or disagreement, then source change would be an ogival (S-shaped) function such

$$\Delta s = \frac{\beta}{[1 + (am)^2]^{1/2}} am \qquad (2.52)$$

These two particular functions are shown in Fig. 2.4b (Fig. 2.4a is the same as Fig. 2.1b).

The Polarity Assumption

Many reinforcement theorists would assert that it is difficult to modify an established attitude. This would be as true of the receiver's attitude toward the source as his attitude toward the object. A model embodying this assumption

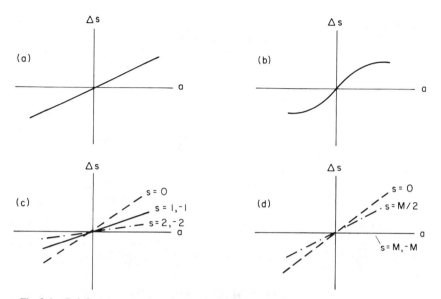

Fig. 2.4. Reinforcement models of source change as a function of attitude toward the object: (a) proportional to agreement, (b) ogival function of agreement, (c) proportional to agreement and adjusted for polarity, and (d) bounded linear agreement.

can be obtained simply by multiplying either of the equations above by a factor such as

$$\text{source polarity multiplier} = 1/(1 + s^2) \qquad (2.53)$$

The effect of this assumption on the linear model of Eq. (2.50) is displayed in Fig. 2.4c.

Absolute Limits

If we are to assume that the object attitude has an absolute upper bound of M, then this carries the implication that all attitudes have this same upper bound. In particular, the receiver's attitude toward the source will have the same absolute bounds as the receiver's attitude toward the object.

Mathematically the models for source change would be modified to impose absolute limits by exactly the same techniques employed to modify attitude change above. To impose an upper bound of M we multiply the source change equation by a factor $\beta(M - s)$, where the magnitude of β is chosen small enough to prevent overshoot. To impose a lower bound L, multiply the equation by the factor $\beta(s - L)$. If both an upper bound and a lower bound are imposed by multiplying by the factor $\beta(M - s)(s - L)$, then a polarity effect is implicitly assumed and the polarity multiplier is superfluous. In particular, to impose an upper bound of $+M$ and a lower bound of $-M$ with an automatic polarity effect, the multiplicative factor is $\beta(M^2 - s^2)$. For example, the linear agreement model becomes

$$\Delta s = \beta am(M^2 - s^2) \tag{2.54}$$

which is shown in Fig. 2.4d.

If the receiver's attitude toward the object is bounded by $\pm M$, then agreement–disagreement is bounded by $\pm mM$ and the asymptotic form of the agreement function is superfluous. In this case, where both attitudes are defined as the probability of a positive statement, the model for source change becomes

$$\Delta s = \beta\left(a - \tfrac{1}{2}\right)ms(1 - s) \tag{2.55}$$

We now consider both attitude and source change together.

ATTITUDE CHANGE AND SOURCE CHANGE

The primary assumption for reinforcement models of attitude change is that a positive message induces positive change and a negative message induces negative change. There are four secondary assumptions. A model for attitude change might or might not assume (1) polarity effects, (2) agreement–disagreement asymmetry, (3) an absolute limit on attitudes, and (4) source credibility effects. Hence it is mathematically possible to have 16 different models of attitude change. Because polarity and absolute limits are not qualitatively independent, this number is reduced to 12. Furthermore, the source credibility effect is an integral assumption of most reinforcement theories. For these theories there are 6 distinct models of attitude change.

The primary assumption for source change is that source change is positive if the source agrees with the subject and negative if the source disagrees with the subject. There are secondary assumptions. A model may or may not assume (1) polarity effects, (2) absolute bounds on the attitude toward the source, or (3) an upper bound on the emotional response produced by agreement–disagreement. Thus it is mathematically possible to have 8 different models of source change. However, the assumption of absolute limits qualitatively includes a polarity assumption and an upper bound on the effect of agreement. Hence there are only 5 distinct models of source change.

The presentation of a message induces both attitude change and source change. Thus a model of the total process must include a model for each. Because the assumptions concerning attitude change are mathematically independent of the assumptions for source change, there are $16 \times 8 = 128$

mathematically possible models of the entire process. However the assumptions are not psychologically independent. If there are absolute bounds on attitudes, then there is only one model for source change and four models for attitude change. If a source credibility effect is assumed, then agreement–disagreement asymmetry is the only technical assumption within models where attitudes are bounded. The other psychological assumption that applies to both models concerns polarity. If polar attitudes resist change, then polarity effects must be assumed in both models. Thus if attitudes are unbounded, there are 16 possible methods of which half do not make the source credibility assumption. In summary, for theories in which the source credibility effect is a technical assumption, there are 4 bounded and 16 unbounded models of source and attitude change. For most reinforcement theories the source credibility effect is an integral assumption that leaves 2 bounded and 8 unbounded models.

Models that assume that an attitude is the probability of a positive response are a special case of models in which attitudes are assumed to be bounded. However, the formulas differ slightly.

CHAPTER 3

Information Processing Theory

INTRODUCTION

Hovland and his many co-workers have nearly always been classified as reinforcement theorists and discussions of their work are usually replate with reference to Hull, Dollard and Miller, Spence, and so on. However, both Insko (1967) and Kiesler *et al.* (1969) ultimately express disillusionment with the results of this classification. The problem is that over a 20-year period the Yale school underwent a complete reversal in orientation from learning theory to cognitive theory. This chapter is concerned with the late stages of this process, that is, what is currently termed "information processing theory."

Hovland, Janis, and Kelley (1953) describe the key attitude change producing process as the receiver's internal comparison of his position with the position advocated by the message. In the course of this comparison the receiver asks himself questions and compares his answers with those presented in the message. When the receiver accepts the new answers in place of his own, attitude change has resulted. Acceptance is produced by "incentives." The primary incentives are the arguments and reasons that support that answer. The receiver is occasionally influenced by secondary incentives such as anticipated rewards or punishments. McGuire (1964, 1966) describes this process in a three-stage form: the receiver must attend to the message, comprehend the message, and yield to the message. More recently, McGuire

(1976) expanded the information processing sequence to include exposure, perception, comprehension, yielding, retrieval and memory search, decision making, and action. Not all theorists agree on the labeling of the sequence; for example, in his work on consumer choice, Bettman (1979) defines the following sequence: processing capacity, motivation, attention and perception, information acquisition and evaluation, memory, decision processes, and learning. Bettman's theory, however, deals specifically with consumer choice and is only tangently related to communication and attitude change. A recent review of information processing approaches to communication and attitude change is given by Cappella and Folger (1980). Generalizations of information processing theory to human behavior are given by Lindsay and Norman (1972).

The early works in the information processing tradition were largely the products of Asch (1948) and co-workers and Hovland (see Hovland, *et al.*, 1953). Later work moved in two directions. The research of McGuire (1960, 1968) and Wyer (1974) on syllogistic/probabilistic relations among beliefs gave rise to cognitive consistency theory. The research on the linear discrepancy hypothesis by Hovland and Pritzker (1957), Anderson and Hovland (1957), and Anderson (1959, 1964, 1971) led to the information processing attitude change model described in this chapter.

The basic assumption in information processing theory is that a receiver reacts to a communication or a set of messages by breaking it into component messages, arguments, or assertions about the object being described. The receiver then compares each argument or assertion with his own corresponding belief. Any argument that agrees with his own belief will have no effect on his attitude toward the object. However, if an assertion is different from the receiver's belief, then the receiver may either reject the message or yield to the argument. If he yields, then there is belief change. This induces corresponding attitude change. Thus only if the receiver initially disagrees with a message will there be any attitude change. The attitude change that does occur is in the direction of the values implied by the belief change.

THE BASIC INFORMATION PROCESSING MODEL

Messages, like attitudes, have an affective value. If attitudes are laid out on a continuum, then every message advocates some position on this scale. Thus a message is a representation of an attitudinal position. This measurement model was proposed by Thurstone (1929) and "aligns" the message on the same continuum as the attitude. Thus it is possible to speak of the discrepancy between them, that is, $m - a$. Because the primary process underlying attitude change in the present models is the receiver's internal comparison of his position with the message, the discrepancy between attitude and message becomes the agent of change and we would expect the factor $m - a$ to enter every model.

Early studies of attitude change and social influence indicates that the magnitude of obtained attitude change induced by a message tends to be proportional to the amount of change suggested [French (1956), Hovland and Pritzker (1957)]. Anderson (1959) and Anderson and Hovland (1957) propose a "distance-proportional" model with the conditions that (1) the magnitude of change is proportional to the discrepancy between the receiver's attitude and the position advocated by the message and (2) the change is always in the direction advocated by the message. These postulates take the form

$$\Delta a = \alpha(m - a), \qquad 0 < \alpha < 1 \tag{3.1}$$

The graph for the linear discrepancy model is illustrated in Fig. 3.1. The sign of Δa is positive if the receiver's initial position is below the message and negative otherwise. Thus, if the receiver's attitude is below the message, he shifts up; if his attitude is above, he shifts down. He always shifts toward the position advocated by the message, and the greater the distance from the message, the

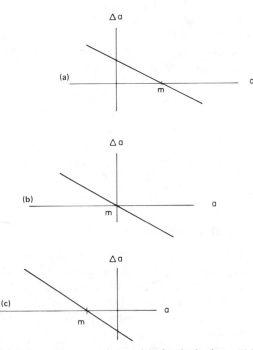

Fig. 3.1. The basic information processing model of attitude change: (a) positive message; (b) neutral message; (c) negative message.

greater the change. This model is formally equivalent to the simple linear servomechanism or homeostat of cybernetics (Ashby, 1956, 1963). The message is analogous to input from the environment and the receiver adjusts his position toward the input value.

INFORMATION PROCESSING MODEL: AN ALTERNATIVE DERIVATION

The preceding derivation of the linear discrepancy model has been accepted by information processing theorists for many years, but it is not complete. The problem is this: the comparison between message and internal state is actually done on the basis of logical content rather than emotional content, that is, the receiver compares the statement made by the speaker to his own belief. If there is a discrepancy, then the listener may or may not change the discrepant belief. Attitude change is then produced by the belief change, if any. The following argument shows that the linear discrepancy model is still appropriate, although as a probabilistic model rather than a deterministic one. That is, the linear discrepancy model emerges from this new argument as a regression equation predicting attitude change from the prior attitude.

The crucial fact is that the message value is only an indirect indicator of logical content. Similarly, the receiver's attitude is only an indirect indicator of whether he will agree with the message or not. The connecting assumption follows from the model as developed here: if beliefs are scaled for emotional content, then the receiver's attitude will be the average of the affective values associated with beliefs.

Suppose that the message value exactly matches the receiver's attitude, that is, $m = a$. This means the emotional content of the message is exactly at the average of the emotional content of the receiver's beliefs. This should maximize the probability of a match between the content of the message and the corresponding belief. If there is a discrepancy, then it could be in either direction. If the receiver yields to the message, then that could mean a change from an old belief with a value that is either higher or lower than the message value. Because the message value is at the mean, the probability should be the same in either direction. Thus, on the average, the belief change could go in either direction and hence the resulting average attitude change would be zero. That is, if we average attitude change across all persons whose attitude is equal to the message value, then the average change will be zero. This result is predicted by the linear discrepancy equation, except we must add the phrase "on the average." That is, on the average,

$$\Delta a = 0 \quad \text{if} \quad a = m$$

If the receiver's attitude has a value higher than the message value, that is, $a > m$, then the probability of a discrepancy between message and belief is higher and a discrepancy is more likely to be in one direction than in the other. That is, because the message value is below the attitude value, it is below the average of the receiver's belief values. Thus if there is a discrepancy, then it is likely that the old belief has an emotional value that is higher than the message value. Thus, on the average, the attitude change will be negative. Again this average is in the direction predicted by the linear discrepancy equation.

If the receiver's attitude has a value lower than the message value, that is, $a < m$, then there is likely to be a discrepancy between belief and message, and the discrepancy is likely to be that the old belief has a value below the value of the message. Thus, on the average, attitude change will be positive. This average change is in the direction predicted by the linear discrepancy equation.

We have now argued that a belief comparison model predicts average attitude change that will be in the direction of the message value. Thus we have shown that the average attitude change will have the algebraic sign given by the linear discrepancy equation. What about magnitude? Will the amount of change increase as the discrepancy between message and attitude increases? As the discrepancy increases, the probability of a mismatch between message and belief increases, that is, the probability of attitude change increases. Furthermore, as the discrepancy increases, the probability of change in the predicted direction becomes greater. Finally, as the discrepancy increases, the difference between the old belief value and the message value increases. Thus an increase in the amount of the discrepancy will mean an increase in the average change in the predicted direction. Hence the linear discrepancy equation should be a very good approximation to the regression equation for attitude change onto prior attitude.

For those who are familiar with psychometric theory, we add the caveat that for actual data the regression line must be corrected for attenuation (see Hunter and Cohen, 1974) due to error of measurement in the attitude. If the regression line is not corrected, then the intercept will be displaced from the message value correspondingly.

For those familiar with stochastic processes, we note that the probabilistic model is a continuous state Markov process.

The above discussion assumed that a set of component messages may change beliefs and that the new attitude is the average of the affective values associated with the new beliefs. A simple average assumes that each message in the set of messages changes attitude irrespective of the order of message presentation and that the impact of each message is reduced in proportion to the number of messages. There are, however, other models of message impact and these are considered next. We discuss three possibilities: simultaneous impact, given order of presentation, and random order. Each is discussed under two conditions: full impact and reduced impact.

MULTIPLE MESSAGES

For the basic information processing model, it is not difficult to obtain the equation for change following a succession of messages. This equation can then be compared to the corresponding equation for reinforcement theory.

The algebra is easiest if we put the equations in predictive form rather than change form. The effect of a single message is to change the attitude from a_n to a_{n+1}, where

$$
\begin{aligned}
a_{n+1} = a_n + \Delta a &= a_n + \alpha(m - a) \\
&= a_n + \alpha(m_{n+1} - a_n) \\
&= (1 - \alpha)a_n + \alpha m_{n+1}
\end{aligned}
\tag{3.2}
$$

The subscript $n + 1$ appears on the message value according to the definition of a_n as the attitude following the nth message, that is, a_{n+1} is the attitude following the $n + 1$th message. This equation shows that the new attitude is a weighted sum of the old attitude and the message value. Because the sum of the weights is

$$
(1 - \alpha) + (\alpha) = 1
$$

the weighted sum is actually a weighted average. That is, the new attitude is a weighted average of the old attitude and the message value. The relative weight of the message is $(1 - \alpha)/\alpha$.

Consider the impact of two successive messages with values m_{n+1} and m_{n+2}:

$$
a_{n+2} = (1 - \alpha)a_{n+1} + \alpha m_{n+2} = (1 - \alpha)^2 a_n + (1 - \alpha)\alpha m_{n+1} + \alpha m_{n+2}
$$

The first part of this equation says that the new attitude is the weighted average of the immediately prior attitude and the most recent message (i.e., with message value m_{n+2}). The second part of the equation says that the new attitude is a weighted sum of the attitude further back in time a_n and the two intervening message values. The sum of the weights is

$$
[(1 - \alpha)^2] + [(1 - \alpha)\alpha] + (\alpha) = 1
$$

thus we see that the new attitude is the weighted average of the older attitude and the two intervening message values. The weights of the two message values differ; the weight of the most recent message value is greater than that of the earlier message value by a factor of $1/(1 - \alpha)$.

This pattern continues as more and more messages are considered. The new attitude is a weighted average of the initial attitude and all of the intervening message values. The weight of the old attitude goes down by a factor of $1 - \alpha$

each time. The same is true of any given message value; as the message moves back in time, its weight is reduced by a factor of $1 - \alpha$ as each new message is received. To see this pattern most clearly, consider an experiment with an initial attitude a_0 and a succession of messages with values $m_1, m_2, m_3, \ldots,$

$$a_1 = (1 - \alpha)a_0 + \alpha m_1$$

$$a_2 = (1 - \alpha)^2 a_0 + (1 - \alpha)\alpha m_1 + \alpha m_2$$

$$a_3 = (1 - \alpha)^3 a_0 + (1 - \alpha)^2 \alpha m_1 + (1 - \alpha)\alpha m_2 + \alpha m_3$$

$$a_4 = (1 - \alpha)^4 a_0 + (1 - \alpha)^3 \alpha m_1 + (1 - \alpha)^2 \alpha m_2 + (1 - \alpha)\alpha m_3 + \alpha m_4$$

$$\vdots$$

$$a_n = (1 - \alpha)^n a_0 + (1 - \alpha)^{n-1} \alpha m_1 + (1 - \alpha)^{n-2} \alpha m_2 + \cdots$$

$$= (1 - \alpha)^n a_0 + \sum_{k=1}^{n} (1 - \alpha)^{n-k} \alpha m_k \tag{3.3}$$

This weighted average formula stands in sharp contrast to the cumulative formula from reinforcement theory:

$$a_n = a_0 + \alpha \sum_{k=1}^{n} m_k \tag{3.4}$$

This becomes even clearer if we consider the simpler case in which we assume that all messages have the same value $m_k = m$. We then have

$$a_n = \begin{cases} (1 - \alpha)^n a_0 + [1 - (1 - \alpha)^n]m & \text{(information processing),} & (3.5) \\ a_0 + n\alpha m & \text{(reinforcement)} & (3.6) \end{cases}$$

If the messages are positive, then reinforcement theory predicts that the impact of a greater and greater number of messages will be to drive the attitude upward without limit. Information processing theory predicts that the new attitude will always be an average of the initial attitude and the message value m. The impact of many messages is to drive the weight given the initial attitude to zero and hence drive the weight of the message value to one. Thus, in the limit, the information processing model predicts that the initial attitude will converge to the message value m.

If the parameter α is large, or if the number of messages is large, then the two models are easy to distinguish. But if the change produced by each message is small, or if the number of messages is small, then the models are not that different. Consider an experiment in which $\alpha = .1$, $m = 1$, and $a_0 = 0$. For three messages, the values predicted by the two models are shown in the accompanying tabulation.

Message	Reinforcement	Information processing
0	0	0
1	.10	.10
2	.20	.19
3	.30	.27

COMPOUND MESSAGES

Most communications can be broken into a succession of component messages. These can then be handled as in the previous section. However, a message such as "The Fiat is an economical, roomy, safe car." may not be processed as three successive messages. Instead, we shall consider two alternative models: simultaneous impact versus random succession.

If three messages have simultaneous impact, then the natural model is to add the impacts

$$\Delta a = \alpha(m_1 - a) + \alpha(m_2 - a) + \alpha(m_3 - a)$$
$$= \alpha[(m_1 + m_2 + m_3) - 3a] = 3\alpha(\bar{m} - a)$$

More generally, the simultaneous impact of n messages would be

$$\Delta a = n\alpha(\bar{m} - a), \tag{3.7}$$

that is, the simultaneous impact of n messages is obtained by using the linear discrepancy equation with the average message value $\bar{m}$ and with the impact parameter α multiplied by the number of messages.

The previous derivation assumes that a message element has the same impact when part of a compound as when it is presented alone. This may not be true. Suppose that the parameter for an element of a compound is reduced in proportion to the number of elements in that compound. For example, each element in a triad would have a parameter of $\alpha/3$ instead of α. The simultaneous effect of n messages would then be the same as the previous equation with α/n replacing α, that is,

$$\Delta a = n(\alpha/n)(\bar{m} - a) = \alpha(\bar{m} - a) \tag{3.8}$$

If the effect of compounding is to reduce the impact of any one element proportionately, then the final result of simultaneous processing is the one-message equation with a message value of $\bar{m}$. That is, if the impact of compound elements is reduced, then the receiver acts as if presented with one message whose message value is the average of the values of the elements compounded.

In the random succession model, it is assumed that the person processes all three messages but in random order. Furthermore, it is likely that the person cycles through the messages several times with only a short consideration of each cycle. If the messages are considered successively, then the impact of three messages would be

$$a_3 = (1 - \alpha)^3 a_0 + (1 - \alpha)^2 \alpha m_1 + (1 - \alpha)\alpha m_2 + \alpha m_3$$

If we average this expression across all possible orders, then within each term all messages occur equally often. Thus the average across orders is

$$a_3 = (1 - \alpha)^3 a_0 + (1 - \alpha)^2 \alpha \bar{m} + (1 - \alpha)\alpha \bar{m} + \alpha \bar{m}$$
$$= (1 - \alpha)^3 a_0 + [1 - (1 - \alpha)^3]\bar{m}$$

The change in a is then given by

$$\Delta a = [1 - (1 - \alpha)^3](\bar{m} - a) \tag{3.9}$$

This too is the linear discrepancy equation with the average message value $\bar{m}$, but the impact parameter α is replaced by the complicated expression $[1 - (1 - \alpha)^3]$. If we expand this expression, we obtain

$$1 - (1 - \alpha)^3 = 1 - (1 - 3\alpha + 3\alpha^2 - \alpha^3) = 3\alpha - 3\alpha^2 + \alpha^3$$

If α is small, say, .1, then $\alpha^2 = 0.1$ and $\alpha^3 = .001$ are much smaller. In this case there is little difference between $1 - (1 - \alpha)^3$ and 3α. The general equation for random successive impact is

$$\Delta a = [1 - (1 - \alpha)^n](\bar{m} - a), \tag{3.10}$$

where

$$1 - (1 - \alpha)^n = n\alpha - \frac{n(n - 1)}{2}\alpha^2 + \frac{n(n - 1)(n - 1)}{1(2)(3)}\alpha^3 - \cdots$$

If α is small, then α^2 is much smaller. So if α is small, then the parameter for the random succession model differs little from $n\alpha$. That is, if the change elicited by a single message is small, then the random succession model cannot be distinguished from the simultaneous impact model.

Again, the preceding model assumed that the element of a compound would have the same impact as it would have if presented alone. If instead the impact is reduced proportionately to the number of messages in the compound, then the equation for random succession would have α/n substituted for α. The equation for successive consideration with reduced impact would be

$$\Delta a = \left[1 - \left(1 - \frac{\alpha}{n}\right)^n\right](\bar{m} - a) \tag{3.11}$$

where

$$1 - \left(1 - \frac{\alpha}{n}\right)^n = \alpha - \frac{(n - 1)}{n}\frac{\alpha^2}{2} + \frac{(n - 1)}{n}\frac{(n - 2)}{n}\frac{\alpha^3}{6} - \cdots$$

For small n or small α, the multiplicative parameter differs little from α and hence the random succession model with reduced impact differs little from the simultaneous consideration model with reduced impact. If n is large, the series above is approximated by the exponential function, that is,

$$\Delta a = (1 - e^{-\alpha})(\bar{m} - a) \tag{3.12}$$

The simultaneous and random succession models with full impact are quite similar in that both predict that change will be governed by the linear discrepancy equation with the average message value. However, they differ in their predictions concerning the impact parameter. If the number of messages is small and if the parameter for a single message is small, then the two models agree that the parameter value for the compound message will be about $n\alpha$, where n is the number of messages. However, if the number of messages is large or if the impact of a single message is large, then the simultaneous model will predict much more change than the succession model. However, under these conditions, it is very unlikely that the receiver can simultaneously consider the messages. Thus the simultaneous impact model should always be considered an approximation to the random succession model.

The simultaneous and successive models are even closer if impact is reduced by compounding. Even for as many as seven elements, a parameter value of $\alpha = .50$ for the simultaneous model would not differ much from a multiplicative parameter of .40 for the successive model. Most compound messages have fewer than seven elements, and values of α for established attitudes are smaller than .50.

The preceding discussion assumed that the value of the impact parameter α was known for the single message. If this were not true, then none of the models could be distinguished empirically. The data would merely show

$$\Delta a = \alpha(\bar{m} - a) \tag{3.13}$$

where α is the impact parameter for the compound message.

The preceding computations could have been done with the reinforcement model. However, because the successive message equation has no order effect for message values, there would be no difference between simultaneous and successive impact equations. The equation for full impact would be

$$\Delta a = \alpha n \bar{m} \tag{3.14}$$

in either case. The equation for reduced impact would be

$$\Delta a = \alpha \bar{m} \tag{3.15}$$

in either case.

NONLINEAR DISCREPANCY CURVES

The basic information processing model for attitude change posits a linear relationship between change and the prior attitude. That is, the greater the discrepancy between attitude and message, the greater the attitude change. However, there are alternative models that predict nonlinear discrepancy relations. Most notable of these is the "inattention" model that assumes that, for extremely discrepant models, the receiver ceases to pay attention to the message and focuses instead on internally constructing counterarguments.

THEORETICAL AND TECHNICAL VARIATIONS

There are other models consistent with information processing theory that can be derived by adding assumptions such as counterargument formation or polarity effects. These will be presented next. A summary of each model for attitude change is presented in Table 3.1.

Inattention to Message Due to Counterarguments Formation

As the discrepancy between the message and the receiver's attitude increases, disagreement between source and receiver increases. To a point this simply increases the amount of attitude change. However, beyond that point further discrepancy might cause the person to cease being a passive receiver during the message. Instead, too great a discrepancy may elicit an active argumentative state in which the receiver is so busy composing retorts that he no longer listens to the message. Wright (1980) presents an extensive review on the role of "message-evoked thoughts" and attitude change. Studies by Eagly (1974) and Olson, Toy, and Dover (1978) find more counterarguments with large discrepancies. If internal argument prevents attitude change, then the simplest equation is

$$\Delta a = \frac{\alpha}{1 + \beta(m - a)^2}(m - a) \tag{3.16}$$

where β measures the tendency to counterargue with increasing discrepancy. If $\beta = 0$, then the receiver pays full attention to the message and $\Delta a = \alpha(m - a)$; however, to the extent that the receiver does not pay attention, then attitude change is less than $\alpha(m - a)$, that is,

$$\frac{1}{1 + \beta(m - a)^2} = \begin{cases} 1 & \text{if} \quad m = a \\ <1 & \text{if} \quad m \neq a \end{cases} \tag{3.17}$$

If $\beta > 0$, then as $(m - a)^2 \to \infty$, the ratio in Eq. (3.17) goes to zero, that is, the greater the discrepancy between m and a, the greater the time spent

TABLE 3.1

Information Processing Attitude Change: Summary

Model	Assumptions
Basic: Linear discrepancy	
$\Delta a = \alpha(m - a), \qquad 0 < \alpha < 1$	Receiver makes internal comparison of attitude with attitude communicated in a message. The magnitude of attitude change is proportional by α to the discrepancy between the receiver's attitude and the attitude conveyed in the message. Change is always in the direction of the attitude conveyed in the message.
Inattention to Message	
$\Delta a = \dfrac{\alpha}{1 + \beta(m - a)^2}(m - a)$	Same as basic model except as inattention to message increases, attitude change decreases; inattention increases as a function of message–attitude discrepancy.
Polarity Effects	
$\Delta a = \dfrac{\alpha}{1 + a^2}(m - a)$	Same as basic model except extreme attitudes exhibit less change; attitudes become more extreme as $a \to \pm\infty$.
Credibility	
$\Delta a = \text{credibility} \cdot \alpha(m - a)$	Credibility of the source affects attitude change; highly credible sources facilitate change; low credible sources inhibit change.
$\text{credibility} = \dfrac{e^{\sigma s}}{1 + e^{\sigma s}}$	Unbounded attitudes toward source s; credibility is 0 at $s = -\infty$ and $+1$ at $s = +\infty$.
$\text{credibility} = \dfrac{s}{[1 + s^2]^{\frac{1}{2}}}$	Same as above except credibility is -1 at $s = -\infty$ and $+1$ at $s = +\infty$. This model allows "boomerang" effects for incredible sources.
Polarity Effects	
$\Delta a = \dfrac{\text{credibility}}{1 + a^2}\alpha(m - a)$	Same as above except extreme attitudes are more resistant to change.

constructing counterarguments instead of paying attention to the message and the less the attitude change. This equation differs only in parameter labels from a social judgment model of attitude change reported in Chapter 4. This model is shown in Fig. 3.2

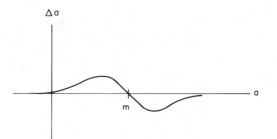

Fig. 3.2. The graph for the inattention (counterargument) model of attitude change derived from information processing theory; shown for a positive message.

Polarity Effects

The proportional change model can also be modified to account for a reduction in persuadability for receivers who held extreme attitudes. For example,

$$\Delta a = \frac{\alpha}{1 + a^2}(m - a) \qquad (3.18)$$

assumes that attitude change is reduced in proportion to the square of polarity and is graphed in Fig. 3.3. The striking feature of this model is the asymmetry of change around the message. That is, equal attitude–message discrepancy differences do not produce the same amount of change in both directions. As discrepancy from the message increases, polarity ultimately also increases and so attitude change tends to zero. This model yields very similar predictions to the social judgment models discussed in Chapter 4, although its premises are quite different.

Source Credibility and Attitude Change

Information processing theorists have given considerable attention to credibility of the source. They expect "credible" sources to be more persuasive and

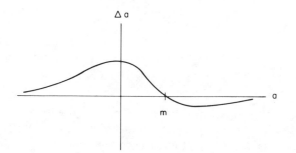

Fig. 3.3. Information processing model with polarity; positive message.

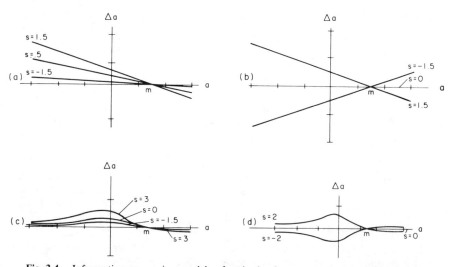

Fig. 3.4. Information processing models of attitude change as a function of premessage attitude and source credibility: (a) proportional change without boomerang; (b) proportional change with boomerang; (c) polarity without boomerang; (d) polarity with boomerang. In all of the graphs, $m = 1.5$.

The polarity models can be modified to show source credibility effects. These models would be

$$
\text{and} \qquad \Delta a = \begin{cases} \dfrac{e^{\sigma s}}{1 + e^{\sigma s}} \alpha \dfrac{(m - a)}{1 + a^2} & (3.27) \\[4mm] \dfrac{s}{\sqrt{1 + s^2}} \dfrac{(m - a)}{1 + a^2} & (3.28) \end{cases}
$$

which are graphed in Fig. 3.4c and d, respectively.

Source Change and the Discrepancy Equation

In our original review of the work in information processing theory, we found no formal models of source change. In fact, information processing theorists seem to have overlooked source change entirely. In contexts such as the evening news, there may be no source change, but in contexts such as political campaigns there is considerable source change. In response to this, we originally derived a speculative model that we thought to be consistent with the spirit of information processing theory.

In the course of the next several years, we carried out two research projects that lead to the development of specifically derived models of source change. The first project was a study of attitude change in an interpersonal context,

TABLE 3.2

Information Processing Source Change: Summary

Model	Assumptions
Mirror model $\Delta s = \beta(m - s)$	Interpersonal communication context. The message m about the source is a direct reflection of what the source says about another person.
Comparison model $\Delta s = \beta(m - a - s)$	Assumes that receivers expect source to evaluate another person on the basis of what they believe about that person.
Mixed (in aggregate data only) $\Delta s = \beta(m - s) - p\beta a$	Assumes that $p\%$ of the receivers use the comparison model and $1 - p\%$ use the mirror model.
Political model $\Delta s = \beta(a - s)$	Message value about the source depends on how the receiver feels about the issue endorsed. The message value is given as the receiver's attitude a toward the issue.
Mixed for individuals $\Delta s = \beta(m - s) - p\beta a$	Assumes that both direct reflection and bias comparison occur in the receiver, with bias comparison occurring $p\%$ of the time.

which will be reported in Chapter 10. The other empirical context was the study of political campaigns, which will be presented in Chapter 11.

The interpersonal models and the political model of source change were both derived from the same general proposition: the content of a message that states the beliefs or feelings of the source is a message about the source as well as the object. If the message value for the source is m_s, then source change will be given by the same discrepancy equation as for any other attitude change,

$$\Delta s = \alpha(m_s - s) \tag{3.29}$$

though the change parameter α may be different for the amount of source change produced by a given message than for the amount of attitude change. That is, if both attitude and source change are considered, then the equations would be

$$\Delta a = \alpha(m - a) \tag{3.30}$$

$$\Delta s = \beta(m_s - s) \tag{3.31}$$

where the shift from α to β represents the potential difference in parameter values for the two messages.

The difference between the various models in the two empirical contexts stems from different theories of how the content of the message is processed to produce the message about the source. So far two contexts have produced four models for this process. It may be that each empirical context will require a different model for deriving the source message value from the content of the message. A summary of the source change models appears in Table 3.2.

SOURCE CHANGE: INTERPERSONAL CONTEXT

The Message: What It Says About the Source

In an interpersonal context, the source is telling the listener about some third person. In this situation, it is common for the listener to think of the message in two ways: what the message says about the object person and what the message says about the source. If the listener derives a message about the source from the message about the object, then that second message will have a message value m_s. Information processing theory would then predict that there would be source change in accordance with the discrepancy equation

$$\Delta s = \beta(m_s - s) \tag{3.32}$$

or one of its variations.

To construct a model of source change is thus to construct a model of message perception that states the rules for deriving a perception of the source from what the source says about a third person. We shall develop two such models. The first can be characterized by the childhood poem "Twinkle, twinkle, little star; what you say is what you are." That is, people who say nice things are nice and people who say nasty things are nasty. That is, this model asserts that $m_s = m$. The second model assumes that the listener relates what the source says to what the listener believes. That is, the listener compares m and a. A source who is nicer or less nasty than the listener is nice and a source who is less nice or nastier than the listener is nasty. This model asserts that the message value for the source is $m_s = m - a$.

From these two models of message perception, we derive three models of a source change: one model assumes $m_s = m$, one model assumes $m_s = m - a$, and the third model assumes that different listeners use different rules. That is, the third model assumes that the listener population consists of two sub-populations: those listeners characterized by $m_s = m$ and those characterized by $m_s = m - a$. An aggregate data analysis across both kinds of receivers would mix the regression equations to form a weighted average of the two models.

The Mirror Model

The mirror model of message perception assumes that receivers expect nice people to say nice things and nasty people to say nasty things. Nice people will either refrain from saying nasty things or will couch negative thoughts in tactful euphemisms. On the other hand, nasty people are believed to say something nice only if they are manipulating another. Thus the meaning of the message as a characterization of the source is a direct reflection of what the source says (hence the phrase "mirror" model): $m_s = m$.

According to information processing theory, the impact of the message on the attitude toward the source should be determined by the discrepancy equation, that is, on the comparison between the message values $m_s = m$ and the current attitude value s. Thus the mirror model of source change is

$$\Delta s = \beta(m_s - s) = \beta(m - s) \tag{3.33}$$

where the parameter β has the same meaning as the α of the linear discrepancy equation though not necessarily the same numerical value.

This model can also be thought of as a message source discrepancy model. The receivers's attitude toward the source will change in the direction of what the source says.

The Comparison Model

The comparison model asserts that people set their expectations for the source on the basis of what they believe about the object rather than on what they believe about the source. Thus if the receiver believes that the third person is nasty, then there is no surprise in hearing the source say that the third person is nasty. The message sounds factual and neutral. But a source who describes a nasty person in neutral terms appears to be warm hearted.

The expected message value is what the listener believes about the object person, that is, the attitude a. The position staked out by the source is the message value m. The implied value of the source depends on whether the source sees people as better than they are or as worse than they are. That is, the implied value of the source is the comparison

$$m_s = m - a$$

The source change implied by information processing theory is then given by

$$\Delta s = \beta(m_s - s) = \beta[(m - a) - s] = \beta(m - a - s) \tag{3.34}$$

The Mixed Model

Suppose that the mirror model works for some people and the comparison model works for others. An aggregate analysis would mix the two kinds of people. If the two subpopulations had the same distribution of attitude toward the object, then the aggregation would result in an averaging of the two regression equations. If the proportion of persons characterized by the comparison model is p and the proportion of persons characterized by the mirror model is $q = 1 - p$, then the average equation or mixed model of source change would be

$$\begin{aligned}
\Delta s &= p(\text{comparison}) + q(\text{mirror}) \\
&= p[\beta(m - s - a)] + q[\beta(m - a)] \\
&= \beta(p + q)m - \beta(p + q)s - p\beta a \\
&= \beta m - \beta s - p\beta a \\
&= \beta(m - s) - p\beta a
\end{aligned} \tag{3.35}$$

There is another model that has the same regression equation; a model that asssumes that both processes take place within the same head. That is, suppose that both perceptual processes take place in the receiver: an alternation between reacting to the source as what he says and reacting to the source in comparison to what the listener believes. The result might be a net impression in which the implied value of the source is a weighted average of the emotional values of the two ways of thinking. That is, the perceptual process might be a mixed model.

$$\begin{aligned}
m_s &= p(\text{comparison}) + q(\text{mirror}) \\
&= p(m - a) + q(m) \\
&= (p + q)m - pa = m - pa
\end{aligned} \tag{3.36}$$

The source change equation is then

$$\Delta s = \beta(m_s - s) = \beta[(m - pa) - s] = \beta(m - pa - s) = \beta(m - s) - p\beta a \tag{3.37}$$

SOURCE CHANGE IN A POLITICAL CONTEXT

According to information processing, source change will occur if the message from the source contains an implicit message about the source. In a political campaign most messages endorse or reject policies. The message about the source can be characterized in terms of the aphorism "What you say is what you'll do." That is, logically cast the message in terms of a position endorsed. The content of the message in regard to the object is "This position is the wise position." The message about the source is "This is the probable behavior of the source." The message value in regard to the object is always positive by construction. The message value in regard to the source depends on how the receiver feels about the position endorsed. That is, the source message value is given by the receiver's attitude a,

$$m_s = a$$

The resulting attitude change is then given by

$$\Delta s = \beta(m_s - s) = \beta(a - s) \tag{3.38}$$

For example, if the head of the Republican party issues the statement "The Republican party favors greatly reduced taxes." then this statement is recoded into "If in power, the Republican party will greatly cut taxes." The value of this message as a description of the Republican party depends on how the voter feels about greatly reduced taxes and the implied cuts in government programs. That is, the implied value of the message is the receiver's attitude toward reduced taxes and reduced programs.

In this message model, it is important to remember that the issue was coded so that the party is endorsing a position. This may mean a reverse coding of the position as it is stated in ordinary discourse. For example, opposition to the MX missile system would be coded as endorsing the position "The MX missile system should be abandoned."

A political campaign is always a bundle of issues. Thus a model for the campaign will require extending the model for single messages to a model for the impact of several messages. Furthermore, the final model must consider not just one but two political parties. These extensions are carried out in the later chapter analyzing panel data from the Butler and Stokes (1969, 1974) longitudinal study of British politics.

SOURCE CHANGE: OTHER CONTEXTS

We have considered two contexts in which information processing theory can be used to derive models of source change. These models are actually models of message perception in those areas. In the interpersonal area, two models of message perception were constructed: the mirror model $m_s = m$ and the comparison model $m_s = m - a$. In the political context, the message model was $m_s = a$. These examples make it clear that a variety of models can be constructed in different areas.

Here we would like to cite just one more area: lab studies of attitude change such as those reviewed in the discussion section of Chapter 10 on the study of the simulated network. For example, in Aronson, Turner, and Carlsmith (1963), the object was the use of alliteration in poetry. The low credibility source was a college student and the high credibility source was T. S. Eliot. Yet the message delivered was very erudite in either case. The probable message about the source in this study was "This source knows a lot about poetry." Thus the well-constructed nature of the message itself sets a high value on the dimension "expertise" for the source of the message. Studies that focus on unfamiliar subject matter would be prone to this problem, whereas studies on topics where the experimental subject regards himself as knowledgeable may have different models. For example, in the network study itself, the objects of the messages are people and the sources did not present messages that set themselves apart from the receivers as experts. In the "network" study (Chapter 10), the message value was that for the interpersonal context.

CHAPTER 4

Social Judgment Theory

LATITUDES OF ACCEPTANCE AND REJECTION

Social judgment theory is a variation of information processing theory. The theory began with studies of message perception reported by Sherif and Hovland (1961), who found that receivers do not react neutrally to messages, rather they judge messages as being acceptable or not. This judgment is highly predictable from the discrepancy between message value and the attitude of the receiver. If the discrepancy between message and attitude is small, then the receiver judges the message to be acceptable. However, if the discrepancy is large, then the receiver will judge the message to be biased or distorted and not acceptable. Sherif and Hovland (1961) describe this phenomenon in terms of "latitudes of acceptance" and "latitudes of rejection." Their general theory of message perception is shown in Fig. 4.1. The latitude of acceptance is centered about the attitude value of the perceiver and represents a region of small message–attitude discrepancy. On either side of the latitude of acceptance there is a latitude of rejection that contains messages that are highly discrepant in one direction or the other.

Social judgment theorists [Hovland, Harvey, and Sherif (1957), Sherif and Hovland (1961), and Sherif, Sherif, and Nebergall (1965)] believe that attitude change depends on message perception. They assert that the extent of attitude change and source change depends on whether the message falls within the latitude of acceptance or not. Attitude change increases with discrepancy as

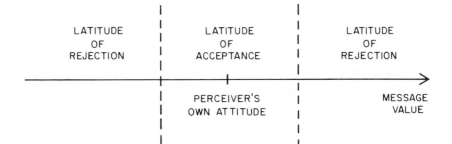

Fig. 4.1. The social judgment theory classification of messages into latitudes of acceptance and rejection.

long as the message falls within the latitude of acceptance, but then it decreases if the discrepancy is so large that the message falls in the latitudes of rejection. Thus attitude change is predicted to be a nonlinear function of discrepancy. If the message falls within the latitude of acceptance, the source is seen to be fair, intelligent, and wise. If the message falls into the latitudes of rejection, then the source is seen as biased, dull witted, and lacking knowledge in the area. Thus social judgment theory predicts that source change will be positive if the message falls within the latitude of acceptance and negative if the message falls within the latitudes of rejection.

The variations of social judgment theory depend on assumptions as to just what happens if the message falls in the latitudes of rejection. One possibility is to assume that as discrepancy becomes larger and larger, the attitude change decreases to zero as the receiver rejects the message more and more completely. This would be consistent with the information processing orientation of the social judgment theorists. However, Hovland *et al.* (1957) hypothesize otherwise. They suggest that if the discrepancy becomes large enough, the receiver might actually change in the opposite direction to that of the message; a change called a "boomerang." However, they offer no theoretical reason for why this would be true (Kiesler, Collins, and Miller, 1969).

It is also possible to introduce source credibility effects into social judgment theory by hypothesizing that the width of the latitude of acceptance depends on the receiver's attitude toward the source. That is, the latitude of acceptance might be larger if the receiver likes the source than if the receiver dislikes the source.

BASIC SOCIAL JUDGMENT MODEL

We believe that boomerang is not native to social judgment theory which is dominated by information processing assumptions. Therefore we shall take the basic social judgment model for attitude change to be one in which change is always in the direction of the message and in which the amount of change increases as long as the discrepancy is small enough to keep the message within the latitude of acceptance but decreases to zero as the discrepancy tends to infinity. If λ is the width of the latitude of acceptance, and d is the message attitude discrepancy (i.e., $d = m - a$), then the simplest equation that meets the assumptions of social judgment theory is

$$\Delta a = \frac{\lambda^2}{\lambda^2 + d^2} \alpha (m - a) \tag{4.1}$$

The graph for this model is given in Fig. 4.2a. Equation (4.1) can be factored into two terms. The term $\alpha(m - a)$ is the amount of change predicted by the linear discrepancy equation, that is, the amount of change that would result from a neutral response to the message. The initial fraction $\lambda^2/(\lambda^2 + d^2)$

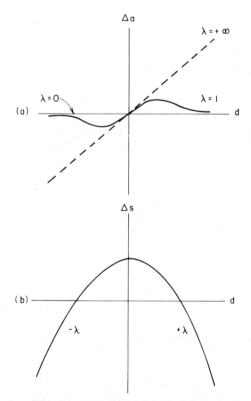

Fig. 4.2. The basic social judgment model: (a) attitude change as a function of discrepancy $(d = m - a)$ at different levels of acceptance latitude λ; (b) source change as a function of discrepancy at different levels of acceptance latitude λ.

TABLE 4.1

SOCIAL JUDGMENT ATTITUDE CHANGE: SUMMARY

Model	Assumptions
Basic	
$$\Delta a = \frac{\lambda^2}{\lambda^2 + d^2}\alpha d$$	Messages in the region of acceptance are assimilated and judged as factual and unbiased. Within this region attitude change obeys the linear discrepancy rule: $\Delta a = \alpha(m - a)$. Messages in the region of rejection evoke a contrast reaction and are judged to be objectionable and propagandistic. In the region of rejection, messages yield diminishing degrees of attitude change with increasing communication discrepancy.
Boomerang	
$$\Delta a = \frac{\beta^2 - d^2}{\beta^2 + 1}\alpha d$$	Highly divergent messages cause "boomerang." The width of the region of acceptance is indirectly specified by β.
Tamed boomerang	
$$\Delta a = \frac{\beta^2 - d^2}{\beta^2 + \gamma d^2}\alpha d$$	Same as above except boomerang effects are asymptotically linearly related to discrepancy; γ is a suitably chosen scaling constant.
Bounded boomerang	
$$\Delta a = \frac{\beta^2 - d^2}{\beta^2 + \gamma|d|^3}\alpha d$$	Same as previous model except boomerang does not increase without bound: boomerang effect levels off at large discrepancies.
No change at extreme discrepancy	
$$\Delta a = \frac{\beta^2 - d^2}{\beta^2 + \gamma d^4}\alpha d$$	Same as previous model except at large discrepancies attitude change approaches zero.
Credibility and latitude of acceptance	
$$\beta = \rho e^\sigma$$	Increases in source credibility increase latitude of acceptance; $\beta \to 0$ as $s \to -\infty$ and $\beta \to +\infty$ as $s \to +\infty$; ρ is a suitably chosen scaling constant $2\beta/\sqrt{3} = \lambda$.

TABLE 4.2

Social Judgment Source Change: Summary

Model	Assumptions
Basic	
$\Delta s = \gamma(\lambda^2 - d^2)$	Sources whose messages fall within the region (latitude) of acceptance exhibit positive change. When the message is outside the region of acceptance, change in attitude toward the source is negative.
Source derogation	
$\Delta s = \gamma \dfrac{\lambda^2 - d^2}{\lambda^2 + 1}$	Unbounded source derogation.
$\Delta s = \gamma \dfrac{\lambda^2 - d^2}{\lambda^2 + \lvert d \rvert + 1}$	Same as above except unbounded derogation is less extreme.
$\Delta s = \gamma \dfrac{\lambda^2 - d^2}{\lambda^2 + d^2 + 1}$	Source derogation levels off at large discrepancies.
$\Delta s = \gamma \dfrac{\lambda^2 - d^2}{\lambda^2 + d^4 + 1}$	Source derogation is asympotically zero.
Source credibility and source change	
$\lambda = \delta e^{\sigma s}$	Assumes λ is not a constant but is a function of the attitude toward the source; δ is less than ρ to the extent that β is less than λ [see Eq. (4.16)].

determines the proportion of that change that is realized after the emotional evaluation of the message.

Sherif and Hovland (1961) and Sherif *et al.* (1965) argue that messages that fall within the latitude of acceptance are viewed as fair and unbiased; those that fall outside of the acceptance latitude, that is, within the latitude of rejection, are viewed as biased, slanted, and unfair. If the source is identified with the message, then message perception will produce source change. Source change is positive if the discrepancy is less than λ in absolute value and negative otherwise. That is,

$$\Delta s > 0 \qquad \text{if} \quad d^2 < \lambda^2$$

The simplest equation with this property is

$$\Delta s = \gamma(\lambda^2 - d^2) \tag{4.2}$$

The graph for the basic source change model is presented in Fig. 4.2b. Table 4.1 presents a summary of the variations in the equation for attitude change, and Table 4.2 presents a summary of the variations in the equation for source change.

THEORETICAL AND TECHNICAL VARIATIONS

Models with Boomerang

Some studies of attitude change have observed boomerang effects, that is, attitude change in the direction *opposite* of that advocated by the message [Wilke (1934), Manske (1937), Russell and Robertson (1947), and Williamson and Remmers (1940)]. The original social judgment theory proposed by Sherif and Hovland (1961) attempted to account for change in the direction of a message, no change, and boomerang effects, that is, change opposite of the message.

Like the basic social judgment model, messages in the region of acceptance are assimilated and judged as factual and unbiased. Within this region attitude change is proportional to the magnitude of the communication discrepancy and direction of the message. Messages in the region of rejection evoke a contrast reaction and are judged to be objectionable and propagandistic. In the region of rejection, such messages yield diminishing degrees of attitude change with increasing communication discrepancy. However, highly divergent messages cause the receiver to change in a direction away from the message, that is, boomerang.

Figure 4.3 displays these assumptions in graphic form. Thus if we start upward to attitudes more positive than the message, change will be toward the message, that is, negative. The change will be greater and greater until the boundary of the latitude of acceptance is reached. At this point change is maximal (the function has a minimum). The amount of change then decreases until the message is no longer assimilated. Past this point the message has a reverse effect, that is, the subject boomerangs and attitude change is positive. If we proceed from the message toward attitudes more negative than the message, similar statements apply. However, below the message, assimilation means that attitude change will be positive whereas boomerang yields negative change.

Thus the function Δa has three zeros and four sign regions. The simplest such function is a cubic. A cubic would be symmetric about the message as was

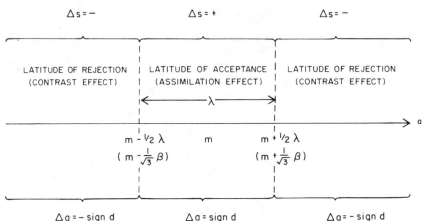

Fig. 4.3. Graphic form of assumptions for source judgment with boomerang: source and attitude change.

assumed by Sherif. This cubic is given by

$$\Delta a = \frac{\alpha}{1 + \beta^2}(a - m + \beta)(a - m)(a - m - \beta) \qquad (4.3)$$

which is displayed in factored form to show the derivation from the zeros. A form that shows its relation to the linear discrepancy model is

$$\Delta a = \frac{\beta^2 - (m - a)^2}{\beta^2 + 1} \alpha(m - a) \qquad (4.4)$$

where $0 < \alpha < 1$, $\beta \geq 0$. The first term in this product can be regarded as a complex manipulation of the sign of the parameter α. The graph of the model is shown in Fig. 4.4b (Fig. 4.4a is a repeat of Fig. 4.2).

The parameter β indirectly specifies the width of the region of assimilation, that is, the region where attitude change is in the direction of the message. It can be directly obtained by computing the maximum and minimum of the cubic. The interval is from $m - (\beta/\sqrt{3})$ to $m + (\beta/\sqrt{3})$ and has length $2\beta/\sqrt{3} = \lambda$.

This model implicitly assumes that (1) the size of the region of indifference is "zero" and (2) the width of the latitude of acceptance is the same for everyone. Assumption 1 may be untenable in certain experimental situations. Sherif *et al.* (1965) finds that, although the latitude of acceptance is constant across the range of attitudes toward the object, the width of the region where the receiver neither marks accept nor marks reject (the latitude of noncommitment) shrinks with polarity of attitude. This is most pronounced if the object has personal importance to the individual.

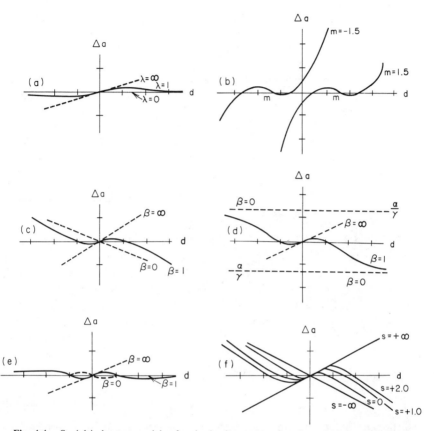

Fig. 4.4. Social judgment models of attitude change as a function of (a) message–attitude discrepancy without boomerang (basic model), (b) premessage attitude with cubic boomerang, (c) discrepancy with asymptotically linear boomerang and with varying latitudes of acceptance, (d) discrepancy with asymptotically constant boomerang and with varying latitudes of acceptance, (e) discrepancy with asymptotic change, no boomerang, and with varying latitudes of acceptance, (f) discrepancy with asymptotically linear boomerang and with varying levels of source credibility.

If the latitude of noncommitment is regarded as a region of mild rejection and hence added to the latitude of rejection, the assumptions of the model are in accord with Sherif's findings.

Because the function for attitude change is symmetric about the message value m, the model could be expressed in discrepancy units rather than attitude units. The origin would now be at the message value, not at $a = 0$. Defining $d \equiv m - a$ and substituting into Eq. (4.4), the new expression is

$$\Delta a = \frac{\beta^2 - d^2}{\beta^2 + 1} \alpha d \tag{4.5}$$

where $d > 0$ implies the message is more favorable than the attitude and $d < 0$ implies the message is less favorable than the attitude.

The two limiting cases of the model occur when the width of the region of acceptance is either zero or infinite. As $\beta \to +\infty$, $\Delta a \to \alpha d$ and the Sherif model reduces to the linear discrepancy model. Because the region of acceptance is infinite in width, any message must be within the region, hence attitude change is proportional to message discrepancy. Suppose the region of rejection is infinitely wide. Then, $\beta \to 0$ and $\Delta a \to -\alpha d^3$. Every message evokes a boomerang in attitude with magnitude proportional to the cube of discrepancy.

Tamed Boomerang

The cubic growth rate of boomerang in the previous model might seem unrealistic; boomerang can be tamed by modifying Eq. (4.5) to read

$$\Delta a = \frac{\beta^2 - d^2}{\beta^2 + \gamma d^2} \alpha d \qquad (4.6)$$

The essential behavior of Sherif's model is intact, but boomerang is, asymptotically, linearly related to discrepancy (Fig. 4.4c).

As before, when $\beta \to \infty$, $\Delta a \to \alpha d$. But, because of the modification, as $\beta \to 0$, $\Delta a \to -\alpha d/\gamma$. That is, with an infinitely wide region of rejection, boomerang is also proportional to message discrepancy.

Bounded Boomerang

The tamed boomerang model still assumes that boomerang increases without bound. Instead, boomerang might only increase up to a point and then level off for larger discrepancies. For example,

$$\Delta a = \frac{\beta^2 - d^2}{\beta^2 + \gamma |d|^3} \alpha d \qquad (4.7)$$

This model is graphed in Fig. 4.4d.

The limiting cases for the region of acceptance are similarly affected. With an infinitely wide latitude of acceptance, $\beta \to +\infty$ and $\Delta a \to \alpha d$. With pure boomerang (infinitely wide region of rejection), $\beta \to 0$ and $\Delta a \to -\alpha/\gamma$ for $d > 0$ and $+\alpha/\gamma$ for $d < 0$.

No Change at Extreme Discrepancy

Alternatively, at some extreme discrepancy, the receiver might simply reject the message and undergo no attitude change. For example,

$$\Delta a = \frac{\beta^2 - d^2}{\beta^2 + \gamma d^4}\alpha d \tag{4.8}$$

Figure 4.4e presents the graph for this model.

As $\beta \to \infty$, $\Delta a \to \alpha d$ for the linear discrepancy model. As $\beta \to 0$, $\Delta a \to -\alpha/\gamma d$. Thus boomerang first increases with discrepancy, then asymptotically decreases to zero.

Source Credibility

The key concepts in the social judgment approach to attitude change are the latitudes of acceptance and rejection. These regions not only identify the conditions under which the message will be maximally effective or result in boomerang but also enable Sherif to explain why attitude change might be either linear or curvilinear with discrepancy. When the latitude of acceptance is relatively broad, even an "extreme" message falls within it, so the observed relationship between attitude change and discrepancy will necessarily be linear. With a narrower latitude of acceptance, the observed data will manifest a curvilinear relationship.

Although the exact numerical size of the latitude of acceptance cannot be predicted, it is not arbitrary. Sherif postulates two variables that restrict the relative width of these latitudes. They are ego-involvement and source credibility. The implications of ego-involvement will not be pursued here.

Sherif and Sherif (1967) concur with previous theorists who argue that the credibility of the source magnifies the degree of attitude change, though he derives this prediction from a different base. Credible sources have a wider latitude of acceptance and, thus, a narrower latitude of rejection. The converse is true for noncredible sources. Thus, for Sherif, credibility is a positive function of the receiver's attitude toward the source and the latitude of acceptance is a positive function of credibility. Because the latitude of acceptance is indirectly represented by β in these models, these assumptions could be expressed in a form such as

$$\beta = \rho e^{\sigma s} \tag{4.9}$$

where ρ is a positive constant determined entirely by the choice of unit for s. This yields a perfectly incredible source with $\beta = 0$ for $s = -\infty$ and a perfectly credible source with $\beta = +\infty$ (as desired) for $s = +\infty$.

With these assumptions, the parametric graphs of Δa as a function of a and s are simply the graphs presented before with varying values of β. This is illustrated in Fig. 4.4f for the Sherif model with boomerang as asymptotically linear function of discrepancy.

SOCIAL JUDGMENT THEORY: SOURCE CHANGE

Social judgment theory does not directly address the issue of change in attitude toward the source. It does state that the receiver's reaction to the source is associated with the discrepancy of the message. Those sources whose messages fall into the latitude of acceptance are characterized as fair and impartial. When the message lies in the latitude of rejection, the source is labeled as biased. Thus it seems reasonable that if a source's message is in the region of acceptance, the receiver's attitude toward the source would shift upward. If the message is rejected, the source would be derogated. Within the latitude of acceptance, the degree of enhancement would be inversely related to message discrepancy. That is, the more consonant the messsage, the more positive his evaluation, But in the region of rejection, a more discrepant message would cause greater disparagement of the source.

In terms of inequalities, this means

$$\Delta s > 0 \quad \text{if} \quad -\lambda < d < +\lambda$$

$$\Delta s = 0 \quad \text{if} \quad d = -\lambda \quad \text{or} \quad d = +\lambda$$

$$\Delta s < 0 \quad \text{if} \quad d > +\lambda \quad \text{or} \quad d < -\lambda$$

These inequalities can be more conveniently written as

$$\Delta s = \begin{cases} + & \text{if} \quad \lambda^2 - d^2 > 0 \\ 0 & \text{if} \quad \lambda^2 - d^2 = 0 \\ - & \text{if} \quad \lambda^2 - d^2 < 0 \end{cases} \tag{4.10}$$

$$\Delta s = \gamma(\lambda^2 - d^2) \tag{4.11}$$

where λ is the region of acceptance if source change is plotted as a function of discrepancy.

Source Derogation

An example of a model with unbounded source derogation is

$$\Delta s = \gamma \frac{\lambda^2 - d^2}{\lambda^2 + 1} \tag{4.12}$$

which is presented graphically in Fig. 4.5a.

A less extreme model with unbounded source derogation is

$$\Delta s = \gamma \frac{\lambda^2 - d^2}{\lambda^2 + |d| + 1} \tag{4.13}$$

which is graphed in Fig. 4.5.

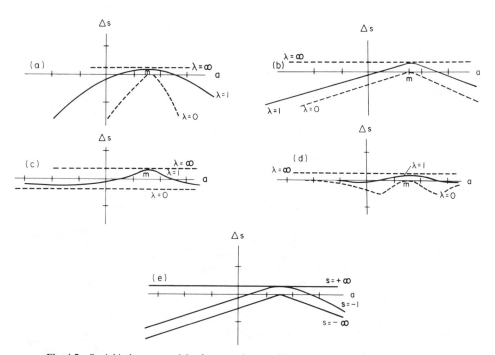

Fig. 4.5 Social judgment models of source change with source derogation an asymptotically: (a) quadratic function of premessage attitude ($m = 1.5$), (b) linear function of premessage attitude, (c) constant function of premessage attitude ($m = 1.5$), (d) zero function of premessage attitude, and (e) linear function of premessage attitude and with a source credibility effect.

An example of a model where source derogation as a function of discrepancy levels off is

$$\Delta s = \gamma \frac{\lambda^2 - d^2}{\lambda^2 + d^2 + 1} \tag{4.14}$$

which is presented in Fig. 4.5c.

An example of a model in which source derogation is asymptotically zero is

$$\Delta s = \gamma \frac{\lambda^2 - d^2}{\lambda^2 + d^4 + 1} \tag{4.15}$$

which is presented in Fig. 4.5d.

Source Credibility and Source Change

If source credibility affects the latitude of acceptance, then the λ in the previous equations for source change is not a constant. On the contrary, λ is a function of the attitude of the receiver toward the source. In particular, the assumption made before for β [Eq. (4.9)] would be rewritten as

$$\lambda = \delta e^{\sigma s} \tag{4.16}$$

where $\delta < \rho$ to the extent that $\beta < \lambda$. The resulting parametric graphs of the change in attitude toward the source as a function of a and s are presented in Fig. 4.5e.

SOURCE CHANGE AND ATTITUDE CHANGE

In this chapter five different equations for attitude change and five different equations for source change were formulated. The uses for each equation are doubled by the possibility of assuming that source credibility is a function of attitude toward the source (or that the latitude of acceptance depends on source credibility).

Each model requires an equation for source change and an equation for attitude change, that is, a coordination of the two. The only determined coordination is that either both or neither will make the source credibility assumption. Furthermore, just as Sherif gives no explicit statement of source change, he gives no explicit statement relevant to the coordination of the two. Moreover, there is no apparent implicit basis for a coordination. Thus any of the remaining combinations are consistent with Sherif's theory.

CHAPTER 5

Affective Consistency: Balance And Congruity Theory

Information processing theory begins by considering the cognitive response to a discrepancy between the logical content of the message and the receiver's beliefs. There is a different kind of discrepancy that has fascinated other theorists: the emotional compatibility or incompatibility between the feelings of the receiver and the source. Attempts to define emotional consistency led to the development of balance theory (Heider, 1946) and congruity theory (Osgood and Tannenbaum, 1955). This chapter will develop simple models that illustrate the general properties of these models, though these models are not the models of the classic literature. The classic congruity models will be derived in the next chapter.

The history of affective consistency theories is well summarized by Brown (1962) and Zajonc (1960). They also provide an excellent overview and comparison of formulations within this class. Briefly, the current consistency models of attitude change trace their origins to theories of group dynamics rather than attitude change per se. Brown proposes that the principles of consistency theory can be attributed to the even earlier work on psychological conflict [Miller (1944), Lewin (1935), and Freud (1909)]. The first statement of the principles of balance was by Heider (1946). These principles were extended and refined by Newcomb (1953), Abelson and Rosenberg (1958), Cartwright and Harary (1956), Feather (1967), and Phillips (1967).

BALANCE THEORY AS NEWCOMB DERIVED IT

Newcomb (1953) developed balance theory in an interpersonal context in which one person is talking to another about some object. What the speaker says influences the listener in two ways: the listener may change his attitude toward the object, and the listener will assess the speaker on the basis of whether the listener likes what the speaker says. That is, we have attitude change and source change. The basic balance theory model can be determined by predicting the processes that take place in the listener.

Consider first the influence process. According to balance theory, if the listener likes the speaker, then the receiver will be influenced in the direction of the message. That is, if the receiver likes the source and the source says nice things about the object, then the receiver will tend to be positively disposed toward the object at that moment. Thus the receiver's attitude will become either more positive or less negative. If the receiver likes the source and the source says nasty things about the object, then the receiver will be negatively disposed toward the object at that moment and attitude change will be negative.

If the receiver dislikes the source, then balance theory makes a more controversial assertion. If the receiver dislikes the source and the source speaks highly of the object, then the receiver is negatively disposed toward the object at that moment. That is, the receiver reacts according to the rule "The friend of my enemy is my enemy." or "If you like it there must be something wrong with it." If the receiver dislikes the source and the source says nasty things about the object, then the receiver is positively disposed toward the object at that moment and attitude change will be positive. That is, the receiver reacts according to the rule "The enemy of my enemy is my friend." or "If you don't like it there must be something good about it." This last rule has come under considerable debate among balance theorists, as will be noted in the chapter on the balance theories of sociometric structure, in the second volume.

The influence process can be sketched in Table 5.1. Examination of the table shows that the algebraic sign of attitude change is given by the algebraic sign of the product of attitude toward the source and message value, that is,

$$\text{sign}(\Delta a) = \text{sign}(sm)$$

Thus the simplest basic model for attitude change derived from balance theory is

$$\Delta a = \alpha ms$$

The source change model is more straightforward. Relations between persons are assumed to be harmonious if friends agree or if enemies disagree. That is, if the source agrees with the receiver, then the receiver is positively

TABLE 5.1

ATTITUDE CHANGE FOR THE BASIC BALANCE MODEL

Attitude toward source s	What source says m	Momentary disposition process	Attitude change Δa
+	+	The friend of my friend is a friend.	+
+	−	The enemy of my friend is an enemy.	−
−	+	The friend of my enemy is an enemy.	−
−	−	The enemy of my enemy is a friend.	+

disposed toward the source at that moment and source change is positive. If the source disagrees with the receiver, then the receiver is momentarily negatively disposed and the resulting source change is negative.

The assumptions for source change are given in Table 5.2. Examination of the table shows that the algebraic sign of source change is given by the product of the algebraic signs of attitude toward the object and message value, that is,

$$\text{sign}(\Delta s) = \text{sign}(am)$$

Thus the simplest basic model for source change derived from balance theory is

$$\Delta s = \beta ma$$

We have now derived a basic model of balance theory in the passive communication context (see Fig. 5.1):

$$\Delta a = \alpha ms \tag{5.1}$$

$$\Delta s = \beta ma \tag{5.2}$$

TABLE 5.2

SOURCE CHANGE FOR THE BASIC BALANCE MODEL

Attitude toward object a	What source says m	Momentary evaluation of source	Source change Δs
+	+	Sharp fellow	+
+	−	What a blockhead	−
−	+	What a blockhead	−
−	−	Sharp fellow	+

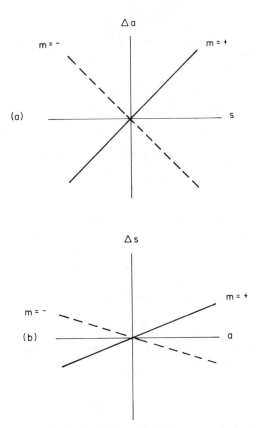

Fig. 5.1. (a) Balance model of attitude change. Solid line represents $m = +$ and $\alpha = 1$; dotted line represents $m = -$ and $\alpha = 1$. (b) Balance model of source change. Solid line represents $m = +$ and $\beta = \frac{1}{2}$; dotted line represents $m = -$ and $\beta = \frac{1}{2}$.

CONGRUITY THEORY AND TWO-STAGE S–R THEORY

Osgood, Tannenbaum, and Suci (1957) believe that their congruity model of attitude change follows from two-stage stimulus–response (S–R) theory. However, the actual content of their derivation has nothing to do with conditioning. Instead they argue that incongruous messages set up an internal pressure that causes change to a less incongruous set of attitudes. This derivation is actually a variation of Gestalt psychology rather than reinforcement theory.

In this chapter we shall attempt to derive congruity theory from conditioning principles rather than from a hypothetical internal pressure mechanism. As it happens, there is no problem for the positive message. We shall derive a simple linear model for the impact of a positive message that is in full agreement with the linear model that we shall derive from the pressure theory in the next chapter. However, there are very great problems with the negative message. In our opinion, the congruity theory model for the negative message cannot be derived from conditioning theory without introducing an internal linguistic translation mechanism that is anathema to traditional S–R theory regardless of the number of stages. On the other hand, the linguistic translation derives directly from balance theory. Thus we believe that the following derivation of congruity theory shows it to be a variation of balance theory rather than a variation of conditioning theory.

Consider the positive message. If the message is positive, then the source is endorsing the object. This is an invitation for the receiver to think about the source and the object together. When the receiver thinks about the object, there is an emotional response whose value is given by the receiver's attitude toward the object, that is, by a. When the receiver thinks about the source there is an emotional response whose value is given by the receiver's attitude toward the source, that is, by s. According to conditioning theory, an emotional response that occurs in the presence of an emotional event will be altered in the direction of that event. Thus the emotional response to the object should be conditioned by the emotional event that is the emotional response to the source. Similarly, the emotional response to the source should be conditioned by the emotional event that is the emotional response to the object. Thus each of the two emotional responses will condition the other. Each of the two emotional responses should change in the direction of the other. Each of the two emotional responses should change in the direction of the other. The simplest mathematical model of such simultaneous conditioning is

$$\Delta a = \alpha(s - a) \tag{5.3}$$

$$\Delta s = \alpha(a - s) \tag{5.4}$$

This is our basic congruity model for the positive message (see Fig. 5.2a).

Consider the negative message (Fig. 5.2c–d). Because the source is talking about the object, one might suppose that the message is an invitation to the receiver to think simultaneously about the source and the object. If this were true, then the conditioning model would predict the same change for the negative message as for the positive message. There is no known data that would fit this prediction. Osgood and Tannenbaum (1955) were well aware of this fact when they proposed a very different process for the negative message. They say that a negative message sets up a dissociation between source and object (as opposed to the association set up by the positive message). They then assert that the receiver's attitude toward the object conditions not to the

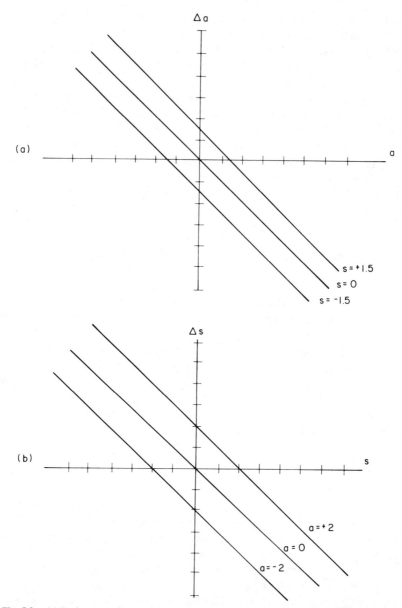

Fig. 5.2. (a) Basic congruity model (positive message) for attitude change when $\alpha = 1$ and $s = +1.5, 0, -1.5$. (b) Basic congruity model (positive message) for source change when $\alpha = 1$ and $a = +2, 0, -2$. (c) Basic congruity model (negative message) for attitude change when $\alpha = 1$ and $s = +1.5, 0, -1.5$. (d) Basic congruity model (negative message) when $\alpha = 1$ and $a = +2$, $a = 0$, and $a = -2$.

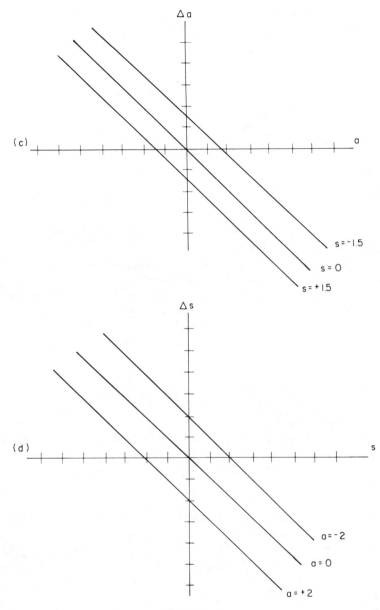

Fig. 5.2. (c–d)

receiver's emotional response to the source but to the exact negative of that value, that is,

$$\Delta a = \alpha[(-s) - a] = \alpha(-s - a) = -\alpha(s + a)$$

They further assert that the receiver's attitude toward the source conditions not to the receiver's emotional response to the object but to the exact negative of that value, that is,

$$\Delta s = \alpha[(-a) - s] = \alpha(-a - s) = -\alpha(a + s)$$

These equations become our simplest congruity theory model for the negative message:

$$\Delta a = -\alpha(s + a) \tag{5.5}$$

$$\Delta s = -\alpha(a + s) \tag{5.6}$$

Does the Osgood and Tannenbaum model for the negative message follow from conditioning theory? There is no process in conditioning theory called "dissociation." Furthermore, their use of the term "dissociation" is not consistent with normal English. The usual meaning of "dissociate" is to break apart. Thus dissociated objects are unrelated to one another, not the opposite of one another. Moreover, their interpretation does not even follow from logic (though derivation from logic is not legitimate in conditioning theory). If a source dissociates himself from an object, he is only claiming dislike, he is not claiming that the two have opposite value. Thus the introduction of opposite emotional reactions has no basis in conditioning theory.

Furthermore, even if the negative phrasing of the message caused the receiver to think of the opposite of his fundamental emotional responses, the link to the two separate congruity equations is not made by conditioning theory. Consider the congruity assertion for attitude change: a conditions to $-s$. Thus the two emotional responses a and $-s$ must be present. But consider the congruity assertion for source change: s must condition to $-a$, and hence both s and $-a$ must occur together. If the two assertions are taken together as is done by the pair of equations representing the dissociative process, then four emotional responses must occur: a, s, $-a$, and $-s$. If each conditions to the other three, then all conditions toward zero. This is not the congruity model.

To obtain any relationship between the congruity equations and conditioning processes, we must make two assumptions. First, the receiver must have two separate responses to the one linguistic experience; there must be separate consideration of the source and the object. There is no basis for this in conditioning theory, but it is perfectly reasonable in any cognitive theory. Second, the receiver must translate the experience "source dislikes object" into the meaning "source and object have opposite values." This translation does not follow from conditioning theory, nor from logic, but it does follow from balance theory. Indeed this translation is the essence of balance theory.

Thus we see that the basic cognitive events in congruity theory are not those of conditioning theory but those of balance theory. The difference between the two models that we have developed is in the manner in which the cognitive implications are translated into emotional change. In the basic balance model, emotional reactions to the message are translated directly into attitude and source change. In the congruity model, the emotional reactions to the message are assumed to set up emotional targets to which the attitudes are then conditioned. This second step leads to the discrepancy equations of the balance model.

CHAPTER 6

Classical Congruity Theory

INTRODUCTION

Osgood and Tannenbaum (1955) believe that their congruity theory could be derived from conditioning theory, but our analysis (see Chapter 5) has shown this to be false. However, to some extent this is a moot point because their derivative had nothing to do with conditioning theory anyway. Their derivation was a mechanical metaphor in which incongruous events set up an internal pressure that in turn caused changes in attitudes that resulted in a decrease in the incongruity.

A careful analysis of the basic procedure that they followed shows that there are two parts. First, they followed certain communication rules that were assumed to govern the receiver's interpretation of linguistic experience. These rules turned out to be the rules of balance theory. Second, they developed a pressure model to translate the linguistic experience into emotional change. This model is the basic equilibrium model of Gestalt psychology. In Gestalt psychology there is the concept of pragnanz—a "good form" in which the parts of some perception or thought or experience are in "proper" relation to each other and form a whole. If there is a discrepancy from pragnanz, then it sets up a psychic tension that generates change in the direction of greater pragnanz.

Osgood and Tannenbaum (1955) also differ from previous theorist in the way in which they think of the message. Rather than scale the message to give it a value comparable to the receiver's attitude, they characterized messages as associative assertions, dissociative assertions, and an unnamed residual category. Thus a message with positive value evokes an association, or positive bond, between the source and object. A negative message evokes a dissociation or negative bond, between source and object. Neutral messages are not discussed.

If the message is positive, the attitudes toward source and object are semicongruous if they have the same sign. They are completely congruous only if the affective values are exactly equal. That is, if two cognitive elements are associated, they should be affectively compatible. If they are not compatible, the association produces a "pressure to congruity" that must be reduced. The pressure is reduced by affective change. Thus the critical discrepancy for congruity theory is the difference between the attitudes toward source and object rather than the difference between attitude and message value. This discrepancy is reduced when the attitude toward the object shifts in the direction of the attitude toward the source (even if the shift is negative), and vice versa.

Congruity theory was stated in three concrete forms in the writings of Osgood and his associates. First, an explicit mathematical model was presented that assumed incongruity was completely resolved. Confronted with data collected by Tannenbaum (1953), the model was modified in several ways. The resulting theory was not mathematically stated but was implicit in their interpretation of the data. With only vague reference to a "congruity learning function" (Osgood *et al.*, 1957), the predicted change was reduced by a factor of five. From the fact that congruity was not completely resolved, they derived the assumption that the pressure of incongruity is less than the discrepancy between attitudes toward source and object (the "correction for incredulity"). From the fact that source change was less than attitude change, they concluded that source change and attitude change are not symmetric (the "assertion constant"). In addition to this implicitly stated model, they had two empirically derived "correction formulas" that they believed to embody the theoretical modifications stated verbally. These empirical formulas are not consistent with the theoretical modifications.

PREVIEW

In each of the congruity theory models to be developed below, the general pattern of derivation is identical and corresponds to the common core of general theoretical assumptions. First, the presentation of the message is assumed to produce a certain "pressure of incongruity." The first state in model construction is to calculate that pressure P from the assumptions to be used in that model. Second, the theory assumes that all the pressure must be relieved, and it must be relieved by source and attitude change. This is represented in the model construction by the equation

$$\text{pressure relieved} = |\Delta a| + |\Delta s| = P$$

Because the sum of attitude and source change is thus known, the two are individually given once any other equation in the two is known. In each case, the natural equation is given by the Osgood and Tannenbaum assumptions concerning the relative resistance of source and object attitudes to change. That is, the assumptions generate an expression for the ratio $|\Delta s|/|\Delta a|$. The proportions of pressure relieved by source change and attitude change are then derived and the calculation of the model equations follows immediately.

In this chapter, the modified version of congruity theory is translated into a family of related models. For the positive message, the first model developed is the original one-step equilibrium model. Here the assumptions are that the pressure of incongruity equals the discrepancy between source and object attitudes,

$$P = |s - a|$$

and that resistance to change is proportional to polarity,

$$\frac{|s|}{|a|} = \frac{1/|s|}{1/|a|}$$

In the next model it is assumed that the discrepancy between source and object produces incredulity. Two plausible alternative assumptions about the amount of incredulity are given. For each, the amount of incredulity is calculated and the resulting or effective pressure of incongruity is then given by

$$P = \text{discrepancy} - \text{incredulity}$$

The derivation is then completed with the original polarity assumptions for the ratio of $|\Delta s|$ to $|\Delta a|$. This derivation accomplishes what Osgood and Tannenbaum attempted to do with their "correction for incredulity." However, it is noted that their correction is actually inconsistent with their primary assumptions.

Next, a model was derived in which the incredulity assumption was not made but where the source attitude was assumed to be relatively more resistant to change than the object attitude. This model embodies what

Osgood and Tannenbaum sought with their "assertion constant." However, their "assertion constant" is noted to be inconsistent with their primary definition of congruity.

Finally, a general model for the positive message is developed using both the assumption of incredulity and the assumption that the relative resistance to source change and attitude change is not symmetric. All the preceding models are shown to be special cases of this last model.

For the negative message, the only change in the derivations is the definition of congruence and hence "discrepancy." Once discrepancy is defined by $|s + a|$, all results are strictly parallel.

Next, some assumptions given by Osgood *et al.* (1957) concerning "intensity of assertion" are formalized. The gist of these assumptions is that the proportion of discrepancy translated into pressure of incongruity will be a positive function of what is defined in the present volume as the polarity of message value $|m|$. The most important consequence of this derivation is the prediction that a neutral message will produce no pressure of incongruity and hence neither source change nor attitude change.

Finally, it is noted that the polarity assumption is not a primary but a technical assumption of congruity theory. As an alternative, the assumption that the relative resistance to change is a constant is offered. The resulting models are linear and the implications of this for an equilibrium analysis are discussed. The general linear model with incredulity and source–object asymmetry is also presented.

THE ORIGINAL CONGRUITY MODEL: ONE-STEP EQUILIBRIUM

The original one-step equilibrium model for the positive message will now be derived in four steps. First, the pressure of incongruity is calculated. Second, the identity relating pressure to total affective change is stated. Third, the relative sizes of Δs and Δa are determined. Fourth, the proportion of pressure relieved by each affective change is computed and the actual change equations follow immediately.

Osgood and Tannenbaum first assumed that the pressure of incongruity was exactly equal to the discrepancy between source and object:

$$P = |a - s| \qquad (6.1)$$

They then assumed that the pressure relieved by an affective change is equal to the size of the change, that is, the pressure relieved by attitude change is $|\Delta a|$ and the pressure relieved by source change is $|\Delta s|$. The total pressure relieved is

$$|\Delta a| + |\Delta s| = \text{pressure relieved}$$

If all pressure must be relieved in the situation, then

$$P = |\Delta a| + |\Delta s| \tag{6.2}$$

They then assumed that attitude change and source change are symmetric and that the relative change is inversely proportional to the intensity of the attitude (polarity). Hence

$$\frac{|\Delta s|}{|\Delta a|} = \frac{1/|s|}{1/|a|} = \frac{|a|}{|s|} \tag{6.3}$$

Let p be the proportion of the total pressure of incongruity relieved by attitude change. Then $1 - p$ is the proportion relieved by source change. That is,

$$pP = |\Delta a| \qquad \text{and} \qquad (1 - p)P = |\Delta s| \tag{6.4}$$

$$|\Delta a| + |\Delta s| = pP + (1 - p)P = P \tag{6.5}$$

Dividing Eq. (6.5) by $|\Delta a|$ and substituting from 6.4, we have

$$1 + \frac{|\Delta s|}{|\Delta a|} = \frac{P}{|\Delta a|} = \frac{P}{pP} = \frac{1}{p}$$

When we substitute from Eq. (6.3), we have

$$1 + \frac{|a|}{|s|} = \frac{1}{p}$$

or

$$p = \frac{1}{1 + |a|/|s|} = \frac{|s|}{|s| + |a|} \tag{6.6}$$

and

$$1 - p = \frac{|a|}{|s| + |a|} \tag{6.7}$$

From these equations, the model follows immediately:

$$\Delta a = \frac{|s|}{|s| + |a|}(s - a) \tag{6.8}$$

$$\Delta s = \frac{|a|}{|a| + |s|}(a - s) \tag{6.9}$$

This model is presented in Figs. 6.1 and 6.2. The postmessage attitude toward

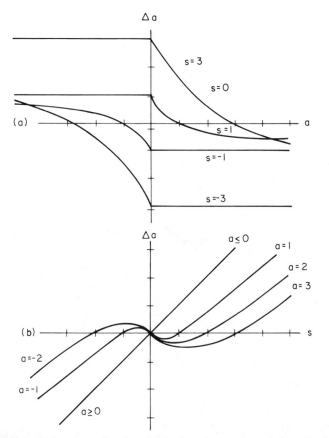

Fig. 6.1. Attitude change as a function of attitude toward source and object for the original congruity model (positive assertion).

the object is

$$a' = a + \Delta a$$

$$= a + \frac{|s|}{|a| + |s|}(s - a)$$

$$= a - \frac{|s|}{|a| + |s|}a + \frac{|s|}{|a| + |s|}s$$

$$= \left(1 - \frac{|s|}{|a| + |s|}\right)a + \frac{|s|}{|a| + |s|}s$$

$$= \frac{|a|}{|a| + |s|}a + \frac{|s|}{|a| + |s|}s$$

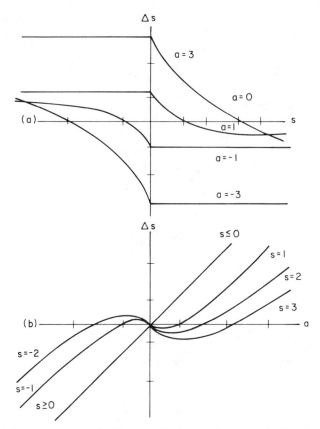

Fig. 6.2. Source change as a function of attitude toward source and object for the original congruity model (positive assertion).

or

$$a' = (1 - p)a + ps. \qquad (6.10)$$

Similarly, the postmessage attitude toward the source is

$$s' = (1 - p)a + ps \qquad (6.11)$$

Thus the postmessage attitudes are equal and completely congruous. Equilibrium has been established. These final attitudes toward source and object are weighted averages of initial attitudes. The weights, though, are not constants but are themselves functions of source and object attitude. A summary of the original congruity model and variations of this model are given in Table 6.1.

TABLE 6.1

Model	Assumptions
Original congruity with one-step equilibrium	
$$\Delta a = \frac{|s|}{|s| + |a|}(s - a)$$ $$\Delta s = \frac{|a|}{|a| + |s|}(a - s)$$	Positive message. Congruity assumptions as specified by Osgood and Tannenbaum (1955). Complete convergence to congruity in one step. Pressure of incongruity is equal to source–object discrepancy.
$$\Delta a = \frac{|s|}{|s| + |a|}(-s - a)$$ $$\Delta s = \frac{|a|}{|s| + |a|}(-a - s)$$	Negative message.
Correction for incredulity	
$$\Delta a = (1 - \alpha)\frac{|s|}{|s| + |a|}(s - a)$$ $$\Delta s = (1 - \alpha)\frac{|a|}{|a| + |s|}(a - s)$$	Positive message. Pressure of incongruity is less than source–object discrepancy; incredulity is proportional to discrepancy $\alpha|a - s|$.
$$\Delta a = (1 - \alpha)\frac{|s|}{|s| + |a|}(-s - a)$$ $$\Delta s = (1 - \alpha)\frac{|a|}{|a| + |s|}(-a - s)$$	Negative message.
Nonlinear correction for incredulity	
$$\Delta a = \frac{1}{1 + |a - s|}\frac{|s|}{|s| + |a|}(s - a)$$ $$\Delta s = \frac{1}{1 + |a - s|}\frac{|a|}{|a| + |s|}(a - s)$$	Positive message. Incredulity increases more than $\alpha|a - s|$; α is a variable rather than a constant; α is an increasing function of discrepancy.
$$\Delta a = \frac{1}{1 + |a + s|}\frac{|s|}{|s| + |a|}(-s - a)$$ $$\Delta s = \frac{1}{1 + |a + s|}\frac{|a|}{|a| + |s|}(-a - s)$$	Negative message.
General congruity	
$$\Delta a = (1 - \varepsilon - \alpha)\frac{|s|}{|s| + \beta|a|}(s - a)$$ $$\Delta s = (1 - \varepsilon - \alpha)\frac{\beta|a|}{|s| + \beta|a|}(a - s)$$	Positive message. Pressure of incongruity is a function of message intensity, $|m|$, source–object discrepancy, and linear incredulity.

TABLE 6.1 (cont.)

Model	Assumptions
$\Delta a = (1 - \varepsilon - \alpha)\dfrac{|s|}{|s| + \beta|a|}(-s - a)$	Negative message.
$\Delta a = (1 - \varepsilon - \alpha)\dfrac{\beta|a|}{|s| + \beta|a|}(-a - s)$	

Congruity without polarity

Model	Assumptions
$\Delta a = \dfrac{1}{1 + \beta}(1 - \alpha)(s - a)$	Positive message. Congruity model without polarity assumption; $\beta = |\Delta s|/|\Delta a|$.
$\Delta s = \dfrac{\beta}{1 + \beta}(1 - \alpha)(a - s)$	
$\Delta a = \dfrac{1}{1 + \beta}(1 - \alpha)(-s - a)$	Negative message.
$\Delta s = \dfrac{\beta}{1 + \beta}(1 - \alpha)(-a - s)$	
$\Delta a = \dfrac{1}{1 + \beta}(1 - \varepsilon - \alpha)(s - a)$	Positive message. Same assumptions as above except pressure of incongruity is a function of message intensity.
$\Delta s = \dfrac{\beta}{1 + \beta}(1 - \varepsilon - \alpha)(a - s)$	
$\Delta a = \dfrac{1}{1 + \beta}(1 - \varepsilon - \alpha)(-s - a)$	Negative message.
$\Delta s = \dfrac{\beta}{1 + \beta}(1 - \varepsilon - \alpha)(-a - s)$	

Source–object asymmetry

Model	Assumptions
$\Delta a = \dfrac{|s|}{|s| + \beta|a|}(1 - \alpha)(s - a)$	Positive message. Source change is always less than that predicted from polarity alone.
$\Delta s = \dfrac{\beta|a|}{|s| + \beta|a|}(1 - \alpha)(a - s)$	
$\Delta a = \dfrac{|s|}{|s| + \beta|a|}(1 - \alpha)(-s - a)$	Negative message.
$\Delta s = \dfrac{\beta|a|}{|s| + \beta|a|}(1 - \alpha)(-s - a)$	

CORRECTION FOR INCREDULITY

The original formulation produces a complete convergence to congruity in one step. This does not happen very often, so Osgood and Tannenbaum modified the theory. The key assumption in their second formulation is that pressure of incongruity will be less than source–object discrepancy by the extent of "incredulity" elicited by that discrepancy. If we assume that incredulity is directly proportional to discrepancy, we have

$$\text{incredulity} = \alpha |a - s| \tag{6.12}$$

and hence

$$P = |a - s| - \text{incredulity} = (1 - \alpha)|a - s| \tag{6.13}$$

If there is no incredulity, α would be zero and Eq. (6.13) would reduce to Eq. (6.1).

After an exactly parallel derivation, the new model is

$$\Delta a = (1 - \alpha)\frac{|s|}{|s| + |a|}(s - a) \tag{6.14}$$

$$\Delta s = (1 - \alpha)\frac{|a|}{|a| + |s|}(a - s) \tag{6.15}$$

These equations are identical to Eq. (6.8) and (6.9) except that they have been multiplied by the fraction $1 - \alpha$. Thus this new model assumes that a and s move $1 - \alpha$ of the distance to the equilibrium values of the previous model. Although all the pressure of incongruity is relieved, a single message does not produce perfect congruity.

This model, with $\alpha = \frac{4}{5}$, is mathematically equal to the model assumed by Osgood and Tannenbaum when they divided all their predicted change scores by five. However, it is obtained here without recourse to an external and otherwise unmentioned "congruity learning principle" (Osgood *et al.* 1957).

To the contrary, this model generates a developmental process that is similar to learning. Thus if the positive message were repeated or if a series of positive messages forced congruity, then the ultimate equilibrium values would not be those specified by the one-step model in Eq. (6.8) and (6.9).

The model above used the simplest version of the Osgood and Tannenbaum assumption that incredulity is a direct function of discrepancy, that is, that if you double the discrepancy, you double the incredulity. Suppose the relation is not so simple. For example, incredulity might increase more than proportionately to discrepancy. Then in the above equations α would not be a constant but would be an increasing function of discrepancy, for example,

$$\alpha = \frac{|a - s|}{1 + |a - s|} \tag{6.16}$$

which is graphed in Fig. 6.3. Because none of the steps in the derivation depend on α being a constant, all equations are unchanged. Thus any correction for incredulity will ultimately multiply the original Osgood and Tannenbaum equations by a common factor. It is worth noting that any "correction" for incredulity that does not ultimately result in the multiplication of Eqs. (6.8) and (6.9) by a common factor will not satisfy the polarity assumption in Eq. (6.3).

Osgood and Tannenbaum proposed a "correction for incredulity" that does not satisfy this criterion. However, their correction was not obtained by direct

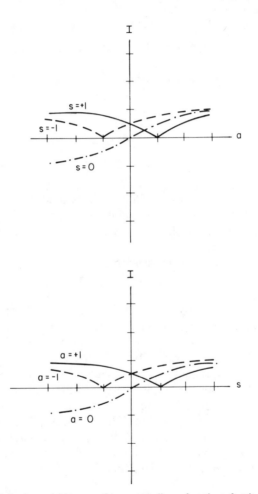

Fig. 6.3.   Incredulity in a positive assertion as a nonlinear function of attitude toward source and object (source–object discrepancy).

mathematical argument from their theoretical assumption but from a post hoc empirical fit to the Tannenbaum (1953) residuals.

The model following from the particular nonlinear incredulity assumption in Eq. (6.16) will now be derived. Because α is not a constant, the resulting model is not simply a proportionate decrease in the old. Thus

$$\Delta a = \frac{1}{1 + |a - s|} \frac{|s|}{|s| + |a|} (s - a) \tag{6.17}$$

$$\Delta s = \frac{1}{1 + |a - s|} \frac{|a|}{|a| + |s|} (a - s) \tag{6.18}$$

This model is graphed in Fig. 6.4 and 6.5. The main effect of the incredulity correction is increasingly to reduce the magnitude of source and attitude change as a function of discrepancy. As a side effect, it produces results reminiscent of the constant change with polarity model. Thus attitude change is always maximum for neutral attitudes ($a = 0$), and source change is always maximal for neutral source ($s = 0$).

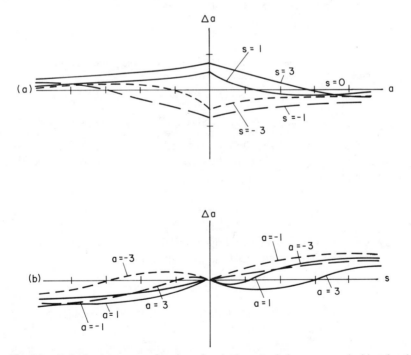

Fig. 6.4. Attitude change as a function of attitude toward the source and object for the congruity model with nonlinear incredulity (positive assertion).

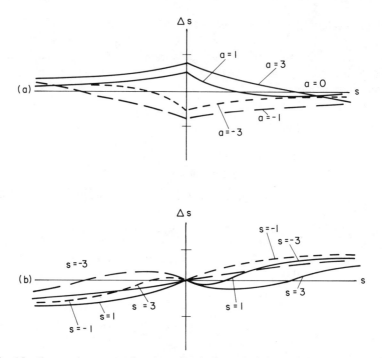

Fig. 6.5. Source change as a function of attitude toward the source and object for the congruity model with nonlinear incredulity (positive assertion).

SOURCE–OBJECT ASYMMETRY

The other modification in the theory dealt with the relative change in source and object. Thus suppose that source change is always somewhat less than would be predicted from polarity alone, say,

$$\frac{|\Delta s|}{|\Delta a|} = \beta \frac{|a|}{|s|} \tag{6.19}$$

where β is less than one if source change is relatively less than attitude change. After the same derivation, the resulting proportions are

$$p = \frac{1}{1 + \beta \frac{|a|}{|s|}} = \frac{|s|}{|s| + \beta |a|} \tag{6.20}$$

and

$$1 - p = \frac{\beta |a|}{|s| + \beta |a|} \tag{6.21}$$

The model is

$$\Delta a = \frac{|s|}{|s| + \beta|a|}(1 - \alpha)(s - a) \tag{6.22}$$

$$\Delta s = \frac{\beta|a|}{|s| + \beta|a|}(1 - \alpha)(a - s) \tag{6.23}$$

where $\alpha = 0$ and $\beta = 1$ yield the original model. If $\alpha > 0$ (constant or not), this model makes the incredulity assumption, and if $\beta < 1$, this model makes an "assertion correction." Figures 6.6 and 6.7 present the model without

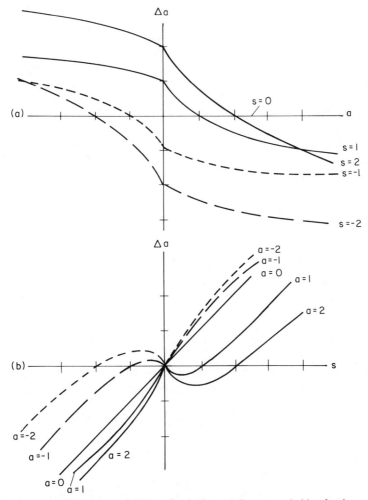

Fig. 6.6. Attitude change as a function of attitude toward source and object for the congruity model with source–object asymmetry (positive assertion).

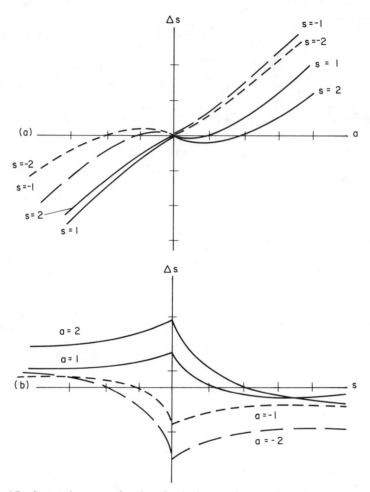

Fig. 6.7. Source change as a function of attitude toward source and object for the congruity model with source–object asymmetry (positive assertion).

incredulity ($\alpha = 0$) and a large source–object asymmetry ($\beta = \frac{1}{2}$). The main feature of these graphs is, of course, the fact that attitude change is much larger than source change.

The effects of this assumption are shown more clearly in the postmessage attitude and source values.

$$a' = \frac{\beta|a|}{|s| + \beta|a|} a + \frac{|s|}{|s| + \beta|a|} s \tag{6.24}$$

$$= (1 - \tilde{p})a + \tilde{p}s \tag{6.25}$$

and

$$s' = \frac{\beta|a|}{|s| + \beta|a|}\,a + \frac{|s|}{|s| + \beta|a|}\,s = a \tag{6.26}$$

where the new weight $\tilde{p}$ is related to the weight p of the original model by

$$\frac{\tilde{p}}{1 - \tilde{p}} = \frac{1}{\beta}\frac{p}{1 - p} \tag{6.27}$$

That is, s is given $1/\beta$ times the weight in the new average that it was given in the original [Eqs. (6.10) and (6.11).]

A congruity model with incredulity given as the nonlinear function [Eq. (6.16)] and with a large source–object asymmetry ($\beta = \frac{1}{2}$) is given in Figs. 6.8 and 6.9. The predominant feature of these graphs is the nonlinear incredulity effect (compare with Figs. 6.4 and 6.5). The source–object asymmetry is less noticeable, particularly when source and object are highly discrepant affectively.

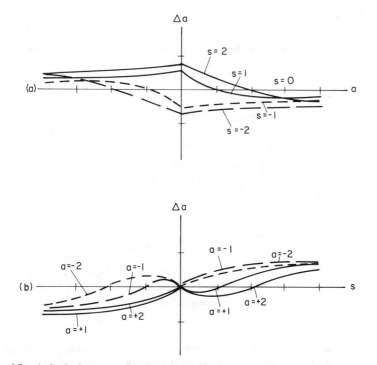

Fig. 6.8. Attitude change as a function of attitude toward source and object for the congruity model with nonlinear incredulity and source–object asymmetry (positive assertion).

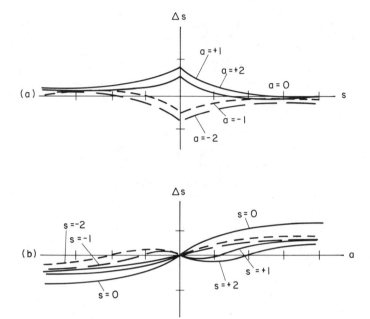

Fig. 6.9. Source change as a function of attitude toward source and object for the congruity model with nonlinear incredulity and source–object asymmetry (positive assertion).

Osgood and Tannenbaum proposed an "assertion constant" to handle the problem of source–object asymmetry. They simply added the constant to attitude change if the message was positive and subtracted it if the message was negative. This cannot be true. If the attitudes were congruent, or nearly so, the assertion constant would produce incongruity! Furthermore, their modification of the model implicitly changes the polarity and incredulity assumptions in nonobvious ways.

THE NEGATIVE MESSAGE

If the message is negative, the attitudes toward source and object are congruous only if they have opposite sign. That is, if two cognitive elements are negatively associated, they should be affectively incompatible. Two dissociated elements are perfectly congruous only if the attitudes are exactly the negative of each other.

The critical difference between positive and negative messages is in the congruity condition and the corresponding discrepancy that measures incongruity. Thus the pressure for attitude change derives from the discrepancy between a and $-s$, that is,

$$D_a = |-s - a| = |-(\Delta + a)| = |s + a| \tag{6.28}$$

The pressure for source change derives from the discrepancy between s and $-a$, that is,

$$D_s = |-a - s| = |-(a + s)| = |a + s| \tag{6.29}$$

Because these are identical, the pressure of incongruity can be unequivocally assumed to be equal to discrepancy again, that is,

$$P = |s + a| = |-s - a| \tag{6.30}$$

From this point the derivation of every model for the negative assertion is identical to the corresponding derivation for the positive model.

The original Osgood and Tannenbaum model is

$$\Delta a = \frac{|s|}{|s| + |a|}(-s - a) \tag{6.31}$$

$$\Delta s = \frac{|a|}{|s| + |a|}(-a - s). \tag{6.32}$$

The postmessage attitudes are given by

$$a' = (1 - p)a + p(-s) \tag{6.33}$$

$$s' = (1 - p)(-a) + ps = (1 - p)a + p(-s) \tag{6.34}$$

where p is the same polarity-weighted proportion as before,

$$p = \frac{|s|}{|s| + |a|} \tag{6.35}$$

Thus the postmessage attitudes are exactly equal in magnitude and of opposite sign, that is, they are congruous (for a negative association).

The assumption thhat incredulity reduces the pressure of incongruity is independent of message value if phrased in terms of discrepancy. If incredulity is a linear function of discrepancy, then

$$\Delta a = (1 - \alpha)\frac{|s|}{|s| + |a|}(-s - a) \tag{6.36}$$

$$\Delta s = (1 - \alpha)\frac{|a|}{|a| + |s|}(-a - s) \tag{6.37}$$

As for the positive message, the assumption that incredulity is a linear function of discrepancy produces a model that simply moves each attitude $1 - \alpha$ of the distance to the equilibrium values generated by the original model [Eqs. (6.33) and (6.34)].

If incredulity increases more than proportionately to discrepancy, then again the α of the previous equations simply shifts to the corresponding function of discrepancy:

$$\alpha = \frac{|a + s|}{1 + |a + s|} \tag{6.38}$$

The new model for nonlinear incredulity is

$$\Delta a = \frac{1}{1 + |a + s|} \frac{|s|}{|s| + |a|}(-s - a) \tag{6.39}$$

$$\Delta s = \frac{1}{1 + |a + s|} \frac{|a|}{|a| + |s|}(-a - s) \tag{6.40}$$

The effect of the incredulity assumption is to reduce greatly the change associated with large discrepancies. It also accentuates the polarity assumption in that maximal change in attitude is at $a = 0$ and maximal source change is at $s = 0$.

The Osgood and Tannenbaum "correction for incredulity" is as counter to their theoretical assumptions for the negative message as for the positive.

The assumption that source change is relatively less than attitude change is also independent of message value. With the same relative constant β, the model for the negative assertion is

$$\Delta a = \frac{|s|}{|s| + \beta|a|}(1 - a)(-s - a) \tag{6.41}$$

$$\Delta s = \frac{\beta|a|}{|s| + \beta|a|}(1 - \alpha)(-a - s) \tag{6.42}$$

where $\alpha = 0$ and $\beta = 1$ yield the original model. Again $\alpha > 0$ (constant or not) is the incredulity assumption, and $\beta < 1$ is an "assertion correction." The major effect of the assertion correction is to make attitude change much larger than source change.

This is shown more clearly in the postmessage attitude equations

$$a' = \frac{\beta|a|}{|s| + \beta|a|} a + \frac{|s|}{|s| + \beta|a|}(-s) \tag{6.43}$$

or

$$a' = (1 - \tilde{p})a + \tilde{p}(-s) \tag{6.44}$$

and

$$s' = (1 - \tilde{p})(-a) + \tilde{p}s = -a' \tag{6.45}$$

The new value for attitude toward the source is exactly the negative of the new attitude toward the object. So this model produces exact congruity in one step. The postmessage attitude is a weighted average of the premessage attitude and the *negative* of source affect, and vice versa. The weight for the asymmetric model β is related to the weight for the symmetric model p by

$$\frac{\tilde{p}}{1 - \tilde{p}} = \frac{1}{\beta} \frac{p}{1 - p} \tag{6.46}$$

that is, source affect is weighted $1/\beta$ times as heavily as before. As for the positive message, the source–object asymmetry is overshadowed by the nonlinear incredulity factor. The difference in the magnitude of source and object change is obscured for large affective discrepancy in source–object attitudes.

The Osgood and Tannenbaum "assertion constant" is as counter to their theoretical assumptions for the negative message as for the positive message.

Thus, once source–object discrepancy is suitably redefined for the negative message, all results are strictly parallel to those for the positive message.

MESSAGE STRENGTH AND THE NEUTRAL MESSAGE

Osgood, *et al.* (1957) note that the pressure of incongruity would be a function of the "intensity" of the assertion. For example, "Reagan advocates peaceful coexistence" should be less incongruous than "Reagan advocates communism." Thus the amount of incongruity is not only proportional to source–object discrepancy but also to message "strength." If the strength or intensity of a message follows the same law as the intensity of attitudes, then it should be a direct function of polarity. For example,

$$\text{message intensity} = |m| \tag{6.47}$$

Pressure of incongruity would then be a direct function of message value as well as source–object discrepancy, that is,

$$P = \begin{cases} f(m)|a - s| & \text{if } m = + & \text{(6.48)} \\ f(-m)|a + s| & \text{if } m = - & \text{(6.49)} \end{cases}$$

Furthermore, because a neutral message is both the limiting case of a weak positive message and the limiting case of a weak negative message, we have

$$f(0)|a - s| = f(0)|a + s| \tag{6.50}$$

or

$$f(0) = 0 \tag{6.51}$$

Thus a neutral message produces no pressure of incongruity and hence no attitude or source change.

On the other hand, consider a message of infinite strength. It should be perfectly assertive. That is, we would have

$$P = \text{discrepancy} \quad \text{if} \quad m = \pm\infty$$

or

$$f(m) = 1 \quad \text{if} \quad m = \pm\infty$$

Thus $f(m)$ begins with 1 at $m = -\infty$, goes to 0 at $m = 0$, and returns to 1 at $m = +\infty$. For example,

$$f(m) = \frac{|m|}{|m| + 1} \tag{6.52}$$

which is graphed in Fig. 6.10.

Thus the pressure of incongruity is only equal to the discrepancy between source and object if the message is "perfectly" or "infinitely" assertive and is less otherwise. Using the same particular function $f(m)$,

$$P = \frac{|m|}{1 + |m|} \cdot \text{discrepancy}$$

$$= \frac{m}{m + 1}|a - s| \quad \text{if} \quad m = +$$

$$= \frac{-m}{-m + 1}|a + s| \quad \text{if} \quad m = - \tag{6.53}$$

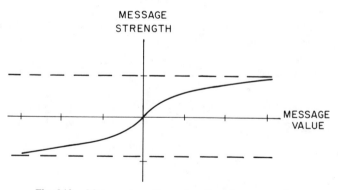

Fig. 6.10.   Message strength as a function of message value.

If we rewrite this equation for the positive message, then

$$P = (1 - \varepsilon)|a - s|, \qquad \varepsilon = \frac{1}{1 + m} \tag{6.54}$$

which is identical to the pressure formula generated by the linear incredulity assumption [Eq. (6.12)] except that α is replaced by ε. The corresponding equations for source and attitude change would of course be identical and are

$$\Delta a = (1 - \varepsilon)\frac{|s|}{|s| + |a|}(s - a) \tag{6.55}$$

$$\Delta s = (1 - \varepsilon)\frac{|a|}{|s| + |a|}(a - s) \tag{6.56}$$

In fact, for an experiment with only one message value, the models are completely confounded.

The negative message is handled by noting that

$$\varepsilon = \frac{1}{1 + |m|} \qquad \text{if} \quad m = - \tag{6.57}$$

and that the model then becomes identical to the linear incredulity model for the negative message:

$$\Delta a = (1 - \varepsilon)\frac{|s|}{|s| + |a|}(-s - a) \tag{6.58}$$

$$\Delta s = (1 - \varepsilon)\frac{|a|}{|a| + |s|}(-a - s) \tag{6.59}$$

In either case, the attitudes shift

$$1 - \varepsilon = \frac{|m|}{|m| + 1} \tag{6.60}$$

of the distance to the equilibrium values.

If we subtract incredulity from the pressure of incongruity, we have

$$P = \frac{|m|}{1 + |m|}(\text{discrepancy} - \alpha \cdot \text{discrepancy})$$

$$P = (1 - \varepsilon - \alpha) \cdot \text{discrepancy} \tag{6.61}$$

whether α is constant or not. Thus the general model for the positive message is

$$\Delta a = (1 - \varepsilon - \alpha)\frac{|s|}{|s| + \beta|a|}(s - a) \tag{6.62}$$

$$\Delta s = (1 - \varepsilon - \alpha)\frac{\beta|a|}{|s| + \beta|a|}(a - s) \tag{6.63}$$

and for the negative message is

$$\Delta a = (1 - \varepsilon - \alpha)\frac{|s|}{|s| + \beta|a|}(-s - a) \tag{6.64}$$

$$\Delta s = (1 - \varepsilon - \alpha)\frac{\beta|a|}{|s| + \beta|a|}(-a - s) \tag{6.65}$$

If $\beta < 1$, this yields source asymmetry and α may be constant or a function of discrepancy. The figures for the models are visually indistinguishable from those of the corresponding incredulity models, although the location of the maximum change is mathematically distinct (i.e., related to discrepancy, etc., by a different function of the parameters).

Thus as Osgood *et al.* noted, these models can only be distinguished in an experiment that varies message value. Furthermore, a positive message–negative message design will not work because, from the point of view of intensity, $|-3| = |+3| = 3$.

The critical test for the assumption that pressure is a function of message intensity is to use a neutral message in a context where the positive and negative messages are eliciting considerable change.

CONGRUITY WITHOUT POLARITY

The original mathematical formulation of congruity theory embodied two sets of principles:

1. the primary definitions of congruity, pressure of incongruity, and the modes of releasing that pressure and

2. three technical assumptions—the equality of pressure and discrepancy, the symmetry of source and object, and the polarity effects of intensity.

Osgood and Tannenbaum ultimately relaxed the equality of pressure and discrepancy by defining incredulity. They relaxed symmetry with the assertion correction. The following models present an alternative to the polarity assumption.

Suppose the relative size of source change is independent of intensities, then

$$|\Delta s|/|\Delta a| = \beta \tag{6.66}$$

where $\beta = 1$ if source and object are symmetric and is less than one if source change is relatively smaller. After a parallel development, the general model for the positive message is

$$\Delta a = \frac{1}{1 + \beta}(1 - \alpha)(s - a) \tag{6.67}$$

$$\Delta s = \frac{\beta}{1 + \beta}(1 - \alpha)(a - s) \tag{6.68}$$

If $\beta = 0$ and $\alpha = 1$, this model produces a simple linear version of the original Osgood and Tannenbaum model:

$$a' = s' = (a + s)/2 \tag{6.69}$$

If $\beta = 1$ and α is a constant, we have the linear proportional change version of this model. This model is presented in Figs. 6.11 and 6.12. In the developmental process generated by repeated messages, this model converges to the same limits as the one step model, that is, the arithmetic average of initial values.

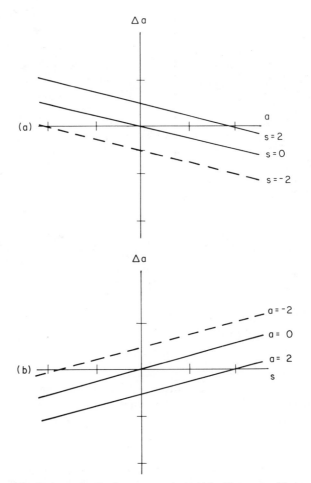

Fig. 6.11. Attitude change for the linear congruity model with source–object symmetry and linear incredulity (positive assertion).

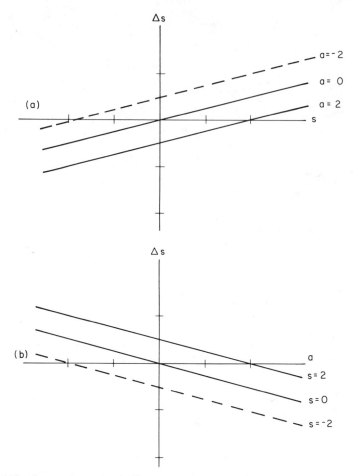

Fig. 6.12.   Source change for the linear congruity model with source–object symmetry and linear incredulity (positive assertion).

If incredulity is proportional to discrepancy (α is a constant) and $\beta < 1$, then the asymmetric model is linear and has equilibrium values

$$a^* = s^* = \frac{s + \beta a}{1 + \beta} \qquad (6.70)$$

which are simple weighted averages of the initial values and are independent of the amount of change produced by one message. This model is shown in Figs. 6.13 and 6.14.

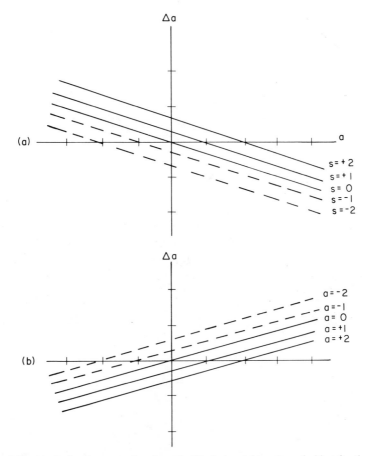

Fig. 6.13. Attitude change as a function of attitude toward source and object for the linear congruity model with linear incredulity and source–object asymmetry (positive assertion).

If incredulity is a nonlinear function of discrepancy [Eq. (6.16)] and source change is smaller than attitude change ($\beta < 1$), we have

$$\Delta a = \frac{1}{1 + \beta} \frac{1}{1 + |a - s|} (s - a) \qquad (6.71)$$

$$\Delta s = \frac{1}{1 + \beta} \frac{1}{1 + |a - s|} (a - s) \qquad (6.72)$$

The equilibrium values are still

$$a^* = s^* = \frac{s + \beta a}{1 + \beta} \qquad (6.73)$$

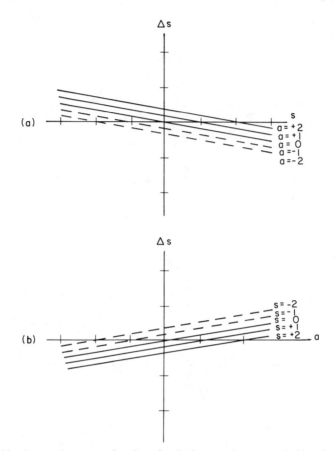

Fig. 6.14. Source change as a function of attitude toward source and object for the linear congruity model, linear incredulity, and source–object asymmetry (positive assertion).

and are independent of the amount of change following any one message. This model is presented in Figs. 6.15 and 6.16. Here both effects are displayed: attitude and source change are greatly reduced for large discrepancy and source change is only half of attitude change.

The critical step in developing the model for the negative message is to note that attitude shifts toward the negative of source affect and source affect shifts toward the negative of the attitude (as was the case with polarity). The general model is

$$\Delta a = \frac{1}{1 + \beta}(1 - \alpha)(-s - a) \qquad (6.74)$$

$$\Delta s = \frac{\beta}{1 + \beta}(1 - \alpha)(-a - s) \qquad (6.75)$$

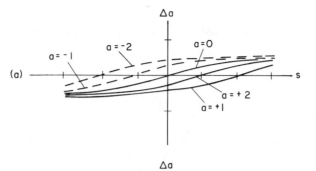

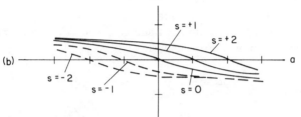

Fig. 6.15. Attitude change as a function of attitude toward source and object for the linear congruity model with nonlinear incredulity and source–object asymmetry (positive assertion).

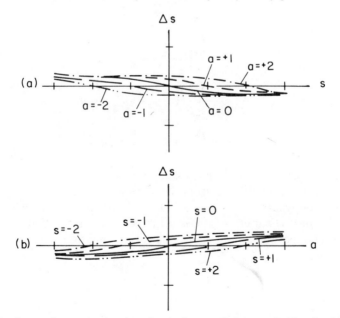

Fig. 6.16. Source change as a function of attitude toward source and object for the linear congruity model with nonlinear incredulity and source–object asymmetry (positive assertion).

where $\beta < 1$ yields the source–object asymmetry and $\alpha > 0$ (constant or not) yields the correction for incredulity. The equilibrium values are

$$a^* = \frac{\beta a - s}{\beta + 1} = \frac{\beta a + (-s)}{\beta + 1} \tag{6.76}$$

$$s^* = \frac{s - \beta a}{1 + \beta} = \frac{s + \beta(-a)}{1 + \beta} = -a^* \tag{6.77}$$

These equilibria are congruous linear weighted averages of each attitude and the negative of the other. As for the positive message, the equilibria are independent of incredulity assumptions.

Finally, if we assume that pressure of incongruity is a function of message "intensity" or "strength," this model undergoes exactly the same modification as did the polarity model. For the positive message,

$$\Delta a = \frac{1}{1 + \beta}(1 - \varepsilon - \alpha)(s - a) \tag{6.78}$$

$$\Delta s = \frac{\beta}{1 + \beta}(1 - \varepsilon - \alpha)(a - s) \tag{6.79}$$

where

$$\varepsilon = \frac{1}{1 + m}$$

For the negative message,

$$\Delta a = \frac{1}{1 + \beta}(1 - \varepsilon - \alpha)(-s - a) \tag{6.80}$$

$$\Delta s = \frac{\beta}{1 + \beta}(1 - \varepsilon - \alpha)(-a - s) \tag{6.81}$$

As for the polarity models, the assumption of less incongruity for "weaker" messages is indistinguishable from the incredulity assumptions in an experiment with a single message value (or balanced positive and negative messages). Intensity must be varied. Again, it is the neutral message that provides the simplest and most direct test of the intensity assumption.

CHAPTER 7

Dissonance Theory

INTRODUCTION

Dissonance theory has often been classified with affective consistency theories [Brown (1962) and Osgood (1960)]. As Kiesler, *et al.* (1969) note, the basis for this is actually rather superficial. Festinger (1957) says that consistency produces dissonance, and reduction of dissonance leads to attitude and source change (among other things). This is analogous to saying that inconsistency produces a pressure of incongruity that is relieved by attitude and source change. However, at a more fundamental level there is no agreement between the theories. For dissonance the inconsistency is produced when a credible source says something at odds with the receiver's belief. That is, dissonance arises from message–object discrepancy, a logical or semilogical contradiction. But for affective consistency theory the inconsistency arises from "incompatible" emotional reactions to associated objects (source–object discrepancy). Thus we view dissonance theory as a variety of information processing theory.

The first exposition of dissonance principles was given by Festinger (1957). The application of dissonance theory to attitude change was made by Festinger and Aronson (1960) and experimentally tested by Aronson, Turner, and Carlsmith (1963). At the end of this chapter we shall present a reinterpretation of Janis's theory of fear arousal in persuasive messages that shows it to be a version of dissonance theory.

The central assertion by Aronson *et al.* (1963, p. 31) was that "... when an individual finds that an opinion advocated by a credible communicator is discrepant from his own opinion he experiences dissonance." Like any other drive, dissonance must be reduced. In the passive communication paradigm, the constraints are such that only two outlets are available for channeling or reducing dissonance—derogation of the communicator and attitude change. By counterbalancing these two outlets, they used dissonance theory to derive nonlinear discrepancy curves for attitude change similar to those of social judgment theory.

The presentation of Aronson *et al.* (1963) suggests that nonlinear discrepancy curves for attitude change follow directly from dissonance theory. This is not true. There are two problems with their derivation: a theoretical problem and a technical problem. The theoretical problem is the linkage between dissonance and message–attitude discrepancy. There is nothing in dissonance theory as developed by Festinger (1957) to guarantee that a receiver will feel dissonance just because someone says something different from what the receiver believes. Indeed, we know people who claim that they find discrepant messages interesting rather than dissonance producing. However, we shall not follow up this problem but shall simply take the Aronson *et al.* (1963) hypothesis to be an axiom added to dissonance theory.

The technical problem is that the nonlinear discrepancy curves do not even follow from the Aronson *et al.* (1963) assumptions. They did not do a formal derivation, just intuitively jumped from assumptions to mathematical curves. When we first took their assumptions and carefully followed their presentation, we came up with a model with linear discrepancy curves. We then went back to dissonance theory and constructed an energy dissipation model. We still did not obtain the Aronson *et al.* (1963) nonlinear discrepancy curves. However, the second model gave us a lead for an alternative energy model that did yield the Aronson *et al.* (1963) curves. Thus, to obtain the Aronson *et al.* (1963) curves from dissonance theory, we had to make a number of additional assumptions. There are many models consistent with dissonance theory that bear little resemblance to the Aronson *et al.* (1963) data.

The primary focus of the Aronson *et al.* (1963) work was attitude change. However, in dissonance theory, there is a direct link between attitude change and source change. Dissonance theory holds only if both equations fit the data because the two equations are derived simultaneously within the theory. Dissonance theory may produce nonlinear attitude change equations similar to those of social judgment theory, but the source change equations are radically different. In particular, dissonance theory never allows for positive source change, whereas social judgment theory predicts positive source charge if the message discrepancy is small enough to allow the message to fall within the latitude of acceptance (see Chapter 4). There is a similar wide departure between the source change equations of information processing theory and those of dissonance theory.

Three models of dissonance theory are presented below. The first parallels the presentation of Aronson *et al.* (1963) who derive attitude change and source change independently and intuitively. The resulting equation for attitude change is identical to the information processing (linear discrepancy) model in which source credibility is a multiplier of linear discrepancy theory (see chapter 3). This model conforms to some but not all of what the authors claim to have derived from dissonance theory. In particular, it does not yield Sherif's nonlinear discrepancy curves.

A second model is constructed using an "energy" calculation of dissonance and its release through source and attitude change. The key assumption in this model is that the relative amount of dissonance released by source change in comparison to attitude change is directly proportional to discrepancy and inversely related to source credibility. The resulting curves for attitude change are nonlinear discrepancy curves with a source credibility effect. However, the curves increase to a finite asymptote rather than decreasing to zero.

This suggested that a more extreme model of the same form in which the relative amount of dissonance reduction produced by source change is still inversely related to source credibility but is proportional to the *square* of discrepancy. The attitude change equation is very close to that of social judgment theory without boomerang. This last model is consistent with the curves that Aronson *et al.* drew in their 1963 paper.

THE INTUITIVE MODEL

The first step in modeling dissonance theory is to calculate the amount of dissonance aroused in the passive communication context. Dissonance is produced when a receiver hears a discrepant message from a credible source. Thus, "The magnitude of dissonance increases as a function of the discrepancy" (Aronson *et al.* 1963, p. 32). The degree of dissonance is also a function of source credibility. For sources with no credibility, discrepant statements elicit *no* dissonance. Thus the amount of dissonance (taken to be a positive quality) is proportional to source credibility and communication discrepancy. That is,

$$\text{dissonance} = \alpha \cdot \text{credibility} \cdot \text{discrepancy}.$$

Because the dissonance theorists see only effective and noneffective sources, credibility is strictly nonnegative and ranges from zero to perfect. One example of these assumptions about credibility is the same model proposed in the section on discrepancy models (see Chapter 3):

$$\text{credibility} = \frac{e^{\sigma s}}{1 + e^{\sigma s}}$$

Finally, this yields

$$\text{dissonance} = \alpha \frac{e^{\sigma s}}{1 + e^{\sigma s}} |m - a| \qquad (7.1)$$

The graph of this function is shown in Fig. 7.1.

The next step in obtaining the intuitive dissonance model is to show how dissonance is reduced through attitude change. For sources with perfect credibility, dissonance is eliminated solely through attitude (opinion) change. "If dissonance is reduced by opinion change alone, the degree of opinion change is a direct function of the extent of the discrepancy" (Aronson *et al.* 1963, p. 32). If the source has zero credibility, there is no dissonance and hence no attitude change. These statements would be consistent with the assumption that attitude change is a direct function of dissonance. The simplest such function is obtained if they are directly proportional. Furthermore, attitude change is always in the direction of the message. Thus

$$\Delta a = \beta \alpha \frac{e^{\sigma s}}{1 + e^{\sigma s}} (m - a) \qquad (7.2)$$

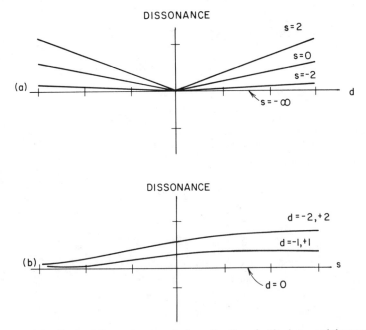

Fig. 7.1. Magnitude of dissonance provoked as a function of attitude toward the source and message discrepancy.

Attitude change is graphed in Fig. 7.2a. This model is identical to the information processing model given by Eq. (3.25).

Dissonance can also be reduced through source change. In particular, source change is always negative, that is, source change is source derogation. "... The tendency to derogate the communicator should likewise increase as a direct function of the extent of the discrepancy" (Aronson et al. 1963, p. 32). For sources with perfect credibility there is no source derogation—source change is inversely related to source credibility. One possible model that embodies these assumptions is

$$|\Delta s| = \gamma(1 - \text{credibility})|m - a|$$

or

$$\Delta s = -\gamma \frac{e^{-\sigma s}}{1 + e^{-\sigma s}} |m - a| \qquad (7.3)$$

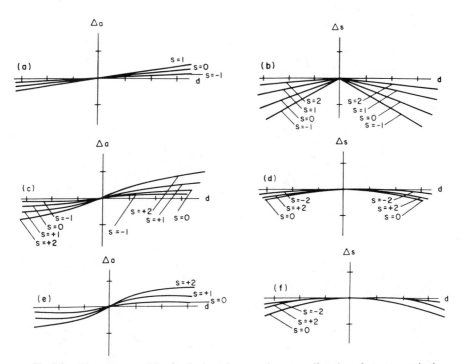

Fig. 7.2. Dissonance, models of attitude and source change as a function of message–attitude discrepancy: (a) intuitive model attitude change, (b) intuitive model source change, (c) first conservation model attitude change, (d) first conservation model source change, (e) second conservation model attitude change, and (f) second conservation model source change.

The term chosen to represent the inverse relation to credibility is bounded by one as credibility goes to zero. This model is graphed in Fig. 7.2b.

Now that attitude change and source change have been specified, we have the intuitive dissonance model

$$\Delta a = \delta \frac{e^{\sigma s}}{1 + e^{\sigma s}}(m - a), \qquad \delta = \alpha \beta \qquad (7.4)$$

$$\Delta s = -\gamma \frac{e^{\sigma s}}{1 + e^{\sigma s}}|m - a| \qquad (7.5)$$

Source change and attitude change can now be discussed together. With credibility held constant, attitude change and source derogation increase directly with message discrepancy. When the source is perfectly credible, $\Delta a = \delta(m - a)$ and $\Delta s = 0$. That is, dissonance is reduced only through attitude change. For a perfectly incredible source, $\Delta a = 0$ and $\Delta s = -\gamma|m - a|$, that is, there is no attitude change but the source is derogated to the extent his message is discrepant. For mildly credible sources, dissonance is reduced through both attitude change and source derogation.

Aronson, *et al.* (1963) come to a different prediction for a mildly credible source delivering a highly discrepant communication than that predicted from Eq. (7.4) and Fig. 7.2a. They argue for a curvilinear relationship between attitude change and discrepancy when the message is presented by a mildly credible source. They assert the following.

> Consider a communicator of mild credibility. Here, both opinion change and derogation can be used to reduce dissonance. If a communication is relatively close to the opinion of the recipient, the existing dissonance can be reduced easily by a slight shift of opinion. On the other hand, if the discrepancy is great, a person can reduce dissonance much more easily by derogating the communicator. That is, if the position advocated by a mildly credible communicator is extreme, it may appear quite unrealistic to the recipient. If this were the case, it is unlikely that he would change his attitude very much. Instead, he might reduce dissonance by deciding that the communicator is unrealistic—or stupid, naive, untruthful, etc. [p. 32].

Basically their argument reduces to this: for extreme discrepancy there will be considerable source derogation. They then implicitly subtract derogation from dissonance and conclude that there will be little attitude change. However, as discrepancy increases, so does dissonance, and if dissonance increases sufficiently, there can be both large source derogation and large attitude change. Thus, in the preceding model, if $s = 0$, credibility is $\frac{1}{2}$ and (ignoring the constant γ),

$$\Delta s = -\frac{1}{2}|m - a| \qquad (7.6)$$

As discrepancy doubles, the derogation of source also doubles. If we quadruple discrepancy, source derogation will increase indeed. But so does dissonance! Thus, for this model (ignoring the constant δ),

$$\Delta a = \tfrac{1}{2}(m - a) \tag{7.7}$$

so even as the tendency to derogate the source doubles, the amount of attitude change also doubles. Hence this model is actually consistent with dissonance theory as they present it. Thus the mere existence of greatly increased source derogation does not permit the dissonance theorists to derive the curvilinear discrepancy curves characteristic of social judgment theory. On the other hand, this model is by no means the only model consistent with their verbal theory. In particular, the models below yield quite different curves for attitude change.

A FIRST CONSERVATION MODEL

The next model relates affective change and dissonance in a strong quantitative law. Assume that the amount of dissonance dissipated is exactly equal to the amount of affective change, that is, attitude plus source change. Then

$$|\Delta a| + |\Delta s| = \text{dissonance} \tag{7.8}$$

This sort of conservation law is implicit in such phrases as "motivate attitude change" and the compensation assumptions relating source change and attitude change. If we continue to assume that dissonance is given by Eq. (7.1), then

$$|\Delta a| + |\Delta s| = \alpha \frac{e^{\sigma a}}{1 + e^{\sigma s}} |m - a| \tag{7.9}$$

Now that the total amount of effective change is fixed, we can no longer consider attitude change and source derogation separately. Rather we must consider either the relative change or the proportion of dissonance released through one channel or the other. The derivative below will begin with relative change, then calculate the proportion of dissonance to be released in each channel. The change equations follow directly.

The critical aspect of this alternative model is to solve for the relative reduction of dissonance by source derogation versus attitude change, or, equivalently, the ratio of Δs to Δa. Suppose we take the assumptions stated above for the absolute amount of source change and restate them as assumptions for relative source derogation. First, the relative tendency to derogate the source is a direct function of discrepancy. Second, the relative tendency to derogate the source is inversely related to source credibility. We can then rewrite Eq. (7.9) for the ratio of Δs to Δa as

$$\frac{|\Delta s|}{|\Delta a|} = \text{dissonance} = \gamma \frac{e^{-\sigma s}}{1 + e^{-\sigma s}} |m - a| \tag{7.10}$$

Let p be the proportion of the total dissonance released through attitude change and $1 - p$ the remaining proportion reduced through source derogation. For a given amount of dissonance D, $|\Delta a| + |\Delta s|$ is fixed and equal to D. Thus, as one component of dissonance reduction increases, the other must necessarily decrease. Now,

$$pD = |\Delta a| \qquad \text{and} \qquad (1 - p)D = |\Delta s| \tag{7.11}$$

or

$$|\Delta a| + |\Delta s| = D = pD + (1 - p)D \tag{7.12}$$

Dividing through Eq. (7.12) by Δa and substituting Eq. (7.11) for Δa yields

$$1 + \frac{|\Delta s|}{|\Delta a|} = \frac{D}{|\Delta a|} = \frac{D}{pD} = \frac{1}{p}$$

Substituting from Eq. (7.10) yields

$$1 + \gamma \frac{e^{-\sigma s}}{1 + e^{-\sigma s}} |m - a| = \frac{1}{p}$$

or

$$p = \frac{1 + e^{\sigma s}}{e^{\sigma s} + 1 + \gamma |m - a|} \tag{7.13}$$

and

$$1 - p = \frac{\gamma |m - a|}{e^{\sigma s} + 1 + \gamma |m - a|} \tag{7.14}$$

Now substituting in Eq. (7.11) yields

$$\Delta a = \alpha e^{\sigma s} \frac{\gamma(m - a)}{e^{\sigma s} + 1 + \gamma |m - a|} \tag{7.15}$$

$$\Delta s = -\frac{\gamma |m - a|}{e^{\sigma s} + 1 + \gamma |m - a|} \frac{e^{\sigma s}}{e^{\sigma s} + 1} \alpha |m - a| \tag{7.16}$$

This model is presented graphically in Fig. 7.2. For a perfectly credible source, $\Delta a = \alpha\gamma(m - a)$ is the linear discrepancy model, and there is no source derogation ($\Delta s \equiv 0$). If the source has no credibility, then there is no attitude change and no source derogation (there is no dissonance). Source derogation is a U-shaped function of attitude toward the source. As discrepancy increases, attitude change increases to an asymptotic level ($\alpha e^{\sigma} e^{s}$), which is in turn an increasing function of source credibility or attitude toward the source.

This is in substantial agreement with Aronson *et al.* except that attitude change does not go to zero as discrepancy goes to infinity for sources of intermediate credibility. Thus we have a second model based on the Aronson *et al.* assumptions that is inconsistent with the predictions they "derived." On the other hand, attitude change was linear in the first model and asymptotically constant in the second. This suggests that a more extreme version of the assumptions in the second model would produce the social judgment curve for attitude change.

A SECOND CONSERVATION MODEL

Assume again that total affective change equals the dissonance released and that the relative tendency to derogate the source is inversely related to source credibility. However, instead of assuming that the relative tendency to disparage the source is proportional to discrepancy, assume that it is proportional to the square of the discrepancy, that is,

$$\frac{|\Delta s|}{|\Delta a|} = \gamma \frac{e^{-\sigma s}}{1 + e^{-\sigma s}} |m - a|^2 \tag{7.17}$$

So, if you double discrepancy, you quadruple the relative tendency to derogate the source rather than change your attitude. If you triple the discrepancy, the relative tendency to derogate is multiplied by nine. Thus for any increase in discrepancy, there is a more than proportional increase in the tendency to disparge the source.

The derivation is identical in form to the first conservation model and yields

$$\Delta a = \alpha e^{\sigma s} \frac{\gamma(m - a)}{e^{\sigma s} + 1 + \gamma |m - a|^2} \tag{7.18}$$

$$\Delta s = -\alpha \frac{\gamma |m - a|^2}{e^{\sigma s} + 1 + \gamma |m - a|^2} \frac{e^{\sigma s}}{e^{\sigma s} + 1} |m - a| \tag{7.19}$$

These models are displayed in Fig. 7.2. Again the perfectly credible source produces a linear discrepancy law for attitude change and no source derogation. Again there is no dissonance produced by the perfectly incredible source and concomitantly no change. Again source derogation is a U-shaped function of source credibility. However, attitude change is also a U-shaped function of discrepancy (whereas source derogation is an increasing function of discrepancy).

This last model is consistent with Aronson, *et al.* The key assumption is mathematical, namely, that the relative tendency to derogate the source grows at a more than proportional rate as a function of discrepancy. On the other hand, the equations for source change in either of the last two models are not consistent with Aronson *et al.* As in the intuitive model they assume that if the source is perfectly incredible, then source change is proportional to discrepancy. In the second and third models, this result does not follow from the basic assumptions. Instead, when credibility is zero, source change is zero. The fact that these models do not make this assumption is not incidental to dissonance theory. Aronson *et al.* also assume that for a perfectly incredible source there is no dissonance. But source derogation is a change in the receiver's attitude toward the source. Thus source change without dissonance is unmotivated attitude change, cognitive change without cognitive dissonance. The second and third models assume instead that if a source is so incredible that a receiver can dismiss a discrepant message without dissonance, then the receiver will dismiss the source without source change.

A summary of the three dissonance models is given in Table 7.1.

TABLE 7.1

DISSONANCE ATTITUDE AND SOURCE CHANGE: SUMMARY

Model	*Assumptions*
Intuitive dissonance $$\Delta a = \lambda \frac{e^{\sigma s}}{1 + e^{\sigma s}}(m - a)$$ $$\Delta s = -\gamma \frac{e^{-\sigma s}}{1 + e^{-\sigma s}}|m - a|$$	Assumptions parallel those given by Aronson *et al.* (1963).
First conservation $$\Delta a = \alpha e^{\sigma s} \frac{\gamma(m - a)}{e^{\sigma s} + 1 + \gamma|m - a|}$$ $$\Delta s = \frac{\gamma|m - a|}{(e^{\sigma s} + 1 + |m - a|)}$$ $$\times \frac{e^{\sigma s}}{e^{\sigma s} + 1}\alpha|m - a|$$	The amount of dissonance is equal to the amount of attitude change plus source change, $|\Delta a| + |\Delta s|$. Source derogation is a direct function of discrepancy and inversely related to source credibility.
Second conservation $$\Delta a = \alpha e^{\sigma s} \frac{\gamma(m - a)}{e^{\sigma s} + 1 + \gamma|m - a|^2}$$ $$\Delta s = -\alpha \frac{\gamma|m - a|^2}{(e^{\sigma s} + 1 + \gamma|m - a|^2)}$$ $$\times \frac{e^{\sigma s}}{e^{\sigma s} + 1}|m - a|$$	Same as above model except source derogation is proportional to the square of discrepancy.

JANIS'S THEORY OF FEAR APPEALS

Although Janis is usually classified as a reinforcement theorist [Insko (1967), Kiesler *et al.* (1969)], the following analysis of his theory of fear-arousing appeals (1967) interprets it as a rather special version of dissonance theory. Janis begins by assuming that the message has produced a state of fear, shame, or guilt in the receiver that must be dissipated. The mechanisms for dissipating the unpleasant state can be broadly classified as either "coping" or "denial" of message validity. In the passive communication paradigm, "coping" would mean attitude change, whereas "denial" of message validity would lead to source derogation. Furthermore, his statements about message properties can be separated into two lines of argument. One line can be summarized as stating that the extent of the fear to be dissipated will be greater if the source is credible, the message is plausible, and the message relies on fear appeals. His other remarks concern conditions that tend to block or encourage the use of coping or denial as the mechanisms of dissipation. Thus the one variable mentioned by Aronson *et al.* (1963) but not mentioned by Janis is discrepancy. However, we submit that he made the discrepancy assumptions in a different guise. First, if the receiver has no and/or would not consider using, say, cigarettes, he will feel no fear. Second, if the message advocates "don't start," it elicits less fear than if it advocates "stop." But these statements taken together are exactly the discrepancy hypothesis. Finally, we note that his discussion of the relative use of denial in "don't start" versus "stop" is exactly parallel to the Aronson, *et al.* (1963) assumptions concerning the relative use of source derogation as a function of increased discrepancy. The one new element added by Janis is the assumption that an appeal to fear, guilt, or shame will have a multiplicative effect on the amount of dissonance aroused.

CHAPTER 8

Summary of Attitude and Source Change Theories

Substantively, the attitude change theories fall in three classes: reinforcement theory, affective consistency theories, and cognitive theories. Reinforcement theories assume that receivers react directly to the emotional content of the message. The cognitive theories assume that it is the "logical" content of the message that produces change, and affective consistency theory assumes that change is produced when the implied emotional reactions are incompatible.

SUMMARY OF ATTITUDE CHANGE THEORIES

Figure 8.1 shows typical attitude change curves for each of the five theories. Graphs (a–c) present typical predictions for the reinforcement theories of attitude change. Here the key assumption is that the receiver's attitude is a response that the source can either reward and reinforce or punish and weaken. Suppose the source delivers a positive message. If the receiver's attitude is also positive, the message–attitude agreement reinforces the attitude and produces positive attitude change. If the receiver's attitude is negative, then the message–attitude disagreement punishes the *negative* attitude and thus produces *positive* attitude change. Hence, as in graphs (a–c), a positive message produces positive attitude change. In similar fashion, a negative message reinforces a negative attitude, punishes a positive attitude,

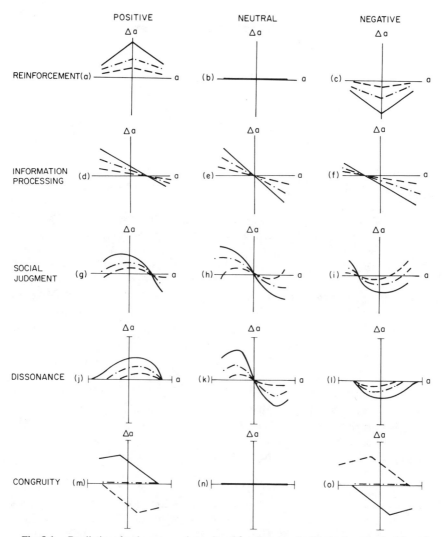

Fig. 8.1. Predictions for the message intensity of five theories of attitude change, where (——) denotes a positive source, (–·–) a neutral source, and (——) a negative source: (a–c) reinforcement; (d–f) information processing; (g–i) social judgment; (j–l) dissonance; (m–o) congruity.

and thus produces negative attitude change. A neutral message has no reinforcement value and produces no change. The graphs also embody two technical assumptions of lesser theoretical significance. The first is that the more positive the receiver's feeling toward the source, the more credible the source will appear and the greater the attitude change will induce. The second is that the more polar the attitude, the less it will change.

Graphs (d–f) in Fig. 8.1 present typical predictions from the information processing models. Here the agent for attitude change is the discrepancy between the positive advocated by the message and the position held by the subject. Attitude change will be proportional to the percentage of arguments in the message on which the receiver yields. Thus the critical prediction for these theorists is that the curves have negative slope and cross the attitude axis at the message value, hence change is toward the message value. The graphs embody the technical assumptions that

1. the more credible the source, the greater the change and
2. the more the receiver likes the source, the more credible the source will appear to be.

Graphs (g–i) in Fig. 8.1 present typical predictions for Sherif's social judgment theory. Like the information processing theories, social judgment theory assumes that the agent of change is the discrepancy between the position advocated by the message and the position held by the receiver. If the discrepancy is not too large, the receiver perceives the message as reasonable and assimilates to it, that is, if the message falls in the receiver's "latitude of acceptance," change is in the direction of message value. As the discrepancy becomes larger, the message is viewed as more and more biased and the degree of attitude change declines to zero. For extreme discrepancies the receiver will actually "boomerang" or change in the direction opposite to that advocated by the message. Boomerang effects are an explicit prediction of the Sherif model; however, our basic social judgment model instead assumes that change merely goes to zero. The graph also embodies the assumptions that

1. the width of the latitude of acceptance is a direct function of the credibility of the source and
2. the credibility of the source is a direct function of how much the receiver "likes" the source.

Graphs (j–l) in Fig. 8.1 present typical predictions for dissonance theory. Dissonance theory also assumes that the agent for change is the discrepancy between the message position and the receiver's attitude. Thus the dissonance produced by the message is proportional to the discrepancy and proportional to the credibility of the source. For small discrepancies or for highly credible sources the dissonance is reduced by attitude change in the direction advocated by the message. For large discrepancies or low source credibility, the dissonance is reduced by derogating the source, and there is little attitude change. Unlike social judgment theory, the difference due to source credibility between the curves is an integral theoretical assumption. However, the assumption that the credibility of the source is a direct function of the receiver's attitude toward the source is a technical assumption.

Graphs (m–o) in Fig. 8.1 present the predictions for congruity theory. Congruity theory posits two different psychological processes: one for positive messages and one for negative messages. If the message is positive, an associative bond is created between the implicit evaluative responses toward source and object and each response will then change in the direction of the other. Thus for a positive message the receiver's attitude satisfies a discrepancy law, however the discrepancy is not between message and attitude but between the receiver's attitudes toward source and object. If the message is negative, then a dissociative bond is created between the implicit evaluative responses toward source and object and each attitude changes toward the negative of the other. Again attitude change obeys a discrepancy law, but again the discrepancy is not that between message and attitude. Attitude change is in the direction of the negative of the receiver's attitude toward the source. The prediction of no change for the neutral message is derived from their assumption that change is a function of "message intensity" and the assumption that message intensity is proportional to message polarity. The nonlinearity of the predicted curves derives from the polarity assumptions and a nonlinear "correction for incredulity." The polarity assumptions have always been presented as integral assumptions, but actually they are completely independent of the process assumptions.

Mathematically there are three main clusters in the theories of attitude change that are most clearly seen in these plots of attitude change as a function of premessage attitude with attitude toward the source parameterized. For the reinforcement theorists the curves are all above the axis for a positive message and all below the axis for a negative message. The information processing theorists, social judgment theorists, and dissonance theorists are all discrepancy theorists. Except for boomerang, attitude change is positive when the message value is above the attitude and negative when it is lower. For congruity theory there is a complex interaction between message value and attitude toward the source. If the message is positive, each curve crosses the axis at the point where $a = s$, is positive below that point, and negative about it. That is, the curves for different source values look like discrepancy curves for different message values. If the message is negative, the curves all cross the axis where $a = -s$ and again resemble discrepancy curves for different message values. For the neutral message, congruity theory and reinforcement theory predict no change.

SUMMARY OF SOURCE CHANGE THEORIES

Figure 8.2 presents the theoretical predictions of change in the receiver's attitude toward the source. Graphs (a–c) present typical predicted source change curves for reinforcement theory. Reinforcement theory assumes that

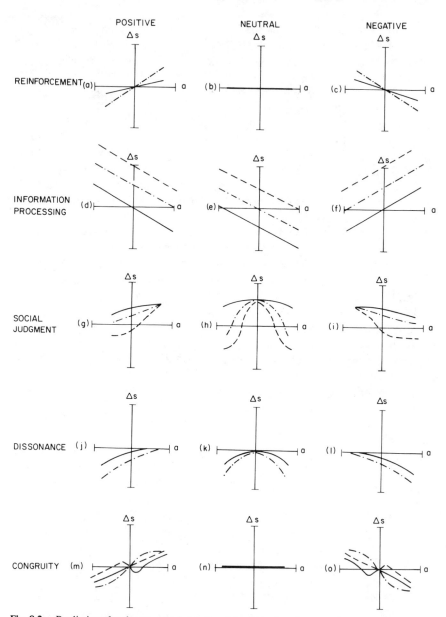

Fig. 8.2. Predictions for the message intensity of five theories of source change, where (——) denotes a positive source, (–·–) a neutral source, and (——) a negative source: (a–c) reinforcement; (d–f) information processing; (g–i) social judgement; (j–l) dissonance; (m–o) congruity.

agreement will strengthen the attitudinal response and that disagreement will weaken it. Thus agreement acts as a positive reinforcer and disagreement as a negative reinforcer. Thus the positive emotional response elicited by agreement should generalize to the source (by classical conditioning) and produce positive source change. In similar fashion the emotional distress produced by disagreement will generalize to the source to produce negative source change. Because a positive message produces agreement for receivers with a positive attitude and disagreement for receivers with a negative attitude, we have the results in graphs (a–c). These graphs embody two technical assumptions. First, it is assumed that the extent of agreement or disagreement is proportional to the polarity of the receiver's attitude toward the object. Second, it is assumed that the more polar the receiver's attitude toward the source, the less the source change.

Graphs (d–f) in Fig. 8.2 present the predicted source change curves for information processing theory. Here it is assumed that the receiver compares the source's message with the receiver's current assessment of the facts. Sources who describe an object more favorably than expected undergo positive source change; sources who describe an object less favorably than expected undergo negative source change.

Graphs (g–i) in Fig. 8.2 present the predicted source change curves for social judgment theory. If the message falls in the receiver's latitude of acceptance, it is judged to be fair and reasonable, and the source change should be positive. If the message falls in the receiver's latitude of rejection, it is judged to be biased, and the source change is negative. The differences between these curves for different values of source credibility are an integral assumption of the theory. However, the assumption that source credibility is a function of the receiver's attitude toward the source is a technical assumption.

Graphs (j–l) present the predicted source change curves for dissonance theory. Because the dissonance not dissipated through attitude change will be dissipated through source derogation, source change will be zero at the message value (zero discrepancy) and will become steadily more negative as discrepancy increases. The nonmonotone ordering of the curves for different attitudes toward the source has a more complicated explanation. If the source has low credibility, then the message produces very little dissonance and hence little source change. On the other hand, if the source credibility is extremely high, all the dissonance is dissipated through attitude change and again there is little source change. The assumption that source credibility is a function of the receiver's attitude toward the source is a technical assumption.

Graphs (m–o) in Fig. 8.2 present the predicted source change curves for congruity theory. In this form it is clear that the congruity predictions for source change are very similar to those for reinforcement theory, although the derivation is quite different. For congruity theory a positive message causes the attitude toward the source to adjust in the direction of the attitude toward the object, and a negative message causes the source attitude to shift toward the negative of the object attitude. The non-monotone ordering of the curves derives from the polarity assumptions.

The theorists are more sharply differentiated in their predictions for source change. For the comparison information processing model for predicting source change, the key assumption is that if a source advocated a position more favorable than expected, there would be source enhancement. Advocating a less favorable than expected position elicits disparagement. For social judgment theory, any message in the latitude of acceptance elicits enhancement, and a message in the latitude of rejection elicits disparagement. Thus source change as a function of attitude will be positive near the message value and negative if the latitude is too discrepant in either direction. The dissonance theorists also predict that source change will be a function of the discrepancy between the attitude and message value. If there is no discrepancy, there is no disparagement. The greater the discrepancy in either direction, the greater the disparagement. Thus, if source change is plotted against attitude, it will be zero at the message value and increasingly negative as you leave that value. For congruity theory there is a complex interaction between attitude and message value. For the positive message, if source change is plotted as a function of source (with attitude parameterized), each curve will cross the axis at $s = a$. Below this point the curves are positive; above it they are negative. For the negative message, the curves cross the axis at $s = -a$, are positive below that point and negative above it. For the neutral message, congruity theory predicts no change.

CHAPTER 9

Cognitive Consistency Theory

INTRODUCTION

The intent of this book is to focus on attitudes rather than beliefs. However, there is one theory that has generated more research than any other program in this area and that cannot be ignored—cognitive consistency theory. This research was reviewed by McGuire (1960a, b, c) and in Wyer (1974) and much of it is cited in Chapter 14, on hierarchically structured sets of attitudes. In addition to extending formal logic to handle subjective probabilities other than zero or one, these researchers[†] have showed that beliefs become more logically consistent over time and that the time path of any observed belief depends in critical ways on related beliefs that may or may not have been observed. These workers predicted and found delayed-action, indirect effects of change in one belief on change in related beliefs.

The purpose of this chapter is twofold. First, the cognitive theory is critiqued, and then, evidence is presented that shows that cognitive consistency theory is a special case of information processing theory. Recent consistency theorists have assumed that subjective conditional probability is as universal as objective conditional probability. Counterexamples show that

[†] See McGuire (1960a, b, c), Watts and McGuire (1964), Dillehay, Insko, and Smith (1966), Nelson (1968), Holt and Watts, (1969), Watts and Holt (1970).

most subjective conditional probabilities do not exist but are created under the special conditions of causation and logical implication. That is, we shall argue that a person will create the subjective probability $P(B \mid A)$ if he believes that event A causes event B or if he believes that statement A logically implies statement B. Also, recent consistency theorists have argued that attitudes are a special kind of belief. This chapter shows affect must be considered separately from belief.

Cognitive consistency theory has been developed as a static theory, a theory predicting belief from other beliefs rather than as change equations predicting belief change from a message. Wyer and Goldberg (1970) claim to have "predicted" belief change, but their procedure is actually an ad hoc test of static consistency rather than true prediction.

This chapter develops models of change using the information processing theory of belief change. Our first model uses the Wyer–Goldberg (1970) cognitive consistency equation and treats information processing theory as an adjunct theory. However, that model is disconfirmed by the ample empirical evidence of inconsistency. An alternative model is derived directly from information processing theory without recourse to the cognitive consistency equation. This "one step" model actually predicts that the cognitive consistency equation arises as the result of repeated change due to a succession of messages. Thus one need not assume the cognitive consistency equation to be true, but we show that it can be derived as an equilibrium condition of information processing theory. Models are also developed for several different message conditions.

LOGICAL CONSISTENCY THEORY AND SUBJECTIVE PROBABILITY

The oldest belief consistency theory is that of logic. Suppose belief A logically implies belief B. If the receiver thinks A is true but B is false, then his beliefs are logically contradictory and the belief system can be made consistent only by changing one of the beliefs, that is, by coming to believe that either A is false or B is true.

Most of the empirical research in the cognitive consistency tradition has stemmed from this logical syllogism. The question is: what will bring contradictions to mind if they exist? What will influence the direction of change? And so on.

The main mathematical problem with the use of logical consistency as a psychological theory is that it can be applied only when the receiver has a definite belief about all propositions in question. That is, the receiver must hold each belief to be either true or false. What of statements where the receiver thinks that the statement is probably true but still has reservations?

The problem as posed by McGuire (1960a–d) is: How can the principle of implication be stated in terms of subjective probabilities? His solution to regard subjective probabilities as consistent if they satisfy the multiplicative rule

$$P(B) = P(B\,|\,A)P(A) \tag{9.1}$$

This rule contains logical implication as a special case. To believe that A implies B is to hold the subjective probability $P(B\,|\,A) = 1$. If $P(B\,|\,A) = 1$, then to believe in A means $P(A) = 1$ and hence there is consistency only if

$$P(B) = P(B\,|\,A)P(A) = (1)(1) = 1$$

That is, there is consistency only if the person also believes B to be true. However, McGuire's model also provides a consistency condition for partial belief. If the receiver is 80% sure of A and 80% sure that A implies B, then his belief in B is only consistent if the subjective probability is

$$P(B) = P(B\,|\,A)P(A) = (.8)(.8) = .64$$

The McGuire product rule was criticized by Wyer (1974) and Wyer and Goldberg (1970) because it embodies as assumption omitted by McGuire. It not only embodies the idea of logical implication but the idea of single causation as well. Consider objective probability theory. To say that $P(B) = P(B\,|\,A)P(A)$ is to say that B will occur only if A occurs. If there are other causes that can produce B, then the McGuire product rule will understate the probability of B. Wyer and Goldberg (1970) propose the objective probability formula as a consistency principle. That is, they assert that subjective probabilities will be stable only if they satisfy the rule

$$P(B) = P(B\,|\,A)P(A) + P(B\,|\,A')P(A'), \tag{9.2}$$

where a prime on a belief such as A' means the logical negation of A, that is, the assertion that A is false. The subjective probability $P(B\,|\,A')$ captures the idea that there may be causes of B other than A.

CAUSATION AND SUBJECTIVE PROBABILITY

The previous discussion was riddled with references to causality. This is not true of the Wyer and Goldberg (1970) formulation of cognitive consistency. Implicit in their presentation is the assumption that the consistency equation for subjective probabilities will have the same universal application as the corresponding objective probability law. They set no limits on the application of that principle (Wyer, 1974). If the person's cognitive structure is only affected by his causal beliefs or by logical implication, then universal application is not possible. Below we argue that if the person believes A is one of the causes of B, then the Wyer model will hold only in the direction of predicting $P(B)$ from $P(A)$. In fact, the reverse subjective probability $P(A \mid B)$ most likely will not exist.

Our argument proceeds from problems in the reversal of conditional probability in objective probability theory. It is true that there is a reversal principle called the Bayes theorem, but the application of that theorem frequently calls for information that is not present. However, application of conditional probability in the assumed causal order usually requires less information, requires information that is readily available, and requires no "tricky" computations.

A concrete example illustrates that argument. The elements of this example are shown in Fig. 9.1, with causal beliefs represented by arrows. Assume that people set a cutoff that classifies people as intelligent or not intelligent. They believe that intelligent people are more likely to make it in high-prestige, high competition universities such as Michigan State University (MSU) whereas low-ability students are better off at a local college such as Lansing Community College (LCC). Finally, people with high ability are more likely to do advanced work and therefore more likely to obtain a Ph.D. We begin by applying the Wyer formula to an inference that follows the assumed causal flow. Suppose people believe that high intelligence tends to produce high school achievement and low intelligence inhibits achievement. Thus, if A is the event "high intelligence," A' the event "low intelligence," and B the event "obtain a Ph.D.," then most people would have subjective probabilities something like $P(B \mid A) = .80$ and $P(B \mid A') = .20$. It is also well known in Michigan that it is much harder to enter Michigan State University than to enter Lansing Community College. Thus most would accept probabilities such as $P(A \mid MSU) = .50$ and $P(A \mid LCC) = .20$. Cognitive consistency theory would then argue that people should use the inference process represented by Wyer (1974) to answer questions such as "How do MSU and LCC compare in

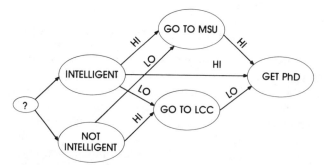

Fig. 9.1 The assumed causal structure for the argument against reversal of subjective conditional probabilities representing causal inference.

terms of how well their graduates do in seeking higher degrees?" The formula goes like this:

$$P(B|MSU) = P(B|A)P(A|MSU) + P(B|A')P(A'|MSU)$$
$$= .8(.5) + (.2)(.5) = .50 \qquad (9.3)$$
$$P(B|LCC) = P(B|A)P(A|LCC) + P(B|A')P(A'|LCC)$$
$$= .8(.2) + (.2)(.8) = .32 \qquad (9.4)$$

Thus, they should predict that MSU graduates are almost twice as likely to obtain advanced degrees.

The preceding example is typical of cognitive consistency theory; the inference is in the direction of assumed causal process. But conditional probability formulas work both ways. Consider the following question: "We have a Lansing graduate who has gone on for a Ph.D. What is the probability that he graduated from MSU rather than from LCC?" According to Wyer (1974), we should have

$$P(MSU|B) = P(MSU|A)P(A|B) + P(MSU|A')P(A'|B). \qquad (9.5)$$

But we believe that real people would find this question far harder than the previous one because the reversed conditional probabilities do not represent causal processes. To see the complexity of this problem, let us assume that the probabilities given above are objective probabilities and then trace through the computation of the reverse conditional probabilities using statistical methods. If $P(B|A) = .80$, then what is $P(A|B)$? The answer depends on the context. Consider first the MSU campus. By definition,

$$P(A|B) = \frac{P(A \text{ and } B)}{P(B)} = \frac{P(B|A)P(A)}{P(B)} = .80 \qquad (9.6)$$

However, on the LCC campus the same formula yields $P(A|B) = (.8)(.2)/.32 = .50$. That is, the conditional probability in the causal direction is $P(B|A) = .80$ (independent of context), whereas the conditional probability against the causal grain changes as a function of the *marginal* probability of the causally *antecedent* event. That is, the probability of A given B depends on the probability of A.

The fact that the probability changes from one content to the other means that in the formula "$P(A|B)$" must be a pooled estimate averaged over the two campuses. Thus yet another number must be given rather than inferred—the relative number of students at MSU and LCC. That is, $P(A|B)$ can vary from .50 (if virtually all graduates are from MSU) to .32 (if virtually all graduates are from LCC). For example, if LCC and MSU have the same number of graduates, then $P(A|B) = .5(.50) + .5(.32) = .41$.

The other necessary conditional probabilities $P(\text{MSU} \mid A)$ and $P(\text{MSU} \mid A')$ are also reverse calculated to be $.5(.5)/.35 = .71$ and $.5(.5)/.65 = .38$. Thus $P(\text{MSU} \mid B) = .61$.

Cognitive consistency theorists assert that objective probability theory can serve as a model for human inference. They also assert that inference is carried out using the Wyer formula. We just showed that these assertions are in fact very unlikely. In those situations in which people find it easy to talk about $P(B \mid A)$, they should be hesitant to talk about $P(A \mid B)$ and should be prone to insist that "it depends $\cdots$." Indeed, given the difficulty of reverse probability computations, it is likely that if they are forced into reverse reasoning, then people would use some nonobjective approximation such as "$P(A \mid B) = P(B \mid A)$," or some other nonobjective rule.

THE RELEVANCE OF THE IRRELEVANT AND VICE VERSA

There is another argument for restricting the Wyer–Goldberg (1970) formula to events in which A is preceived as a cause of B. The argument below presents the usual method for assessing the indirect effect of belief change when the belief that changes is causally antecedent to the belief that is indirectly affected.

What is the impact of such change on the subjective probabilities associated with an irrelevant belief? We shall show that if the Wyer formula is true for irrelevant beliefs, then the rules for belief change are immensely more complicated than has been assumed by cognitive consistency theorists at this time.

The theory of persuasion as presently developed from cognitive consistency theory differs little from classic logic. If a person believes that A is a causal determinant of B, then an argument in favor of A will be an argument in favor of B. For example, assume that a survey finds that the citizens of Blacksburg, Virginia, believe that if their nuclear power plant was properly constructed (hereafter referred to as "A"), then it is probably safe (hereafter referred to as "B"), that is, $P(B \mid A) = .90$. However, the same survey indicates that the Blacksburg citizens thinks that if their nuclear power plant was improperly constructed, then it is probably not safe, that is, $P(B \mid A') = .10$. At the present, all citizens belief that their nuclear power plant was properly constructed, that is, $P(A) = 1.00$.

Suppose, however, that an unscrupulous environmental club issues the following message: "Our local nuclear reactor was constructed by the Poof Corporation, which has been long known for its illegal corner cutting on public projects." If 40% of the Blacksburg citizen accept this message, then the percentage of safe ratings will drop from .90 to .58, that is,

$$P(B) = P(A)P(B|A) + P(A')P(B|A'),$$

$$.90 = (1.00)(.90) + (.00)(.10) \qquad \text{before message} \qquad (9.7)$$

$$.58 = (.60)(.90) + (.40)(.10) \qquad \text{after message}$$

Let us now consider an irrelevant belief that existed before the message about the Poof Corporation. In front of the nuclear power plant is a large sign reading "Zoom Electric Company," However, in the years since the plant was built, the sign has peeled and faded. There is talk among the citizens as to whether the management of the power plant is sufficiently compulsive to repaint the sign, but no one in the town believes that a newly painted sign (or the sign left as is) has any bearing on the safety of the nuclear reactor, if A_2 is the belief "The sign will soon be painted," then we would have something like

$$P(B) = P(A_2)P(B|A_2) + P(A'_2)P(B|A'_2)$$

$$.90 = (.60)(.90) + (.40)(.90) \qquad (9.8)$$

The irrelevance of the sign to the safety of the reactor is given by $P(B|A_2) = P(B|A'_2) = P(B)$. That is, the Blacksburg citizens think that their reactor is safe regardless of whether the sign will or will not be painted.

Let us now assume that the message about the "cost cutting policies" of the Poof Corporation has been received by the citizens of Blacksburg. We showed that safety ratings change from .90 to .58, that is, the citizens after the message think their reactor is *less* safe after receiving the message than before. But what happens to beliefs in Eq. (9.8)? Does $P(A_2)$, $P(B|A_2)$, and $P(B|A'_2)$ change? If not, then there are gross inconsistencies between the two predictions of the safety ratings $P(B)$. If so, then the message about the "cost cutting" policies of the Poof Corporation not only changed $P(B)$ but so did beliefs that are irrelevant to $P(B)$. The Poof Corporation message should not have any effect on the belief $P(A_2)$ about the sign being painted. But, if the Wyer–Goldberg (1970) model is correct, then all irrelevant conditional belifs. must have changed from .90 to .58, that is

$$P(B) = P(A_2)P(B|A_2) + P(A'_2)P(B|A'_2)$$

$$.58 = (.60)(.58) + (.40)(.58) \qquad (9.9)$$

If irrelevant, subjective, conditional probabilities are carried around in the receiver's head, then the Poof Corporation message must have changed all of them to .58 even though the message had nothing to do with sign painting or other irrelevant beliefs. Cognitive consistency theory according to Wyer therefore must make the following remarkable prediction: "After readinng that the reactor had been built by a cost cutting contractor, the citizens changed their probability that a painted sign leads to a safe reactor from .90 to .58."

Furthermore, if a message has an effect on one belief A that is relevant to belief B, then it must also have an effect on an unknown number of other conditional probabilities, namely, those beliefs that are not relevant to belief B. That is, if cognitive structure takes the form claimed by the Wyer (1974) theory, then the primary impact of any message is on those beliefs to which it is entirely irrelevant.

ATTITUDE AS A SPECIAL KIND OF BELIEF

Some cognitive consistency theorists have gone beyond the realm of belief and belief consistency to consider the issue of attitude change. They stake out a radical position: attitudes are just a special case of beliefs. They believe that to say that Joe has a positive attitude toward his wife is to say that Joe believes that his wife is good. That is, they believe that the statement "I love Betty." means nothing more than the belief "Betty is good." We shall consider two versions of this theory—the Jones–Gerard (1967) theory and the Wyer–Goldberg (1970) theory and shall show that each leads to severe difficulties.

Jones and Gerard (1967) attempt to derive a syllogistic theory of attitudes based on McGuire's (1960) work. They define a person's attitude toward x as the set of all syllogisms whose conclusion is "x has value v," where v is either good, bad, or indifferent. Each syllogism has the form x has property P, P has value v, therefore x has value v. They note that this definition requires perfect attitudinal consistency, that is, "x has value v" must be the conclusion of all syllogisms that conclude in a value for x. Although they admit that this might not be true of a given object x at one point in time, they hypothesize that such inconsistency is transient. That is, they assume that the person will either alter his conclusion (the value of x) to make all the values the same or will alter the premise (x has property P) of each syllogism that yields an "inconsistent" value.

Unfortunately, Jones and Gerard give no definition of attitude during the "temporary" phase when there are inconsistent syllogisms in the person's mind. This is very inconvenient in cases such as that of Joe Fidelis. Joe was heard to complain of Betty that she always made him wait when he came to take her on a date. Throughout their married lives, Joe was continually apologizing for being late with the irritated remark that "Betty takes too long getting dressed." Betty died shortly after their fiftieth anniversary and Joe "pined away" in less than 3 months. Joe always professed great love for Betty, but he also subscribed to the following syllogism: "People who make their friends wait needlessly are selfish. Betty will neither move faster nor start earlier. Therefore Betty is selfish." Thus, in Jones and Gerard's theory, his attitude toward Betty was "temporarily" undefined. Did Joe love Betty? Those using the Jones and Gerard definition will never know.

Wyer and Goldberg (1970) try to push the Jones–Gerard syllogism to a logical extreme: they attempt to reduce attitudes to beliefs of the form "x is good." They handle the Jones and Gerard inconsistency problem by going to subjective probabilities. If the subjective probability for Betty is less than 1.00, then Joe need not reject every statement that implies Betty is not good.

However, the Wyer–Goldberg model becomes troublesome if one combines their subjective probability model for attitude with their consistency equation. Consider the following situation. It is the heyday of the war in Vietnam. Sam believes that the war in Vietnam is evil. Sam believes that the war in Israel is good. When asked about war in general, Sam says that war is neither good nor bad per se. This can be coded in terms of subjective probabilities as recommended by Wyer–Goldberg: P(war in Vietnam is good) $= 0$, P(war in Israel is good) $= 1.00$, P(war is good) $= .50$. No problem in the simple coding.

But these three concepts (war, war in Vietnam, and war in Israel) are related logically in that the two specific wars are logical instances of the class wars. Thus we have

$$P(\text{war in Vietnam is good} \mid \text{war is good}) = 1.00$$

$$P(\text{war in Vietnam is good} \mid \text{war is not good}) = 0$$

Therefore we can compute Sam's attitude toward war from the Wyer cognitive consistency formula, where B is the belief "war in Vietnam is good" and A is the belief "war is good." We then have

$$\begin{aligned} P(B) &= P(B \mid A)P(A) + P(B \mid A')P(A') \\ &= 1.00(.50) + 0(.50) \\ &= .50 \end{aligned} \tag{9.10}$$

Thus cognitive consistency theory requires that Sam's attitude toward the war in Vietnam be indifferent rather than negative.

Similarly, cognitive consistency theory implies that Sam's attitude toward the war in Israel must be indifferent rather than positive. In fact, the cognitive consistency principle as stated by Wyer requires that Sam's attitude toward all wars be exactly .50. Thus the Wyer and Goldberg model does not solve the problem of Jones and Gerard, it extends the problem to intermediate attitude values.

There is another problem for the Wyer–Goldberg model that again stems from the consistency formula. Sally loves the color pink, that is, $P(X$ is good $\mid X$ is pink$) = 1.00$. But Sally hates greasy things, that is, $P(X$ is good $\mid X$ is greasy$) = 0$. How then does Sally feel toward pink greasy hot dogs? Affective theories have an additive principle for composing competing reactions. But cognitive consistency has no need for such principles in dealing with beliefs.

There appear to be many problems associated with treating attitudes as special cases of beliefs. Part of the problem stems from the fact that affect is truly bipolar (good and bad) whereas subjective probability is fundamentally unipolar (true or false = not true). To say that a belief is not true is not to say that the opposite of the belief is true. To say that the statement "X is good" is false is not necessarily to say that "X is bad;" X could be neutral.

PROBLEMS IN THE WYER–GOLDBERG PREDICTION OF CHANGE

Cognitive consistency, like balance theory, has been developed as an equilibrium theory. It states when beliefs will not change rather than when and how much they will change. Without a dynamic theory specifying what change will take place when beliefs are inconsistent, cognitive consistency theory is incomplete. A dynamic theory is presented in the section entitled "Cognitive Consistency as a Predicted End State," where we shall use the information processing theory of belief change to derive cognitive consistency theory. But first we would like to clear up a misunderstanding that has arisen from the work of Wyer and Goldberg (1970), who claim to show that their model "predicted change." What they show is that the consistency formula continued to fit the data after change as well as it fit before. However, they do not predict the change in any belief. This is spelled out below.

Let $P(A)$ be the subjective probability of some proposition A and $P(A \mid X)$ the subjective probability of A given some other proposition X. If X is any proposition related to A and X' is the proposition "not X," then the subjective probabilities are consistent if and only if

$$P(A) = P(A \mid X)P(X) + P(A \mid X')P(X') \tag{9.11}$$

This leads to a nonlinear static prediction equation

$$P(\hat{A}) = P(A \mid X)P(X) + P(A \mid X')P(X') \tag{9.12}$$

where $P(\hat{A})$ is the predicted rather actual value. Differences between $P(A)$ and $P(\hat{A})$ represent inconsistencies in the person's probabilities. If most people are consistent and if inconsistencies tend to be "random," then the equation for $P(\hat{A})$ can be used as a regression equation for predicting $P(A)$. Wyer and Goldberg (1970) show this regression equation to work reasonably well on their data. However, this is not the prediction of future values, it is a check on consistency among contemporaneous values.

Does their model predict belief change? It does not, and their claim that it does is based on a subtle but important error. Their data consist of five pretest measures: $P(A_1)$ and the other four subjective probabilities necessary to test their regression equation; and the five posttest scores: $P(A_2)$ and the four related posttest measures. Thus they could produce four scores. From the pretest data they obtain an observed value for $P(A_1)$ and a "predicted" value $P(\hat{A}_1)$ that is obtained from the nonlinear regression equation above. From the posttest data they obtain an observed value for $P(A)$ and a "predicted" value $P(\hat{A}_2)$ by applying the nonlinear regression equation to the other four *posttest* scores. They then form and correlate the differences $P(A_2) - P(A_1)$ with $P(\hat{A}_2) - P(\hat{A}_1)$ and find the correlation to be high enough to be "quantitative predictions of belief change" (see also, Wyer, 1970). The problem here is in their "prediction" of $P(A_2)$. The variable $P(\hat{A}_2)$ is not predicted from pretest scores, it is calculated from the five posttest scores, that is, $P(\hat{A}_2)$ is a post hoc measurement, just as $P(A_2)$ is.

Nor is this a trivial comment. Because their prediction of the postmessage belief was post hoc, it was unnecessary to relate change to such variables as, say, message value. Indeed, Wyer and Goldberg (1970) have no such discussion. Wyer (1970, 1972) experimentally manipulates $P(X)$ and $P(A|X)$ to produce changes in $P(A)$, but this model does not predict the changes in $P(X)$ and $P(A|X)$, so his test of the model uses the same post hoc "predictions" of $P(A_2)$ as did Wyer and Goldberg (1970).

On the other hand, in a truly predictive model, if one is given several pretest measures, say, x_0, y_0, z_0, and the level and value of the message, then one must be able to predict all of the posttest scores from these initial values. This is a critical point. If a model predicts the post message belief, then one can use that predicted belief to predict beliefs at a still further point in time. Thus one can extend the predictions to generate the long-term effects of a succession of messages using sequences if the change is discrete or differential equations if the change is continuous.

MODELS OF BELIEF CHANGE

The models of belief change to be derived below are consistent with cognitive consistency theory in spirit but introduce additional assumptions to predict the amount and direction of change due to external messages or internal inconsistency. The change theory used throughout is information processing theory. The first section derives the information processing model of simple belief change. The following sections derive models of change in causally consequent beliefs. Much of this work can be easily extended to change in behavioral intentions (see Chapter 13).

Information Processing Theory

The word "belief" is often used in an ambiguous manner. Belief may refer to a statement such as "Nuclear power plants have been proven safe." A statement may or may not be espoused by the receiver. However, if a statement is referred to as one of the person's beliefs, then it is both a statement and is assumed to be espoused by the person. That is, the word "belief" could refer to a statement or to the extent to which the receiver believes the statement to be true. Thus we split this ambiguity by using capital letters as statements and small letters for subjective probabilities. For example, if A is a statement, the related belief a would be the subjective probability that A is true, that is,

$$a = P(A)$$

Beliefs, then, are numbers between zero and one, where zero means the person believes the statement to be false and one means the person believes the statement to be true.

According to information processing theory, belief change will be produced by an external message only if the message challenges the belief. That is, there must be a discrepancy between the content of the message and the person's current belief. The receiver compares the message with his current belief. If there is a difference, then the receiver either yields or rejects the message. If the message argues that the belief is true, then the receiver will change only if his subjective probability is less than one. If there is change, then it will be an increase in subjective probability. Let us denote the belief subjective probability by p. A message that argues that thc bclicf is true has a message value of $m = 1$. Thus the information processing model would be

$$\Delta p = \alpha(1 - p) \tag{9.13}$$

where the parameter α measures the strength of the message.

If the message argues that the belief is false, then the receiver will change his belief only if his subjective probability is greater than zero. If there is change, then it will be a decrease in subjective probability. The corresponding model is

$$\Delta p = -\alpha p = \alpha(0 - p) \tag{9.14}$$

That is, if the message argues that the belief is false, then the message value is zero. Thus the model is a special case of linear discrepancy theory.

The two models above can be expressed in terms of linear discrepancy theory:

$$\Delta p = \alpha(m - p) \tag{9.15}$$

where $m = 1$ if the message argues "true" and $m = 0$ if the message argues "false."

Indirect Effects If Beliefs Are Always Consistent: Two-Step Change

Cognitive consistency theory has no explicit model of change, but it has been written as a theory of indirect change. The key assumption is that if two beliefs are linked by the consistency equation, then change in the logically prior belief will induce change in the implied belief to bring about consistency. Let us denote the subjective belief toward the causally prior belief by a, that is, let $a = P(A)$. Let us denote the causally posterior belief by b; that is, let $b = P(B)$. Then the Wyer and Goldberg (1970) consistency equation is

$$P(B) = B(B|A)P(A) + P(B|A')P(A')$$

which can be written

$$b = P(B|A)a + P(B|A')(1 - a) \tag{9.16}$$

After the external message, beliefs $P(A)$ and $P(B)$ will be changed. If the new beliefs are consistent, then they must satisfy the equation

$$\text{new } P(B) = P(B|A)\,\text{new } P(A) + P(B|A')\,\text{new } P(A') \tag{9.17}$$

After the message, the new probabilities will be denoted by $a + \Delta a$ and $b + \Delta b$. The change in a is given by the information processing model for direct message effects:

$$\Delta a = \alpha(m - a)$$

The change in b must be derived from the consistency equation for "new $P(B)$". That is, if the new beliefs are to be consistent, then they must satisfy the Wyer–Goldberg equation

$$\begin{aligned}
b + \Delta b &= P(B|A)(a + \Delta a) + P(B|A')[1 - (a + \Delta a)] \\
&= P(B|A)a + P(B|A)\Delta a + P(B|A')(1 - a) - P(B|A')\Delta a \\
&= [P(B|A)a + P(B|A')(1 - a)] + [P(B|A) - P(B|A')]\Delta a \quad (9.18)
\end{aligned}$$

The first term of this last equation is just b according to the consistency equation. Thus

$$\Delta b = [P(B|A) - P(B|A')]\Delta a = \alpha[P(B|A) - P(B|A')](m - a) \tag{9.19}$$

This derivation follows the McGuire or Wyer–Goldberg reasoning exactly. The message about A produces change in the belief $a = P(A)$. The receiver thinks about B in relation to A. This then produces change in $b = P(B)$. The initial change produced by the message is

$$\Delta a = \alpha(m - a) \tag{9.20}$$

whereas the indirect change in B is given by

$$\Delta b = [P(B|A) - P(B|A')]\Delta a = [P(B|A) - P(B|A')]\alpha(m - a) \tag{9.21}$$

Hereafter, Eq. (9.21) will be called the two-step model.

COGNITIVE INCONSISTENCY

The model just derived has a severe problem: it assumes that beliefs are always consistent. This section reviews evidence showing that there may be considerable inconsistency among beliefs. The existence of inconsistency opens the door to alternative models. As it happens, the search for alternative models was more fruitful than originally thought. The information processing model derived below predicts the cognitive consistency equation. That is, cognitive consistency theory is derived as a special case of information processing theory.

There is a great deal of evidence that appears to show the presence of cognitive inconsistency. All the studies by McGuire or by Wyer and co-workers show correlations between actual and predicted subjective probabilities that are considerably less than one. However, an appreciable proportion of the variation in these equations could be due to errors of measurement. Most of these studies report no assessment of reliability of measurement. Furthermore, the error of measurement enters equations nonlinearly and require special estimation procedures for adequate control (Hunter and Cohen, 1974) if the reliability of measurement is low.

There is also indirect evidence for the presence of inconsistency, that is, there are studies showing differences in the extent of consistency. For example, there is evidence of inconsistency in the studies showing the "Socratic effect." These studies find that as people think about premises that lead to specific conclusions, the consistency between premises and conclusions increases. McGuire (1960c) argues that people have a "natural tendency" to restructure thoughts toward greater consistency when given the chance; repeated measurements of syllogistically related beliefs provide this opportunity. That is, for measures of related beliefs that are repeated over time, subsequent measures produce more consistent results than initial measures. Rosen and Wyer (1972) find some support for the hypothesis that those who are more aware of belief relatedness will produce greater consistency.

Inconsistency is required to account for the Socratic effect findings of Dillehay *et al.* (1966), Rosen and Wyer (1972), McGuire (1960a, b, c), Watts and Holt (1970), and Wyer and Goldberg (1970). Had there been no inconsistencies, there would be no Socratic effects and no postmessages follow-up effects to detect.

Krugman (1965, 1968) makes a similar argument to explain inconsistencies between beliefs and attitudes or between beliefs and behavior. He argues that consistency will come about only if the person is induced to think about the related elements.

INDIRECT EFFECTS: A ONE-STEP MODEL

This section derives a model of "indirect" belief change directly from information processing theory. However, this model does not assume a two-step change process. Rather, the model assumes that change in the implied belief is produced directly by the message, hence the name "one-step" model.

The one-step model does not use the cognitive consistency equation in its derivation. However, it predicts that the cognitive consistency equation plays a special role in the model—as an equilibrium state. That is, the one-step model predicts the cognitive consistency equation as the result of a long sequence of messages.

The cognitive consistency theorists have been largely concerned with the effects of material implication on belief change. Thus they have focused on examples in which there is a large content difference between the belief statements A and B. In such a case, it seems plausible to assume that the receiver responds to the message about A by thinking about A. Any change in B must then come in a second step in which the receiver thinks about B in relationship to A. However, if the link between A and B is strong enough, then the receiver might think of the message as being a message about B. If this were true, then the message might produce change in B directly.

Consider the advertising model derived by Danes and Hunter (1980) using a version of cognitive consistency theory derived from Wyer (1970) by Jaccard and King (1977). For Danes and Hunter, belief B is a behavioral intention to purchase, such as "I should buy a Fiat" and belief A is a related attribute assertion, such as "The Fiat is an economical car." We think it quite likely in this context that a receiver would respond to a message arguing that the Fiat is economical as a message urging him to change his purchase intention.

If the receiver interprets a message about A to be a message about B, then, according to information processing theory,

$$\Delta b = \alpha(m_b - b) \tag{9.22}$$

where m_b is the message value about B. These indirect message values can be stated as subjective conditional probabilities. That is, a message that argues that A is true is saying that "$P(B) = P(B|A)$." A message that argues that A is false is saying that "$P(B) = P(B|A')$." Thus, according to cognitive consistency theory, the message value is

$$m_b = \begin{cases} P(B|A) & \text{if message argues A is true} \\ P(B|A') & \text{if message argues A is false} \end{cases} \tag{9.23}$$

PRESERVATION OF CONSISTENCY BY THE ONE-STEP MODEL

We now show that the cognitive consistency equation can be derived from the one-step model. This will be done in two parts. This section presents the proof that cognitive consistency is "preserved" by the one-step model. That is, this section proves that the one-step model predicts that if the beliefs are consistent before the message, then the new beliefs will be consistent after the message.

The one-step model assumes that if A is seen as causally prior to B, then presentation of a message relevant to A will produce changes in both beliefs. In each case, change is predicted by the linear discrepancy equation

$$\Delta a = \alpha(m - a) \quad \text{and} \quad \Delta b = \alpha(m_b - b) \tag{9.24}$$

If a and b change according to these equations and if a and b satisfy the cognitive consistency equation before the message, then they satisfy the cognitive consistency equation after the message.

We shall show this only for the "A is true" message because the algebra for the "A is false" case is essentially the same. The one-step model assumes that

$$\Delta a = \alpha(1 - a) \quad \text{and} \quad \Delta b = \alpha[P(B|A) - b] \tag{9.25}$$

whereas the previous two-step model assumes

$$\Delta a = \alpha(1 - a) \quad \text{and} \quad \Delta b = [P(B|A) - P(B|A')]\Delta a \tag{9.26}$$

We now show that if the beliefs are consistent before the message, then the two-step model equation for Δb is algebraically equivalent to the one-step model equation for Δb:

$$\begin{aligned}
\Delta b &= [P(B|A) - P(B|A')][\alpha(1 - a)] \\
&= \alpha[P(B|A)(1 - a) - P(B|A')(1 - a)] \\
&= \alpha[P(B|A) - P(B|A)a - P(B|A')(1 - a)] \\
&= \alpha\{P(B|A) - [P(B|A)a + P(B|A')(1 - a)]\} \\
&= \alpha[P(B|A) - b] \tag{9.27}
\end{aligned}$$

as claimed

COGNITIVE CONSISTENCY AS A PREDICTED END STATE

In this section we prove that the one-step model predicts cognitive consistency as an end state. We do this by proving that the one-step model predicts that the difference between actual belief b and the value of b computed from the cognitive consistency decays exponentially to zero. That is, we prove that, according to the one-step model, a sequence of messages will produce cognitive consistency.

If beliefs a and b are continually changing, then the cognitive consistency equation is also a dynamic equation. Let us define a variable b^* to be the value of b given by the cognitive consistency equation. The value of b^* is

$$b^* = P(B|A)a + P(B|A')(1 - a) \tag{9.28}$$

The extent of cognitive inconsistency can then be measured by the difference between the actual and given values of b. Let us denote this discrepancy by d, that is, let d be defined by

$$d = b - b^* \qquad (9.29)$$

We now prove that the one-step model predicts that successive messages drive the discrepancy to zero exponentially. The proof will be given only for the case where the message argues that A is true.

From the linearity of the change operator, we have

$$\Delta d = \Delta b - \Delta b^* \qquad (9.30)$$

The one step-model predicts

$$\Delta b = \alpha[P(B|A) - b] \qquad (9.31)$$

The change in b^* is what was computed as the predicted change in b in the section assuming that beliefs are always consistent. That is,

$$\Delta b^* = [P(B|A) - P(B|A')]\Delta a$$
$$= \alpha(1 - a)[P(B|A) - P(B|A')] \qquad (9.32)$$

Therefore,

$$\Delta d = \alpha[P(B|A) - b] - \alpha(1 - a)[P(B|A) - P(\mathrm{B}|A')]$$
$$= \alpha[P(B|A) - (1 - a)P(B|A) + (1 - a)P(B|A') - b]$$
$$= \alpha\{[P(B|A)a + P(B|A')(1 - a)] - b\}$$
$$= \alpha(b^* - b)$$
$$= -\alpha d \qquad (9.33)$$

After n messages, the discrepancy will be

$$d_n = d_o(1 - \alpha)^n \qquad (9.34)$$

which is an exponential decay time function. Therefore, the discrepancy between actual and required values of b decays exponentially to zero.

We just showed that the one-step model predicts the cognitive consistency equation to be the end product of a succession of messages. Thus the cognitive consistency equation need not be assumed as a new theory; it is a special case of the information processing theory of belief change.

CONSISTENCY PRODUCING PROBE MESSAGES

Where does inconsistency come from in the first place? There are two answers compatible with information processing theory. First, the receiver might be presented with a message about A but not think about B. A specific model that assumes that this will happen under certain circumstances shall be presented in the next sub-section, "Transfer Discrepancy." Second, the receiver might hear a message about B. For most beliefs, the fact that A implies B does not mean that B implies A. Because A is not implied by B, there is no reason that the receiver should think of A when presented with a message about B. Thus it is likely that a message about B will produce change in b without producing change in a. If the beliefs were consistent before the message, then the change in b would make the beliefs inconsistent after the message.

There is one kind of message that should always reduce inconsistency a probe message that asks the receiver to think about B in relation to A. Logically, because B is consequent to A, information processing theory predicts that this probe message will produce change in b:

$$\Delta b = \alpha(m_b - b)$$

where m_b is the message value about B produced by thinking about B in relation to A. Because probability theory is a branch of logic, information processing theory predicts that the message value will be

$$P(B) = P(B|A)P(A) + P(B|A')P(A')$$

That is, the message value about B given from thinking about A is the cognitive consistency equation. Thus the message value is

$$m_b = b^* \tag{9.35}$$

and the change equation is

$$\Delta b = \alpha(b^* - b) \tag{9.36}$$

This is the linear discrepancy equation with b^* as the target. Because a does not change, the value of b^* does not change. Therefore, a succession of probe messages will cause b to converge exponentially to b^*.

Again information processing theory predicts the cognitive consistency equation as the end state of a succession of messages rather than a process in its own right.

The above discussion does not assume the Wyer–Goldberg model to be a general model with universal application. Rather, it assumes that the model applies in specific cases, that is, those in which the receiver is asked to think about B in relation to A and when A implies B either by logical implication or causation. Moreover, the value b^* is not a predicted belief but is a perceptual target value derived when the person thinks about B in relation to A.

TRANSFER DISCREPANCY

The one-step model assumes that the receiver always thinks about B after receiving the message about A. But suppose that the receiver thinks only about A and never considers its implications for B. In this case, there could be change in A without the concommitant change in B. This could produce inconsistency in the two beliefs. This section presents two "transfer discrepancy" models that assume that the receiver will fail to think about B under certain conditions: awareness of discrepancy and awareness of belief change.

Awareness of Discrepancy

Danes and Hunter (1980) and Danes and McEwen (1981) assume that the receiver will think about the related belief B only if the receiver is aware of the discrepancy between the message and the antecedent belief A. That is, if the receiver is not aware of the discrepancy, then there will be no consideration of belief B.

Because the content of the message is an argument for or against A, the transfer discrepancy model assumes that there is always change in the subjective probability of A, that is,

$$\Delta a = \alpha(m - a)$$

If there is change on B, then that change is governed by the one-step information processing model

$$\Delta b = \alpha(m_b - b)$$

where m_b is either $P(B|A)$ or $P(B|A')$, depending on whether the message is pro or con in regard to A. However, this model differs from the one-step model in that it assumes that change on B does not always take place. Instead, this model assumes that after the receiver has considered A, there is only a reconsideration of B if the receiver is aware of the message discrepancy. That is,

$$\Delta b = \begin{cases} \alpha(m_b - b) & \text{if receiver aware of discrepancy} \\ 0 & \text{if receiver is not aware of discrepancy} \end{cases} \qquad (9.37)$$

In aggregate data, the observed change in b would be the average of the two regression lines, that is, if p is the probability of being aware and $q = 1 - p$, then

$$\Delta b = p[\alpha(m_b - b)] + q(0) = p\alpha(m_b - b) \qquad (9.38)$$

The probability of being aware of discrepancy is not likely to be the same for all receivers. Rather, the discrepancy is likely to be more noticeable if it is large than if it is small. If the probability of awareness is proportional to the size of the discrepancy, then we would have

$$p = \beta|m - a| \qquad (9.39)$$

The size of β can be obtained by consideration of a special case. If the message argues that A is true but the receiver believes that A is false, then

$$p = \beta(1 - 0) = \beta \qquad (9.40)$$

Because it stretches credibility to believe that the receiver will not notice the difference between absolutely true and absolutely false, we have

$$\beta = p = 1$$

Thus the first set of transfer discrepancy equations is

$$\Delta a = \alpha(m - a) \qquad \text{and} \qquad \Delta b = \alpha|m - a|(m_b - b) \qquad (9.41)$$

AWARENESS OF BELIEF CHANGE

The awareness of belief change model assumes that the simple discrepancy between the message and the antecedent belief is insufficient. For this model the key variable for the transfer of change from one belief to another is the degree to which the receiver is aware that the antecedent belief has changed. That is, after the receiver has considered A, there is only a reconsideration of B if the receiver is aware that A has changed, that is,

$$\Delta b = \begin{cases} \alpha(m_b - b) & \text{if} \quad \text{receiver is aware of } \Delta a \\ 0 & \text{if} \quad \text{receiver is not aware of } \Delta a \end{cases}$$

In aggregate data, the observed change in b would be the average of the two regression lines, that is, if p is the probability of being aware and $q = 1 - p$, then

$$\Delta b = p[\alpha(m_b - b)] + q(0) = p\alpha(m_b - b) \qquad (9.43)$$

The probability Δa of being aware of belief change is likely to be more noticeable if the change is large than if it is small. If the probability of noticing Δa is proportional to the size of change, then

$$p = \beta(\Delta a) = \beta\alpha(m - a) \qquad (9.44)$$

As for the awareness of the discrepancy version of the transfer model discussed above, the size of β can be obtained by consideration of the special case of $\Delta a = 1$. If a person initially believed "false," and after a message believed "true", then

$$p = \beta(\Delta a) = \beta\alpha(1 - a) = \beta(1) = \beta \qquad (9.45)$$

Because it is quite unlikely that a person would not notice maximum change, we have

$$p = \beta = 1.$$

TABLE 9.1

Model	Assumptions
Wyer–Goldberg $$P(B) = P(\hat{B}) = P(B \mid A)P(A) + P(B \mid A')$$	Beliefs are related by the laws of objective probability. Beliefs are consistent only if $P(B) = P(B)$.
Information processing for belief change $$\Delta p = \alpha(m - p); \qquad 0 \leq \alpha \leq 1$$	Belief is denoted by p and message about the belief by m. The receiver compares the message with his current belief. If there is a difference, the receiver either yields or rejects the message. Message acceptance is governed by α, a measure of message strength.
Change in consistent beliefs: two-step $$\Delta b = \alpha(m - a)[P(B \mid A) - P(B \mid A')]$$	Change in target belief is given by the information processing model for belief change $\Delta a = \alpha(m - a)$. All other beliefs b that are caused by or are implications of a change to be consistent with the new a; belief change occurs in two steps.
Basic information processing: one-step $$\Delta b = \alpha(m_b - b)$$ $$m_b = \begin{cases} P(B \mid A), & \text{if message argues } A \\ & \text{is true} \\ P(B \mid A'), & \text{if message argues } A \\ & \text{is false} \end{cases}$$	A message about a relief that implies b is interpreted as either $P(A \mid B)$ or $P(A \mid B')$. Change in target belief is given as $\Delta a = \alpha(m - a)$.
Probe message $$\Delta b = \alpha(b^* - b)$$	b^* is given by the Wyer–Goldberg equation. The effects of "just thinking" about beliefs and conditional beliefs derive an internal message b^*. Stated beliefs b converge exponentially to b^* as the number of probe messages increase.
Transfer discrepancy $$\Delta a = \alpha(m - a)$$ $$\Delta b = \alpha \lvert m - a \rvert (m_b - b)$$	Target change is given by the information processing model. Derived change in b is given by one-step model and modified by receiver's awareness of the discrepancy between m and a.
$$\Delta a = \alpha(m - a)$$ $$\Delta b = \alpha^2 \lvert m - a \rvert (m_b - b)$$	Same as above except change transferred from a to b depends on the receiver's awareness of Δa.

The awareness of change equations for the transfer model are

$$\Delta a = \alpha(m - a)$$
$$\Delta b = p\alpha(m_b - b) = \alpha^2|m - a|(m_b - b) \qquad (9.46)$$

CONCLUSION

Information processing theory fits past data much better than the traditional cognitive consistency model. First, information processing theory specifies conditions under which there will be inconsistency. Given a pair of beliefs related in order A to B, inconsistency will be produced if messages are directed at B or if a message directed at A fails to cause the receiver to think about B. However, information processing theory also predicts consistency in just those situations in which it has been observed: situations in which the receiver has been encouraged to think about the relationship between A and B. A brief summary of the models in this chapter is given in Table 9.1.

PART II

ATTITUDE CHANGE STUDIES

The next four chapters present empirical studies showing how models can be pitted against one another. The simulated social network study in Chapter 10 is an experiment designed to test all the models of attitude change derived in Part I. This chapter also contains a review of the research on source change and a discussion of source credibility findings. Both present and past data tend to fit the information processing models. Chapter 11, on political attitudes, shows how to convert attitude change models to test them against longitudinal survey data. The model that best fits the British data gathered by Butler and Strokes (1974) was the information processing model. Chapter 12 tests various information processing models of belief change. The data show that a message produces less change in receivers who have accumulated a large amount of information about the topic than in receivers who are relatively uninformed. Chapter 13 extends cognitive consistency theory to a belief-behavior model; a model of advertising and purchase intention.

CHAPTER 10

Attitude and Source Change in a Simulated Social Network

The present study was designed to test the models of attitude and source change derived from reinforcement, information processing, social judgment, congruity, and dissonance theory. The experimental paradigm for the test was passive communication (Chapter 1) in a simulated social network. Summaries of the models tested are presented in Chapter 8; full discussions of the models appear in Chapters 2–7. For attitude change, the data gathered by the experiment support the basic information processing model. The results for source change support the mixed information processing model. For both attitude and source change, the results from this experiment reject all models from reinforcement and congruity theory.

METHOD

Subjects

Two hundred and nineteen students who enrolled in introductory psychology courses were recruited by telephone to participate in the study. Each subject was paid $3.00 for participating. Most of the subjects were at the freshman and sophomore class level.

An Overview of the Experimental Procedure and Objectives

The fit of the models was tested with data generated from a simulated social network experimental design in which the attitude change materials were 20 interpersonal messages obtained when each of five hypothetical persons was asked to describe each of the other four. Five amateur thespians at Michigan State University were hired to portray the roles of the stimulus persons. The experimenters claimed to have interviewed the members of a drama club and their faculty advisor; the interpersonal messages were said to be based on the material collected in these interviews.

In reality, the interpersonal material was constructed without any resource to empirical data. The material for each stimulus person consisted of a biographical resume ("prepared by the advisor"), a personal sketch or self-description, and four interpersonal sketches—statements about the stimulus person from each of the other people. Although the material was fictitious, it had been written to resemble protocols that might have been obtained from real-life interviews.

Each actor (stimulus person) was first introduced by the biographical sketch. Next the actor delivered a self-description and finally talked about the other four group members. The self-description and interpersonal sketches had been prerecorded on videotape prior to the experimental sessions.

Subjects in the experiment read the five biographical resumes and then rated each stimulus person on several evaluative semantic differential scales. Next the videotaped personal sketches were shown, after which subjects again completed the evaluative scales for each stimulus person. Subjects then viewed 20 interpersonal sketches. In each of these sketches, one of the five actors (the "source" for that message) described one of the other actors (the "object" of the message). After each sketch, subjects rated the source and object of the sketch on the evaluative scales. Subjects then made final ratings of the five drama club members.

To summarize, *de novo* attitude toward five hypothetical stimulus persons were formed through a series of preliminary printed sketches. Each stimulus person then gave a brief videotaped self-portrait. Thus two messages and concomitant evaluations of the stimulus persons took place before the data to be analyzed for attitude change were gathered. In the attitude change material each person delivered a message describing each of the other four persons. Thus, in these messages, each person "appeared" eight times: four times as the source of a message and four times as the object of a message.

We hoped to accomplish three goals by this procedure. First, we held the subject's interest while presenting a rather large number of attitude-change-inducing messages. Second, we hoped to make source change and attitude change commensurate, that is, we hoped to avoid the sharp distinctions between source and object characteristic of most attitude change designs. Third, and above all, we hoped to obtain sufficient source change to distinguish the models.

Our greatest concern at the time of the pilot study was that the procedure might prove confusing. However, the fact that the stimulus persons were identified by photographs from the beginning seemed to eliminate completely such problems. Our second main concern was that subjects might be bored by the experiment. However, subjects uniformly reported that they found the experiment absorbing, and most said it was "fun."

Warm Up and Habituation

At the beginning of the session, subjects were given a short introduction to the experiment. They were told that they would be presented with considerable information about five members of a drama club. They were told that in a previous study the experimenters interviewed the five members of an actual drama club and their faculty advisor. The experimental messages were said to be based on the material collected in these interviews but played out by actors from a Michigan State University drama club.

The subject was then introduced to each actor by a biographical sketch "prepared by the advisor" with an accompanying photograph. The subject filled out a semantic differential on each actor after reading the biographical sketch. The material in these sketches serves to preset attitudes toward the members. The biographical material was selected to produce maximal variance in the initial attitudes toward each group member and thus to guarantee varying degrees of communication discrepancy when the interpersonal sketches were presented. The biographical sketches also furnished experience with the experimental task and the rating instruments.

Each actor then presented a self-description. The self-descriptions were "prepared by the member himself" and presented reasons and objectives for joining the drama club. These sketches were delivered by the student actors on videotape. The visual personal sketches familiarized the subject with the "live" group (until this point, the subject had only read printed material about the group and seen a photograph) and stabilized an impression of each member prior to the interpersonal message phase of the study. These videotaped sketches further fixed the identity of each stimulus person and helped to eliminate the transient reactions the subject might have had upon viewing the stimulus persons for the first time when delivering an interpersonal sketch. After the personal sketches, the subject again filled out semantic differential scales on each actor. The warm up and habituation phase of the experiment were then complete.

The Experimental Messages: The Simulated Social Network Design

After "warm up" was complete, the subject entered the main experimental section of session. This was designed to fit the following social network paradigm. Suppose the subject views two individuals *A* and *B* who successively talk about one another. When *A* describes *B*, *A* becomes a *source* of information and *B* becomes the *object* of this information. The subject forms an impression of *B* based on what *A* says and, at the same time, forms an impression of *A*. These impressions can be translated into evaluative ratings of *A* and *B*. Subsequently, when *B* talks about *A* their roles are now reversed, with *B* the source and *A* the object. Given the *A* and *B* are unfamiliar stimuli to the subject prior to the experiment, one might expect that

1. the evaluative ratings acquired by *A* and *B* would be determined by what they say about each other;

2. the evaluative ratings could be manipulated through message content, thus providing experimental control over attitude and source change;

3. source and object are strictly comparable and are relatively equal in terms of potential change; and

4. subjects should find "people talking about other people" interesting and engaging.

This paradigm can be generalized to a set of people talking about one another, thus providing a natural base for replications and varied message values. For this study five amateur thespians at Michigan State University were hired to portray the roles of stimulus persons. The stimulus persons were five members of a hypothetical drama club. A "message" consisted of a short monologue on videotape in which one of the stimulus persons described one of the others. Because each of the five actors described each of the other four, there were 20 such interpersonal messages.

Wrap Up and Debriefing

After the last interpersonal sketch, the subject made a final rating of each member in the acting club. The experimenter then entered and explained that the material had been constructed rather than actually obtained from a campus drama club. The experimenter described the purpose of the study and answered questions about the experiment. Before leaving, subjects were requested not to reveal or discuss the contents of the experiment with anyone until the end of the school term.

The Sociogram

Because it was anticipated that the experimental material would be delivered by student actors, members in a hypothetical drama club were selected for stimulus persons. This decision permitted the student actors to provide first

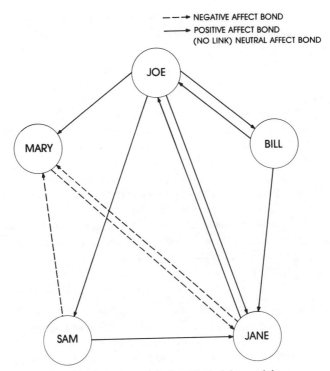

Fig. 10.1.   Sociogram of the hypothetical drama club.

hand knowledge in the construction and testing of materials. In addition, such a hypothetical group seemed to provide diverse stimulus person attributes and interactions. The size of the group was set at five.

A hypothetical sociogram was defined for the group; sociometric choices were not symmetrical (see Fig. 10.1). The sociogram was designed to provide a rich variety of evaluative material (messages) with positive, neutral, and negative affect.

For each member a kernel caricature was composed. The facts in this caricature were maintained in the interpersonal sketches, although the source was free to interpret these facts in a fashion appropriate to the sociogram. The source might also "add facts" if these were consistent with the caricature. This procedure generated interpersonal sketches that contained consistent information about the objects from message to message yet reflected the sources' evaluations of the objects.

Advisor Biographies and Self-Descriptions

Biographical sketches about each member were "prepared by the faculty advisor to the drama club." The material in these sketches served to preset attitudes toward the members. The biographical material was selected to produce maximal variance in the initial attitudes toward each group member and thus guarantee varying degrees of communication discrepancy when the interpersonal sketches were presented. The biographical sketches also furnished subjects with experience on the experimental task and the rating instruments.

The self-descriptions were "prepared by each member," who presented reasons and objectives for joining the drama club. These sketches were delivered by the student actors and presented by videotape. The visual personal sketches familiarized the subject with the "live" group (until this point, the subjects had only read printed material about the group) and stabilized an impression of each member prior to the interpersonal message phase of the study. It was also intended that these videotaped sketches would further fix the identity of each stimulus person and would also eliminate from the *interpersonal* sketches the transient reactions the subject might have had upon viewing the stimulus persons for the first time.

Interpersonal Sketches

With the group size at five, there were 20 possible interpersonal messages. All 20 were constructed and videotaped. Each sketch was intended to reflect the positive, negative, or neutral association from the source to the object. In writing negative or positive sketches, highly complimentary or highly derogatory material was introduced into the sketch, consistent with the caricatures and biographies. In neutral sketches, an attempt was made to avoid highly polar material. Weakly positive statements were balanced by weakly negative statements when necessary. In all cases the positive and negative material was logically consistent, that is, it referred to different attributes such as talent and warmth.

Two orders of presentation for the interpersonal messages were devised. In one order, each member in turn successively talked about the other four members—same source about multiple objects (SSMO). In the second order, four members talked about the same member, then four members talked about another member, and so on—multiple sources about same object (MSSO). The MSSO order was introduced to check for any unanticipated order effect in SSMO (see Table 10.1).

Ratings of Source and Object

All attitudes were measured by the semantic differential technique. The adjective pairs in the present study were friendly–unfriendly, warm–cold, selfish–unselfish, ungenerous–generous, modest–arrogant, vain–humble, dishonest–honest, and trustworthy–untrustworthy. Reliability coefficients for

TABLE 10.1

EXPERIMENTAL SEQUENCE FOR THE
SSMO AND MSSO CONDITIONS

Condition	
SSMO	*MSSO*
Mary	Mary
Joe	Joe
Bill	Bill
Jane	Jane
Sam	Sam
Mary	Mary
Joe	Joe
Bill	Bill
Jane	Jane
Sam	Sam
Mary about Bill	Jane about Sam
Mary about Jane	Bill about Sam
Mary about Joe	Joe about Sam
Mary about Sam	Mary about Sam
Joe about Bill	Sam about Jane
Joe about Jane	Bill about Jane
Joe about Mary	Joe about Jane
Joe about Sam	Mary about Jane
Bill about Jane	Sam about Bill
Bill about Joe	Jane about Bill
Bill about Mary	Joe about Bill
Bill about Sam	Mary about Bill
Jane about Bill	Sam about Joe
Jane about Joe	Jane about Joe
Jane about Mary	Bill about Joe
Jane about Sam	Mary about Joe
Sam about Bill	Sam about Mary
Sam about Jane	Jane about Mary
Sam about Joe	Bill about Mary
Sam about Mary	Joe about Mary
Mary	Mary
Joe	Joe
Bill	Bill
Jane	Jane
Sam	Sam

the pre-message evaluative ratings of source and object were estimated by the application of the Spearman–Brown formula to the average correlation among the eight evaluative scales. The reliabilities ranged from .70 to .94 with an average of .89.

The Scaling of Messages

Messages were written with the intended message values of the sociogram (see Fig. 10.2). Three scaling studies were conducted to assess the actual message values: messages were scaled when viewed in context (VIC), read in context (RIC), and read out of context (ROC). The average correlation between the methods was .93. The message values used in analyzing the source and attitude change in the main study were the majority-rule values assigned by the three scaling methods. The correlation between intended and actual sociogram was .84. (They agreed on 16 of the 20 links or messages.) On a scale from -3 to $+3$, the average message values for positive, neutral, and negative messages were 1.53, $-.16$, and -1.40.

RESULTS: CHANGE IN ATTITUDE TOWARD THE OBJECT

This section presents the results for attitude change. The first analysis is a full regression of attitude change on premessage attitudes toward source and object. This analysis was performed to bring out all the anticipated non-linearities and source–object interactions. However, this analysis uses a rather unorthodox mixture of within and between variance. Therefore, two further analyses will be presented: one that looks only at group means and one that looks at the data for each message separately. The results of these analyses support the information processing model for attitude change.

An Overview of the First Analysis

The basic data for this analysis were the evaluative ratings of the source and object on the 20 interpersonal sketches (messages). These data provided the necessary information for constructing the regression function relating attitude change to the subject's prior attitudes toward source and object.

Attitudes toward source and object could theoretically range from -3 to $+3$. The range was divided into four intervals: -3.00 to -1.50, -1.49 to 0.00, $+0.01$ to $+1.49$, and $+1.50$ to $+3.00$. These intervals are referred to as highly negative (HN), moderately negative (MN), moderately positive (MP), and highly positive (HP). The number of categories could not be increased without an intolerable number of empty and near-empty cells in the bivariate premessage distribution.

The four intervals on each attitude continuum partitioned the premessage bivariate distribution of s and a into 16 cells. For each cell, the associated mean postmessage attitudes were calculated. These means were used to arrive at the estimated regression function.

A preliminary message-by-message analysis of the results proved to be inadequate. In several of the messages, over 50% of the cells were empty. Many of the cell frequencies were too small to protect against large sampling errors.

Therefore, the data for the individual messages were pooled. Nine positive messages went into the positive message table, seven neutral messages into the neutral message table, and four negative messages into the negative message table. The pooling procedure used was equivalent to averaging means across messages with any particular cell weighted by the frequency of that particular cell. At this stage, the pooled tables were computed separately for the SSMO and MSSO conditions. Within each condition, some of the extreme corner cells were empty or contained only a few observations. The remaining cells displayed similar results in the two conditions. Consequently, the SSMO and MSSO data were pooled.

Figures 10.2–10.4 present the results for the positive, negative, and neutral messages, respectively. These figures show little departure from linearity and

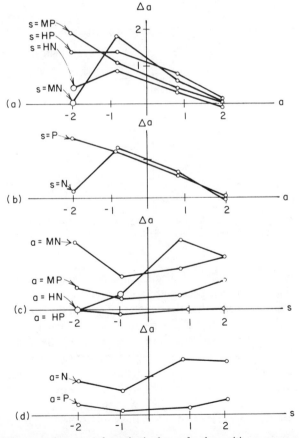

Fig. 10.2.   The regression curves for attitude change for the positive message as a function of premessage attitudes toward source and object.

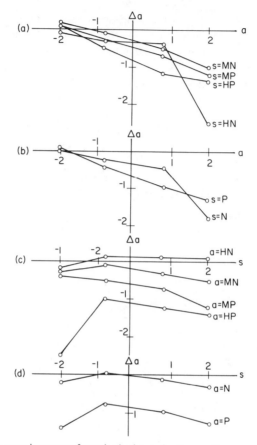

Fig. 10.3. The regression curves for attitude change for the negative message as a function of premessage attitudes toward the source and object.

no evidence of source credibility effects. An extensive analysis (not reported here) shows that the circled points are all from extreme cells with very low frequencies. Thus it appears that the departures are all due to sampling error. In any case, although some of the departures from linearity or some of the apparent source effects tend to support other models, these departures are coherent. That is, one departure might suggest dissonance theory but another favors balance theory. Furthermore, the departures that fit a given model are not corroborated by the results for cells with large frequencies. None of the models in this book fit the data with the low frequency cells data taken as is. If the cells with low frequencies are deleted, the source effects and nonlinearities vanish.

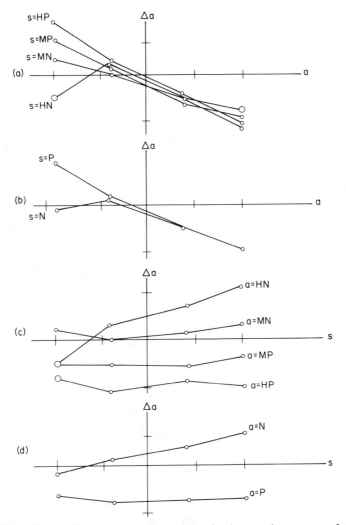

Fig. 10.4. The regression curves for attitude change for the neutral message as a function of premessage attitudes toward the source and object.

Because there were no source effects, we averaged the curves across source values. Figure 10.5 presents the data for attitude change as a function of premessage attitude toward the object for positive, negative, and neutral messages. The departures from the linear discrepancy model are trivial in magnitude and not statistically significant. The average slope is approximately .40.

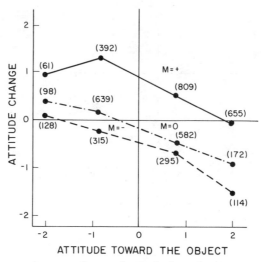

Fig. 10.5.   The regression curves for overall attitude change by message type as a function of premessage attitude toward the object (cell frequencies in parentheses).

Thus analysis of the individual level data reveal no nonlinearities and no source effects of any kind. The data fit the simple linear discrepancy equation of information processing model.

An Analysis Using Only Group Means

The fact that the preceding analysis revealed so little nonlinearity or interaction came as a surprise. However, there are certain blessings in this outcome. If the nonlinearities are small in relation to the entire range of premessage attitudes, then they are even smaller in relation to the restricted ranges found for single messages. Thus the group means for single messages should be related in much the same way as the scores for individual subjects. In particular, if the attitude change for individual subjects is a linear function of message value and premessage attitude, then the group means follow exactly the same function. That is, if individual scores satisfy $\Delta a = \alpha(m - a)$, then the means satisfy $\overline{\Delta a} = \alpha(\bar{m} - \bar{a})$. Thus, in the present study, we can legitimately do that which is usually done without justification—test a model derived for individuals against group means. From the data for the first experimental message in the SSMO condition ($N = 141$), we can calculate four means—the mean premessage attitudes toward the object, the mean premessage attitude toward the source, the mean attitude change, and the mean source change. A fifth number representing this message is the message value from the ROC scaling study. In similar fashion, we can obtain five "scores" for each of the

TABLE 10.2

PREMESSAGE PARAMETER RELATIONSHIPS

Means		S. D.	Correlations				Partial correlations			
Variable value			$\bar{a}$	$\bar{s}$	m	Δa	$\bar{a}$	$\bar{s}$	m	Δa
$\bar{a}$	.44	.86	1.00	−.18	.48	−.09	1.00	−.27	—	−.63
$\bar{s}$	.58	.76		1.00	.11	.20		1.00	—	.17
m	.45	1.29			1.00	.67			—	—
Δa	.02	.59				1.00				1.00

other 19 messages in the SSMO condition. Another set of means can be calculated from the 72 subjects in the MSSO condition. Again, for each of 20 experimental messages, there are five "scores." Thus altogether we formed a data table that was 5 variables wide by 40 messages long. This data table was then subjected to a regression analysis as if the 40 messages were 40 subjects. Table 10.2 presents the basic results pertinent to the regression function for attitude change. The crucial results are that message value correlates .67 with mean attitude change whereas the partial correlations with message value removed are −.63 for mean premessage attitude toward the object and .17 for mean premessage attitude toward the source. Thus the linear regression accounts for a substantial portion of the variance, and the contribution of the premessage attitude toward the source is negligible. The actual regression equation is $\Delta a = .42m - .37a - .01s - .009$, and the multiple correlation is .82. This substantiates the equation $\Delta a = .4(m - a)$ derived by the previous analysis.

The Within-Message Correlations

Because the nonlinearities and interactions are small relative to the restricted range of premessage attitudes for any one message, the simple correlations for each message should be indicative of the extent to which there are any effects due to the premessage attitude toward the source. In particular, if a positive source has more impact than a negative source, then the correlations between the premessage attitude toward the source and attitude change $r_{s,\Delta a}$ should be positive for positive messages and negative for negative messages. The correlations between attitude change and the premessage attitudes were calculated for each of the 20 experimental messages in the SSMO condition ($N = 141$) and each of the 20 messages in the MSSO condition ($N = 72$). These 80 correlations were then averaged within message value groups. The means

TABLE 10.3

ATTITUDE CHANGE CORRELATIONS[a]

Message value	N	Mean $r_{a,\Delta a}$	Mean $r_{s,\Delta a}$
Positive	18	−.47	.10
Neutral	14	−.48	−.08
Negative	8	−.39	.14
Average		−.45	.05

[a] Correlations between attitude change and pre-message attitudes toward source and object for the 40 experimental messages averaged by message value.

are presented in Table 10.3. The source correlations are not only small but are positive for both positive and negative messages.

Thus there is no evidence of a multiplicative source effect in the data, and the linear estimate given by the overall average (.05) is applicable. This confirms the negligible regression weight for source in the previous analysis and the inconsistencies of the source effect in the main analysis.

The mean correlation of −.45 between premessage attitude toward the object and attitude change is, in part, spurious. Indeed, because the average reliability of an attitude measurement is .89 in this study, a spurious correlation of about −.22 could have arisen from the fact that a and Δa share a common error term (Hunter and Cohen, 1974). On the other hand, if the linear model had held exactly for individual subjects, then the effect of unreliability would have been to reduce the correlation from a true −1.00 to an observed −.79. Thus, although the model accounts for a substantial portion of the nonerror variance in individual scores, there is considerable residual.

Order Effects

We now question whether order effects might invalidate the previous analyses. We first note that there are three main sources of order effects that have been controlled. First, if a subject encounters a message at a different point in time, his premessage attitude toward the source will be different, hence the message might have a different impact. Because this attitude was measured and used as an independent variable in each analysis above, these "order effects" have been taken into account. Second, at a different point in time, the subject's premessage attitude toward the object may differ. In an experiment in which attitude change varies as a function of premessage attitude (the typical case), this will produce "order effects." Again, the premessage attitude toward the object was measured and used as an independent variable and thus these "order effects" were controlled. Third, the same message at two points in time is heard against two different backgrounds. If the different contexts produce different message values, then those differing values will induce differing amounts of attitude change, hence "order effects." A check on this possibility was made at the time of message scaling. The messages were either read out of context (ROC) or viewed in context (VIC). The correlation between the two sets of scale values was .93. Thus there is little room for "order effects" due to differences in message values as a function of context.

Regarding order effects that were not controlled, the multiple correlation .82 for the model applied to group means places a rather sharp limit on the extent of such effects.

RESULTS FOR SOURCE CHANGE

Chronological Background

The analysis of the results for source change will follow the same pattern as that for attitude change. However, the fact that these analyses are actually widely separated in time is relevant to the source change results because the original analyses lead to different interpretations of the results. Our first analysis is oriented to the detection of the complicated nonlinearities that we find in our theoretical analysis (see Chapters 2–7). The only apparent complications turn out to be sampling error associated with very low frequency cells. Source change appears to be a linear function of the message value and the premessage attitude toward the source. The data appear to satisfy a simple source–message discrepancy model reminiscent of the linear discrepancy model of information processing theory. We then formulate the mirror model of source change and seek to test that model against all the other relevant data sets that we can find. We find the data for four out of five studies to confirm the mirror model and find the Tannenbaum data to be equivocal. In revising our original manuscript, we note that because the data fit a linear model, we can do a much more powerful analysis of the data using group means that will eliminate the problems of small cell frequencies. However, this linear analysis reveals a different regression equation. Instead of the mirror model $\Delta s = .3(m - s)$, we obtain the equation $\Delta s = .3(m - s) - .23a$. That is, the linear analysis shows that source change depends on the premessage attitude toward the object. At this point we formulate the comparison model of source change and the mixed population model. When we go back to our original analysis we find that the premessage effect has been there all along. It is just that it is so much weaker than the source and message effects that it is not visible to our naive eye.

The Search For Nonlinearities

The main analysis of change in attitude toward the source is parallel to that of change in attitude toward the object. The data from the 20 messages is pooled into three message classes: positive, negative, and neutral. Within each class, the bivariate distribution of premessage attitudes is partitioned into a 16 cell grid. The data for SSMO and MSSO are quite similar and are therefore pooled. Figures 10.6–10.8 present the results for source change for the positive,

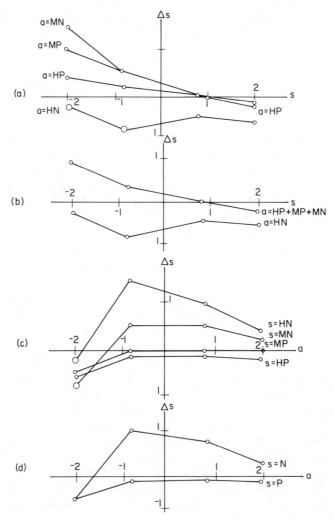

Fig. 10.6. The regression curves for source change for the positive message as a function of premessage attitudes toward the source and object.

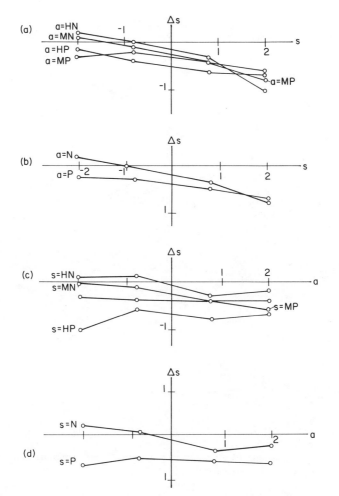

Fig. 10.7. The regression curves for source change for the negative message as a function of premessage attitudes toward the source and object.

negative, and neutral messages. The circled points are low-frequency cells. An extensive analysis (Not reported here) shows that all the departures from linearity stem from these low-frequency means. According to this analysis, the departures from linearity are due to sampling error.

Because there are no interactions, the key relationships should show up in the main effects. These main effects are obtained by averaging, with suitable deletion of low-frequency cells. The two-way interaction graphs are shown in Fig. 10.9. Figure 10.9a clearly shows the impact of message value and the impact of premessage attitude toward the source. This figure taken alone

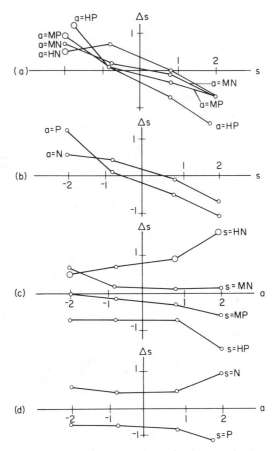

Fig. 10.8. The regression curves for source change for the neutral message as a function of premessage attitudes toward the source and object.

represents very close fit for the mirror model of source change. Figure 10.9b shows the two-way effects of message value and premessage attitude toward the object. This is the figure that we originally misinterpreted. The message effect is clear in this table, but the attitude effect is not. We looked at this figure and asserted that there was no effect for premessage attitude toward the object. However, with the hindsight of the linear analysis as a guide, we now note that all three of the lines in Fig. 10.9b show a negative slope. The slope for the neutral message is about −.125. The slope for the neutral message in relationship to premessage attitude toward the source is about −.44. Thus the mixed model of source change is indicated with an estimate of $p = .28$.

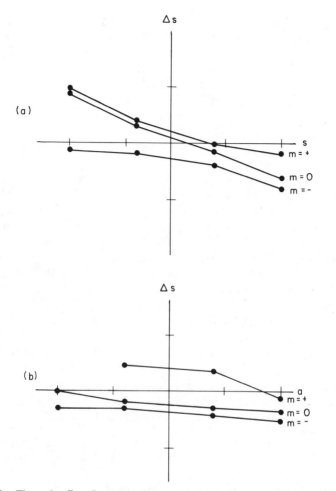

Fig. 10.9. The main effects for source change with the low-frequency cells deleted from the analysis.

An Analysis of Source Change Using Only Group Means

Because gross nonlinearities and interactions are anticipated in the source change regression curves, it is necessary that the regression curves extend over the full range of each premessage attitude. Therefore, previous analysis was performed on data pooled across the messages within each message class. However, because these nonlinearities and interactions are in fact quite small, it is possible to separate the "between and within variance." The analysis below is performed on the group means. For each of 20 messages under each of two conditions, there are three means: the mean premessage attitude toward the object, the mean premessage attitude toward the source, and mean source change. We then add a fourth variable, the ROC message.

We can now look at the multiple regression of mean source change on the three predictors: message value and the mean premessage attitudes toward source and object. If the mirror model fits the data for individuals, then from $\Delta s = \beta(m - s)$, we have the following equation for group means: $\overline{\Delta s} = \beta(m - \bar{s})$. Thus the multiple regression function for the means should be approximately $\Delta s = .30m - .30\bar{s}$ (if the main analysis is to be corroborated). Table 10.4 contains the basic statistics from which the observed regression function is calculated. The key results are that message value correlates .47 with source change, whereas the partial correlations with message value held constant are $-.49$ for premessage attitude toward the source and $-.29$ for the premessage attitude toward the object. The regression function is $\overline{\Delta s} = .25m - .31\bar{s} - .23\bar{a} + .06$, and the corresponding multiple correlation coefficient is $R = .75$. The coefficient for premessage attitude toward the object is not zero but $-.23$, or about two-thirds the size of the coefficient for premessage attitude toward the source. If premessage attitude toward the object is removed from the analysis, the regression equation becomes $\Delta s = .17m - .25\bar{s} - .03$, and the multiple correlation decreases to .64, a decline of 22% in goodness of fit. Thus there is little doubt that the regression coefficient for a is not zero. On the other hand, the standard error for this coefficient is .13. Thus, if a larger study were conducted that fully filled in the distribution of premessage attitude means, it is possible ($p \leq .40$) that the coefficient of $\bar{a}$ might only be $-.20$ and not inconceivable ($p \leq .07$) that it might be only $-.10$. These differences may seem small in absolute terms, but in

TABLE 10.4

PREMESSAGE ATTITUDE RELATIONSHIPS[a]

Mean	S. D.	Correlations				Partial correlations			
		$\bar{a}$	$\bar{s}$	m	Δs	$\bar{a}$	$\bar{s}$	m	$\overline{\Delta s}$
Variables Value									
$\bar{a}$ .44	.86	1.00	$-.18$	.48	.01	1.00	$-.27$	—	$-.29$
$\bar{s}$ .58	.76		1.00	.11	$-.38$		1.00	—	$-.49$
m .45	1.29			1.00	.47			—	—
Δs $-.10$	.43				1.00				1.00

[a] Means, standard deviations, and correlations between mean premessage attitude toward the object a, mean premessage attitude toward the source $\bar{s}$, ROC message value m, and mean source change Δs for the 40 experimental messages generated by entering the SSMO and MSSO means separately.

relative terms they represent the difference between a coefficient for $\bar{a}$ two-thirds the size of that for source and a coefficient only one-third the size of that for source.

The analysis of the group means suggests that the proper model for source change is *not* $\Delta s = \beta(m - s)$ but the *mixed* information processing model $\Delta s = \beta(m - s) - \beta pa$, where p is a fraction that was .74 in the overall regression function. This corroborates the basic finding of the main analysis: the main component of source change is the source–message discrepancy.

Correlations between Source Change and the Premessage Attitudes within Single Messages

Because the regression of source change on the premessage attitudes is largely linear, there is much to be gained by looking at the correlations within a single message. Because the SSMO and MSSO data must be analyzed separately, there are 40 such correlations between source change and each of the premessage attitudes. These are averaged within each message type and the resulting averages are presented in Table 10.5.

The main features of this table is that the correlations between source change and premessage attitude toward the source are consistently negative and relatively large. This corroborates the findings that the main component in source change is the source–message discrepancy. On the other hand, the correlations between source change and premessage attitude toward the object are inconsistent in sign and relatively small. However, the correlation for premessage attitude toward the source will be $-.22$ if the spurious error component is present in source change. Thus the ratios of the correlations in Table 10.5 are badly biased by this spurious component. It can be shown that these ratios for perfectly reliable measures will approximately 50% greater than those shown. In particular, the ratios will be .31 for the neutral message

TABLE 10.5

CORRELATIONS WITHIN SINGLE MESSAGE[a]

Message	Number of messages	Average correlations	
		$r_{s,\Delta s}$	$r_{a,\Delta s}$
Positive	18	$-.38$	$+.05$
Neutral	14	$-.44$	$-.10$
Negative	8	$-.37$	$-.08$
Average	40	$-.40$	$-.04$

[a] Correlations within single messages between source change and premessage attitudes averaged by message type

and .34 for the negative message. This ratio of .33 between the regression weight for premessage attitude toward the object and the regression weight for premessage attitude toward the source is exactly intermediate between the $p = .28$ of the main analysis and the $p = .74$ of the analysis of group means.

All three analyses agree on the main finding of this study. The dominant term in source change in these data is not agreement–disagreement but rather the discrepancy between the message value and the subject's premessage attitude toward the source. Thus all three analyses agree that in this study reinforcement theory, social judgment theory, dissonance theory, and congruity theory are all quantitatively and qualitatively disconfirmed.

The differences in the analyses revolve around whether the deviations from the message–source model $\Delta s = \beta(m - s)$ are as "negligible" as we believed at the end of the main analysis or as large as those of the mixed discrepancy model, $\Delta s = \beta(m - s) - \beta pa$, which fits the group means.

OBSERVATIONS

Attitude change satisfies a simple linear discrepancy model. The subject changes his attitude toward the object by a constant fraction of the distance to the position advocated by the message. Attitude change is largely independent of the subject's attitude toward the source.

Source change also satisfies a simple linear discrepancy model. The receiver's attitude toward the source changes in proportion to the difference between the receiver's feeling toward the source and the affect expressed in the source's statement. There are small lawful deviations from this prediction. These deviations are positive if the receiver's attitude toward the object is negative and negative if the receiver's attitude is positive. Thus, for the most part, source change is independent of whether or not the receiver and source agree or disagree about the object. The only exception to this is the case where the message is positive and the receiver's attitude toward the object is extremely negative. In these cells, the source is derogated. Finally, there is one other unexplained finding: the slope for the neutral message is steeper than the other message types.

In the era dominated by consistency theory, the most startling result is that source change and attitude change are almost completely independent.

Reinforcement Theorists

Reinforcement theorists assume that attitude change is primarily a function of message value alone and is dependent on attitude only to the extent that there may be increased resistance at the extremities. This is completely at odds with the relativistic message effects of the discrepancy model and hence the present data. Furthermore, reinforcement theory predicts that source change will be a direct function of whether the source agrees or disagrees with the receiver. This, too, is strongly disconfirmed in our data.

Congruity and Balance Theory

Congruity theory assumes that the heart of the communication paradigm is the relation between attitude toward source and attitude toward object. For a positive message, the discrepancy between source and object affect should decrease. Attitude and source change should be almost perfectly negatively correlated. For the negative message, these attitudes should each change toward the negative of the other, and the resulting changes should therefore be almost perfectly positively correlated. Congruity theory fails on all three counts:

1. it posits the wrong discrepancy (source–object) for attitude change (object–message);

2. it posits the wrong discrepancy (source–object) for source change (source–message); and

3. it posits a near perfect correlation between attitude change and source change.

We find attitude and source change to be independent.

The weak or qualitative form of congruity theory is balance theory, which posits the same critical discrepancies without predicting the specific form of the remedy. The critical failure of balance theory is in its predictions for the negative message. All change is toward the negative source–negative object combination that is unbalanced for the negative message.

Dissonance Theory

Dissonance theory assumes that object–message discrepancy is the cause of attitude change. Thus it gives good qualitative fit to the attitude change results. However, the predicted source derogation does not occur. Dissonance theory could interpret this as a negation of the assumption that source credibility is a function of the subject's affect toward the source. Moreover, if source credibility is not only independent of the subject's attitude toward the source but generally very high, then dissonance theory will degenerate to the linear discrepancy model for attitude change. However, if source credibility is independent of source affect, source change is a function of object–message discrepancy and independent of attitude toward the source. Furthermore, the greater the credibility, the greater the dissonance and, for equal discrepancy, the greater the source derogation (ignoring extreme values). Source enhancement such as occurs for the positive and neutral messages is impossible within dissonance theory.

Social Judgment Theory

Sherif assumes that message–object discrepancy is the very core of the communication situation. Furthermore, if ego involvement is so low that social judgment theory degenerates to the linear discrepancy law of attitude change, there should be no source credibility effect. Thus the attitude change results are predictable. But if the latitude of acceptance is so wide that there are no nonlinearities, then there should be no source derogation. Furthermore, source change, when it occurs, should be a function of object–message discrepancy not source–message discrepancy.

Information Processing Models

The most elemental form of the information processing models of attitude change is the simple linear discrepancy law without credibility effects. Thus the information processing theories fit the data for attitude change without special assumptions.

The natural question for information processing is, what does the message say about the source? One answer is that the message indicates how the source feels about other people. Thus a positive message is an indication that the source likes other people and hence is a nice guy, whereas a negative message indicates that the source tends to dislike other people, and hence, is "nasty". So a message from the source is a message about the source and should even have about the same value. A second answer is that a comparison of the message with the subject's own belief can be interpreted as an indication of the source's bias in responding to other people. This suggests that the source message value is the difference between the object message value and the subject's own attitude toward the object. Both answers are compatible with information processing theory and indeed both may coexist within the same subject. The information processing models are the only class of models that account for both attitude change and source change in the present data.

Source Credibility

Studies of attitude change data are not unusual in supporting the discrepancy hypothesis. Reviews of other studies with similar findings are found in Whittaker (1967), Insko (1967), and Kiesler, *et al.* (1969). The fact that there is no source credibility effect was more surprising.

There are at least two possible explanations for the fact that we find so little difference in attitude change as a function of the subject's attitude toward the source. First, one might suppose that there really is source effects but that we do not see them. Perhaps there is a distinction between the subject's feeling toward the source as a person and the subject's assessment of the ability of the source as a judge of character. It is the first of these that we measure, but perhaps it is the second of these that functions as the "credibility" determiner. However, the halo effect in person perception correlations shows that these two assessments will in fact be highly correlated. We believe it is impossible for the correlation to be so low as to attenuate large credibility differences. Furthermore, the fact that the multiple correlation for the group means reaches .82 means that there is little room for such effects.

Instead, we are inclined toward a hypothesis related to one put forward some years ago by Asch (1948). He argues that source credibility effects per se do not exist. Rather, they are artifacts traceable to other aspects of the experiment. In particular, he notes that many experimental messages are highly ambiguous, so adding an author's name gives phrases and allusions an entirely different meaning. Can the apparent source credibility effects in all studies be explained by similar artifacts?

Consider the excellent study reported by Rhine and Severance (1970). One of the issues debated in the experimental messages is park acreage for another city in another state (they wanted low "ego involvement"). What may we assume of these subjects? First, the subjects know almost nothing about the city government involved, the tax situation in that city, the business requirements, or other possibly relevant facts. Second, and even more important, they know they do not know. Therefore, when they are presented with a message, they have two problems:

1. whether or not the arguments presented are acceptable and
2. whether or not the arguments touched on all the relevant dimensions of the issue.

Their response to the first problem is what the experimenters wanted to study. But the subject's postmessage attitude necessarily reflects his resolution of the second problem as well. He has no objective way to decide the second problem for himself. Thus his only rational response is to transform it into a problem that he can consider: Is the source trustworthy enough and knowledgeable enough to have presented a full case? That is, the experiment is designed so that the subject lacks the information to form his own opinion and thus forces him to consider ad hominem arguments. This in turn creates apparent "source credibility" effects.

What about our study? The issue is: how likable is the stimulus person? This is an issue that the subject has "studied" for years. Furthermore, the dimensions are of his own choosing and he knows them well. Thus he knows whether a message is complete or not and he knows whether the information left out would or would not be as relevant as what he has heard. He need not guess at what the source might have said. Finally, we note that the subject has had years of practice in dissecting statements by people about other people, that is, years of practice in differentiating between the conclusions of the source and the "evidence" cited by the source in support of those conclusions. The subject need not let the source do his reasoning for him.

It is of interest that although Rhine and Severance (1970) find credibility effects on the park issue, they do not find credibility effects on the issue of increasing student tuition. They attribute the failure to high "ego involvement." But, in fact, tuition is yet another topic on which students have (or think they have) some expertise.

Tannenbaum's Data

There are two sets of findings that are most closely related to the present study: Tannenbaum's (1953) dissertation that served as the basis for congruity theory and the studies designed to test dissonance and social judgment theory by simultaneously varying source credibility and discrepancy.

The material in Tannenbaum's study was "newspaper articles" in which a prominent person or political institution was reported to have endorsed or opposed some civic or cultural policy. The articles were carefully written to be free of actual arguments of justifications of the reported position. Premessage attitudes toward source and object were classified into three intervals: positive, negative, or neutral. For each of the resulting nine cells, he reports the mean source change and attitude change for 15 observations. Tannenbaum's actual results are presented in Fig. 10.10 in the same scale as the results for the present study. They differ from our results both qualitatively and quantitatively.

The principal problem in the attitude change data for other models is the "boomerang" for negative source on the positive message. If this one small negative number is ignored (and it may not even be statistically significant), then reinforcement theory with polarity gives almost perfect fit to the data. The same is true for social judgment theory. The source change goes from positive to negative at $a = 0$, which is precisely the point at which attitude change was maximal in both messages, that is, at the boundary of the latitude of acceptance.

By comparison, congruity theory shows poorer fit to the data. It does predict the source change results. It also predicts the attitude change curves for the positive source. However, the attitude change for the negative source is much too weak in the positive message and is zero for the negative message. On the other hand, the attitude change for the neutral source is not zero but is positive for the positive message and negative for the negative message. However, these last results are small in magnitude.

The information processing model fits the data if the credibility effect is extreme and we add an assumption of polarity effects. Dissonance theory also fits the data for attitude change if the one point of boomerang is regarded as zero. However, the source enhancement for both messages is directly opposed

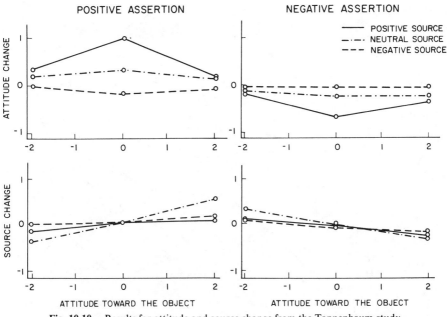

Fig. 10.10. Results for attitude and source change from the Tannenbaum study.

to the dissonance prediction. Even if source change is treated as zero, dissonance theory would be in trouble. The amount of source disparagement is woefully short of dissonance predictions, particularly for large discrepancies.

The attitude change in Tannenbaum's data is of marginal magnitude. The models could only be fit qualitatively. Every model had places where it assumed certain points were zero and all these assumptions are reasonable statistically ($N = 15$ for any given point). Source change was even smaller, and in fact, hypothesis that there was none is not completely unreasonable.

Tannenbaum's data bring out the fact that many of the models are very similar, and unless the magnitude of source change and attitude change is substantial, distinguishing among competing models can be difficult.

Studies That Manipulated Both Source Credibility and Discrepancy

Figure 10.11 presents the basic results for attitude change and source change in four often-cited studies. The procedures used by Bergin (1962), Aronson *et al.* (1963), and Bochner and Insko (1966) are reviewed by Insko (1967) and Kiesler, *et al.* (1969) and will not be stated here. The Rhine–Severance (1970)

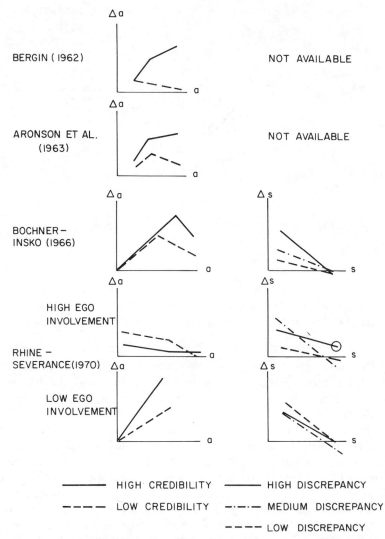

Fig. 10.11.   Results for attitude and source change in the source credibility–discrepancy studies.

high ego involvement study employed tuition increase as the issue with either a professor or an army private as source. Their low ego involvement issue was increased park acreage for a city in another state and the source was either a government committee or a hair stylist.

The attitude change results in all studies are discrepancy curves. Thus the data on attitude change fits information processing theory (with counterargument to account for the nonlinearities), social judgment theory, and dissonance theory. The data disconfirm reinforcement and congruity (or balance) theory.

As noted by these researchers, the source change data do not support dissonance theory. Where there is source change, it is positive. Moreover, it is the less credible source who is enhanced; the more credible source undergoes little change. These results are also in opposition to the predictions of social judgment theory. For social judgment theory, source change should be a function of discrepancy, not the initial attitude toward the source.

These findings on source change are in perfect agreement with information processing theory, namely, the source–message discrepancy hypothesis proposed above. The only exceptional value is the point (which is circled) in the Rhine–Severance high ego involvement data.

The only theory that fits both the data on attitude change and the data on source change is information processing theory. Thus all the data that we know of except the Tannenbaum data support information processing theory. The Tannenbaum data is not disconfirmatory but equivocal because of its combination of small sample size and little change.

CHAPTER 11

Change in Political Party and Issue Attitudes

Contributed by T. Daniel Coggin and John E. Hunter

INTRODUCTION

Political voting is largely determined by three factors: the political party of the candidate, the stance of the candidate toward salient political issues, and the candidate's personal characteristics such as warmth or trustworthiness. Multiple regression analysis has usually suggested that party identification and political attitudes are the strongest predictors of vote; though these two variables are themselves correlated. The focus of this chapter is on the causal determination of these two attitudes and the explanation for the correlation between them.

   The causal theories to be tested here assume that the primary determinant of political identification and political attitudes is the messages emitted by the parties as to their stands on various issues. The specific theories are derived from theories of attitude change. In these theories the political party is given the role of the source of messages, where the content of the message is the stand taken by the party. The voter is given the role of the receiver and his attitude is his own position toward the issue addressed by the party message under consideration. The overall impact of the set of messages presented by the party can be assessed by cumulating the impacts across the various issues. This leads to the formation of two variables: party identification (attitude toward the source) and a political attitude index (attitude toward the object).

The relations between these attitudes over time are derived from the attitude theory predictions about the individual messages. For example, congruity theory asserts that when a candidate endorses a certain issue, the voter's attitude toward that issue will change in the direction of the voter's attitude toward the candidate. Thus, according to congruity theory, there should be a causal arrow from attitude toward the party to attitude toward issues. On the other hand, information processing theory asserts that change in the voter's attitude toward the issue will depend on the discrepancy between the message value and his current stand. Thus information processing theory posits no causal arrow from party attitude to issue attitude.

The communication models to be derived here cannot be tested using cross-sectional data. Each predicts a correlation between party identification and political issue attitudes. However, the models can be tested with longitudinal data because the direction of causal arrows then becomes directly observable. However, the models cannot be tested in the form of attitude change theories because the messages heard by each candidate are not known. Instead, they will be subjected to only a crude test in the form of three wave path analysis models. However, each of the four models considered here has a distinct form because they make qualitatively different predictions. Thus there is adequate base for differential testing of the models in the data considered. The best longitudinal data available at the time of this study was the Butler and Stokes (1969, 1974) study of British politics. These data were reanalyzed to test the models and that analysis is presented here.

We present three formal mathematical models of the relationship between attitudes toward political parties and attitudes toward political issues in an election campaign. The models are derived from three prominent theories of attitude change in the psychological literature: congruity theory, information processing theory, and reinforcement theory.

There is one model that will not be formalized here but that can be identi-fied with a path model: the reference group model of attitude change. The term "reference group" was coined by Herbert Hyman (1943), though the theory was developed earlier by Sherif (1936) and has been extended (Sherif, 1953). Shibutani (1955) defines a reference group as "... that group whose outlook is used by the actor as the frame of reference in the organization of his perceptual field." The concept of reference groups has figured quite prominently in the literature on political attitude change, beginning with the work of Lazarsfeld, Berleson, and Gaudet (1944), Berleson, Lazarsfeld, and McPhee (1954), and Campbell, Converse, Miller, and Stokes (1960). In their national study of political attitudes in the 1956 U.S. presidential election, Campbell and co-workers continually argued the importance of the political party as a major reference group in the formation of political attitudes (especially for those with low political involvement, which included a large segment of the electorate).

They argued that political issues were virtually irrelevant to voting and to party attitudes. Thus any model that predicts a casual arrow in only the direction from party attitude to issue attitudes and not vice versa will be called the "SRC model," after the Survey Research Center at the University of Michigan where those authors then resided.

The other missing model is the spatial model of party competition by Downs (1957) and others. The spatial model is a static theory that ignores the inertia of party attitudes, hence it ignores the whole issue of political socialization. The spatial model asserts that the voter will assess each party in terms of how closely it fits his issue attitudes and vote for the party with the better fit. Thus it can be viewed as a special case of information processing theory.

Chapter 1 of this volume formalized theories of attitude change in an experimental context called the passive communication paradigm. In this context a source (communicator) issues a message (communication) to a receiver about some attitude object. Two attitudes may be influenced by this message; the receiver's attitude a toward the object of the message and the receiver's attitude s toward the source of the message. The phrase "attitude change" is used to denote the change in the receiver's attitude toward the object, and the phrase "source change" is used to denote the change in the receiver's attitude toward the source. In this chapter the source of the message will always be taken to be a political party and the object of the message will always be assumed to be a political theory or issue. For issue i let a_i be the voter's attitude on issue i, s_1 the voter's attitude toward party 1, s_2 the voter's attitude toward party 2, and N the total number of issue attitudes.

A political party will take positions on a number of salient issues. On each issue, the attitude change is specific to that issue, but the source change is always change in the same attitude—attitude toward the party. To create one variable to assess attitude toward issue, we create an attitude index $\bar{a}$ formed by summing across the relevant issue attitudes. Change on any attitude then results in a change in the index. Furthermore, it can be shown that, for each of the three psychological theories, we can ignore issues upon which the parties take a common stand if we model only the party differential, which we define as $D = s_1 - s_2$, and score the issue attitudes so as to match (by arbitrary choice) party 1.

CONGRUITY THEORY

Congruity theory was formulated by Osgood and Tannenbaum (1955) and extended by Osgood *et al.* (1957). They argue that if a source presents a positive message about an object, then that positive message evokes a positive association or bond between the source and object. If the source disparages the object, then that negative message evokes a dissociative, or negative, bond between source and object.

For a positive message, two affective responses are elicited by the message: the attitude toward the sources and the attitude toward the object a. These affective responses each generalize to the other, that is, each response is conditioned in the direction of the other. Thus each attitude changes in the direction of the other. Chapter 5 shows that the simplest mathematical model for this process is

$$\Delta a = \alpha(s - a) \quad \text{and} \quad \Delta s = \beta(a - s). \tag{11.1}$$

If the source disparages the object, then two distinct processes take place. When the receiver thinks about the object, two affective responses are elicited: the receiver's affective response to the object and a response derived from his attitude toward the source. Because the source disparages the object, the receiver's affective response derived from the source is the exact opposite of his attitude toward the source. The receiver's affective response then conditions to the affective response generated by the negation of the affective response toward the source. That is, if the receiver dislikes the source that disparages the object, then the source-generated effective response toward the object is positive. In similar fashion, when the receiver thinks about the source, then the generated affective response from the object is the exact opposite of his feeling toward that object. Thus if the receiver dislikes the object that is disparaged by the source, then the generated response toward the source is positive. The affective response toward the source then conditions to the generated affective response derived from the object. Thus each attitude changes in the direction of the negative of the other. Chapter 5 shows that the simplest mathematical model for this process is

$$\Delta a = \alpha(-a - s) \quad \text{and} \quad \Delta s = \beta(-s - a). \tag{11.2}$$

The previous presentation assumes that there is a natural way to score a message, and hence there is a sharp difference drawn between positive and negative messages. However, most political issues can be scored in either direction. Thus, for any given issue and party position, the issue can be scored so that the party is endorsing the issue as stated. If the issue is reverse scored, then the equations for the negative message given above transform into the equation given for the positive message. That is, if all issues are scored in the direction endorsed by a given party, then the change equations for congruity theory are always of the form

$$\Delta a = \alpha(s - a) \quad \text{and} \quad \Delta s = \beta(a - s).$$

These equations are those for a single issue and a single party. The actual situation to be modeled entails two parties and a multiplicity of issues.

One Party, Multiple Issues

Assume that all issues are mentiond equally often and that only one party is speaking. If all issues are scored in the direction endorsed by the party, the discussion of issue i elicits the change

$$\Delta a_i = \alpha(s - a_i) \quad \text{and} \quad \Delta s = \beta(a_i - s). \tag{11.3}$$

Let the attitude index be the average of the attitude values

$$\bar{a} = \frac{1}{N} \sum_i a_i. \tag{11.4}$$

After all N issues have been discussed, then each attitude will have been influenced by exactly one message. The resulting change in the attitude index is then

$$\Delta\bar{a} = \frac{1}{N} \sum_i \Delta a_i = \frac{1}{N} \sum [\alpha(s - a_i)]$$

$$= \frac{1}{N} \left(\sum_i \alpha s - \sum_i \alpha a_i \right)$$

$$= \frac{1}{N} (N\alpha s - N\alpha\bar{a})$$

$$= \alpha(s - \bar{a}). \tag{11.5}$$

On the other hand, after discussion of all issues, the party attitude has changed N times. The total change is thus given by

$$\Delta s = \sum_i \Delta s = \sum_i \beta(\bar{a}_i - s)$$

$$= \sum \beta\bar{a}_i - \sum \beta s = N\beta\bar{a} - N\beta s$$

$$= N\beta(\bar{a} - s). \tag{11.6}$$

Thus the change elicited by messages about N issues is

$$\Delta\bar{a} = \alpha(s - \bar{a}) \quad \text{and} \quad \Delta s = N\beta(\bar{a} - s). \tag{11.7}$$

Two Parties, Multiple Issues

If there are two parties taking stands on the issues, then there are two sources, s_1 and s_2, to be considered. For each source there will be change equations such as those derived above. However, there is one complication that must be overcome before both equations can be written at the same time: the direction of scoring on each attitude issue must be determined in the same way for both parties. That is, the equation derived in the previous section assumed that issue attitudes were scored in the direction adopted by the party. But with two parties there would be two such conventions.

To break the deadlock, let us define the scoring of the issue attitudes so as to match one of the parties, say, party 1. Then the change in attitude toward party 1 will be

$$\Delta s_1 = N\beta(\bar{a} - s_1). \tag{11.8}$$

However, the corresponding equation for the second party, that is,

$$\Delta s_2 = N\beta(\bar{a} - s_2), \tag{11.9}$$

will not be true because the issues are not scored to match the second party's stands. Suppose that the two parties were directly opposed on every salient issue. Then the "$\bar{a}$" for the second party would be exactly the reverse of the "$\bar{a}$" for the first party. That is, if only issues on which the parties differ are considered, then the change equation for the second party would be:

$$\Delta s_2 = N\beta(-\bar{a} - s_2) \tag{11.10}$$

when the issues are scored in the direction endorsed by party 1.

Can we ignore the issues on which the parties take a common stand? No, not if we wish to consider the attitudes toward each party separately. However, if we model only the party differential $s_1 - s_2$, then congruity theory predicts that issues with a common stand are irrelevant. Define the variable D to be the party differential,

$$D = s_1 - s_2. \tag{11.11}$$

Because of the linearity of the change operator, the change in D is the difference of the changes in the two party attitudes. That is,

$$\Delta D = \Delta s_1 - \Delta s_2. \tag{11.12}$$

When this difference is expanded into summations, the terms corresponding to issues on which the parties take a common stand cancel each other out. Thus we have

$$\begin{aligned} \Delta D = \Delta s_1 - \Delta s_2 &= N\beta(\bar{a} - s_1) - N\beta(-\bar{a} - s_2) \\ &= N(2\beta\bar{a} - \beta s_1 + \beta s_2) \\ &= [2\beta\bar{a} - \beta(s_1 - s_2)]N \\ &= N\beta(2\bar{a} - D). \end{aligned} \tag{11.13}$$

The change in the attitude index is the net effect of the two sets of messages received from the two parties. If we let the two changes be denoted $\Delta\bar{a}_1$ and $\Delta\bar{a}_2$, then the equations of the last section would read

$$\Delta\bar{a}_1 = \alpha(s_1 - \bar{a}) \quad \text{and} \quad \Delta\bar{a}_2 = \alpha(s_2 - \bar{a}). \tag{11.14}$$

However, this was under the convention of scoring attitudes in accordance with the party under consideration. Thus for this equation the "a_2" is reverse scored from a_1. The correct equation is thus given by

$$\Delta\bar{a}_2 = -\{\alpha[s_2 - (-\bar{a})]\}$$
$$= -\alpha(s_2 + \bar{a}). \tag{11.15}$$

The attitude change elicited by the two parties is thus

$$\Delta\bar{a} = \Delta a_1 + \Delta a_2 = \alpha(s_1 - \bar{a}) + [-\alpha(s_2 + \bar{a})]$$
$$= \alpha s_1 - \alpha\bar{a} - \alpha s_2 - \alpha\bar{a}$$
$$= \alpha(s_1 - s_2) - 2\alpha\bar{a}$$
$$= \alpha(D - 2\bar{a}). \tag{11.16}$$

Thus the full model for two parties and multiple issues is

$$\Delta\bar{a} = \alpha(D - 2\bar{a}) \qquad \text{and} \qquad \Delta D = N\beta(2\bar{a} - D). \tag{11.17}$$

These equations are very similar to those for the single message. The difference is that the role played by the simple source attitude s in the equations for the single message is played by the variable $D/2$ in these equations. That is, the congruity prediction is that the attitude index a will change in the direction of the variable $D/2$ and the variable $D/2$ will change in the direction of the attitude index $\bar{a}$.

In particular, congruity theory predicts that a path model for these variables would have a causal arrow from differential party identification D to attitude

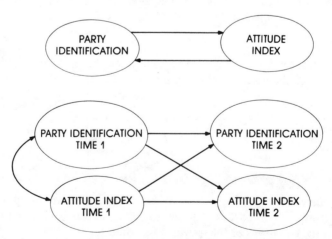

Fig. 11.1. A comparison of cross-sectional and longitudinal path models derived from congruity theory: (a) the nonrecursive cross-sectional model; (b) the recursive longitudinal model.

index $\bar{a}$ and a causal arrow from attitude index $\bar{a}$ to political identification D. In a cross-sectional study this would imply a two-way arrow and would mean that the path model would have to be nonrecursive. However, in a longitudinal model, the arrow from party identification to attitude index would be from identification at time 1 to attitude at time 2. The arrow from attitude to identification would be from attitude index at time 1 to party identification at time 2. Thus the arrows would not be two way arrows and the model would be recursive. This distinction is shown in Fig. 11.1. Figure 11.1a shows the cross-sectional model with two causal arrows connecting party identification and attitude index. Figure 11.1b shows the causal arrows spread over time. The curved arrows connecting party identification and attitude index at time 1 does not represent the impact of the current messages but does represent the cumulative impact of past messages.

INFORMATION PROCESSING THEORY

Hovland *et al.* (1953) describe the key attitude change process as being the receiver's internal comparison of his own position with that advocated by the message. The receiver, in effect, quizzes himself concerning the object and compares his response to those presented in the message. If the receiver accepts the answers offered by the message in place of his own, then attitude change has occurred. Thus, as described by McGuire (1964, 1966), the process is one of three stages: the receiver must attend to the message, comprehend the message, and yield to the message. Chapter 3 classifies the general information processing model as one of a class of models characterized by the linear discrepancy hypothesis. It notes that the emotional content of a message can be scaled, hence each message has an affective value "m." That is, messages are representations of attitudinal positions. If we adopt the measurement model proposed by Thurstone (1929) and align messages on the same continuum as attitudes, we can then speak of discrepancy or distance between the message and the attitude:

$$\text{discrepancy} = |a - m|.$$

French (1956), Hovland and Pritzker (1957), Anderson and Hovland (1957), and Anderson (1959) propose a "distance-proportional" model that incorporates two major conditions:

1. the magnitude of change is proportional to the discrepancy between the receiver's attitude and the position presented in the message and

2. the change is always in the direction of the position advocated by the message.

Anderson and Hovland (1957) formalize this to take the form

$$\Delta a = \alpha(m - a).$$

The discussion in Chapter 3 presents two models of source change derived from information processing theory. For the interpersonal model, it is argued that a message from Mary stating "Joe is a creep," has two implications: first, there is the message "Joe is a creep," which will influence the listeners' attitude toward Joe. But second, there is an implied message "Mary is the kind of person who would call Joe a creep," which is a message about Mary rather than Joe. Thus the discussion in Chapter 3 asserts that the basic message can be interpreted as an explicit message about the object and an implicit message about the source. The source change model is

$$\Delta s = \beta(m_s - s),$$

which is the standard information processing model, where s is the attitude under change. The key to the derivation is to quantify the value of the message as it pertains to the source, that is, to find the implied value of m_s. The specific model derived for the interpersonal context is not applicable to the political context, but a similar derivation is given below.

The crucial step in deriving a model of the political impact of a party position from information processing theory is to recognize the fact that a single message may contain several logically distinct propositions. For example, if the leader of the Democratic party in the House came out of a party caucus in September 1957 and announced, "The Democratic party urges the President to send troops to Little Rock to settle the riots there," then two messages could logically be derived from that statement. First, there is the message "Sending troops to Little Rock is a good thing to do." This is the message that is the basis of the influence that the party exerts over the receiver with regard to his attitude toward the issue of whether or not to use troops to stem the riots. We denote this message m_i. The value of this message with regard to the stated issue is determined entirely from the content of the message and is strongly positive in this case. The value of this message with respect to the Democratic party cannot be immediately derived from the message content itself. Instead, the message value must be derived from the implied statement (the second logical proposition) "The Democratic party should have the same value as does the policy of sending troops into Little Rock," that is, the value of the message as it pertains to the party is the value the receiver places on the issue position adopted by the party, that is, the issue attitude a. We denote this message m_s.

The standard (linear) information processing equation for change in attitude toward the source (party) is

$$\Delta s = \beta(m_s - s), \tag{11.18}$$

where m_s is the message value that is usually denoted by m. The discussion in the previous paragraph shows that the information processing model implies that the message value m_s would be given by

$$m_s = a_1, \tag{11.19}$$

and it follows that

$$\Delta s = \beta(a_i - s). \tag{11.20}$$

Similarly, if the party rejects issue i, then it will reject such endeavors, that is,

$$m_s = -a_i \tag{11.21}$$

and

$$\Delta s = \beta(-a_i - s). \tag{11.22}$$

The complication of two equations for source change derives from the assumption of an arbitrary direction for the issue. If the issue is scored in the direction that the party endorses, then the equations for the information processing model become

$$\Delta a = \alpha(m - a) \quad \text{and} \quad \Delta s = \beta(a - s). \tag{11.23}$$

It is important to note that s does not appear in the change equation for a. This means that issue attitude change does not depend on the voter's attitude toward the party. Thus, according to information processing theory, there is no causal arrow from attitude toward the party to attitude toward the issue.

The extension of the equations for the single message to a model with two parties and multiple issues is given in the next section.

One Party, Multiple Issues

If issues are all scored in the direction of endorsement by the party, then for each issue we have

$$\Delta a_i = \alpha(m_i - a_i) \quad \text{and} \quad \Delta s = \beta(a_i - s), \tag{11.24}$$

where m_i is the exact position taken by the party on issue $_i$. As all issues are discussed, each attitude is affected by one message and hence the change in the attitude index is given by

$$\Delta \bar{a} = \frac{1}{N} \sum_i \Delta a_i = \frac{1}{N} \sum_i \alpha(m_i - a_i)$$

$$= \frac{1}{N} \sum \alpha m_i - \frac{1}{N} \sum \alpha a_i$$

$$= \alpha \bar{m} - \alpha \bar{a}$$

$$= \alpha(\bar{m} - \bar{a}). \tag{11.25}$$

On the other hand, each message has an impact on the party attitude, hence

$$\Delta s = \sum_i \Delta s = \sum_i \beta(a_i - s)$$
$$= \beta \sum a_i - \beta \sum s$$
$$= N\beta\bar{a} - N\beta s$$
$$= N\beta(\bar{a} - s). \tag{11.26}$$

Thus the impact of multiple messages from a single party is

$$\Delta\bar{a} = \alpha(\bar{m} - \bar{a}) \qquad \text{and} \qquad \Delta s = N\beta(\bar{a} - s). \tag{11.27}$$

Two Parties, Multiple Issues

If there are messages by two parties, then the impact on the attitude index will be the sum of the two impacts. Let us denote them $\Delta\bar{a}_1$ and $\Delta\bar{a}_2$, respectively. Then

$$\Delta\bar{a}_1 = \alpha(\bar{m}_1 - \bar{a}) \qquad \text{and} \qquad \Delta\bar{a}_2 = \alpha(\bar{m}_2 - \bar{a}). \tag{11.28}$$

If we consider only issues on which the parties have exactly opposed views, then $\bar{m}_2 = -\bar{m}_1$, and the total impact is

$$\Delta\bar{a} = \Delta\bar{a}_1 + \Delta\bar{a}_2 = \alpha(\bar{m}_1 - \bar{a}) + \alpha(\bar{m}_2 - \bar{a})$$
$$= \alpha(\bar{m}_1 + \bar{m}_2) - 2\alpha\bar{a}$$
$$= -2\alpha\bar{a}. \tag{11.29}$$

The derivation for the change in the party differential is complicated by the scoring conventions for the two groups. When this is taken into account, the equations for the change in attitude toward each party are

$$\Delta s_1 = N\beta(\bar{a} - s_1) \qquad \text{and} \qquad \Delta s_2 = N\beta(-\bar{a} - s_2). \tag{11.30}$$

The change in the party differential is then the difference

$$\Delta D = \Delta s_1 - \Delta s_2 = N\beta(\bar{a} - s_1) - N\beta(-\bar{a} - s_2)$$
$$= N\beta\bar{a} + N\beta\bar{a} - N\beta s_1 + N\beta s_2$$
$$= 2N\beta\bar{a} - N\beta(s_1 - s_2)$$
$$= N\beta(2\bar{a} - D). \tag{11.31}$$

The final results are

$$\Delta\bar{a} = -2\alpha\bar{a} \qquad \Delta D = N\beta(2\bar{a} - D). \tag{11.32}$$

Although $\bar{a}$ appears in the change equation for D, the party differential does not appear in the change equation for $\bar{a}$. Thus, according to information processing theory, there is a causal arrow from attitude index to party

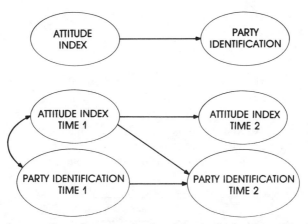

Fig. 11.2. A comparison of cross-sectional and longitudinal path models derived from information processing theory: (a) the recursive cross-sectional model; (b) the recursive longitudinal model.

identification but not vice versa. That is, even in a cross-sectional study, the path model for information processing theory is recursive. The longitudinal model is also recursive but takes on a different form. The path models are shown in Fig. 11.2.

REINFORCEMENT THEORY

The fundamental assumption of reinforcement theory, as argued by Miller and Dollard (1941), Doob (1941), and others, is that agreement strengthens an attitude, whereas disagreement weakens it. The specific mathematical consequences of this assumption are derived in Chapter 2 and are presented in the accompanying tabulation.

a	m	Response	Δa
$+$	$+$	$+$ Strengthened	$+$
$+$	$-$	$+$ Weakened	$-$
$-$	$-$	$-$ Strengthened	$-$
$-$	$+$	$-$ Weakened	$+$

The key point to note is that strengthening a negative affect results in attitude change that is algebraically negative, whereas the weakening of a negative response is algebraically positive. From this tabulation we see that the algebraic sign of attitude change is always given by the algebraic sign of the message value m. The simplest equation for such a model is the basic reinforcement model

$$\Delta a = \alpha m.$$

There is always a second side to any reinforcement situation, the response to the reinforcing agent. If the source agrees with the receiver, then he is administering reward, whereas disagreement is punishment. This will result in change in attitude toward the source as well as change in attitude toward the object of the message. The source change predicted by reinforcement theory is presented in the accompanying tabulation (see Chapter 2).

a	m	Process	Δs
+	+	Reward	+
+	−	Punishment	−
−	−	Reward	+
−	+	Punishment	−

From this tabulation we see that the algebraic sign of the source change is given by the sign of the product of the attitude toward the object and the message value. The simplest such model is

$$\Delta s = \beta m a.$$

The equations for the impact of a single message are

$$\Delta a = \alpha m \qquad \text{and} \qquad \Delta s = \beta m a. \tag{11.33}$$

Although a appears in the change equation for s, the variable s does not appear in the change equation for a. Thus, according to reinforcement theory, there is a causal arrow from issue attitude to party identification but not vice versa.

The derivation of the model for two parties and multiple issues is presented later.

One Party, Multiple Messages

The change equations for message i are

$$\Delta a_i = \alpha m_i \qquad \text{and} \qquad \Delta s = \beta m_i a_i.$$

If all messages are scored so that the party endorses the issue, then all message values m_i have the same algebraic sign. If all messages have the same intensity, then we have

$$m_i = \mu,$$

where μ is the constant message value given the scoring convention.

If all issues are discussed equally, then after all issues have been discussed, each attitude will have changed once. The change in the attitude index is then

$$\Delta \bar{a} = \frac{1}{N} \sum_i \Delta a_i = \frac{1}{N} \sum_i \alpha m_i = \frac{1}{N} \sum_i \alpha \mu = \alpha \mu. \tag{11.34}$$

After all messages have been heard, the party attitude will have changed N times. The total change will be

$$\Delta s = \sum_i \beta m_i a_i = \sum_i \beta \mu a_i = \beta \mu \sum_i a_i = N \beta \mu \bar{a}. \tag{11.35}$$

Thus, after all the issues have been discussed, the resulting attitude change will be

$$\Delta \bar{a} = \alpha \mu \quad \text{and} \quad \Delta s = N \beta \mu \bar{a}. \tag{11.36}$$

Two Parties, Multiple Messages

If we apply the scoring convention so that party 1 endorses all issues, then the impact of party 1 is

$$\Delta \bar{a}_1 = \alpha \mu \quad \text{and} \quad \Delta s_1 = N \beta \mu \bar{a}. \tag{11.37}$$

If we consider only issues on which the parties are exactly opposed, then the impact of party 2 is

$$\Delta \bar{a}_2 = \alpha(-\mu) = -\alpha \mu \quad \text{and} \quad \Delta s_2 = N\beta(-\mu)\bar{a} = -N\beta\mu\bar{a}. \tag{11.38}$$

The change in the attitude index is then given by the sum

$$\Delta \bar{a} = \Delta \bar{a}_1 + \Delta \bar{a}_2 = \alpha \mu + (-\alpha \mu) = 0. \tag{11.39}$$

The change in the party differential is given by the difference

$$\Delta D = \Delta s_1 - \Delta s_2 = N\beta\mu\bar{a} - (-N\beta\mu\bar{a}) = 2N\beta\mu\bar{a}. \tag{11.40}$$

Thus the change equations resulting from the two-party campaign are

$$\Delta \bar{a} = 0 \quad \text{and} \quad \Delta D = 2\alpha\mu N \bar{a}, \tag{11.41}$$

where μ is a message strength parameter. In this model the variable $\bar{a}$ appears in the change equation for D, but D does not appear in the change equation for $\bar{a}$. Thus, according to reinforcement theory, there is a causal arrow from attitude index to party identification but not vice versa. Thus even the cross-sectional path model is recursive.

Figure 11.3 shows the cross-sectional and longitudinal path models derived from reinforcement theory. Comparison of Fig. 11.3 with Fig. 11.2 shows that the qualitative path diagrams for information processing theory and reinforcement theory are identical. Thus these two theories must be differentiated quantitatively.

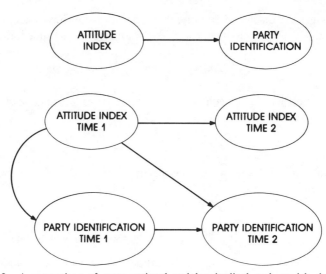

Fig. 11.3. A comparison of cross-sectional and longitudinal path models derived from reinforcement theory: (a) the recursive cross-sectional model; (b) the recursive longitudinal model.

QUANTITATIVE DIFFERENTIATION BETWEEN INFORMATION PROCESSING AND REINFORCEMENT THEORIES

The qualitative path diagrams for information processing theory and reinforcement theory are identical. However, the actual change equations are quite different, as seen in the following tabulation.

Information processing	Reinforcement
$\Delta \bar{a} = -2\alpha\bar{a}$	$\Delta \bar{a} = 0$
$\Delta D = N\beta(2\bar{a} - D)$	$\Delta D = 2\alpha\mu N\bar{a}$

If we could make observations under the controlled conditions assumed in these equations, then we could distinguish between the models on the basis of the course of issue attitudes alone. According to reinforcement theory, the attitude index will not change over time. According to information processing theory, the attitude index will converge to a neutral state.

However, these equations assume that everyone in the sample has heard exactly the same messages, with exactly the same number of messages devoted to each issue by each party. These conditions will be substantially violated in any real political study. Thus we must look for differentiation between the stochastic equations generated when error terms are added to the model. Let us shift from change equations to probabilistic prediction equations in which we add a disturbance term u_n for the attitude index and a term v_n for party identification. The stochastic difference equations for the information processing model are

$$\bar{a}_{n+1} = (1 - 2\alpha)\bar{a}_n + u_n \quad \text{and} \quad D_{n+1} = N\beta 2\bar{a}_n + (1 - N\beta)D_n + v_n.$$
$$(11.42)$$

From these equations it can be shown that the variance of both the issue attitude index $\sigma^2_{a_n}$ and the party differential $\sigma^2_{D_n}$ will, under nearly all conditions, converge to an equilibrium value over time.

The stochastic difference equations for the reinforcement model are

$$\bar{a}_{n+1} = \bar{a}_n + u_n \quad \text{and} \quad D_{n+1} = 2\alpha\mu N\bar{a}_n + D_n + v_n. \quad (11.43)$$

From these equations we see that both the variance of the issue attitudes index and the party differential will continually increase over time, allowing reasonable assumptions.

Thus the information processing model mathematically predicts that the variances of the attitude clusters will ultimately converge to a pair of equilibrium values, and the reinforcement model mathematically predicts that the variances will continually increase over time. These predictions allow us to distinguish between the models by looking at the pattern of change in the variances over time.

THE BRITISH PANEL DATA

Butler and Stokes (1969, 1974) began with a representative cross section of persons 20 years of age or older living in private households or institutions in England, Wales, and Scotland in 1963, when no general election was held. Three more waves of interviewing followed the general elections of 1964, 1966, and 1970. The total, unweighted number of subjects included in the study is 2,922.

We decided to drop from our analyses anyone who either identified with or voted for a party other than the Conservative or Labour party. This decision is the result of the fact that it is not clear where one would place the minor parties (i.e., the Liberals, the Welsh Nationalists, the Communists, and the Scottish Nationals) on a continuum of liberal to conservation (Beer, 1973). Furthermore, because most of the issue index questions were not asked in 1963, our analysis applies only to the 1964–1966–1970 portion of the Butler–Stokes data. There were 831 people who responded to all three administrations of the survey. Of them, 546 met our criterion of never voting for a minor party.

Design of the Analysis

Figure 11.4 presents the path diagrams for four models across three waves of data. The path diagrams for information processing theory and reinforcement theory are identical. Thus only three diagrams are shown. The congruity model has causal arrows from both variables to each other. The other models have one-way causation. Information processing and reinforcement theory have arrows only from the attitude index to political identification. The SRC model, or reference group model has arrows only from political identification to attitude index. If the path analysis supports the one-way arrow from attitude index to party identification, then the information processing and reinforcement models would be tested against each other by assessing the pattern of change in variances over time.

The purely path-analytic test of the congruity model can be misleading because it contains the other models as special cases. That is, the difference

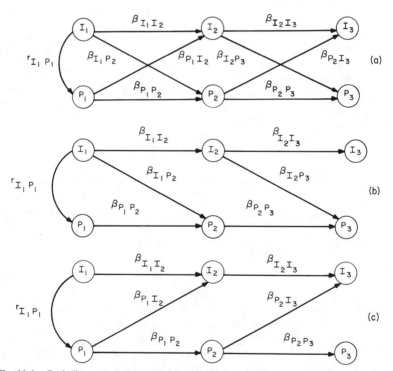

Fig. 11.4.   Path diagrams: I_1, I_2, and I_3 represent issue attitudes at times 1, 2, and 3; P_1, P_2, and P_3 represent party attitudes at times 1, 2, and 3, for (a) congruity model, (b) information processing and reinforcement model, and (c) SRC model.

between the information processing model (or reinforcement model) and the congruity model is that it postulates that the arrow from party attitude to issue attitude will be null. But the path-analytic test of the congruity model will accept a beta weight of 0 for that arrow with only slightly poorer fit than the information processing model (and no difference in fit at all if the sample beta weight were actually 0). The difference between the congruity model and the SRC model in path analytic terms is that the SRC model postulates that the beta weight for issue attitude onto party attitude will be 0. Again this is a special case of the congruity equations. Thus the true test of the congruity model requires not only that it fit the correlations to within sampling error but that both cross-beta-weights be positive.

The model equations are true score equations; they assume all variables to be perfectly measured. Although attitudes cannot be perfectly measured in reality, we worked hard to obtain the best multiple indicators that we could within the study at hand. We also used cluster analytic methods (Hunter, 1977) to obtain correlations corrected for attenuation. However, longitudinal data have several additional potential problems, which are discussed at length in a paper by Tosi *et al.* (1976). This includes transient factors [see also Cronbach (1951) and Heise (1969)] and specific factors. We developed methods from Tosi *et al.* (1976) to correct the test–retest correlations to eliminate the specific factors (Hunter, Coggin, and Gerbing, 1981). We would like to have used the Heise formula to correct for transient factors, but our models are sharply bivariate and hence our data should not satisfy his assumptions. Otherwise, all parameters (with one exception which is discussed in detail below) were estimated using conventional OLS statistics.

The Issue Attitudes Index

The British issue attitudes index was formed from a total of 12 political issue questions asked in the 1964–1966–1970 waves of the panel. The 12 questions were scored according to scales of lengths varying from two to four responses, in what amounts to a variation on the Likert notion of the "agree–disagree" scale type. The 12 issues can be broken into two groups, domestic and foreign-policy issues. The 9 domestic issues concerned respondent's opinion on nationalizing industry, death penalty, power of trade unions, social services spending, reduce taxes or increase social services, power of big business, trade union ties to the Labour party, importance of the royal family, and immigration.

Our initial cluster analyses (Hunter, 1977) reveals that a unidimensional cluster is formed from five of the domestic issues. The five issues are those concerning nationalizing industry, the power of trade unions, social services spending, reduce taxes or increase social services spending, and the power of big business, that is, attitudes on economic policy. The three foreign-policy issues correlated very weakly with party attitudes over time and were, therefore, not good predictors of change in party attitudes. Hence, when we speak of the domestic issue index, we are referring to the five issues listed above, unless otherwise indicated.

The Party Attitudes Index

The British party attitudes index was formed from four items measured in the 1964–1966–1970 waves of the panel. The first item is the party self-image question in which the respondent classifies himself as either Conservative, Labour, Liberal, other, or none. We deleted anyone who classified himself as other than Conservative or Labour. The second item is the respondent's vote choice in the general elections for the three waves—the possible choices being Conservative, Labour, Liberal, Welsh Nationalist, Communist, or Scottish National. We included only those who chose the Conservative or Labour party. The third and fourth items are the respondent's choice on two questions asking about the best party for foreign and domestic affairs. These four items were found to be unidimensional.

Relevant Subgroups of the Population

In addition to testing our models on the entire sample of 546 panel respondents, we split the data into four subgroups of theoretical interest.

We formed subgroups using socioeconomic status. Sociologists believe that class is the most salient dimension of British party politics [e.g., Alford (1963) and Pulzer (1967)] and that occupation is the major dimension of social stratification in Britain. Butler and Stokes (1969, 1974) argue that head of household's occupation is the best predictor of the class location of a respondent. They use a seven-point scale:
1. residual state pensioner;
2. unskilled manual;
3. skilled manual;
4. lower nonmanual;
5. skilled or supervisory nonmanual;
6. lower managerial or administrative;
7. higher managerial or professional.

For a discussion of the reliability and validity of this scale, see Kahan *et al.* (1966). Our breaking point was 3.5, which corresponds to the basic division between the manually and the nonmanually employed. This has traditionally been viewed by British sociologists as the major class dividing point.

We formed subgroups using media exposure. Converse (1962) and Butler and Stokes (1969, 1974) found that level of media exposure is related to stability of partisan preference and issue attitudes. The media exposure score (MES) was formed by Butler and Stokes from questions relating to exposure to newspapers, conversations with other people, and exposure to television and radio. We divided the sample at the mean—those with scores above 2.29 ($N = 315$ for "high media exposure") and those with scores at or below 2.29 ($N = 231$ for "low media exposure"). The correlation between the occupation score and the media exposure score is .13.

The Fit of the Models to the British Data

Table 11.1 presents the corrected correlation matrices for the British issue and party attitude indices. The correlations in Table 11.1 have been corrected for both random and specific sources of measurement error and serve as the basis for the path analytic tests of the models.

The Congruity Model

Table 11.2 presents a summary of each path analysis carried out on the corrected correlations in Table 11.1 for the entire sample and four subgroups. Table 11.1 shows that we have a high degree of multicollinearity between the predictors I_1 and P_1, and I_2 and P_2. With predictors correlated in the high .80s and .90s, we can expect a good deal of instability in our path coefficients. Sampling error probably accounts for the several negative path coefficients, all but one of which are not significant at the .05 level. Traditional tests of significance are not straightforwardly applicable to coefficients calculated from corrected (for attenuation) correlations. We include them in our tables simply to give some indication of sampling error.

The path coefficients in Table 11.2 for the high SES group are not the observed beta weights $\beta_{I_1I_2} = .14$ and $\beta_{P_1I_2} = .78$. We reversed these weights for several reasons. First, the OLS values do not fit any theory and are contrary to findings anywhere else in the data. For example, the corresponding beta weights for the time 2 to time 3 predictions are .70 and .19, which are almost exactly the reverse of the time 1 to time 2 beta weights. Second, we know that we have extreme multicollinearity ($r_{I_1P_1} = .92$) with correlations corrected for attenuation. Thus these beta weights are subject to massive sampling error and a high degree of indeterminacy. For example, the observed nonsense weights yield a predictive efficiency of $r^2 = .90$. The reversed weights that make sense reduce the predictive efficiency only to $r^2 = .85$. Thus the weights that make sense fit the data almost exactly as well as the OLS weights that make no sense. For a further discussion of the notion of using prior

TABLE 11.1

CORRECTED CORRELATION MATRICES FOR THE BRITISH ISSUE AND
PARTY ATTITUDE CLUSTERS[a]

Subjects included	N	Issue			Party		
		1964	1966	1970	1964	1966	1970
All	546						
1964		100	91	86	95	91	88
1966			100	95	88	84	88
1970				100	83	79	86
1964					100	75	90
1966						100	90
1970							100
r_{xx}							
Issues		.53	.55	.54			
Parties					.93	.93	.93
All issues	546						
1964		100	91	93	88	84	80
1966			100	97	81	74	78
1970				100	75	74	77
1964					100	95	90
1966						100	90
1970							100
r_{xx}							
Issues		.53	.53	.54			
Party					.92	.93	.93
High SES	195						
1964		100	83	75	92	88	88
1966			100	85	88	92	89
1970				100	80	81	85
1964					100	96	96
1966						100	93
1970							100
r_{xx}							
Issues		.51	.51	.58			
Party					.91	.91	.91
Low SES	323						
1964		100	89	81	91	86	93
1966			100	82	78	76	78
1970				100	75	66	81
1964					100	90	90
1966						100	
1970							100
r_{xx}							
Issues		.42	.47	.40			
Party					.90	.92	.91
High media exposure	315						

Subjects included	N	*Issue*			*Party*		
		1964	*1966*	*1970*	*1964*	*1966*	*1970*
1964		100	93	88	95	92	89
1966			100	92	91	89	90
1970				100	86	82	88
1964					100	95	91
1966						100	91
1970							100
r_{xx}							
Issues		.58	.58	.57			
Party					.93	.93	.93
Low media	231						
exposure							
1964		100	88	79	95	87	86
1966			100	95	84	86	84
1970				100	76	79	81
1964					100	92	88
1966						100	87
1970							100
r_{xx}							
Issues		.41	.50	.50			
Party					.91	.91	.91

[a] All correlations are Pearson's *r*. The inter-issue and inter-party attitude cluster correlations have been corrected for attenuation and specific factors. The intra-attitude cluster correlations have been corrected for attenuation. The symbol r_{xx} is the reliability as measured by Cronbach's coefficient alpha for each attitude cluster for the three time periods, that is, the reliabilities used to correct the intra-attitude cluster correlations for attenuation.

information to constrain parameter estimates in the face of high multicollinearlity, we refer the reader to Johnston (1972).

Finally, there is the two-wave analysis. In predicting time 3 from time 1, the OLS estimates are $\beta_{I_1 I_3} = .72$ and $\beta_{P_1 I_3} = .09$.

The Information Processing and Reinforcement Models

Table 11.3 presents the variances for the British attitude clusters over time. An inspection of Table 11.4 reveals that the variances of both attitude indices appear stable over time with minor oscillations about an equilibrium value. This pattern is predicted by the information processing model, which predicts that the variances for both attitude indices will ultimately converge to an equilibrium value. This finding disconfirms reinforcement theory.

Table 11.4 presents a summary of the path analyses for the information processing, or reinforcement model. The fit of this model is quite good; better

TABLE 11.2

CONGRUITY MODEL[a]

Subjects included	N	ρ^2_{ISSUES}	ρ^2_{PARTY}	$\beta_{I_1I_2}$	$\beta_{I_2I_3}$	$\beta_{P_1P_2}$	$\beta_{P_2P_3}$	$\beta_{I_1P_2}$	$\beta_{P_1I_2}$	$\beta_{I_2P_3}$	$\beta_{P_2I_3}$	$r_{I_1P_1}$	Average squared deviation
All	546	1.00	.95	.76	.99	.88	.55	.08	.16	.43	$-.03^b$	.95	.0003
High SES	195	.94	.93	.78	.70	1.00	.74	$.00^b$	.14	.23	.19	.92	.002
Low SES	323	.90	1.00	1.00	.76	.69	.97	.24	−.18	.05	.09	.91	.005
High media exposure	315	.93	.79	.66	.91	.76	.52	.18	.27	.43	$.01^b$	.95	.002
Low media exposure	231	1.00	.91	.84	1.00	.95	.57	$-.04^b$	$.04^b$	.35	$-.01^b$	.95	.003

[a] The β's are standardized regression coefficients; I_1, I_2, and I_3 are issue attitudes in 1964, 1966, and 1970; P_1, P_2, and P_3 are party attitudes in 1964, 1966, and 1970.

[b] Values are for betas *not* significant at the .05 level. The ρ^2 are estimates of the test–retest reliability using Heise's (1969) formula.

TABLE 11.3

VARIANCES FOR THE BRITISH ATTITUDE CLUSTERS[a]

Subjects included	N	Issue Cluster			Party Cluster		
		1964	1966	1970	1964	1966	1970
All	546	8.62	9.70	9.50	12.98	13.55	12.97
High SES	195	7.98	7.69	8.06	8.52	9.54	7.13
Low SES	323	7.31	8.71	8.29	10.93	10.88	11.41
High media exposure	315	9.47	10.18	10.11	13.41	14.17	13.40
Low media exposure	231	7.27	9.04	8.46	12.27	12.49	12.07
All (all issues)	546	19.16	19.48	18.48	12.98	13.55	12.97

[a] To make these variances comparable across groups, all subgroup variances were calculated using the standard deviations for the total sample in 1964 as a baseline.

than the congruity model. The path analysis together with the variance pattern tends to support the information processing model.

The source change parameter $\beta_{I_2 P_3}$ from issues in 1966 to parties in 1970 is a good deal larger than the source change parameter $\beta_{I_1 P_2}$ from issues in 1964 to parties in 1966. This could be the result of an increase in the number of messages received by the British electorate in 1966. Moreover, Harrison (1966) notes that in 1966 the number of households with television in Britain rose above 90%. For the 1966 campaign, the BBC devoted a full 10% of its evening programming to politics.

The SRC Model

Table 11.5 presents the path model summaries for the SRC model. The fit of the SRC model is poorer than the fit for the other two models. Thus, for our data, the SRC model clearly receives the least empirical support.

OBSERVATIONS

Table 11.6 summarizes the results of the tests of our models in the British panel data. Table 11.6 shows that the information processing model is clearly the best-fitting model to the British data. The only apparent exception to this pattern is the high SES group, which is the group with strange OLS parameter estimates.

The information processing model fits the British electorate for the period studied; it predicts a gradual move to neutrality toward both parties and issues over time. This would explain the decline in party identification in Britain noted by Crewe *et al.* (1977) and Crewe (1977).

TABLE 11.4

Information Processing and Reinforcement Path Models

Subjects included	N	ρ^2_{ISSUES}	ρ^2_{PARTY}	$\beta_{I_1I_2}$	$\beta_{I_2I_3}$	$\beta_{P_1P_2}$	$\beta_{P_2P_3}$	$\beta_{I_1P_2}$	$\beta_{I_2P_3}$	$r_{I_1P_1}$	Average squared deviation
All	546	1.00	.95	.91	.95	.88	.55	.09	.43	.95	.0002
High SES	195	.94	.93	.83	.85	1.00	.74	.00ᵃ	.23	.92	.011
Low SES	323	.90	1.00	.89	.82	.69	.97	.24	.05ᵃ	.91	.004
High media exposure	315	.93	.79	.93	.92	.76	.52	.18	.43	.95	.001
Low media exposure	231	1.00	.91	.88	.95	.95	.57	-.04ᵃ	.35	.95	.002

ᵃ Denotes betas *not* significant at the .05 level.

TABLE 11.5

The SRC Model

Subjects included	N	ρ^2_{ISSUES}	ρ^2_{PARTY}	$\beta_{I_1I_2}$	$\beta_{I_2I_3}$	$\beta_{P_1P_2}$	$\beta_{P_2P_3}$	$\beta_{P_1I_2}$	$\beta_{P_2I_3}$	$r_{I_1P_1}$	Average squared deviation
All	546	1.00	.95	.76	.99	.95	.90	.16	-.03ᵃ	.95	.004
High SES	195	.94	.93	.78	.70	.96	.93	.14	.19	.92	.005
Low SES	323	.90	1.00	1.00	.76	.90	1.00	-.18	.09	.91	.001
High media exposure	315	.93	.79	.66	.91	.95	.91	.27	.01ᵃ	.95	.005
Low media exposure	231	1.00	.91	.84	1.00	.92	.87	.04ᵃ	-.01ᵃ	.95	.010

ᵃ Denotes betas *not* significant at the .05 level.

TABLE 11.6

SUMMARY OF THE FIT OF THE MODELS TO THE
BRITISH PANEL DATA

Subgroup	N	Best-fitting model
All	546	Information processing
High SES	195	Congruity
Low SES	323	Information processing
High media exposure	315	Information processing
Low media exposure	231	Information processing

CHAPTER 12

Belief Change and
Accumulated Information

Contributed by Jeffrey E. Danes, John E. Hunter, and Joseph Woelfel

INTRODUCTION

Many theorists argue that "established" beliefs are more difficult to change than de novo beliefs [Cantril (1946), Anderson and Hovland (1957), Roberts (1972), Hovland (1972), and Saltiel and Woelfel (1975)]. Two theories have been advanced to explain such a finding. Cantril (1946) argues for a polarity effect, that is, the more extreme the belief, the greater its resistance to change. Hovland (1972) and Anderson and Hovland (1957) argue that the greater resistance to change stems from the greater amount of information that people have for established beliefs. This argument follows from information processing theory if we assume that people with more information spend more of the message time attending to internal counterarguments.

This chapter reports a study done to test these hypotheses: Are established beliefs more difficult to change? If so, is the increased resistance due to polarity effects or due to accumulated information?

We begin by developing models of change incorporating polarity and information effects in the information processing model of belief change. We could derive similar models from other attitude change theories but the literature on belief change has consistently confirmed discrepancy theory. Our data also show linear discrepancy functions, hence we do not formalize the other theories.

POLARITY

If there are no polarity effects, then the information processing model of belief change is a discrepancy equation. We shall consider only the basic linear model

$$\Delta b = \alpha(m - b),$$

where the message value m is one if the message argues for true and zero if the message argues for false.

Because the midpoint for certainty is .50 for subjective probability, polarity is the distance from .50 rather than the distance from zero, that is,

$$\text{polarity} = |b - .50|$$

Change is reduced from that predicted by the simple discrepancy model to the extent of polarity in the belief. The word "reduced" in this sentence means "reduced in absolute value" and hence the reduction is multiplicative rather than additive. Thus we represent the reduction mathematically by dividing by a number greater than one. The simplest divisor would be

$$\text{divisor} = 1 + \beta\text{polarity} = 1 + \beta|b - .50|$$

Thus the simplest polarity model of belief change is

$$\Delta b = \frac{\alpha(m - b)}{1 + \beta|b - .5|}$$

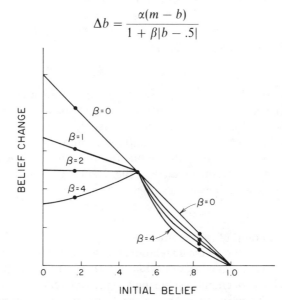

Fig. 12.1. The predicted relationship between belief change and initial belief for the information processing model with polarity effect (message argues for true) for four different values of the parameter β.

Parameter β measures the strength of the polarity effect. If $\beta = 0$, then there is no polarity effect, and the polarity model reduces to the simple linear discrepancy model.

The polarity model is plotted in Fig. 12.1 for various values of β under the assumption that the message argues for true. Polarity effects will be much larger at extremely discrepant initial beliefs than for beliefs already in the direction of the message. The large dots on each curve are plotted for reference to empirical data plots. If the belief range is split into three regions (.00–.35, .35–.65, and .65–1.00), then the corresponding average belief values would be .17, .50, and .83, respectively. If these three points are considered in isolation, then the qualitative prediction of the polarity model is that the points are concave downward, that is, the middle point lies above the straight line connecting the upper and lower points.

ACCUMULATED INFORMATION

Information processing theory predicts that belief change will be reduced to the extent that the receiver attends to internal counterarguments rather than the external message (Roberts and Maccoby, 1973). If people with more information about the belief topic are more likely to generate counterarguments than people with little information, then belief change should reduce to the extent of accumulated information.

If there were no accumulated information, then the belief change will be given by the linear discrepancy equation

$$\Delta b = \alpha(m - b).$$

Belief change will be reduced to the extent that the receiver attends to counterarguments. The presence of counterarguments is assumed to be a function of the amount of accumulated information. Therefore, belief change is reduced to the extent of such information. Because "reduced" here means "reduced in absolute value," the reduction is multiplicative rather than additive. Thus we divide the predicted belief change by a factor greater than one. The simplest such divisor is

$$\text{divisor} = 1 + \lambda I,$$

where I is the amount of information.

Figure 12.2 shows the predicted relationship between initial belief and belief change for the accumulated information model. The figure assumes that the data have been broken into subgroups with different amounts of prior information on the belief topic. That is, the data show all three curves, one for each information subgroup. The three large dots on each curve represent the values for the belief subgroups, that is, $b = .17, .50,$ and $.83,$ respectively.

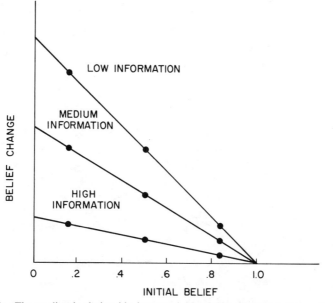

Fig. 12.2. The predicted relationship between initial belief and belief change for different amounts of accumulated information according to information processing theory (message argues for true).

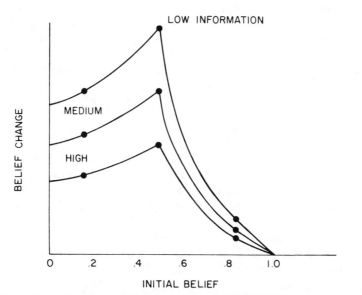

Fig. 12.3. The predicted relationship between initial belief and belief change for the hybrid information polarity model for $\beta = 4$ and a message that argues for true.

HYBRID MODEL

The polarity and accumulated information effects explanations are not logically contradictory. Thus both effects could occur. The "hybrid" model is obtained by dividing the linear discrepancy equation by both the polarity factor and the information factor. This hybrid model is

$$\Delta b = \frac{\alpha(m - b)}{(1 + \beta|b - .5|)(1 + \lambda I)}.$$

Figure 12.3 shows the predicted curves of the hybrid model for $\beta = 4$. The curves for each information subgroup all have the same shape because the value of β is the same for all curves. The curve for each subgroup is concave downward.

EMPIRICAL STUDY

Design

A study was run to test the information processing model and to see if established beliefs are more resistant to change than nonestablished beliefs. The study was a conventional pre–post attitude change study replicated across two belief topics. Prior information was measured in two ways: first, subjects were asked four items to assess their perception as to their state of knowledge; second, subjects were asked four questions as to the number of messages to on the topic to which they had been exposed. The first measure is referred to as the confidence measure of information and the second as the count measure of information. The plan was to break down the data by initial belief and information and compare the regression of belief change with that predicted by the various models.

Message-Belief Topics

The following belief statements were used for the experiment: (i) the nuclear production of electricity is potentially more dangerous than conventional methods of producing electricity, and (ii) the U.S.S.R. military forces are becoming superior to the military forces of the U.S.A. Hereafter the first belief topic is referred to as the "nuclear" belief and the second as the "military" belief. The messages dealt specifically with these beliefs, both argued for "true," and both were abstracted from actual news stories presented in the March 8, 1976, issue of *Time*: "The struggle over nuclear power" and "That alarming Soviet build-up."

To ensure that the "truth" argument came across clearly, each of the news stories was modified slightly; included in the nuclear experimental message was "... nuclear power is potentially more dangerous than conventional sources of power ... To those in the antinuclear camp, the danger is clear, 'the nuclear production of electrical power poses a severe threat to the lives and health of millions of Americans.'" For the military message similar modifications were made; included in the military experimental message was "Whether the Soviets actually plan to attack the Western world, one thing is clear according to NATO Commander in Chief ..., 'The massive Soviet build-up clearly indicates that the U.S.A. is becoming the weaker of the two military giants.'"

Procedure

The subjects were 134 students solicited from the Communication Department subject pool at Michigan State University. Each subject was given a questionnaire booklet that was made up of three parts. The first part contained the belief and information scales which the subject was to fill out for the pretest. The middle section was one of two messages. The subject was asked to "carefully read and underline the main points of the article." The third section consisted of the same belief and information scales which the subject was asked to fill out again as the posttest scores. For the purpose of double checking reliability, a third questionnaire was given one week later. In this design, those subjects who were randomly assigned the nuclear message acted as a control group to those subjects assigned the military message, and vice versa.

Instruments

The belief index was composed of six items. Three were bipolar scales from unlikely to likely, improbable to probable, and false to true. The other three items used a different format. First, the subject was asked to make a forced choice between two endpoints such as true or false, and then to rate his/her confidence in that rating on a 6-point Likert scale from "just guessing" to "certain." This pair of responses was then combined to provide a scale starting from .5 for "just guessing" and counting either up or down in steps of .1 to either one for certain and true or zero for certain and false. The three items of the compound type used the same endpoints as did the three bipolar scales. All six items proved correlationally equivalent when subjected to confirmatory factor analysis. All six items were scored from zero for false to one for true.

The information hypothesis assumes that resistance to persuasion stems from counterarguments that the receiver produces internally. Accumulated information is important because it produces the raw material for counterarguments. For this purpose it does not matter whether or not the information is correct. Therefore, we did not use an achievement test to assess information. Instead, we asked for subjective confidence ratings. The four confidence measures of information were global ratings on 7-point bipolar scales: "know a little–know a lot," "not aware–aware," "not informed–informed," and "not knowledgeable–knowledgeable." The count information items asked the number of times the belief topic had been heard on each of the four media categories: television and radio, newspapers and magazines, books, and personal contacts. In a pilot study these counts did not relate linearly to the subjective information judgments. The maximal linear correlation was found for the logarithmic transformation. In the main study each numerical count was transformed by the formula $x' = \ln(x + 1)$, where ln is the natural log function.

RESULTS

Scale Construction

Because all measurement was done with multiple indicators, reliability could be assessed by Cronbach's (1951) alpha coefficient. The reliability of initial belief was .97 for the nuclear belief and .96 for the military belief. The reliability of the confidence information measure was .85 for the nuclear belief and .80 for the military belief. The reliability of the count measure of information was .97 for the nuclear belief and .96 for the military belief. A confirmatory factor analysis showed that all constructs were measured by unidimensional indicators.

Message Effect

The means and standard deviations for the pretest, posttest, and belief change are shown in Table 12.1. For those who read the nuclear message, there is a mean change of .126 units on a zero–one scale; for those who did not read this

TABLE 12.1

PRETEST, POSTTEST, CHANGE MEANS, AND STANDARD DEVIATIONS FOR THE VARIOUS SUBGROUPS[a]

Message	Condition	Sample size	Pretest	Posttest	Belief change
Nuclear	Message	66	.663(.217)	.789(.264)	.126(.187)
	Control	68	.646(.270)	.642(.267)	−.004(.153)
Military	Message	68	.611(.262)	.657(.264)	.046(.163)
	Control	66	.564(.237)	.540(.264)	−.024(.145)

[a] Standard deviations are presented in parentheses.

message, there is a mean change of .004 units. The point biserial correlation for this message effect is .36, which is significant ($F = 19.62, df = 1, 132; p < .001$). For those who read the military message there is a mean change of .046 units; for those who did not read this message there is a mean change of $-.024$ units. The point biserial correlation for this message effect is .21, which is significant ($F = 6.42; df = 1, 132; p < .01$), though only two-thirds as large as the effect for the nuclear message.

The Pooled Information Measure

The count and confidence information measures are not independent. Corrected for attenuation, the count and confidence measures correlate .81 for the nuclear belief and .73 for the military belief. Thus the two measures were pooled for the first analysis.

Table 12.2 presents belief change as a function of initial belief and accumulated information, using both the confidence and count information measures. The initial belief regions were .00–.35, .35–.65, and .65–1.00. Weighted averages were computed by weighing cells by their sample size whereas unweighted means each cell was given equal weight.

Figure 12.4 presents the change for the nuclear belief in graphic form. The information curves are all discrepancy functions which differ only trivially

TABLE 12.2

BELIEF CHANGE MEANS USING POOLED MEASURES[a]

Initial belief level	Accumulated information			Weighted average	Unweighted average
	Low	Medium	High		
The Nuclear Belief					
False	.539(2)	.263(2)	.117(1)	.344(5)	.306
Uncertain	.271(18)	.117(5)	.027(1)	.229(24)	.138
True	.070(11)	.010(21)	.012(5)	.029(37)	.034
Weighted ave.	.217(31)	.047(28)	.036(7)	.126(66)	
Unweighted ave.	.293	.130	.055		
The Military Belief					
False	.250(3)	.127(4)	.003(6)	.095(13)	.127
Uncertain	.108(17)	−.060(5)	—	.069(22)	.024
True	.069(6)	.000(22)	−.002(5)	.013(33)	.022
Weighted ave.	.115(26)	.007(31)	.001(11)	.046(68)	
Unweighted ave.	.142	.022	.001		

[a] Belief change means and sample sizes for three levels of accumulated information using the pooled measure and three levels of initial belief.

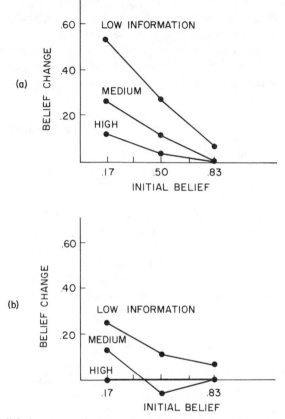

Fig. 12.4. Belief change as a function of accumulated information using the confidence information measure for (a) nuclear belief, (b) military belief.

from straight lines. In each case the departure is concave upward, the opposite to that predicted by the polarity model. Fig. 12.4b presents belief change for the military belief. Although the impact of sampling error is greater against this background of smaller overall change, the impact of information is still large, and the curves are clearly discrepancy functions. Only two curves have a middle point and in both cases the curve is concave upward, the opposite of the prediction for polarity effects.

Both of the experiments show a strong belief by information interaction. Thus main effects are not expected to be meaningful. Problems with main effects in the face of interaction are especially noticeable in the weighted average main effects for the nuclear message. Although all three information subgroups show concave upward curves, the weighted means are concave downward. The unweighted means across information are concave upward as expected.

According to the polarity model, there should be no differences between information subgroups, yet these differences are massive. According to the hybrid model, each information group should have a discrepancy curve that is concave downward. All five are concave upward. In fact, numerical estimates of β would be negative in all five cases. Thus the simple polarity model is disconfirmed and the hybrid model that assumes polarity effects superimposed on information effects is disconfirmed as well. There are no polarity effects in the regression analyses using the pooled measure of accumulated information.

The regression of belief change onto initial belief and accumulated information measured by the pooled measure of information shows virtually perfect fit to the information processing model, with resistance to persuasion increasing with increased accumulated information.

The Count Measure of Information

Table 12.3 presents belief change as a function of initial belief and accumulated information using only the count information measure. Shown are both belief change for the nuclear belief and belief change for the military belief.

TABLE 12.3

BELIEF CHANGE MEANS USING COUNT MEASURES[a]

Initial belief level	Accumulated information			Weighted average	Unweighted average
	Low	Medium	High		
The Nuclear Belief					
False	.772(2)	.128(1)	.025(2)	.344(5)	.308
Uncertain	.282(17)	.115(2)	.092(5)	.229(24)	.163
True	.034(12)	.025(8)	.028(17)	.029(37)	.029
Weighted avg.	.218(31)	.051(11)	.041(24)	.126(66)	
Unweighted avg.	.363	.089	.048		
The Military Belief					
False	.378(3)	.037(3)	−.001(7)	.095(13)	.138
Uncertain	.094(10)	.075(6)	.021(6)	.069(22)	.063
True	.017(2)	.020(12)	.008(19)	.013(33)	.015
Weighted avg.	.140(15)	.038(21)	.009(32)	.046(68)	
Unweighted avg.	.163	.044	.009		

[a] Belief change means and sample sizes (in parenthesis) for three levels of accumulated information using the count measure and three levels of initial belief.

Figure 12.5a presents belief change for the nuclear belief. All curves are discrepancy curves. The curves differ greatly for different information subgroups. The curve for low information is concave upward, but the other two curves are concave downward. This pattern is contrary to the hybrid model, but it does not completely disconfirm the hypothesis of polarity effects.

Figure 12.5b presents belief change for the military belief. The results are similar to those for the nuclear belief, though the amount of belief change is much smaller throughout. The low information curve is concave upward and the other two curves are concave downward. Thus the medium and high information curves show evidence of polarity effects, though the pattern does not fit the hybrid model.

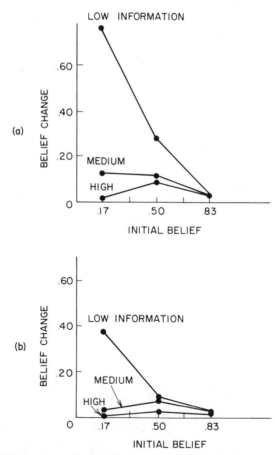

Fig. 12.5.   Belief change as a function of accumulated information using the count measure of information for (a) nuclear belief, (b) military belief.

The sample sizes within cells are very small. This opens the possibility that the small polarity effects within certain information subgroups may be due to sampling error. However, the effects are replicated across beliefs. For both beliefs it is the low information group that is concave upward and the medium and high information groups that are concave downward.

OBSERVATIONS

Theoretically, one would expect the count measure to be indirectly related to belief change, because resistance to change is caused by counterarguments. Mere exposure to information does not mean learning. People who are not interested in an issue can tune out or pass over "boring" messages. Thus a high count of exposures to information is a necessary condition for enough learning to construct counterarguments, but it is attentive exposure that counts in the final analysis. On the basis of this theoretical analysis, we are inclined to disregard the weak and inconsistent polarity effects of the count measure analysis.

The empirical test of the models was not as strong as one would desire. For a nonlinear model, certain cells are more important than others. In our study, the crucial cells are those for receivers whose initial belief was false. Because of the direction of our messages, these cells are minority cells. Thus trying to break the data down simultaneously for the information measures reduces sample sizes to atoms. The study could be redone on an issue about which people tend to hold polar views with little basis for them or in a context where a large sample of people with the right views can be drawn from a much larger initial population.

Other Theories

Because source attitude was manipulated to be positive (i.e., *Time* magazine), this study cannot distinguish between the discrepancy curves of information processing theory and those of social judgment theory or dissonance theory. Furthermore, these other theories are both cognitive in nature and compatible with the information effects found here. Thus social judgment theory and dissonance theory fit the present data as well as information processing theory.

Behavioristic reinforcement theory specifically denies the importance of thought as an epiphenomenon. Thus behavioristic reinforcement theory predicts that counterarguments are irrelevant. We see no other explanation for the information effects in this study within reinforcement theory.

Given a positive source, balance theory predicts change in the direction of the message, as was found here. But we see no basis in balance theory for the information effect. That is, we see no way to derive the prediction of increased resistance to persuasion because of high amounts of accumulated information.

Congruity theory is difficult to extend to this situation. Which source–object discrepancy is to be reduced? Also if congruity theory is to stay as close as possible to conditioning theory, then it too would predict no information effect.

CONCLUSION

This study fits the predictions of information theory and its "cousins," social judgment and dissonance theory. Belief change is predominantly determined by the discrepancy between message and initial belief. However, beliefs based on a large amount of information are more resistant to change, presumably because the receiver is more likely to attend to internal counterarguments.

CHAPTER 13

Cognitive Inconsistency and Change in Purchase Intention

Contributed by Jeffrey E. Danes, John E. Hunter, and O. Karl Mann

INTRODUCTION

Single acts are not only subject to massive random error but to transient situational factors as well (Chapter 16). Thus it is sometimes desirable to funnel psychological causal factors through a stable mediating determinant of behavior: the behavioral intention. Dulaney (1961, 1968) argues for the behavioral intention in the learning domain and presents several studies showing that intentions mediate the impact of prior factors such as reinforcement history and contingency hypotheses. Fishbein and Ajzen (1975) apply this theory to the prediction of behavior from beliefs and attitudes. The theory is cast in the language of cognitive consistency theory by Jaccard and King (1977). Danes and Hunter (1980) use this early work to build a theory of purchase intention. In their work the first dynamic theories of purchase intention are developed, theories that ultimately evolve into the information processing theory presented in Chapter 9.

This chapter presents two studies of intention change. The first compares four models of intention change: the cognitive consistency model and three models of cognitive inconsistency [the basic information processing model and the two transfer models, awareness of discrepancy and awareness of belief change (see Chapter 9)].

PURCHASE INTENTION

The word "intention" is used in two somewhat contradictory ways. As a qualitative or semantic word, intention means a proposition such as "I should buy a Fiat." As a quantity, intention means the extent or strength of the proposition. The cognitive consistency theorists resolve this dilemma in the same manner as for any other belief, by defining the quantitative meaning of intention as the subjective probability of the corresponding intention proposition. That is, if B is the proposition "I should buy a Fiat," then the intention to buy a Fiat is the subjective probability of the proposition, that is, $P(B)$.

Purchase intention usually depends on the attributes of the product. The presence of an attribute can be defined by a statement such as "The Fiat is economical." The extent of belief can then be measured as the subjective probability of that statement. The importance of the attribute to the product can be measured by comparing two subjective conditional probabilities: the probability of purchase if the attribute is present versus the probability of purchase if the attribute is absent. If B is the proposition "I should buy a Fiat" and A is the proposition "The Fiat is economical," then the importance of economy to purchase intention can be measured by comparing $P(B|A)$ and $P(B|A')$. The cognitive consistency equation for purchase intention is

$$P(B) = P(B|A)P(A) + P(B|A')P(A')$$

or

$$b = P(B|A)a + P(B|A')(1 - a) \tag{13.1}$$

in the notation of Chapter 9.

ADVERTISING AND CHANGE IN PURCHASE INTENTION

Most advertisements can be regarded as an argument that the product has a certain attribute such as sex appeal. The message may then have two effects: it may alter the attribute belief a and/or it may alter the purchase intention b. If one message argues for "true," that is, $m = 1$, and if beliefs and intention are consistent before and after the message, then the change in b would be given by the two-step cognitive consistency change equation reported in Chapter 9,

$$\begin{aligned}
\Delta b &= \alpha(1 - a)[P(B|A) - p(B|A')] \\
&= \alpha[p(B|A) - b] \\
&= \alpha\{p(B|A) - [ap(B|A) + (1 - a)p(B|A')]\} \tag{13.2}
\end{aligned}$$

If beliefs and intention are inconsistent before and after the message, then the change in b could be given by one of the three models of inconsistency reported in Chapter 9: the one-step or basic information processing model,

$$\Delta b = \alpha[P(B|A) - b] \tag{13.3}$$

or one of the two versions of the transfer model—awareness of discrepancy (AOD),

$$\Delta b = \alpha(1 - a)[p(B|A) - b] \tag{13.4}$$

or awareness of belief change (AOC),

$$\Delta b = \alpha^2(1 - a)[p(B|A) - b] \tag{13.5}$$

The study presented next was designed to compare these four models.

THE FIRST STUDY

The first study was designed to compare four of the change models presented in Chapter 9: the two-step change model (derived from cognitive consistency theory), the one-step change model (the basic information processing model), and the two transfer discrepancy model (the models for awareness of discrepancy and for awareness of change). The first model assumes consistency before and after the message, and the last three allow for inconsistency before and after one message. For this study, the target belief is a product–attribute association such as "Hunter Vitamins" and "reduce stress." The purchase intention is the subjective purchase probability of buying "Hunter Vitamins."

Design

For the study, receivers were given bogus information describing 10 products, and this information was used to create base-line measures. The base-line measures included purchase intention for each of the 10 products, conditional purchase intentions, and belief ratings. The study design consisted of the following steps: product descriptions, pretest (base-line) measures, messages, and posttest measures.

The data for the first study were obtained from 100 undergraduate students enrolled in introductory marketing classes at Virginia Polytechnic Institute and State University. Students from other marketing classes were used to identify products that most students did not necessarily use but nonetheless may have been of interest to other college students. The products and messages for the study are given in Table 13.1.

The subjects were told that they were involved in "part of an ongoing, nationwide survey of America's colleges and universities ... investigating

TABLE 13.1

PRODUCTS AND MESSAGES USED FOR FIRST STUDY

Product	Message
Kool-Rite Cooler	Lightweight (2 lb.)
Perfect match dating service	Reasonable price ($20 for 4 meetings)
Wagner study guide	Clear and well written
Stutz steam valet	Quick drying
Hunter vitamins	Reduces stress and tension
Karman washer/dryer	Capacity of large washer/dryer
Lilac fabric softener	Added at start of wash cycle
Jeffy wall thermometer	Indoor and outdoor readings
Allied cordless phone	Most inexpensive of all cordless phones ($48.95)
Murry bike basket	Easy installation and removal

products to make life in college easier." Product descriptions were provided for all 10 products, and an example *description* for the vitamins is as follows:

> The FDA has approved a new vitamin tablet that supplies all of the minimum daily requirements recommended for the average adult. The vitamins are fortified with Iron and Niacin to meet additional health benefits. The vitamins are low in price compared to other multi-vitamins and are sold at the Corner Drug Store, Eckerd Drug, Revco, and Food Town. They are currently being sold under the Hunter brand name.

After reading each product description, the receivers responded to the pretest (base-line) measures. Once completed, the experimental messages were introduced. An example *message* for "Hunter Vitamins" is the following:

> The Hunter Vitamin tablets interact with the body enzymes to REDUCE STRESS AND TENSION. The stress relievers interact with the natural body chemistry to reduce the tension of daily college life. Other students surveyed said that these vitamins significantly reduced stress and tension.

All messages argued that the product had the attribute in question, that is, for all messages $m = 1$ (see Table 13.1). Posttest questions were administered immediately after the receivers read the 10 different messages. Multiple measurement was used for all variables. To measure each of the ten purchase intentions, three bipolar scales were used: a 9-point scale for likely–unlikely, a 7-point scale for probable–improbable, and a 5-point scale for I would buy–I would not buy. The same scale and bipolar descriptors were used for the conditional purchase intentions. To measure each of the 10 beliefs, three bipolar scales were used: a 5-point scale for true–false, a 7-point scale for probable–improbable, and a 9-point scale for likely–unlikely. The reliabilities for all constructs estimated by Cronbach's (1951) alpha were .90 and above.

Means Analysis

The study design could be treated as 10 studies, each with 100 subjects. Thus the analysis would require the individual as the unit of analysis in ten separate analyses: one for each product. We opted, however, to follow the approach recommended by Wyer (1974). That is, we used the product as the unit of analysis with the mean response as data. The table of means is given in Table 13.2.

To compare the four models, we jackknifed the correlations (betas), slopes, and intercepts [Tukey (1958), Gray and Schucany (1972), and Fenwick (1979)]. That is, we found the above parameters for all 10 products and for each of the 9 products with one product removed. These parameters are given in Table 13.3. The first row (first three columns) of Table 13.3 give the beta, slope, and intercept using all 10 products for the basic information processing model. These values are .594, 1.12, and .029, respectively. The second row (first three columns) give the beta, slope, and intercept with the cooler product deleted from the estimation sample. These values are: .597, 1.13, and 0.29, respectively. Pseudo values were found by

$$J_i^* = 10J - 9J(i)$$

where J is the parameter estimate for 10 observations and $J(i)$ the parameter estimate with the ith observation deleted. The jackknifed parameter is given as the average of the 10 pseudo values (see Gray and Schucany, 1972).

The jackknifed parameters indicate that only the one-step (basic information processing model) fits the data. The jackknifed beta is .635 and significant ($t = 3.44$, $p < .01$). None of the other three betas are significantly different from zero (.05 level). Additionally, the slope for the one-step model is not different from one ($t = .041$) and the intercept is not different from zero ($t = 1.08$). Thus the one-step model appears to fit the data reasonably well. The second best-fitting model is the awareness of discrepancy (AOD) version of the transfer model.

THE SECOND STUDY

The first study in this chapter found the one-step (basic information processing) model of Chapter 9 to be a better predictor of intention change than the other three change models. The second best predictor of intention change was the awareness of discrepancy version of the transfer model. The second study compared the four models using the compound message models given in Chapter 3.

Two principles lead to six models of the effect of compound messages. First, the compound message can be processed in three ways: it can be broken into

TABLE 13.2

Mean Purchase Intention, Belief, and Conditional Intentions ($N = 100$)

Product	Before message				After message				α^a
	b	a	$P(B\|A)$	$P(B\|A')$	b	a	$P(B\|A)$	$P(B\|A')$	
Food cooler	.395	.577	.519	.154	.495	.818	.579	.161	.570
Study guide	.115	.387	.153	.015	.161	.664	.151	.061	.452
Dating service	.478	.675	.605	.047	.582	.793	.664	.106	.363
Steam valet	.316	.556	.373	.092	.407	.781	.445	.123	.507
Vitamins	.376	.351	.537	.254	.547	.640	.607	.247	.491
Washer/dryer	.230	2.75	.383	.185	.290	.665	.367	.157	.534
Fabric softener	.220	.556	.412	.181	.396	.766	.472	.165	.477
Thermometer	.190	.390	.372	.217	.345	.737	.442	.199	.569
Cordless phone	.239	.468	.390	.124	.301	.705	.392	.121	.445
Bike basket	.166	.518	.274	.157	.204	.752	.281	.166	.485

^{a} The variable α was estimated from $\Delta a = \alpha(\bar{m} - \bar{a}) = \alpha(1 - \bar{a})$, that is, $\alpha = (\bar{a}_{n+1} - \bar{a}_n)/(1 - \bar{a}_n)$.

TABLE 13.3

RESULTS FOR CHANGE MODELS COMPARED IN FIRST STUDY

Product	$\Delta b = \alpha[p(B\mid A) - b]$			$\Delta b = \alpha(1 - a)[p(B\mid A) - p(B\mid A')]$		
	Beta	Slope	Intercept	Beta	Slope	Intercept
All	.594	1.12	.029	.311	0.83	.049
Cooler	.597	1.13	.029	.360	1.16	.036
Dating service	.499	1.09	.032	.186	0.51	.074
Study guide	.615	1.19	.022	.310	0.84	.050
Steam valet	.632	1.33	.012	.315	0.85	.050
Vitamins	.621	1.03	.028	.154	0.39	.070
Washer/dryer	.710	1.33	.024	.430	1.16	.036
Fabric softener	.507	0.88	.039	.506	1.19	.018
Thermometer	.503	1.03	.034	.390	0.98	.034
Phone	.603	1.15	.032	.334	0.87	.052
Basket	.597	1.03	.041	.070	0.21	.093
Jackknifed parameter	.653	1.13	.026	.361	0.97	.028
Jackknifed standard error	.1897	0.3162	.0240	.3811	0.9720	.0636

Product	$\Delta b = \alpha(1 - a)[p(B\mid A) - b]$			$\Delta b = \alpha^2(1 - a)[p(B\mid A) - b]$		
	Beta	Slope	Intercept	Beta	Slope	Intercept
All	.442	1.21	.059	.391	1.89	.068
Cooler	.443	1.22	.059	.391	1.89	.068
Dating service	.334	0.95	.072	.284	1.39	.081
Study guide	.482	1.14	.049	.434	2.26	.059
Steam valet	.454	1.35	.052	.395	2.02	.065
Vitamins	.385	0.95	.062	.383	1.62	.065
Washer/dryer	.682	2.05	.041	.634	3.38	.053
Fabric softener	.443	1.05	.057	.410	1.70	.063
Thermometer	.305	0.93	.066	.218	1.24	.076
Phone	.467	1.24	.063	.396	1.84	.073
Basket	.417	1.05	.071	.363	1.60	.079
Jackknifed parameter	.449	1.36	.057	.393	1.85	.076
Jackknifed standard error	.2912	0.9454	.0277	.3053	1.7081	.0256

component messages by considering each attribute in the order that the attribute is mentioned (the "given order" hypothesis), it can be reacted to in a random cycle of thoughts about each component (the "random succession" hypothesis), or the message components can be considered simultaneously. Second, the effect of the message components can be as large as the components are when considered alone (full effect), or the effect might reduce when the component is considered in combination (reduced effect). The three processing hypotheses are logically independent of the two impact hypotheses. Thus there are six combinations to act as compound message models.

Study Design

The data used for the second study were collected by Danes and Hunter (1980). The study looked at the impact of two compound messages on purchase intention toward the Fiat 131. The positive message argued in favor of three attributes: the Fiat is safe, roomy, and affordable. The negative message argued against five positive attributes: the Fiat does not come with a radio, has no rear window defroster, comes only in a two-door model, has poor color and paint, and has poor gas economy.

The pretest measurement was the same for all receivers. First, beliefs were measured for 11 attributes: the three attributes of the positive message, five attributes of the negative message, and three control or filler attributes not mentioned in either message (size, choice of transmission, and sporty styling). Second, purchase intention was measured in both conditional and unconditional form. This required assessment of 23 subjective purchase probabilities: the overall or unconditional purchase probability and, for each of the 11 attributes, two conditional probabilities—the purchase probability with and the purchase probability without the attribute.

All receivers were then presented with a bogus article from *Consumer Reports*; 63 receivers saw the positive message and 45 receivers saw the negative message. Following this message, all the beliefs and purchase intentions were measured again.

Measurement

All variables were measured on multiple scales. Purchase intention was measured on four bipolar scales: likely–unlikely, I would–I would not, probable–improbable, and I might–I might not. The reliability for the four scales was .97 (alpha coefficient, Cronbach, 1951). Each attribute probability was measured on three bipolar scales: true–false, likely–unlikely, and probable–improbable. The average reliability was .93. The "if present" and "if absent" conditional purchase intentions were each measured on three bipolar scales: yes–no, likely–unlikely, and probable–improbable. The average reliability was .96.

Each bipolar scale had 11 points and was originally scored from 0 to 10. Scale scores were added and divided by the total number of points to create subjective probability scores ranging from zero to one.

Attribute Change

The mean change in attribute probabilities is shown in Table 13.1. Mean change on the targeted attributes was .353 for the positive message and $-.630$ for the negative message. Mean change on the nontargeted attributes was .028 for the positive message and $-.049$ for the negative message. Thus the messages had large impact on the targeted attributes and little impact on the attributes not mentioned.

Table 13.4 also shows the discrepancy between the mean pretest attribute belief and the message value. The ratio of mean change to message discrepancy provides an estimate of the parameter value α in the information processing model. The average value of α was .75 for the positive message and .92 for the negative message. These values are very large in comparison to most change studies and reflect a very powerful impact for the bogus *Consumer Reports* messages.

Intention Change

The models of intention change were tested by using them to predict the posttest purchase intention from the pretest intentions and attribute beliefs. This can be done in 25 ways. First, there are four models of purchase intention change. Each of these can be used with any of the six compound message models. Thus there are 24 particular models combining change and message models. Finally, a twenty-fifth model can be obtained by simply predicting that posttest intention is the same as pretest intention, that is, by assuming no changes at all.

TABLE 13.4

ATTRIBUTE CHANGE

Message topic	Average observed belief change	Average belief discrepancy	α
Positive message			
Safety	.298	.403	.739
Roomy	.441	.565	.781
Affordable	.319	.438	.728
Average	.353	.469	.750
Negative message			
Radio	$-.702$	$-.740$	.948
Defroster	$-.620$	$-.660$	.941
Doors	$-.541$	$-.590$	.916
Color	$-.619$	$-.744$	.832
Economy	$-.671$	$-.709$	.947
Average	$-.630$	$-.688$	.920

TABLE 13.5

Correlations, Slopes, and Intercepts for Predicted Postmessage Intention and Actual Postmessage Intention for Compound Message Models

Impact	Model	Order	Positive message			Negative message			Average		
			r	Slope	Intercept	r	Slope	Intercept	r	Slope	Intercept
Reduced	One-Step	Simultaneous	.51	.583	.222	.37	.584	−.019	.44	.584	.102
		Ordered	.51	.595	.224	.53	.788	−.087	.52	.692	.069
		Random	.52	.602	.242	.52	.745	−.087	.52	.674	.078
	Two-Step	Simultaneous	.45	.538	.245	.32	.511	.000	.39	.525	.113
		Ordered	.43	.542	.265	.37	.582	−.040	.40	.562	.113
		Random	.44	.546	.263	.36	.545	−.039	.40	.546	.112
	AOD	Simultaneous	.55	.627	.269	.46	.703	−.066	.51	.665	.112
		Ordered	.54	.610	.284	.53	.731	−.082	.54	.671	.101
		Random	.54	.609	.286	.51	.880	−.062	.53	.745	.112
	AOC	Simultaneous	.54	.598	.298	.48	.713	−.074	.53	.656	.112
		Ordered	.53	.584	.309	.53	.715	−.081	.53	.650	.114
		Random	.53	.583	.309	.51	.837	−.023	.52	.710	.143
Full	One-Step	Simultaneous	.24	.143	.425	−.33	−.079	.139	−.05	−.064	.282
		Ordered	.42	.438	.267	.25	.529	.092	.34	.484	.180
		Random	.47	.512	.231	.31	.479	.015	.39	.496	.123
	Two-Step	Simultaneous	.46	.380	.268	−.07	−.025	.137	.20	.142	.203
		Ordered	.42	.435	.269	.25	.529	.092	.34	.482	.181
		Random	.47	.509	.233	.31	.487	.015	.39	.498	.124
	AOD	Simultaneous	.47	.406	.293	−.35	−.117	.145	.06	.115	.219
		Ordered	.52	.567	.236	.21	.398	.089	.37	.483	.163
		Random	.54	.610	.220	.29	1.361	.083	.42	.986	.152
	AOC	Simultaneous	.52	.540	.241	−.34	−.127	.149	.09	.207	.195
		Ordered	.54	.619	.228	.22	.414	.083	.38	.321	.116
		Random	.55	.635	.225	.32	2.220	.064	.44	1.428	.144
		(No change)	.46	.456	.389	.54	.547	−.028	.50	.502	.185

The fit of the 25 models was assessed in three related ways. First, we correlated the predicted posttest intentions with the actual posttest intentions. Second, we found the slopes for each model, and third we found the intercepts. The results are given in Table 13.5.

The results of the analyses for the positive and negative messages are roughly similar, but differ in fine detail. Therefore, we averaged the results, and these values are given in the last three columns of Table 13.5. The average predicted–actual posttest correlation for the "no change" model is .50. One clear result is that none of the full impact models fit the data better than the no change prediction; all full impact correlations are less than .50. Eight of the reduced impact models fit better than .50. However, none of these eight are substantially larger than .50.

The slope for the no change model is .502 and the intercept is .185. Two of the better fitting reduced impact models are the awareness of discrepancy random processing model (slope = .745, intercept = .112) and the one-step, ordered, processing model (slope = .692, intercept = .067). The difference in slopes, .053, is indeed small. However, the difference in intercepts is substantial. The intercept (.112) for reduced, random, awareness of discrepancy model is more than 1.6 times larger than the intercept (.067) for the reduced, ordered, one-step model. Based on both slope and intercept, the reduced, ordered, one-step model appears to fit the data better than the other 24 models. The second best-fitting model appears to be the reduced, random, one-step model. This model has a slope equal to .674 and an intercept equal to .078.

The results of this study tend to lend support to the one-step model as the best predictor of change in purchase intention. Furthermore, when compound messages are communicated, it appears that the impact of each component message is *reduced* in proportion to the number of component messages in the compound message. Moreover, most of the subjects in this study apparently read the component messages in the given order of presentation; others apparently read them in "random" order.

OBSERVATIONS

Both studies reported in this chapter found support for the one-step (basic information processing) model developed in Chapter 9. This model evolved from the earlier work by Danes and Hunter (1980), who developed the original transfer discrepancy model (what we have termed the awareness of discrepancy version). Both studies show that the one-step model is a better predictor of purchase intention. The first study demonstrates superiority with single messages, and the second study suggests the same to be true with compound messages. In that study, the best-fitting model appears to be the one-step model with reduced impact that assumed that receivers read the component messages in the given order of presentation.

PART III

RELATIONS BETWEEN ATTITUDES

Attitudes toward related concepts tend to be correlated. This part of the book seeks to explain some of these correlations in terms of theories developed to explain attitude change in the simple passive communication paradigm. That is, this part of the book seeks to extend the attitude change theories of Part I to a theory of attitudes toward logically related concepts. The first chapter develops the simplest such theory: a theory in which all concepts are logical subsets of one another. The theory begins with a hierarchy of concepts related to one another as superordinate or subordinate concepts. A review of the literature suggests that these attitudes will be related to each other because attitudes toward superordinate concepts act as the source of internal messages about subordinate concepts. The first chapter derives the predictions of information processing theory under these assumptions. This chapter also reviews the literature on indirect attitude change and decay or stability in attitude change in relation to the predictions of the hierarchical model. The second chapter presents an empirical test of the hierarchical model. The third chapter extends the hierarchical model to a theory of the relationship between attitudes and behavior.

The last chapter of the section considers hierarchical models derived from other theories of attitude change, with special emphasis on reinforcement theory. The standard reinforcement theory without extinction makes bizarre predictions about hierarchically related attitudes. Even with a strong extinction parameter, the predictions of reinforcement theory are far from current research findings. Social judgment theory and dissonance theory in this context make the same predictions as information processing theory. Balance theory makes the same predictions as reinforcement theory without extinction. Congruity theory is very problematical. Because attitude change in congruity theory is always in the direction of attitude toward the source, it is hard to know what to do with internal messages. If the source is viewed as the self, then all change tends to be dominated by self-esteem and change in each attitude is independent of other attitudes. However, this theory not only predicts correlations within hierarchies but across all hierarchies. Yet there is little correlation between attitudes in completely separate content domains.

Chapter 14 also reviews the relevant literature on individual differences in belief structure. There is also a relationship between the hierarchical model of change and the distinction between persuasibility and dogmatism. The available literature suggests that both traits can be identified with parameters of the hierarchical model.

Attitude Change in Concept Hierarchies*

Contributed by John E. Hunter, Ralph L. Levine, and Scott E. Sayers

Attitudes toward logically related concepts are correlated. This chapter seeks to explain some of these correlations within the context of information processing theory. The basic assumption of the model is that change is determined by internal as well as external messages. An attitude toward a logically superordinate concept (such as "war in general") acts as a source of messages about the given concept (such as "war in the Middle East"). Thus the attitude toward the superordinate concept influences the attitude toward the subordinate concept. This model makes predictions about the decay or stability of attitude change that appears to fit the empirical literature.

CONCEPT HIERARCHIES

Concepts can be frequently organized into logical classes or subclasses that form the superordinate–subordinate relationship with each other. For example, consider the hypothetical belief system in Fig. 14.1. We see from the figure that the concepts are arranged on different levels from the most concrete

* This chapter is an edited version of "Attitude change in hierarchical belief systems and its relationship to persuasibility, dogmatism, and rigidity," by J. E. Hunter, R. L. Levine, and S. E. Sayers, *Human Communication Research*, 1976, **3**: 3–28.

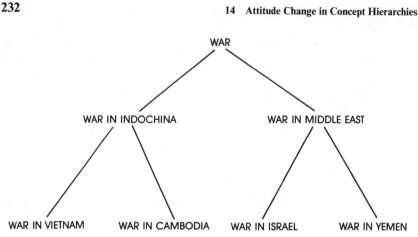

Fig. 14.1   The hierarchical structure of concepts associated with war in general.

and specific to the most abstract and general, and if we wanted, we might find additional levels in both directions. We shall assume that attitudes can be associated with concepts found at all levels. Moreover, it is assumed that one could attempt to change attitudes by presenting independent messages about concepts at any level in the hierarchy. The structure found in Fig. 14.1 is only one of many types of organizations possible, but it seems to be a good starting point in studying belief structures.

What are the implications of having attitudes and beliefs organized into various levels? The main implication is that the attitudes are not independent of one another. That is, if an attitude was completely isolated from other attitudes, then the only method of changing that attitude would be present a series of messages about that concept. On the other hand, if the attitude is embedded in an organized system, then the other attitudes may also function as agents of change.

TOP DOWN INFLUENCE

We have a structure such as that in Fig. 14.1, then there would be three possible directions of influence: upward, downward, and sideways. We now show that these three directions do not have equal status in terms of logic (i.e., Aristotelian logic). Consider the relationship between the person's attitude toward war in general and toward the war in Indochina. Logically, if all wars are bad, then the war in Indochina is bad. Thus logic predicts a strong downward influence. On the other hand, if the war in Vietnam is bad, then logically one could only conclude that *some* wars in Indochina are bad, that is, there is no logical reason that the war in Cambodia might not be good. Thus, logically, upward influence is much weaker than downward influence.

What about sideways influence? Consider the previous example of a person who believes that the war in Vietnam is bad but that the war in Cambodia is good. This in itself is not illogical. Concepts that are located side-by-side in a concept hierarchy represent mutually exclusive sets. Thus, from a purely logical point of view, there is no sideways influence.

From the point of view of logical influence, there is a gross discrepancy between upward and downward influence and there is no sideways influence at all. Do the corresponding psychological asymmetries exist? For example, one would not require a detailed search of the literature to find dozens of instances in which side-by-side attitudes are highly correlated. But the question is: Is the partial correlation between coordinate attitudes still positive when the attitude toward the superordinate concept is held constant?

As of now there are two empirical studies that have been expressly designed to test the top down hypothesis. Poole and Hunter find the predicted pattern of correlations in a cross-sectional study of a hierarchy of attitudes toward sexual behavior in various situations. In Chapter 15 we present a second study by Poole and Hunter on attitudes toward government agencies that report both cross-sectional correlational data that fit the top down pattern and longitudinal experimental data that fit as well.

Much of the factor analytic literature on personality is also relevant. Many personality tests are specific attitude questionnaires where the object is a class of actions such as responding assertively to verbal assault or spending leisure time with other people. Vernon (1951) notes that the correlations conform to a model of hierarchical organization by content. That is, the correlations between relatively specific behavior classes vanish when the corresponding abstract factor is held constant.

There is considerable literature showing that downward influences are quite strong in terms of belief consistency (see the papers by McGuire, Watts, Holt, Wyer, and Goldberg cited below). In each case the syllogism A, A implies B, B is studied. In each case the usual top-to-bottom logical influence was upheld. That is, if either the probability of A or the probability that A implies B is increased, then the probability of B increases. Unfortunately, a study to determine whether or not there are any upward influences in belief systems has not yet been found. That is, if the probability of B is increased by some argument that is independent of A, then there is no logical necessity that the probability of A should increase, and we have seen no empirical study that suggests that such nonlogical processes exist.

Indeed, there is some promise in this literature that such nonlogical processes will be very weak. Holt and Watts (1969) presented arguments intended to increase the "*A* implies *B*" portion of various syllogisms. They then not only looked at possible increases in the subjective probability of the conclusion *B*, but at possible increases in the subjective probability of the premise *A*. An increase in the conclusion *B* would be what we have termed a downward influence and is in the direction of logical consistency. An increase in the premise is not predicted by logical consistency and is somewhat like what we called an upward influence. Holt and Watts find that if the pretest triplet (*A*, *A* implies *B*, *B* probabilities) is presented as a syllogism and hence are measured together, then when the posttest measures are obtained in random order, there are large increases in the "*A* implies *B*" probability that directly reflects the persuasive message, somewhat smaller increases in the conclusion, but no change in the probability of the premise *A*; that is, strong downward influence and no upward influence. However, if the pretest probabilities are assessed with the members of the syllogistic triplet scattered randomly among the 24 probabilities measured, then in addition to the downward influence, there is an increase in the premise of *A* of about half the size of the increase in the conclusion. Thus in this latter condition there are small upward influences. McFarland and Thistlethwaithe (1970) found this so intriguing that they performed three experiments to tease out the exact magnitude of these nonlogical effects. In all three experiments, there are no such effects! This suggests that the apparent increase in *A* in the Holt and Watts (1969) study is due to sampling error, thus arguing that *A* did not increase "*A* implies *B*" and arguing for "*A* implies *B*" did not increase *A*. On the other hand either argument will produce the downward influence, that is, an increase in the conclusion *B*.

MODELS OF CHANGE

In this section we present two hierarchical models for attitude change:

1. a double comparison model that assumes that internal change immediately follows externally produced attitude change and

2. a double comparison model with a time delay, that is, a model in which there is a time delay between external and internal change.

Chapter 15 presents two more alternative models:

3. a pullback model and

4. a generalization model.

In that chapter, all four models are compared against a set of empirical data.

All models assume that attitudes can be influenced by attitudes about concepts at higher levels in the hierarchy. That is, we assume that change in any given attitude is produced by two possible agents: a direct external message or the attitude toward the concept immediately above the given concept in the hierarchy. If we run an arrow from one variable to another to indicate a causal influence, then we obtain the picture shown in Fig. 14.2. Ashby (1956) calls such a picture an "immediate effects diagram."

The critical feature of this diagram is that it enables us to deduce the ultimate causal relations among the variables shown. That is, by tracing along the graph we can see the second-order, third-order, etc. effects of one variable on another. If we do this, then we see that the person's attitude toward the war ultimately affects every other attitude. His attitude toward the war in Indochina, however, affects only his attitudes toward the war in Vietnam and the war in Cambodia. Because there is no backward effect from the war in Indochina to his attitude toward war, there can be no effect on either his attitude toward war or the war in the Middle East, and so forth.

If we trace this graph backward, then we make a very important discovery. If we start at the war in Yemen, then we see that it is never affected by any attitudes except those toward the war in the Middle East and war in general. If we start at the war in the Middle East, then the only attitude that affects it is the person's attitude toward war in general. Finally, the person's attitude toward war is affected by no other attitude. What this means is that if we take a string of attitudes starting from the top of the hierarchy and moving down, then that string can be considered in isolation from the other attitudes. That is, if we consider a string starting from the top of the hierarchy, then the attitudes in that string have an effect on many other attitudes but are not themselves affected. Thus, because of the top down assumption, each string that starts at the top can be analyzed separately.

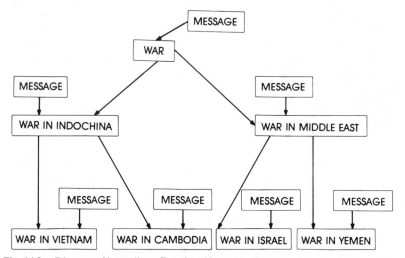

Fig. 14.2. Diagram of immediate effects for a hierarchical structure. The term "message" has a different meaning for each box, that is, the "message" for war in Cambodia means "message about the war in Cambodia." A message about a specific concept has a direct effect on that concept.

THE DOUBLE COMPARISON MODEL

In the previous section we used the diagram of immediate effects to deduce the fact that, in our theory, if we select a chain running down from the highest concept through a succession of lower-order concepts, then that chain can be studied without reference to any other concepts. For example, the subsystem war, war in Indochina, and war in Vietnam can be studied in isolation. More generally, suppose that X, Y, and Z are concepts such that X contains Y and Y contains Z. Let x, y, and z be the attitudes associated with concepts X, Y, and Z. Top down models can then be represented by the following set of functional relations among the variables:

$$\text{change in } x = \Delta x = f_1(x, M_x)$$

$$\text{change in } y = \Delta y = f_2(y, M_y, x) \qquad (14.1)$$

$$\text{change in } z = \Delta z = f_3(z, M_z, y),$$

where M_x, M_y, and M_z are messages sent about X, Y, and Z, respectively, and f_1, f_2, and f_3 are functions associated with changes in the three attitude.

The change functions can be derived from almost any attitude change theory. This chapter derives the change functions from information processing theory. Chapter 17 will discuss other theories.

Information processing theory assumes that there are two messages that elicit two comparison processes. If there is an external message, then the receiver compares his beliefs with those expressed in the external message. However, there is also an internal message that relates the concept to its immediately superordinate concept. The value of the internal message is equal (on the average) to the attitude toward the superordinate concept. Thus the receiver also compares his current belief with that expressed in the internal message about the immediately superordinate concept. Thus there are two comparisons and two discrepancies possible: a discrepancy between the current attitude and an external message (if any) and a discrepancy between the current attitude and the immediate superordinate attitude. A model with messages present at all three levels is

$$\Delta x = \alpha(M_x - x)$$

$$\Delta y = \alpha(M_y - y) + \beta(x - y) \qquad (14.2)$$

$$\Delta z = \alpha(M_z - z) + \gamma(y - z)$$

where $0 < \alpha, \beta, \gamma < 1$. If there is no external messages about, say, Y, then the entire term $\alpha(M_y - y)$ will be dropped from the equation for Δy. The relative sizes of α, β, and γ reflect the relative impact of external messages, messages from the top, and messages from the second level, respectively. We can see no reason why the internal message parameters β and γ will be different, though we leave open that possibility.

These equations make three other implicit assumptions. First of all they assume that the person perceives the link as definite. If the person regards a link as only tentative, then presumably the corresponding influence of superordinate on subordinate will be proportionately reduced. That is, if a link is only tentative, then a term such as $\beta(x - y)$ will be replaced by $p\beta(x - y)$, where p is the subjective probability of that link (i.e., $0 \leq p \leq 1$).

The other implicit assumption is that change is a linear function of discrepancy. Reviews such as Whittaker's (1967) indeed find this to be true under all but extreme conditions. As we note, non-linearities for extreme discrepancies do not affect the main predictions of the model.

The third implicit assumption is that the sources always have the same credibility. Again this is a convenience for explication rather than a substantive requirement of the model.

Although the model is stated in terms of the effect of a single message, the applications that are of primary concern in this chapter are those that involve a long succession of messages. Therefore, the next several sections are concerned with the ultimate effect of a succession of messages which all have the same message value. In each case that follows, the model predicts that all the attitudes converge to some asymptotic value. That asymptote is called the "equilibrium value" for the attitude in question.

ASYMPTOTIC VALUES IN SPECIAL CASES

Case 1. Messages Sent to X Only

Assume that a receiver is given a series of messages at the highest level, that is, messages about X. Messages M_x are also assumed to be a set of messages aimed at X and having the same value, that is, we assume that, although the sender may not be giving identical messages each time, the positive or negative message value will always be the same. By assumption, there will be no terms for external messages about Y or Z. Thus the general model reduces to

$$\Delta x = \alpha(M_x - x)$$
$$\Delta y = \beta(x - y) \tag{14.3}$$
$$\Delta z = \gamma(y - z)$$

An analysis is performed to predict the final resting state of the system after an extremely large number of messages have been sent. Where is the system of attitudes going? In this system the set of attitudes reaches a point of equilibrium where the system will not change. From the mathematical point of view, no change implies that the left side of the equation equals zero. Thus

$$0 = \alpha(M_x - x) \qquad \text{or} \qquad x = M_x$$

$$0 = \beta(x - y) \qquad \text{or} \qquad y = x \qquad (14.4)$$

$$0 = \gamma(y - z) \qquad \text{or} \qquad z = y$$

Solving separately for x, y, and z, we find that in this situation the receiver's feeling about concept X ultimately equals M_x, his attitude about Y equals x, and finally his feelings about Z have the same value as y. Thus y and z also converge to the same value M_x. Eventually the whole system is tuned to the value of the message that was sent and we see that one can control the entire system by giving input at the most abstract level.

The model can also be used to predict the step-by-step time path of the attitudes. A computer program to generate predictive curves for various parameter values was written (Levine *et al.* 1972) and one example is shown in Fig. 14.3. This figure represents a situation in which x, y, and z start together at

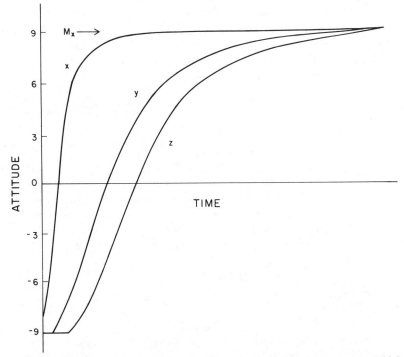

Fig. 14.3.   Predicted change in attitude over time when receivers are given messages a highest level only and α, β, and γ equal .5, .2, and .4, respectively. The initial values of x, y, and z were -9, -9, and -9.

-9, $\alpha = .5$, $\beta = .2$, and $\gamma = .4$, and a succession of messages about X is received by the subject. All messages are assumed to have the value $+9$. We see that, even when the receiver starts with very negative feelings about X, Y, and Z, messages sent at the highest level quickly reverse his feelings toward the three objects in question. Ultimately, all three curves move toward M_x.

One interesting property of this case is that the stable equilibrium point of the system is independent of the initial values of x, y, and z. This will not be true of cases where messages are directed at lower levels of the hierarchy.

Case 2. Messages Sent to Y Only

If the only external messages are directed at Y, then our model simplifies to

$$\Delta x = 0$$
$$\Delta y = \alpha(M_y - y) + \beta(x - y) \qquad (14.5)$$
$$\Delta z = \gamma(y - z)$$

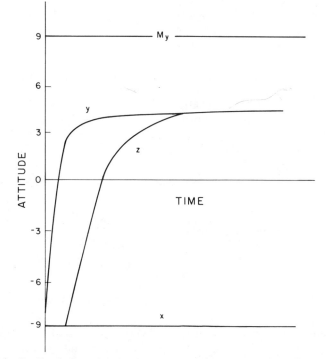

Fig. 14.4. Predicted change in attitudes over time when receivers are given messages at the intermediate level only.

If these are set equal to zero, then the equilibrium values are

$$x = x_0$$

$$y = \frac{\alpha M_y + \beta x}{\alpha + \beta} = \frac{\alpha M_y + \beta x_0}{\alpha + \beta} \tag{14.6}$$

$$z = y = \frac{\alpha M_y + \beta x_0}{\alpha + \beta}$$

Figure 14.4 shows a case where x, y, and z start together at -9 and $M_y = +9$. These equilibrium values show several interesting features. First, the value of x never changes from $x = x_0$, that is, the concept X is never affected by the messages directed at Y. Second, we note that the equilibrium value of y is a weighted average of x_0 and M_y. Thus, no matter how many messages about Y the person receives, his attitude will never reach the value of M_y. Because M_y is the value that is predicted for an isolated attitude by discrepancy theory, an unwary investigator might interpret this lack of change as supporting another theory. Finally, we note that the equilibrium value for z is the equilibrium value of y. This again represents the fact that if there are no external messages directed at a lower level attitude, then eventually the lower-order attitudes come to be consistent with the higher-order attitudes.

Case 3. No External Messages, Internal Messages Only

Even if no external messages are given at all, our model predicts that attitudes will change in directions determined by higher-order concepts. In particular, our model becomes

$$\Delta x = 0$$

$$\Delta y = \beta(x - y) \tag{14.7}$$

$$\Delta z = \gamma(y - z)$$

where the equilibrium values are

$$x = x_0$$

$$y = x = x_0 \tag{14.8}$$

$$z = y = x_0$$

Thus, given no external messages to "interfere" with internal processing, a receiver's attitudes all become the same as his attitude toward the most abstract concept. This is a quantitative version of perfect logical consistency in the long run.

THE GENERAL RESULTS OF THE EQUILIBRIUM ANALYSIS

Because each of the three messages M_x, M_y, and M_z may or may not be given, there are eight possible input conditions for this model. The equilibrium values for each of the eight conditions are shown in Table 14.1. In the first four conditions there are no messages directed at the top concept X and the top attitude never changes x_0. In the last four conditions there is a steady stream of messages directed to the top, all of which have the value M_x. The resulting equilibrium value for x is the message value M_x. These results reflect the fact that the top attitude is never affected by any of the lower attitudes.

Conditions 1, 2, 5, and 6 have no messages directed at Y, and in each case the equilibrium value of y is the same as the equilibrium value for x, that is, if there is no message directed at Y, then y adjusts to the value of x. In conditions 3, 4, 7, and 8, a stream of messages with value M_y is directed at Y, and in each case the equilibrium value of y is a weighted average of the message value M_y and the equilibrium value of x. Thus direct external messages about Y "interfere" with the tendency of the system to develop perfect top down consistency.

Conditions 1, 3, 5, and 7 have no messages directed at Z and in each case the equilibrium value of z is the same as the equilibrium value of y. That is, if there are no external messages directly concerning Z, then z becomes consistent with y. In conditions 2, 4, 6, and 8 there is a stream of messages with value M_z directly concerned with Z. In each case the equilibrium value of z is a weighted average of the message value M_z and the equilibrium value of y. Thus again a stream of direct messages about a lower-order concept "interferes" with the tendency of the system to develop perfect top down consistency.

TABLE 14.1

Final Values of x, y, and z under Eight Special Cases of External Input

Condition	Equilibrium values[a]		
	x_∞	y_∞	z_∞
1 No messages	x_0	x_0	x_0
2 M_z only	x_0	x_0	$rM_z + sx_0$
3 M_y only	x_0	$pM_y + qx_0$	y_∞
4 M_y, M_z	x_0	$pM_y + qx_0$	$rM_z + sy_\infty$
5 M_x only	M_x	M_x	M_x
6 M_x, M_z	M_x	M_x	$rM_z + sM_x$
7 M_x, M_y	M_x	$pM_y + qM_x$	y_∞
8 M_x, M_y, M_z	M_x	$pM_y + qM_x$	$rM_z + sy_\infty$

[a] $p = (1 - q) = \alpha/(\alpha + \beta)$ and $r = (1 - s) = \alpha/(\alpha + \gamma)$.

A TWO-PHASE MODEL OF EXTERNAL
MESSAGE EFFECTS

The double comparison model presented previously assumes that all the effects of an external message occur simultaneously. Later research suggests that this is not true. The research presented in the next chapter shows that the effects of an external message occur in two phases. In the first phase the receiver is so dominated by the external message that only the change due to the external message takes place. However, immediately following the reception of the external message, there is an internal message phase during which attitudes affect one another.

For example, if a message were directed at the attitude toward the concept at the second level (i.e., Case 2), then the change equations for phase one would be

$$\Delta x = 0$$
$$\Delta y = \alpha(M_y - y) \qquad (14.9)$$
$$\Delta z = 0$$

and the change equations for phase two would be

$$\Delta x = 0$$
$$\Delta y = \beta(x - y) \qquad (14.10)$$
$$\Delta z = \beta(y - z)$$

Furthermore, during the pretest–posttest interval, there may be more than one internal change cycle.

The compound change equations for both phases differ only slightly from the simultaneous change equations presented previously. The slight difference can be detected in a careful experiment, as is shown in Chapter 15. However, the difference is not important in the large scale. In particular, the remainder of this chapter is written with the simultaneous equations in mind. However, the discussion holds equally well for the two-phase model.

THE DYNAMICS OF ATTITUDE CHANGE

We have presented an equilibrium analysis of the stability of attitudes in time and represented efforts to predict terminal behavior under a variety of input conditions. This analysis shows the terminal values of attitudes, but it does not say anything about how they got there or how fast attitudes move. We saw in Figs. 14.3 and 14.4 some examples of the dynamics of attitude change in this multivariate model under specific parameter values. We note from these curves that the higher levels can affect lower-level attitudes, but it takes time to have that effect. As a matter of fact, it takes x one time unit to affect y, two time units to affect z, and so on. The farther away any two levels are from each other, the longer the lag will be.

How long is this time "unit"? It is the length of time between messages. That is, the primary agent for change is a message about one of the concepts; the other effects are the secondary results of the activity produced by the message. This means that the time required for indirect effects will be much shorter for concepts embedded in a frequently referenced hierarchy than for concepts that are rarely considered.

The dynamics of the model can be obtained by converting Eqs. (14.2) to predictive equations. This is a translation of the basic model from emphasizing change to finding the values of x, y, and z on the next trial or time period from knowing what happened during the present time period.

Probe Messages and Simply Thinking

The statement that the time unit is the time between messages is deliberately ambiguous because the concept of "message" differs between theories. All the theorists considered in this book agree that there will be no attitude change unless there is some active process or thought about the concept in question. The untested convention in the field is that there will be no change unless there is an external message. For classical reinforcement theory, there will be no change unless there is an external persuasive message. The information processing model developed here assumes that change can be produced by either external or internal messages.

Consider a probe message such as "What do you think about the invasion of Lebanon?" Change produced by this probe message would be governed by the equations of Case 3, the case of no external message. The assumption is that the probe message sets off the same internal messages that would be produced by a persuasive message.

Probe messages need not be external. Consider the subject of an experiment who is lying in bed reviewing the events of the day. Thinking about the experiment seems likely to be equivalent to an internal probe message. Thus the equations for no external message can be assumed to apply to any time when the person thinks about any concept in the hierarchy.

LONG-LASTING EFFECTS OF ATTITUDE CHANGE

A particularly important problem in theoretical and applied research on attitude change deals with the stability of attitude change. In many cases it is relatively easy to change attitudes in an experimental setting only to have them return to the original values once the initial experiment is terminated. Oddly enough very little research has been done on this topic, perhaps because the results of the studies have been rather complex. In their review of early work,

Hovland *et al.* (1953) cite study after study in which attitude change decayed over time. They interpret this largely as a "retention" loss analogous to decay over time in verbal learning. On the other hand, they also cite the work on sleeper effects by Hovland and Weiss (1951) and many others that shows a considerably greater complexity in the retention of attitude change than in simple list learning. This has been further borne out by the interaction of primary–recency with retention studied by Miller and Campbell (1959) and Insko (1964). Moreover, Watts and McGuire (1964) note that decay is not a universal finding. They cite studies by Annis and Meier (1934) and Smith (1943) in which there was no decay over very long periods of time. Furthermore, they cite several studies using complex materials or indirect methods in which the attitude change only appears after a lapse of time [Cohen (1957), McGuire (1960b), Scotland *et al.* (1959)].

How can one explain "decay" in attitude change? The most common agent for producing "decay" is postexperimental messages. Thus, in their classic studies of political behavior, Lazarsfeld *et al.* (1948) and Katz and Lazarsfeld (1955) note that back-sliding is largely a function of returning to a reference group that will provide counterarguments. Newcomb's longitudinal study of attitude change (1961) also finds that attitudes toward politics, for example, remain relatively constant when subjects remain in the same reference group. Because external messages are involved, these results are easily predicted by the present model.

There have also been some ingenious hypotheses about self-administered post-experimental messages. For example, Festinger (1957) postulates that people will seek out and, if necessary, invent messages to fit their emotional feelings. However, Sears (1968) finds the empirical evidence to be equivocal. Another example is part of McGuire's (1964) "inoculation theory." He hypothesizes that when subjects are threatened with an attacking message, they will gather supporting arguments in preparation. However, Freedman (1968) says he has data to show that they do not.

In any case, postexperimental messages seem an unlikely candidate for explaining the decay found by Miller and Campbell (1959) or Insko (1964) because the stimulus materials in both studies are trial transcripts. However, the abstract "retention" curves implicitly or explicitly in use by both authors to explain their findings beg the issue by being circular, as is true of the concept of "retention loss" used by Hovland *et al.* (1953).

A more promising hypothesis is proposed by Watts and McGuire (1964). They argue that for certain aspects of attitude change, the initial learning of the message not only supports the original change but is necessary to maintain that change. They define such aspects as being subject to "functional dependence." They then proceed to argue that some aspects of attitude change will achieve "functional autonomy" (Allport, 1937) and will not be subject to retention losses. The hypothesis is sharpened by Hunter and Cohen (1972) who argue that it is not the aspects of attitude change that are dependent or autonomous but the attitudes themselves. In trial studies, syllogism studies, and most other studies that use true–false as the dependent measure, Hunter and Cohen (1972) note that the subject does not report an immediately felt attitude; instead he constructs his response on the basis of what he recovers from his memory of prior messages, what he concludes from other beliefs, and so on. They postulate that "retention" losses will not occur for attitudes that have an independent existence (e.g., racial prejudice, attitudes toward the war in Vietnam).

Consider an example. Your friend asks you "What do you think about Emily Dank?" You respond "Who's that?" He says "The woman running for the city council on the temperance ticket." You respond "She's an old witch." The next day another friend asks "What do you think about Emily Dank?" You respond "Who's that?" Has your attitude decreased from high negative to neutral? The attitude you express has decreased, but this does not reflect a decrease in an internal variable. Your initial "attitude" toward Emily Dank was instantaneously created by the question and statement of your friend and vanished immediately thereafter. That is, your attitude toward Emily Dank is solely a creature of the sentence describing her which may or may not be retained at any given instant of time. On the other hand, your attitude toward temperance workers is an immediately felt response of long standing, that is, an attitude that exists in its own right. It is this second kind of attitude that is "functionally autonomous."

A related view is expressed by Converse (1964, 1970) in relation to attitude change data obtained in election panel studies. Converse (1970) finds that his data fit a model in which some subjects "have no attitude" and respond randomly whereas the other subjects show little or no change over 4 years. Converse (1964) also compares the level of correlation between attitudes for congressional candidates and the general public. For the congressional candidates the domestic issues correlate .53 whereas for the masses the correlation drop to .23. He interprets this in terms of the large number among the general public who have no attitude. We interpret his finding that certain subjects "have no attitude" to mean that, for these subjects, these attitudes have no functional autonomy. However, we can explain the lower level of correlation in the general public in two ways.

1. in terms of the lack of functional autonomy or
2. by the assumption that less-educated people are more likely to "lack" the abstract superordinate concepts that produce the correlations among opinions. That is, for uneducated people the abstract concepts do not have functional autonomy and hence do not function as entities in the person's hierarchical nets.

The importance of the assumption of functional autonomy becomes evident if we consider the implications of existing univariate models of attitude change. For example, consider the univariate version of the information processing model:

$$\Delta z = \alpha(M_z - z) \qquad (14.11)$$

In the case where M_z is first given, we know that z will approach M_z in the limit. However, when the receiver leaves the experiment and obtains no new messages, we see that z will remian at M_z and never change unless a new value of M_z comes along. This univariate model predicts no decay under any conditions! Thus as Hunter and Cohen (1972) note, most univariate theories of attitude change implicitly assume that the attitude in question is autonomous. The same assumption is made in the present multivariate model.

Does the present model predict that autonomous attitudes will undergo no decay? That depends on whether the autonomous attitude is isolated or not. First, if any autonomous attitude is completely isolated from other attitudes (e.g., de novo concepts), then the present model reduces to univariate discrepancy theory and therefore predicts no decay. Second, because the present model assumes only downward causal influences, the most abstract concept in a hierarchy will act like an isolated attitude and will change only when external messages are directed at that concept.

Can the present model predict decay in an autonomous attitude? Consider Case 2: messages sent to Y only. A stream of messages directed at a second concept Y will produce change in the corresponding autonomous attitude y but not in the autonomous attitude toward the highest-order concept X. Thus the value of x remains x_0 throughout the "acquisition" phase of the experiment. When all external messages are cut off, the appropriate version of our model is Case 3: no external messages. That is, we predict that x will remain at x_0 and y will converge to x, that is, y will shift toward x_0. Thus our model predicts that attitude change in y will not stop when messages cease to arrive. Will the new change in y appear to the experimenter as a "decay" in the attitude change? That depends on the initial value of y. If the receiver's initial attitude toward y is consistent with his attitude toward X, then $y_0 = x_0$. Thus the original change in y is away from $y_0 = x_0$ and the subsequent change is back to $x_0 = y_0$, that is, decay. Because our model predicts that y will be consistent with x if there is no external interference, this model thus predicts decay for most people. However, it is theoretically possible that a situation exists where there is considerable discrepancy between the initial values of x and y. If the experimenter presents messages between these initial values, then the change toward x_0 after the experiment is actually in the same direction as the change toward M_y during the "acquisition" period.

Thus, under appropriate conditions, our model predicts that an autonomous attitude may show either stability or decay. Can it predict the third kind of finding cited by Watts and McGuire (1964), that is, can the model predict delayed attitude change? Consider the case of indirect argument: the experimenter seeks to change the receiver's attitude toward Y by presenting messages about X. During the acquisition phase, the receiver's attitude toward X will be immediatley affected. However, until x has undergone considerable change, little of this change will be passed on to y. On the other hand, the receiver's attitude toward X will not change when the messages cease. Instead, x will stay at the last value attained and will exert a pull on y until y changes to the same value as x. This is precisely the delayed attitude change reported for indirect messages.

A particularly clear cut example of this result is the study by Rokeach (1971a,b), in which he capitalizes on the inconsistencies in many receiver's attitudes toward freedom and equality to produce a feeling of selfishness in some of those people. As a result, the value they place on equality increased, while their attitudes toward civil rights remained unchanged. However, after 3 to 5 months, a strong positive shift in their attitudes toward civil rights was recorded, and this shift become still stronger after 15–17 months. During the same period there was only a negligible increase in their attitude toward equality. Because "equality for Negroes" is a subcategory of "equality," Rokeach's results are exactly what the model predicts. We note in passing that Rokeach's distinction between "value" and "attitude" seems essentially the same as what we are calling higher- and lower-order concepts.

The previous statements are all very reminiscent of McGuire's (1968a) statement that "the human information processing mills may grind exceedingly slowly, but ... they grind out their logically required results quite well." The striking resemblance bears out the contention of Chapter 3 that discrepancy theory is a quantitative analog of information processing theory. Indeed, if receivers' reactions to the syllogisms used by McGuire (1960a,b,c) could be regarded as autonomous attitudes, then, not only his results, but the work of Holt and Watts [Holt and Watts (1969), Holt (1970), Watts and Holt (1970)] can be claimed as evidence for the present model. They find that change in related beliefs is greater after a time delay.

INDIVIDUAL DIFFERENCES IN COGNITIVE STRUCTURE

There are two kinds of individual differences in this model: differences in structure and differences in parameter. Each has very different applications.

If we focus on a particular attitude, then the critical individual differences in structures are those that involve the potential existence or nonexistence of superordinate concepts for the object in question. For example, one person might classify "U.S. involvement in Vietnam" under "wars of liberation," whereas a second person might classify the same concept under "wars of subjugation." The present model will apply in either case and will make the common sense prediction: the first person's attitude will assimilate to a positive superordinate attitude and (barring external messages) become positive whereas the opposite is true of the second person.

The next most important question of individual differences for a particular attitude is whether or not the object under consideration is important to the individual. Consider a football fan who is indifferent to basketball. The concept "football" will not only occur as a subordinate to "sports" but as a subordinate to "high-priority entertainment items" and probably to "things I do with my friends" as well.

The more important the object, the greater the likelihood that the object is linked to a superordinate concept. If the object is linked to a superordinate concept, then that superordinate attitude will produce "interference" for any external message that the investigator may introduce. Thus, on the average, this model predicts that those people who are most involved with an object will show the least attitude change [Sherif and Hovland (1961), Sherif et al. (1965)].

This last observation has an implication that is very important for our model. If one curve is plotted relating attitude change to message–attitude discrepancy, then discrepancy and initial position are necessarily confounded. In particular, the large discrepancies involve subjects with extreme attitudes toward the object. The subjects with extreme attitudes usually feel more "intensely" about the issue (Cantril, 1946), that is, they view the object as more important (Sherif and Hovland, 1961). Thus, as we note above, they are more likely to have a superordinate attitude that reduces the amount of change in the observed attitude. That is, many of the observed nonlinearities in discrepancy curves may be artifacts produced by the failure of most experimenters to control for superordinate attitudes.

Let us turn next to the static correlational study of a set of related attitudes. What does this model predict for the factorial structure? The answer depends on three items. First, how many concepts stand superordinate to the entire set? If the great majority of subjects see trade unions and professional organizations as being two different things, then the factor structure of attitudes toward associations will have at least two such general factors. If the majority of people think instead in terms of rich unions and poor unions, then there would be only one general factor for the set with a weak group factor running through the powerful unions such as the American Medical Association, the New York electricians, and so on, and a second group factor for the less powerful unions such as the Memphis garbage men, the California grape pickers, and so on. The second critical question is the general "age" of the set of concepts. For most high school students, trade associations are concepts to which they have only been recently introduced, hence the structural connections have only been in operation for a short time. Thus each attitude will be largely a function of the particular messages about that organization that the subject has heard rather than his attitudes toward superordinate concepts. Except for the rare cases where all the messages about a set of objects have come from the same source, there is likely to be little correlation between the messages pertaining to different concepts. This "random element" in these messages will lower the correlations between that attitude and the others. In this case the model will predict a large unique factor for each concept. The third critical feature of the set for the present model is the person's involvement with the concepts in the set. If the concepts in question are important, then the person will frequently think of them spontaneously and the only influences on his attitudes will be internal ones. Thus the greater the involvement of the average person in the concepts in the set, the greater the overall strength of the common factors in the set (or subset).

If we consider a particular local portion of the person's belief structure, then the present model makes predictions that have been either implicitly or explicitly made by many cognitive theorists, for example, Lewin (1936), Kounin (1941), Rokeach (1960), Scott (1962, 1965), and McGuire (1968a). If a portion of the receivers's belief system is highly differentiated (i.e., many concepts with few links), then an external message will have a great impact on the concept that it describes but little or no effect on other attitudes. If a portion of the receiver's belief system is highly integrated (i.e., few concepts with many links), then the impact will be quite variable. If the message concerns one of the many subordinate concepts, then the external message will have only a small and transient impact. However, if the message is directed at the top of a hierarchy, then it will have an impact, and that impact will spread over time to all the subordinate attitudes.

In particular, then, this model predicts the findings of Scott (1962, 1963, 1965) in his study of attitudes toward nations. Scott uses a number of sorting tasks and questionnaires to assess "cognitive complexity" in this domain and this ultimately leads to definitions of several dimensions of complexity (Scott, 1966a). Of interest here is "dimensional complexity." This is essentially a count of the number of distinct hierarchies that an individual subject uses to classify the nations. Scott finds that high dimensional complexity of the belief structure is associated with a large number of factors in the attitude correlation matrix, that is, a low degree of intelligence or sophistication will be associated with a tendency toward either xenophobia or xenophilia (Scott, 1965). That is, people of low intelligence simply react to "foreigners."

Does this model predict global individual differences in cognitive structure? Early cognitive theorists follow Lewin's (1936) lead in equating such differences with intelligence. Thus Kounin (1941) seeks an extremely high degree of differentiation among the feeble minded, and Goldstein (1949) expects extremely concrete individuals to be brain damaged. Their reasoning is essentially that forming cognitive objects or concepts is a primitive function, whereas forming links appears later phylogenetically. Therefore, it should be easy for even young or unintelligent persons to form a great many cognitive objects. Thus there should be relatively small individual differences in the number of objects in a belief system, but large differences in the number of connections between them. However, later analyses such as that by Cattell and Winder (1952) noted that the flexibility of intelligence can arise from many things unrelated to the number of cognitive links. Thus later cognitive theorists who are familiar with the literature on intelligence such as Scott (1966b) are loathe to make such predictions.

Actually one might think that any model such as the present theory tends to make the opposite prediction to the theorists who view structure in terms of links between objects. After all, to maintain the same degree of connectedness among the objects in a mathematical graph, when the number of objects is doubled, the number of links must be quadrupled. Now consider a child who learns objects at one rate and links at another. If we measure the number of objects and links at age n and then at age $2n$, then both numbers will double. But because the number of links has only doubled instead of quadrupled, the degree of connectedness has decreased by half. This tendency is further exaggerated by the fact that connections between objects are frequently not formed directly but are generated by adding a new abstract concept to the old system. In similar fashion, if a more intelligent person learns objects and links twice as fast as an unintelligent person, then he will know twice as many of both at any given age. However (again), twice as many links means only one-half the degree of connectedness. Thus larger belief systems will be less well connected and more intelligent people will have less well integrated structures. Although this hypothesis reverses the sign of the correlation between differentiation and intelligence, it is still consistent with the notion that the dimension of "cognitive complexity" is the same as general intelligence.

Many writers confuse the issue by asserting that the good guys are both more highly differentiated and more highly integrated [Rokeach (1960), Harvey (1966)]. Thus it is not surprising that they seek a dimension of cognitive complexity that is distinct from general intelligence.

The empirical literature appears to bear out the writers who associate cognitive structure with intelligence. In Vannoy's (1965) factor analytic study, the only measure of cognitive complexity that show any generality are precisely the intelligence tests. The problems in the literature on "cognitive complexity" are strongly reminiscent of the great difficulty that people in differentiating a general factor of "creativity" from intelligence (McNemar, 1964).

Do local structures tend to become more integrated over time? McGuire's (1960, 1968a) wishful thinking principle predicts that likely events become linked to positive ones, that is, structures become more integrated. An even more extreme version of this hypothesis was tested by Phillips (1967). He notes that most indexes of degree of balance not only predict the growth of links between liked objects but between disliked objects as well. On the other hand, Abelson (1959) argues from balance theory and Kelman and Baron (1968) argue from dissonance theory that "inconsistencies" will frequently be resolved by compartmentalization or differentiation. Thus these theorists would predict a decrease in integration over time. There appears to be no longitudinal data available on the issue.

The present model explicitly assumes that belief structures exert a strong influence on attitudes, but it implicitly assumes that attitudes do not affect beliefs. Thus it is technically neutral toward the issue of increasing or decreasing integration. If no assumptions are added to the theory, then it tends to be compatible with what Abelson (1968a) calls a "minimalist" theory. But the theory is not logically incompatible with assumptions of belief ramification such as those presented by Weick (1968), that is, with additional assumptions this model can become a "maximalist" theory.

PERSUASIBILITY AND DOGMATISM

Three of the variables most often avoked in a discussion of individual differences in attitude change are persuasibility, dogmatism, and rigidity. In this section we propose to identify persuasibility with individual differences in the "external reactivity" parameter α and to identify dogmatism with individual differences in the "internal consistency" parameter β. After we show these to be operationally distinguishable, we note that if they are negatively correlated, then they reflect a general dimension of "attitudinal rigidity."

Persuasibility

Two people who have different belief structures will change differently in ways that were discussed above. Thus the amount of attitude change will be comparable only if structures are held constant. If two people with the same conceptual structure change by different amounts, then do they necessarily differ in persuasibility? Not in this model. First of all, this model is a discrepancy theory. Thus, if it holds, then receivers of the same persuasibility will show the same amount of attitude change only if they hold the same initial attitudes. If their initial attitudes differ, then the discrepancy differs and the elicited change will be different. Second, it depends on whether the object of the message has a superordinate concept or not. If the object is either isolated or at the top of a hierarchy, then the previous analysis will be sufficient. But if there are one or more superordinate concepts, then the observed change is influenced by the superordinate attitudes. The extent of that influence is assessed by the "internal message" parameters β, γ, and so on. Here we must consider three points. First, if the object is important to the person, then his spontaneous thinking has already brought his attitude toward the object equal to his superordinate attitude and hence its influence will be in direct opposition to that exerted by the message. If the object is not important, then there is likely to be some discrepancy and the influence of the superordinate concept may be in any direction. Thus individual differences in the internal parameters tend to act as differences in antipersuasibility or resistance. Although the effects of internal and external messages are generally opposed, they will not always be so. Thus the internal influence must be regarded as distinct from persuasibility.

Second, there is the question of time intervals between message and posttest. The model predicts that the immediate impact of the message is to produce a discrepancy between the object attitude and the superordinate attitude. The internal processes then act to reduce that discrepancy. Thus the observed strength of the internal processes will be greater if there is a delay between message and posttest, that is, the relative importance of individual differences in the internal parameters is greater in "follow-up" studies.

Third, we note that the internal process in this model is also a discrepancy theory. Thus, unless people are matched on superordinate attitude, the internal influence is not a direct measure of the parameter β.

To sum, there are two kinds of parameters in this model. There are the parameters that represent internal quasi-logical influences (β and γ) and a parameter α that represents the influence of the external message. If the message object has no superordinate, then differences in attitude change will be a function of differences in attitude–message discrepancy and the multiplicative parameter. If the message object has a superordinate concept, then differences in change will also depend on the superordinate attitude— message attitude discrepancy and on differences in the multiplicative parameter β.

If there are individual differences in α, then there must be consistent differences in attitude change that are independent of subject matter. Thus, if there are individual differences in the external parameter, then α will correspond to a general dimension of persuasibility [Janis and Field (1959), McGuire (1968b)]. That is, an α of zero represents the ultimate in "no sensitivity to evidence" or "strength of conviction," whereas an α of one represents a perfect state of "intellectual flexibility" or "total gullibility." The only direct evidence for such a variable continues to be the classic study by Janis and Field (1959). They find a weak general factor in a correlation matrix for the change produced by both pro and con messages on a very heterogeneous set of topics. On the other hand, the large correlations are within (crude) content areas and may thus reflect the impact of higher-order concepts rather than persuasibility per se.

Is there indirect evidence for a general persuasibility factor? If persons of low self-esteem are found to show greater attitude change in situations of both self-relevant and non-self-relevant content, then this will be indirect evidence for two propositions, that is, that there be a general factor of persuasibility and that persuasibility be negatively correlated with self-esteem. Indeed, this hypothesis is proposed in steadily more and more complicated forms by Janis and Hovland (1959), Hovland and Rosenberg (1960), and McGuire (1968b, c). The increasing complication reflects the fact that various studies find all degrees of correlation between self-esteem and attitude change (McGuire, 1968b, p. 1159). Furthermore, three major reviews in this area find similar results for other personality variables [Glass (1968a), McGuire (1968b), Steiner (1966)]. Thus there is enough positive evidence to support optimism in the hope of explaining the negative evidence in terms of interactions with various situational determinants (McGuire, 1968b, c) or in the hope that as yet untried variables such as defensiveness (Glass, 1968b) or Machiavellianism [Epstein (1966), Steiner (1968)] will suffice. On the other hand, there is also sufficient evidence to sustain Abelson's (1968b) pessimism.

In contrast to poor results relating personality variables to persuasibility, there are strong and consistent findings in the related area of conformity. In these studies, the subject is not confronted with a persuasive message but with an indication that some individual or reference group holds a different position. Strong evidence for a general factor in this domain is summarized by Cohen (1959) and Steiner (1966). Furthermore, consistent evidence has been gathered showing conformity to be related to low self-esteem [Cohen (1959), Marlowe and Gergen (1969)], need for approval [Crowne and Marlowe (1964), Marlowe and Gergen (1969)], and authoritarianism [Wright and Harvey (1965), Steiner (1966)]. The critical question is this: How much of the observed conformity is attitude change and how much is merely overt compliance? Steiner and Vannoy (1964) find that the correlation between the receiver's conformity score after a session with a confederate and his subsequent private "conformity" score is only .16. Yet the reliability of each score is high (.68–.82) and the measures related to the receiver's evaluation of the confederate correlate from .51 to .74 over time. Thus their study strongly suggests that the substantial evidence for the generality of confirmity is not evidence for the generality of persuasibility.

Actually, the weakness of the literature on persuasibility suggests that there are no appreciable individual differences in the "external" parameter α. However, most of the studies are run on the cognitively homogeneous population of college students.

Dogmatism

The other parameters of this model are the "internal" parameters, β, γ, and so on. Because we see no reason to assume that these parameters are not all equal, we shall assume that they are equal and shall hereafter refer to "the" internal parameter. If there are individual differences in the internal parameter, then they correspond to a dimension of internal "cohesiveness" or "differentiation."

If $\beta = \gamma = 0$, then we have a state in which superordinate attitudes have no influence on subordinate attitudes. For such a subject, if external messages are not correlated, then all attitudes will be unrelated to one another or "completely differentiated." Formerly such a person would have been termed "simple minded." If $\beta = \gamma = 1$, then all lower-order atttudes are instantly assimilated to higher-order concepts. This sort of total consistency is described by industrial workers as "ivory tower" or "theoretical." And indeed this dimension appears to be related to the "abstract–concrete" continuum defined by Goldstein (1947).

Actually, it is our tentative position that the internal parameter β is (or is highly correlated with) dogmatism. We do this in response to Rokeach's (1960) identification of dogmatism with intolerance of ambiguity and the need for consistency. Thus it is our contention that a dogmatist is characterized by his tendency to assimilate his concrete attitudes to his abstract attitudes. This is also consistent with Harvey's (1966, 1967) findings that his "higher" system three and four people are characterized by low dogmatism scores.

Readers who are accustomed to interpreting dogmatism as rigidity and hence low persuasiveness may find our contention puzzling. Actually, Rokeach (1960) never identifies dogmatism with a concept of total rigidity. For example, Kemp (1960) predicts that, on issues that are consistent with his other beliefs, the dogmatist should change *more* than the nondogmatist. This is tested by looking at long term change (6 years) in the Allport–Vernon scale of values for 104 students at a religious college. Dogmatists show the largest increase on "religious" and the largest decrease on "social," while showing the least decrease in "economic" (none). They are also the only group to show no increase on "theoretical." Several other examples of cases where dogmatists are predicted to show greater change are found in the review by Miller and Rokeach (1968).

Indeed, this model shows a complex relation between differences in the internal parameter and differences in attitude change. First, if the message object has no superordinate, then differences in change are solely a function of message–attitude discrepancy and persuasibility. In principle, then, it would be possible for a total dogmatist ($\beta = 1$) to be completely persuaded by an external message if the message is directed to the top of one of his hierarchies and if his persuasibility is maximal ($\alpha = 1$). Thus even an extreme dogmatist may appear quite flexible if the right topic is discussed.

Now we consider the case in which the message object has exactly one superordinate concept. Let two people be matched in their attitudes toward both objects and matched for persuasibility. Then there are two cases. If there is a discrepancy between the superordinate and subordinate attitudes and if the superordinate attitude is in the same relative direction as the message, then the person with the larger internal parameter will change most. Thus a message that brings out a discrepancy in the dogmatist's attitudes will produce considerable "pressure toward consistency."

If there is no superordinate–subordinate attitude discrepancy, then the initial impact of the message will be independent of the size of the internal parameter. However, the message thus produces a superordinate–subordinate discrepancy that is exactly equal in size and opposite in direction to the change elicited by the message. Subsequent thought will then cause the reduction of the message impact in proportion to the size of the internal parameter. Thus a message directed toward an already consistent section of a dogmatist's attitude structure meets great resistance or rigidity.

Consider now two people who impose the same hierarchical structure on a set of objects. Assume that the set of objects is equally important (or unimportant) to both people, so that they seek (or are subjected to) the same number of external messages about the set and, above all, so that they spontaneously think about the set equally often. Our model predicts that the attitudes of both people converge to the value of the attitude toward the object at the top of the hierarchy, but not at the same rate. The larger the internal parameter, the more rapid the assimilation of lower-order attitudes to their superordinates. Indeed, if there are no external messages, then the percentage decrease in the variance of the receiver's attitudes will be approximately equal to 2β [actually $(1 + \beta)^2 - 1$], if β is not small. Thus, if both receivers begin a time period with equally heterogeneous attitudes, then at the end of that period the dogmatist will be the more homogeneous of the two. Thus a dogmatist tends to feel the same way about all the objects in a given set, that is, "sees things in black and white." Tentative support for this is found in studies by Newcomb (1963), Steiner and Johnson (1963), and Foulkes and Foulkes (1965).

ESTIMATION OF PARAMETERS

Finally, we discuss the measurement of the internal and external parameters for individual receivers. We first consider the persuasibility parameter. One strategy is a slight modification of that used by Janis and Field (1959). Construct a set of objects of heterogeneous content to two criteria. First, as close as possible, choose objects that are either isolated from other concepts or are at the top of their hierarchies. Second, and above all, see that the objects do not have common superordinates. Now construct and scale persuasive messages about each object. In fact, if time permits a sequential study, there are enormous advantages in following the lead of Janis and Field (1959) by constructing both a pro and con message for each object. If there are no superordinates and if there is no unreliability, then each attitude x_i will satisfy the equation

$$\Delta x_i = \alpha(\mu_i - x_i) = \alpha d_i \qquad (14.12)$$

where μ_i is the message value and d_i the signed discrepancy. In principle, one can now calculate α by dividing Δx_i by d_i. In fact, this estimate is very unstable in the face of error, and the following regression technique is much more stable. According to discrepancy theory, if change is plotted against discrepancy for each receiver, then the regression will be a line through the origin with slope α. This slope can be estimated by the ordinary least squares formula in which central moments are not subtracted:

$$\alpha = \sum \Delta x_i d_i / \sum d_i^2 \qquad (14.13)$$

If some of the concepts do have relevant superordinate concepts, then there will be corresponding deviations in the amount of observed change that will act as "errors" about the regression line. Should these errors be independent of one another, the slope is not affected in size; the estimate simply becomes a probabilistic estimate of persuasibility (i.e., it is a less than perfectly reliable measure). Thus the application of this formula for *estimating* persuasibility does not require the complete absence of relevant superordinate concepts, but it does require that the objects studied not have a common superordinate.

This formula for persuasibility can be related to *alternative* recommended procedures only if very stringent experimental conditions are met. If the pretest attitudes have only a slight variance across receivers, if the message values are all so extreme as to be outside the range of pretest attitudes, and if the attitudes are all scored in the direction of positive message discrepancy, then the previous formula reduces to

$$\alpha \approx \text{constant} \cdot \sum \Delta x_i \qquad (14.14)$$

That is, under these conditions persuasibility is approximately proportional to mean change or (even less accurately) to the measure used by Janis and Field (1959), the number of changes in the advocated direction.

The internal parameter can also be measured by an attitude change experiment. First, select a heterogeneous set of objects that, as nearly as possible, have exactly one superordinate each. After a pretest measurement of each pair of attitudes, say, x_i and y_i, ask the receiver to write a paragraph on the relation between the pair of concepts. If x is the superordinate attitude, then our model predicts that the change in the subordinate attitude will be

$$\Delta y_i = \beta(x_i - y_i) = \beta d_i \tag{14.15}$$

where d_i is the signed discrepancy between superordinate and subordinate attitudes. Thus, again, the model predicts a linear regression of change on "discrepancy" and β is estimated from the regression formula

$$\beta = \sum \Delta y_i d_i / \sum d_i^2 \tag{14.16}$$

Roughly speaking, this means that β is the amount of attitude change when there is no external message.

If both of the preceding experiments are carried out on the same receivers, then it will be possible to

1. test the model and
2. if the model holds, obtain independent estimates of α and β for each individual. These are then correlated with each other or with other variables. If β is in fact a measure of dogmatism, then a negative correlation between α and β will reflect a general factor of "attitudinal rigidity." However, the evidence gathered by Scott (1966b) suggests that this correlation may well be zero.

We note in passing that it is possible in principle to estimate α and β simultaneously by presenting external messages in the situation described for assessing dogmatism. The parameters are given by applying a modified version of multiple regression to the equation

$$\Delta y = \alpha(\mu_i - y_i) + \beta(x_i - y_i) \tag{14.17}$$

However, this is multiple regression within each receiver and requires extremely high reliability and an extremely apt choice of objects. Furthermore, the probable correlation between the two discrepancies $\mu_i - y_i$ and $x_i - y_i$ greatly complicates testing the model.

ADDITIONAL OBSERVATIONS

An Operational Definition of the Highest Level

In making predictions from our model, the specification of the level of a given attitude is critical. For example, the prediction of decay or stability depends on whether or not the attitude in question is at the top of a hierarchy. Thus, in this model, the problem of finding the highest level relevant for the situation is critical. From the stability analysis we see that we can tell immediately if X is at the top of the line by giving repeated messages about X. If eventually x equals M_x, then we know that X is at the most abstract level. If x asymptotes at some value other than M_x, then there must be a higher level concept that is "interfering" with the external messages. A second test is provided by "retention" data. If X is at the top of the hierarchy, then changing the value of x will lead to a permanent change in the person. That is, attitudes toward X change according to the value of the message and stay there even after external input ceases.

Stochastic Models

When the hierarchical model is tested empirically, then the model must be made stochastic to account for individual differences in parameters and relevant experience outside the lab that is not observed or measured by the experimenter. This stochastic conversion is described in the next chapter.

The stochastic model also provides for an additional test as to whether the top of the hierarchy observed is indeed the top concept or whether the observed hierarchy is embedded in a larger hierarchy. This test is described in the next chapter. In a nutshell, the true top attitude will be a first order autoregressive process. If, instead, the observed top concept is subordinate to an unobserved higher-order concept Q, then the correlations will not satisfy a first-order equation because later attitudes will be influenced by Q as well as by their immediately preceding value.

Subjective Probability

At the point where the model equations are introduced, it is claimed that the general conclusions do not depend on the assumption that subjective probabilities are either zero or one. We now make that point more precisely. The predictions discussed above are based on the equilibrium predictions of the model. The key to these predictions is that the equilibrium value for an attitude is a weighted average of the value of the messages directed toward that attitude (if any) and the equilibrium value of the superordinate attitude (if any). This key fact is still true if all the links are weakened by subjective probabilities. The weakening of the internal link means that the equilibrium value for an attitude is comparatively closer to the message directed toward that concept (if any) than to the superordinate attitude, but it is still between them. This leaves the qualitative predictions unchanged.

Nonlinear Discrepancy Curves

A similar argument applies to the alteration of the model to handle reduced attitude change for large discrepancies, that is, messages that lie in the "latitude of rejection" [Sherif and Hovland, (1961), Sherif, Sherif and Nebergall (1965)]. As long as there is no boomerang, the equilibrium values are only different in degree rather than kind. For example, if an attitude is extremely discrepant from a superordinate attitude, then it has an equilibrium value in which the relative weight of the superordinate concept is reduced from that predicted by the linear model. But the equilibrium value is still a weighted average of superordinate attitudes and message value (if any) and hence the qualitative predictions of the model still hold. Similar statements apply to messages that are extremely discrepant.

Should a situation ever be found in which there is boomerang or total message rejection, then the present model would be qualitatively wrong.

A Longitudinal and Experimental Test of the Hierarchical Model of Attitude Change[†]

Contributed by M. Scott Poole and John E. Hunter

OVERVIEW

The purpose of this study was to test empirically the hierarchical model developed in Chapter 14. There are two traditional ways to test a model: introduce an intervention and see if the means change in the predicted manner or study the pattern of individual differences and see if correlations follow the predicted pattern. Both methods were used in this study. The design used was pretest–pretest–message–posttest–posttest. The mean change produced by the message could be tested against the model, especially that part of the model dealing with the impact of an external message. The correlational predictions could be studied using a four-wave longitudinal analysis. However, to carry out our analysis of the data, we were forced to make major

---

[†] This chapter is an edited version of "Change in hierarchical systems of attitudes," by M. S., Poole, and J. E., Hunter, in *Communication Yearbook III*, D. Nimmo (Ed.), New Brunswick, New Jersey: Transaction Press, 1979.

innovations in both methodology and theory. These innovations make up a large portion of this chapter.

To test experimentally the top down hypothesis, we used two message groups. One group received a message designed to change the attitude at the top of the hierarchy and the second group received a message aimed at one of the four concepts at the bottom of the hierarchy. According to the top down influence hypothesis, the message at the bottom should have an impact only on the attitude toward the concept considered in the message, and even that impact should decay during the interval from immediate posttest to followup posttest. On the other hand, change introduced at the top of the hierarchy should spread down to all attitudes. The change at the top should not decay at the followup posttest and change should increase for subordinate attitudes.

Complications arose in both analyses. For our sample sizes (76 and 54), the longitudinal path analysis broke down for both ordinary least squares analysis and full information maximum likelihood estimation. We have seven variables across four time periods which produced a 28 × 28 correlation matrix. Multiple regression with seven highly correlated predictors gave dramatically unstable results, so we devised a straightforward method of estimating the internal change parameter β by averaging a large number of multiple regression analyses that we could test for homogeneity. However, though the causal parameters could be estimated with high precision, we were faced with massive sampling error in the correlations between exogenous variables. In a longitudinal model, all the time 1 variables are exogenous variables. In our case this meant that there were 21 correlations between exogenous variables. The sampling error from these correlations builds up cumulatively as the model projects over time. So we devised a new method to estimate the exogenous correlations in a dynamic path model. This method appears to be applicable to all dynamic path models because it makes no use of the special properties of the hierarchical model.

The analysis of mean change also turned up some problems. First, the top attitude did not satisfy the operational definition of the top of a hierarchy, that is, change decayed from immediate to followup posttest. So we devised a correlational test to detect the presence of an unmeasured concept Q that is superordinate to the top of the observed hierarchy. This test also showed the observed hierarchy to be embedded in a larger hierarchy.

Furthermore, there were problems with the original model of the impact of the external message. Even when we corrected the equations to take into account the impact of an unmeasured superordinate concept Q, there were small but significant errors of fit. We then invented several alternative models of message impact. The model that showed best fit overall assumes that the impact of the external message occurs in two phases rather than one. That is we originally believed that the external message would simultaneously affect the attitude toward which the message was directed in accordance with linear discrepancy theory and affect all other attitudes in accordance with the internal change equations (i.e., each attitude would be changed in the direction of the attitude to which it is subordinate). Our data suggest that these changes take place in two phases. In the first phase, the message impacts on only that attitude that is the subject of the message. In the second phase, the internal change process modifies that attitude and all others. The difference between the simultaneous model and the two-phase model were small but detectable in our data.

Finally, to test the model against data, one must transform the deterministic model of Chapter 14 into an appropriate stochastic model. Consideration of the sources of random error showed that this is not just a matter of adding an error term. We show that consideration of outside influences adds a constant term to the regression equation as well as disturbance term and lowers the parameter for initial attitude. Furthermore, correlations must be corrected for attenuation before the stochastic model will work (a fact that is true of all path models).

INTRODUCTION

Theories of attitude change and memory have long and parallel histories. Thus it is not surprising that during a decade in which theories of memory are dominated by hierarchical structure based on the class inclusion principle [Wood (1972), Shevell and Atkinson (1974)], there should appear a new theory of attitude organization that is based on the same hierarchical principles. Chapter 14 reviews the literature on attitude change, retention, and decay and asserts that most of the existing literature on attitude organization could be fit to a simple model in which the influence between attitudes is confined to causal paths along the lines of concepts organized into logical hierarchies.

Figure 15.1 shows a hierarchy of concepts. The concept at the top of the hierarchy logically includes those at the second level of the hierarchy, these logically include those at the third level, and so on. The impact of logical implication follows the same lines: If federal bureaucracies are efficient, then so are regulatory commissions. If the Justice Department is corrupt, then so is the Bureau of Prisons. However, in contrast to this down-the-hierarchy path of logical influence, there is no such up-the-hierarchy mode of inference and there are no sideways influences.

Does psychological causality follow logical influence? Chapter 14 cites many studies showing downward influence and some studies that consider nonlogical processes like the upward influence in a hierarchy model, and these studies find no upward influences. Poole and Hunter's (1976) study was

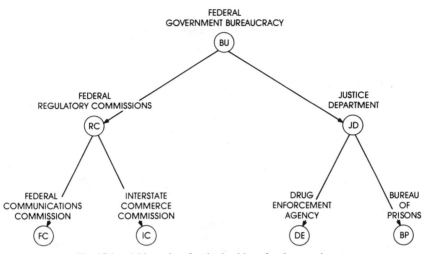

Fig. 15.1. A hierarchy of attitude objects for the experiment.

designed to test this assertion on a hierarchy of attitudes toward sex with various categories of partners. They find that their message directed toward the bottom of the hierarchy elicits change in that attitude but change in none of the attitudes above it. In a follow-up posttest the other attitudes in the hierarchy remain unchanged whereas the attitude that had been changed "decays" back in the direction of its immediately superordinate attitude in the hierarchy. Poole and Hunter (1976) interpret these data as showing good fit of the general model with parameter values of $\alpha = .4$ and $\beta = .2$. However, their message directed at the top of the hierarchy elicits no attitude change, hence no test of the model assumptions concerning downward or sideways influences can be performed.

The present study has two objectives. First, it provides a test of the general logic of the hierarchical model (Chapter 14): (a) that messages impacted at the top of the hierarchy will indirectly change all the attitudes in that hierarchy, whereas (b) messages directed to the bottom of the hierarchy will have no indirect effects and will decay back to an equilibrium with the immediately superordinate attitude. Second, it provides a detailed empirical test of the specific mathematical model offered in Chapter 14.

This chapter compares four hierarchical models: the simultaneous and delayed-change models presented in Chapter 14 and two others (a "pullback" and a "generalization" model). The experimental data support the pullback model, that is, the double comparison model with delayed internal influence and an unmeasured superordinate concept.

CHANGE WITHOUT MESSAGES:
THE INTERNAL INFLUENCE MODEL

In Chapter 14 it is assumed that the influence of one attitude on another is produced by internal messages elicited by any reference to one or more of the concepts in the hierarchy. The effect of such an internal message is to cause the subordinate attitude in question to change in the direction of its superordinate attitude. Let x be the attitude toward the concept at the top of the hierarchy, y the attitude toward one of the second-level concepts, and z the attitude toward one of the third-level concepts that is subordinate to the second level concept already chosen (for example, in Fig. 15.1, a suitable triplet of attitudes are the attitudes toward BU, RC, and IC). Then the equations for internal change are

$$\Delta x = 0$$
$$\Delta y = \beta(x - y) \tag{15.1}$$
$$\Delta z = \beta(y - z)$$

Because x is at the top of the hierarchy, there is no superordinate attitude for it to change toward, y changes toward x, and z changes toward y. For the seven attitude hierarchy, the equations become

$$\Delta BU = 0$$
$$\Delta RC = \beta(SU - RC)$$
$$\Delta FC = \beta(RC - FC)$$
$$\Delta IC = \beta(RC - IC) \tag{15.2}$$
$$\Delta JD = \beta(BU - JD)$$
$$\Delta DE = \beta(JD - DE)$$
$$\Delta BP = \beta(JD - BP)$$

For the analyses reported below, it is convenient to recast these equations in predictive form, that is, to predict the new attitude from the old attitudes instead of predicting the change. Moreover, it is even more convenient to cast this in matrix terms:

$$
\begin{bmatrix} BU_2 \\ RC_2 \\ FC_2 \\ IC_2 \\ JD_2 \\ DE_2 \\ BP_2 \end{bmatrix}
=
\begin{bmatrix}
1 & 0 & 0 & 0 & 0 & 0 & 0 \\
\beta & 1-\beta & 0 & 0 & 0 & 0 & 0 \\
0 & \beta & 1-\beta & 0 & 0 & 0 & 0 \\
0 & \beta & 0 & 1-\beta & 0 & 0 & 0 \\
\beta & 0 & 0 & 0 & 1-\beta & 0 & 0 \\
0 & 0 & 0 & 0 & \beta & 1-\beta & 0 \\
0 & 0 & 0 & 0 & \beta & 0 & 1-\beta
\end{bmatrix}
\begin{bmatrix} BU_1 \\ RC_1 \\ FC_1 \\ IC_1 \\ JD_1 \\ DE_1 \\ BP_1 \end{bmatrix}
\tag{15.3}
$$

If the vector of attitudes is denoted X and the matrix of coefficients is denoted B, then the equation above can be reduced to

$$X_2 = BX_1 \qquad (15.4)$$

If projection farther into the future is desired, it is accomplished by further substitution such as

$$X_3 = BX_2 = BBX_1 = B^2X_1 \qquad (15.5)$$

$$X_4 = BX_3 = BB^2X_1 = B^3X_1 \qquad (15.6)$$

The transition matrix B has certain properties that dictate the form of transition matrices used to test the model. First, all nonzero coefficients below the diagonal are equal. This reflects the assumption that $\beta = \gamma$, that is, the strength of influence in the hierarch does not depend on how far up or down the hierarchy a given superordinate attitude is located. Second, a large number of the nondiagonal entries in the matrix are zero. This is because influence in the hierarchy is assumed to move only downward and along specific paths from more to less general attitudes. A zero where a coefficient should be is equivalent to assuming that there is no path of influence from one attitude to another. Third, coefficients in any row sum to one. Fourth, coefficients in the first row of the matrix are a one and six zeros. This reflects the assumption that the top attitude BU of the hierarchy is independent or functionally autonomous of other attitudes, that is, BU does not change over time. If, instead, BU were not the top of the hierarchy but had a superior attitude Q, we would expect change in BU:

$$\Delta BU = \beta(Q - BU) \qquad (15.7)$$

So the transition matrix would have a coefficient $1 - \beta$ in its upper left corner instead of one.

CHANGE WITH MESSAGES:
EXTERNAL MESSAGE MODELS

In this section we shall discuss four models of message effects on hierarchies of attitudes. With each model we shall first lay out the assumption underlying the model and then describe each of them

Double Comparison with Simultaneous
Internal Influence

This model assumes that the internal influence process and the external message influence process occur simultaneously. For the three-attitude hierarchy,

$$\Delta x = \alpha(M_x - x)$$

$$\Delta y = \alpha(M_y - y) + \beta(x - y) \qquad (15.8)$$

$$\Delta z = \alpha(M_z - z) + \beta(y - z)$$

if M_x, M_y, and M_z are messages aimed at x, y, and z, respectively. If we assume that only attitude x gets a message, we have

$$\Delta x = \alpha(M_x - x)$$

$$\Delta y = \beta(x - y) \qquad (15.9)$$

$$\Delta z = \beta(y - z)$$

Note here that the only attitude that is directly influenced by the message is that for the concept contained in the message. Change induced in an upper-level attitude by a message will later filter down to lower levels because of internal processes, but there will be no direct influence by the message on lower attitudes. If a message is impacted at the lowest level of the hierarchy, it will have no effect at all on other attitudes, because change does not move up a hierarchy.

If no more messages are received, the next transition of the hierarchy will be governed by the internal influence process outlined previously.

Double Comparison with Delayed Internal Influence

This model differs from that above in one important respect—it assumes that when a person receives a message, he considers the full implications of the change produced by the external message before the message is integrated into the hierarchy. After this is done the internal comparison process occurs and internally produced change results. As opposed to the "instantaneous" model, which assumes that external and internal change happen simultaneously, the delayed model separates hierarchical attitude change into two phases. First, the external message is integrated into the hierarchy; then the internal change process occurs. If only x receives a message, we have the following model.

Phase 1: $\Delta x = \alpha(M_x - x)$

$$\Delta y = 0 \qquad (15.10)$$

$$\Delta z = 0$$

Phase 2: $\Delta x = 0$

$$\Delta y = \beta(x^* - y) \qquad (15.11)$$

$$\Delta z = \beta(y - z)$$

and so on, where x^* is the new value of x from phase 1. In phase 1 the attitude directly addressed by the message is changed by the message and all other attitudes in the hierarchy remain the same. In phase 2 the internal influence process of the hierarchy model occurs. The attitude changed in phase 1 exerts influence on its subordinate attitudes based on the new value resulting from phase 1.

In phase 1 of the transition the message changes the attitude. In phase 2 the attitude is changed by the attitude directly above it in the hierarchy, and this either increases or decreases the apparent message effect. Normally the premessage attitude would be at or near the corresponding superordinate attitude. If so, then after the message, that superordinate will act in exactly the opposite direction of the message and hence produce "decay" in the attitude change produced by the message. Only if the premessage attitude was not adjusted to its superordinate attitude and only if the premessage superordinate–subordinate attitude discrepancy was in the same direction as the message–attitude discrepancy would the postmessage change actually amplify the change produced by the message. If the attitude in question has no superordinate attitude, the message effect would be unaltered.

Pullback Model

Up to now we have assumed that x is the top of the hierarchy, but suppose this is false. If there is a superordinate concept above x, then the hierarchy models would make different predictions, normally "decay" in any attitude change observed in x. The existence of a superordinate concept to x in conjunction with the two-phase message effect model will be called the "pullback" model. This model is exactly the same as the delayed change hierarchy model during phase 1. But during phase 2, x is influenced by its superordinate attitude. If we assume that x is in equilibrium before receiving the message, then the superordinate attitude will be equal to the value of x prior to the message, that is, $Q = x_0$. Thus, in phase 2, after the message, $\Delta x = \beta(Q - x^*) = \beta(x_0 - x^*)$, where x^* is the value of x as a result of the message. Changes in other attitudes follow the internal model described previously. If internal processes take place before x is observed, then the observed value of x will be different from the actual value of x when the message is first incorporated into the hierarchy. The observed value results from the effects of the superordinate attitude on x during phase 2 of the transition. These internal effects will usually dampen the message effect but they may increase it under the above conditions.

If no message is impacted on x, it will be expected to change somewhat with each transition until it was in line with its superordinate attitude. If x is in line with its superordinate attitude before the experiment, then no change in x will be observed.

Generalized Model

The generalization model posits individual differences in message reaction among those who receive a message. Given that the attitudes in a hierarchy are usually logically and semantically related, it is possible for a message aimed at one attitude to be generalized and applied to all attitudes in the hierarchy. The degree to which this happens depends in part on the nature of the message and in part on the people who receive the message. If the message is somewhat ambiguous in terms of the object of its praise or indictments, these might be generalized to apply to every attitude in the hierarchy. Moreover, certain people might be more likely to generalize messages than others. For example, a person who distrusts the government might interpret a message that says "the Bureau of Prisons is bad" as saying "the Bureau of Prisons is bad and so are all other government agencies." Thus this model assumes that a certain proportion of those hearing a message generalize it to the whole hierarchy. Assume that 50% of all people generalize a certain message. Assume also that the coefficient α for message effect is .50. If the message is directed at x, we will observed two sorts of message effects in the group regression lines:

$$\Delta x = .50(M_x - x) \tag{15.12}$$

for the target attitude, and

$$\Delta k = .25(M_x - k) \tag{15.13}$$

for all other attitudes in the hierarchy. The message coefficient is .25 for the other attitudes because only 50% of the group in question generalizes, hence the resulting average message coefficient is only half as large.

The "generalization" model assumes the two-stage message impact model for the generalized message effect. No unknown superordinate concept is assumed. In general:

Phase 1: $\Delta a = \alpha(M_a - a)$

$$\Delta b = p\alpha(M_a - b) \tag{15.14}$$

where a is the attitude the message is directed at, b all other attitudes, and p the proportion of people who generalize.

Phase 2: $\Delta x = 0$

$$\Delta y = \beta(x - y) \tag{15.15}$$

$$\Delta z = \beta(y - z)$$

Thus this model differs from the modified hierarchy model principally in terms of the assumptions made about phase 1.

STOCHASTIC MODELS

It is important to consider the nature of the error terms for the model. In most models, error terms are simply assumed to be random error pertaining to variables that are transient over time and unrelated to the observed variables. Undoubtedly there are errors of this type in the present data. However, the present model also predicts several kinds of systematic error. The nature of this will be spelled out for only one illustrative case but other cases are similar.

If people hear only one internal message during the observed time interval, then the change in the second-rank attitudes would be given by

$$\Delta y = \beta(x - y) \tag{15.16}$$

But suppose that some people heard an external message about y during that time interval. If we denote by m the message value heard by those who heard such a message, then for those people the change equation will be

$$\Delta y = \alpha(m - y) + \beta(x - y) \tag{15.17}$$

Because such messages are not observed by the experimenter, these various change equations will be pooled in the data and averaged in the overall regression equation. Suppose that the proportion of people who hear a message is p and suppose that the average message value heard μ is independent of the listener's position (i.e., m is uncorrelated with y), then the overall regression of the second score onto the first will be

$$y_2 = y_1 + \beta(x_1 - y_1) + p\alpha(\mu - y_1) \tag{15.18}$$
$$= (1 - p\alpha - \beta)y_1 + \beta x_1 + p\alpha\mu$$

instead of the usual

$$y_2 = y_1 + \beta(x_1 - y_1) \tag{15.19}$$
$$= (1 - \beta)y_1 + \beta x_1$$

That is, the errors in this model will probably be correlated with the variable being considered, and the errors may well have nonzero expected values (i.e., $p\alpha\mu$ instead of zero).

The preceding argument has two main implications. First, estimation of the internal influence parameters should be done with constant terms in the regression equation; though a purely deterministic model would predict that there be no constants for the best-fitting line when no message is received. The error term $p\alpha\mu$ would be expected to show up as at least part of the constant. Second, although the sum of coefficients in a pure deterministic model is always one, the diagonal coefficients (those for y_2 from y_1) will be depressed somewhat (in this case by at least a factor of $p\alpha$) and thus the row coefficients will sum to less than one. This is an important consideration in estimating the transition matrix $\hat{B}$ for the model.

The models just presented are not deterministic; the data used to test them are stochastic. We find random perturbations in observed values of the attitudes. As discussed, these are due to other internal and external messages not involved in the study but still received by the receivers. The number and nature of these messages differ from person to person, and so, assuming people are independent, they show up as random error. Although the model has the form

$$X_{n+1} = BX_n$$

the data statisfy

$$X_{n+1} = BX_n + U_n \tag{15.20}$$

where U_n is a random error term.

ESTIMATION AND TESTING

Statistical methods for estimating and testing the model were dictated by the stochastic nature of the data. If the model is correct and there is no error in the data, we would obtain a perfect prediction of time $n + 1$ from time n. However, as we note, there are several sources of error in the data. Because of them prediction will be less than perfect in two senses. First, errors in the data can cause misspecification of model parameters, making correct prediction difficult from the start. Second, perturbations in the data from time n to time $n + 1$ can cause even a correct prediction to deviate from observed scores. The model might then be rejected even though it is in fact true. Because of these problems, care must be taken to correct for error as much as possible in estimating and testing the model. Methods for estimating the parameters of the models and for testing the fit of the models to the data are presented next. First, we shall consider the estimation of B, the internal transition matrix. Second, we shall discuss testing the internal influence model and the estimation procedures required by that test. Finally, we discuss the problem of incorrect specification of time period for the model.

Estimation of B

The normal procedure for establishing the coefficients of the transition matrix is to regress the variables at each time onto those at the prior time. However, in this study this procedure could not be used. First, correlations among predictor variables were very high. This makes the regression coefficient unstable. Second, in each regression equation there would have to be at least seven predictors to estimate the transition matrix. With so many predictor variables an extremely large subject pool—on the order of 300 subjects per group—would be needed to avoid bias in the regressions. The number of subjects in the experiment was 76 in one group and 54 in the other. So direct use of regression for estimating the coefficient of B is ruled out. A combination of regression and other procedures is used.

A review of the model reveals special features that can be used in estimating B. First, 36 of the 49 elements in B are zero. Second, if we assume that $\beta = \gamma$, six of seven diagonal elements are equal, whereas all of the nondiagonal elements are equal. Third, the coefficients in any row sum to one. Thus there are many fewer path coefficients to be estimated than if ordinary seven-variable regressions are used. The following method was used to estimate B: regressions were done for the no-message intervals—time 2 onto time 1 and time 4 onto time 3. In these equations the predictors were those variables that the model specified as having nonzero coefficients. The regressions were performed using all variables at time 2 and time 4 as dependent variables. The time 2 onto time 1 and time 4 onto time 3 regressions ought to yield path coefficients for the internal influence process that are free of message effects. The coefficients from the regressions were averaged to give a more stable estimate of the model parameters than a single regression coefficient can give. Because of unobserved internal and external messages subjects receive, in the course of the experiment, the diagonal entries of $\hat{B}$ will be less than the model prediction hence the rows must sum to less than unity. The resulting estimated transition matrix B is then used to test the internal influence model.

Testing the Internal Influence Model

The method used to test the model is a version of path analysis and utilizes the correlation matrices of the observed scores. When causal paths are specified in path analysis, the correlation matrix of the variables in the model can be estimated using the path coefficients, and the estimated matrix can be compared with the correlation matrix of the observed variables. If the fit of the two matrices is good, the model is judged to the correct. In this case the observed correlation matrix at time n is multipled by the estimated transition matrix to yield an estimate of the correlation matrix at time $n + 1$. This estimate is then compared with the observed matrix to ascertain how well the model fits:

$$\hat{B}R_{11} = \hat{R}_{21} \tag{15.21}$$

where B is the transition matrix R_{11} the observed correlation matrix of time 1 scores, and $\hat{R}_{21}$ the estimated correlation matrix of time 1 and time 2 scores.

Just as before, to obtain $\hat{R}_{31}$ we multiply R_{11} by B^2.

$$\hat{R}_{31} = B\hat{R}_{21} = B^2 R_{11} \tag{15.22}$$

To obtain R_{41}, we multiply R_{31} by B to obtain

$$\hat{R}_{41} = B\hat{R}_{31} = B^3 R_{11} \tag{15.23}$$

We can also generate R_{22} from R_{11} as

$$\hat{R}_{22} = BR_{11}B + D \tag{15.24}$$

where D is a diagonal matrix of error variances. So, from a starting correlation matrix such as R_{11}, we can generate $\hat{R}_{12}, \hat{R}_{13}, \ldots, \hat{R}_{1n}$ and $\hat{R}_{22}$ and compare the estimated matrices with the observed matrices.

It is important to use the most reliable measurement feasible in any given study. Even a small amount of measurement error can cause observed values to deviate significantly from perfect measurements. These deviations can lead the researcher to reject a correct model mistakenly because its predictions do not conform to the data, when in fact the data are biased due to error. In particular, irrelevant variables may turn out to have nonzero regression weights (above and beyond chance deviations due to sampling error). Our study used attitude indices that had reliabilities in the 90s. However, where the amount of individual differences in change is not exceptionally large, even this level of reliability does not warrant using the data without correction for attenuation. Note that correction for attenuation is a perfect method only for population statistics; it yields only imperfect corrections when applied to sample correlations. In our study all correlation matrices were corrected for attenuation using Cronbach's coefficient alpha before any other computations were carried out. This procedure, however, does not eliminate the effects of sampling error.

In a typical path analysis the difficult estimation problem is the beta weights, which are many and which require a great many subjects for estimation. The correlations between those variables that serve as exogenous variables are usually few in number and are usually based on relatively large sample sizes. In this study the situation is reversed; there is only one parameter β to be estimated and it appears in 12 independent regression equations, each of which can be computed on the entire sample of 130 subjects. Thus the matrix B is easily estimated for the model. However, the matrix of correlations between the variables that act as exogenous is the matrix of correlations at time 1. There are 21 such correlations and they must be separately estimated for each subsample, that is, for sample sizes of only 54 and 76. Faced with problems of large sampling error, it was decided that the usual path analytic procedure of ignoring the error in the exogenous correlations would not work here.

Two steps were taken to reduce the effects of sampling error in the exogenous correlations. First, projection forward in time was done from each possible starting time separately. That is, time 1 was used as the starting value for projecting $\hat{R}_{21}$, $\hat{R}_{31}$, and $\hat{R}_{41}$; but R_{22} was separately estimated for projecting to $\hat{R}_{32}$ and $\hat{R}_{42}$; $\hat{R}_{33}$ was independently estimated in projecting to $\hat{R}_{43}$. Second, the raw initial correlation matrix R_{11} (or whatever time is taken as the "initial" time in a given calculation) was not used as the estimate of the population matrix Σ_{11}. Instead, Σ_{11} was estimated from R_{11}, R_{21} and R_{22} as shown in the following equations.

The initial correlation matrices Σ_{ii} for the estimation were derived by taking a weighted average of the first three observed correlation matrices in the series (R_{11}, R_{12}, and R_{22}, for example). If we perceive R_{11} as being composed of the true correlation matrix and a matrix of error terms, the three matrices may be defined as

$$R_{11} = \Sigma_{11} + E_1$$
$$R_{21} = B\Sigma_{11} + E_2 \qquad\qquad (15.25)$$
$$R_{22} = B\Sigma_{11}B' + D + E_3$$

where D is a diagonal matrix of estimated errors. If we solve for Σ_{11} we obtain

$$\hat{\Sigma}_{11} = \tfrac{1}{3}[R_{11} + B^{-1}R_{21} + B^{-1}(R_{22} - D)B'^{-1}] \qquad (15.26)$$

where $\hat{\Sigma}$ is then used as the start value and as an estimate of R_{11}. This procedure has the effect of averaging out errors present in any one of the first three correlation matrices. The other initial correlation matrices $\hat{\Sigma}_{22}$ and $\hat{\Sigma}_{33}$ were estimated using the same procedure. In summary, then, the internal influence model will be tested as follows.

1. The estimated transition matrix $\hat{B}$ will be specified using the constraints on parameters suggested by the model. Parameter sizes will be established by using regression.

2. Estimates for observed correlations will be generated by multiplying a starting correlation matrix by the transition matrix. The start matrix $\hat{\Sigma}$ will be derived from the first three matrices in any series.

3. Fit of the model will be ascertained by comparing the estimated correlation matrices with the observed correlation matrices.

METHOD

Overview

The models were tested by measuring the changes that occur in a hierarchy of attitudes over four time periods. The hierarchy used is the one pictured in Fig. 15.1. In the federal government bureaucracy (BUR) group a message was impacted on the attitude at the top of the hierarchy to observe effects of changing this attitude on the rest of the hierarchy. In the interstate commerce commission group (ICC) group a message was directed at an attitude at the bottom of the hierarchy. The original model predicts that changing an attitude at the bottom of the hierarchy will have little effect on the other attitudes. Changes in attitudes during intervals when no message was presented are considered to determine the nature of the internal attitude change process.

Design

A two-group design was used to test the models. The first group received a message directed at the "federal government bureaucracy, and the second group received a message directed at the "Interstate Commerce Commission. For each group data were collected at three separate sessions, approximately one week apart. The design for both groups is depicted in Table 15.1.

Because both groups have an identical experience before the message is given, this design permits a maximal number of subjects for use in testing the internal process model on the time 1–time 2 data. The analysis of the regression of the second pretest onto the first pretest should thus provide a basis for estimating the internal parameter. The time 3–time 4 data can be similarly used, though with a bit more caution. If the full message effect has not taken place at the time of the immediate posttest (time 3), as would be true if the receivers spent time outside the experiment remembering the experimental message or parts of it, then the regression of time 4 onto time 3 might not be purely internal process data.

The follow-up posttest (time 4) is crucial to the design. Almost every study that has found indirect effects in attitude change has found such changes in follow-up data rather than in immediate change data.

At session 1 attitude measures for the seven objects were taken along with measures of amount of information associated with each attitude. At session 2, attitude measure were taken again (pretest 2); receivers then read a message about either the federal government bureaucracy or the Interstate Commerce Commission. Those people who received a message about the federal government bureaucracy make up the BUR group, whereas those who

TABLE 15.1

BASIC PROCEDURE FOR EACH GROUP IN
EXPERIMENT

Session 1	Session 2	Session 3
Pretest 1	Pretest 2	Posttest 2
	Message	
	Posttest 1	

received a message about the Interstate Commerce Commission make up the ICC group. Following the message, receivers were asked to judge the value of the message, to estimate how much the message increased their knowledge of the attitude object, and to provide information about their academic interest and possible family ties with the federal government. Finally, they filled out posttest attitude measures (posttest 1). At session 3, one week later, subjects again filled out the attitude measures (posttest 2) and ranked the agencies in the hierarchy in order of importance to them and in order of their generality. This final ranking was designed to allow a check of whether the attitudes fall into the hierarchy as expected.

At session 1, receivers were told that the study was designed to explore the effects of peoples' beliefs on their processing of information. In addition, at each session, they were told that they would see the same questions at several points during the study. They were asked to consider each question independently of the others. They were not to try to remember their previous answers but to look into themselves and give their present feelings about each question. The instructions were designed to minimize reactivity on the part of receivers; emphasis was laid on eliciting present feelings, whether or not they corresponded to past responses. Independence of subjects was insured by (a) randomly administering treatments, and (b) cautioning subjects not to talk to one another about the experiment while it was in progress. Response sets on multiple-item questions were avoided by alternating the attitudinal adjective pairs with pairs of adjectives unrelated to evaluation, such as unknown–well-known; common–rare; and large–small.

The message aimed at federal government bureaucracy was positive and the message aimed at the Interstate Commerce Commission was negative. Both messages consisted of a short introduction and six arguments supporting either the positive or negative conclusion. In the bureaucracy message the last four arguments were subpoints of a major argument that the federal government bureaucracy maximizes equality and democratic control by the citizens of the United States. In the ICC message the last three arguments were subpoints of a major argument that the Interstate Commerce Commission was against the best interests of the people of the United States. The bureaucracy message contained eight examples or concrete illustrations, whereas the ICC message contained ten. They were approximately the same length, requiring about 15-min reading time for an average receiver.

Instruments

Attitude is defined as an affective response toward an object. Attitudes were measured as responses to concepts on a seven-point semantic differential scale (Osgood *et al.* 1957). Four bipolar pairs of adjectives were chosen to tap evaluative response: good–bad, valuable–worthless, beneficial–harmful, and desirable–undesirable. Message value was measured by the receiver's judgment of the content of the message toward its object along the same four semantic differential scales.

Subjects

Subjects consisted of 130 students from nine Communication Arts 101 classes at the University of Wisconsin–Madison and the Communication 100 subject pool at Mighican State University. Of these, 76 made up the BUR group and 54 were assigned to the ICC group. Approximately 230 people made up the original data pool but only the data for the 130 people who had attended all three sessions were included in the analysis.

RESULTS

Background

The two message groups were tested for similarity in biographical traits. No significant differences were found in the composition of the groups in terms of age, sex, academic experience relevant to the attitudes in question, or political position as measured by the Radical–Conservation Scale (Robinson and Shaver, 1973). There also were no significant differences between the two groups in the amount of information associated with each of the attitudes in the hierarchy.

Each of the eight attitude measures is the sum of four semantic differential scales. Thus it is possible to calculate a reliability for each measure at each point in time using Cronbach's coefficiant alpha (Cronbach, 1951). The reliabilities ranged from .842 to .946, with an average of .904. A reliability for each attitude can also be calculated from the test–retest correlations for each attitude using Heise's (1969) formula, although that formula makes assumptions that are not met in the present data. These stability coefficients ranged from .694 to .922, with an average of .815. In general, reliabilities are very high and the stability coefficients are somewhat lower. This would be expected because a fairly large amount of change occurs in the attitudes across time.

Subjects were asked to rank the attitudes in terms of their generality. The most general attitude was to receive a "1" and less general attitudes were to be given higher ranks. Equally general attitudes were to be given the same rank. The mean rankings fall in the expected order: BU is ranked the highest at 2.29, RC and JD have intermediate positions at 3.03 and 3.38, and FC, IC, DE, and BP receive the lowest ranking at 3.70, 3.64, 3.77, and 3.67.

The Top of the Hierarchy

The correct equations for *BU* differ quite drastically if *BU* is the top of an isolated hierarchy as opposed to the top of a subhierarchy of some larger and unobserved system. If *BU* is the top of isolated hierarchy, then it should be a "first-order autoregressive process." That is, in regression terms *BU* at time t should depend only on *BU* at time $t - 1$ and not on *BU* at times $t - 2$, $t - 3$, ... However, the regression weights in Table 15.2 show that *BU* at time t also depends on its values at times $t - 2$ and $t - 3$. Therefore *BU* is not the top of an isolated hierarchy; there must be a superordinate attitude for *BU*. The "federal government" in general could be such an concept, because it would include all the concepts in question. The means for the BUR group also support this conclusion. There is a marked decay of the change induced in *BU* by the message (-1.67 points from time 3, immediately after the message, to time 4). This decay could be the product of internal influence as *BU* moves back toward a more negative superordinate attitude. Although the hierarchy is structured as it should be, it is not an isolated hierarchy but rather a subhierarchy within some larger system.

Test of the Internal Influence Model

The internal process parameters can be estimated from beta weights of the regression of each attitude onto itself and its superordinate attitude at the preceding time during an interval in which there is no message. In this study that would mean either regressing time 2 onto time 1 or regressing time 4 onto time 3. Both were done. Further, because no message is given during these time intervals, the data for both message groups are entirely comparable and so were pooled for this analysis. All correlations were corrected for attenuation before regressions were calculated.

The average of 12 beta weights for the regression of later attitude onto its earlier superordinate attitude was .09. The average beta weight for an attitude onto its own earlier value was .75. The average multiple correlation was .73.

TABLE 15.2

STANDARDIZED REGRESSION WEIGHTS FOR *BU*
VARIABLE PREDICTED WITH LAGS[a]

Message	Regression Weight			
	$\beta_{x_4 x_2}$	$\beta_{x_4 x_1}$	$\beta_{x_3 x_2}$	$\beta_{x_3 x_1}$
BUR	.61	.16	.77	$-.23$
ICC	.55	.39	.60	.32

[a] $X_4 = BU4$, $X_3 = BU3$, $X_2 = BU2$, $X_1 = BU1$.

The variation in the beta weights is no greater than would be expected from sampling error, given a sample size of only 130 with highly correlated predictors ($\chi^2 = 10.91$ with 11 df, $p > .50$ for the off-diagonal values; $\chi^2 = 11.67$ with 11 df, $p > .40$ for the diagonal values). Therefore, the average beta weights were taken as estimates of the internal process parameters. After making some runs to assess the fit of the model to the attitude correlation matrices, these provisional estimates were revised from .75 to .85 and from .09 to .10.

Reproducing the Observed Correlation Matrices

The usual method of testing a structural equation or path model is to see if the model correctly reproduces the observed correlation matrix. In the present case, the full correlation matrix is 28×28, corresponding to seven variables measured at four times. However, it is much more convenient to break this matrix up into 16 blocks, each 7×7, corresponding to the correlations between 7 measurements at one time with seven measurements at a second time. Denote each such matrix of correlations R_{ij}, where i is the time for the row variables and j the time for the column correlations. Then R_{ij} would be the correlations between the seven variable at time i.

From the regression equation

$$X_{n+1} = BX_n \tag{15.27}$$

we can derive the predicted values of the nondiagonal blocks of the correlation matrix to be

$$R_{21} = BR_{11} \tag{15.28}$$

$$R_{31} = B^2 R_{11} \tag{15.29}$$

$$R_{41} = B^3 R_{11} \tag{15.30}$$

$$R_{32} = BR_{22} \tag{15.31}$$

$$R_{42} = B^2 R_{22} \tag{15.32}$$

$$R_{43} = BR_{33} \tag{15.33}$$

In the deterministic model, these equations could be further reduced to predictions entirely based on R_{11} by the following:

$$R_{22} = BR_{11}B' \quad \text{if deterministic} \tag{15.34}$$

$$R_{33} = B^2 R_{11}B^{2'} \quad \text{if deterministic} \tag{15.35}$$

$$R_{44} = B^3 R_{11}B^{3'} \quad \text{if deterministic} \tag{15.36}$$

However, these equations do not hold in the probabilistic case because of the variance of the error terms. The alternative form is

$$R_{22} = BR_{11}B' + D \qquad (15.37)$$

where D is a diagonal matrix of error variances. Predictions for the model were thus tested only for Eqs. (15.28)–(15.33).

Even though the reliabilities of single measurements were in the .90s, all correlations were corrected for attenuation to avoid the steady cumulation of errors for long time intervals, which would be quite severe in this case.

Each of times 1, 2, and 3 was used to start a series of projections to test the model. The initial matrix for each series was estimated using Eq. (15.36). That is, $\hat{\Sigma}_{11}$, $\hat{\Sigma}_{22}$, and $\hat{\Sigma}_{33}$ were used for the estimates $\hat{R}_{11}$, $\hat{R}_{22}$, and $\hat{R}_{33}$ and to predict the "cross" correlations:

1. using R_{11}, R_{12}, and R_{22} to determine the initial matrix $\hat{R}_{11}$, $\hat{R}_{12}$, $\hat{R}_{13}$, $\hat{R}_{14}$, $\hat{R}_{22}$ were generated;
2. using R_{22}, R_{23}, and R_{33} to determine and initial matrix, $\hat{R}_{22}$, $\hat{R}_{23}$, $\hat{R}_{24}$ and $\hat{R}_{33}$ were generated;
3. using R_{33}, R_{34}, and R_{44} to determine the initial matrix, $\hat{R}_{33}$, $\hat{R}_{34}$ and $\hat{R}_{44}$ were generated.

Fit of the model was determined in terms of two criteria. First, the proportion of predicted correlations that deviated significantly from observed correlations using a 95% confidence interval was computed. Sampling error would make this proportion about .05 even if the model was a perfect description of the population. Second, the root mean squared error of predicted from observed correlations was calculated. Of particular interest are the root mean squared deviations of the matrices for times 3 and 4 as predicted from time 1 and for time 4 as predicted by time 2. It is through prediction across more than one time period that the greatest amount of error should appear.

Table 15.3 contains the number and proportion of "significant" deviations out of 420 predicted correlations. The proportion of "significant" errors was

TABLE 15.3

PROPORTION OF DEVIATIONS SIGNIFICANTLY
GREATER THAN ZERO FOR ALL PREDICTED
CORRELATION MATRICES.[a]

Group	Number	Proportion
BUR	17/420	.040
ICC	23/420	.054

[a] Diagonal valves for symetric matrices are not included in the totals.

.040 for the BUR group and .054 for the ICC group, that is, chance level in both groups. Thus it is plausible to regard all the "significant" errors as due to sampling error.

Table 15.4 contains the root mean square of the errors in predicting the correlation matrices for various time combinations. The root mean squared deviation for the BUR group was .1024 overall and .1202 for the three matrices predicted across more than one time period, $\hat{R}_{13}$, $\hat{R}_{14}$, and $\hat{R}_{24}$. The root mean squared deviation for the ICC group was .1287 and .1513 for the three matrices predicted across more than one time period. In both matrices, the terms near the diagonal have the least percentage deviation, and the percent deviation increases as one moves toward the lower-left-hand corner. This is natural because $\hat{R}_{14}$ is predicted across three time periods and $\hat{R}_{13}$ and $\hat{R}_{24}$ are predicted across two time periods.

A second test of the adequacy of the model was conducted using an averaged pretest score (times 1 and 2) and an averaged posttest score (times 3 and 4) which were calculated for purposes of looking at mean attitude change.

TABLE 15.4

Root Mean Squared Deviations (R_{ij}) of Predicted from Observed Correlation Matrices for Test of Internal Process[a]

			j		
Group	i	1	2	3	4
BUR	1	.091			
	2	.091	.083		
			(.164)		
	3	.111	.076	.059	
				(.088)	
	4	.138	.111	.065	.154
ICC	1	.098			
	2	.097	.142		
			(1.24)		
	3	.156	.140	.063	
				(.202)	
	4	.164	.134	.070	.155

[a] The figures in parentheses are the deviations for matrices that can be estimated in two ways: (a) the figure in parentheses is the deviation in the matrix when it is projected, and (b) the figure not in parentheses is the deviation when that matrix is estimated as an initial matrix.

Averaging doubles the effective time period between the pretest and posttest scores and hence doubles the internal change coefficient (where β before was .10, it is now .20).

The matrices that could be predicted were $\hat{R}_{11}$, $\hat{R}_{12}$, and $\hat{R}_{22}$, where 1 corresponds to the average pretest measure and 2 corresponds to the average posttest measure. Out of 91 correlations for the BUR group, no deviation between observed and predicted scores was significantly greater than zero. For the ICC group 5 out of 91 deviations were significant for a level of .055. The average root mean squared deviations were .071 for the BUR group and .137 for the ICC group. The root mean squared error is smaller for the averaged pretest and posttest scores than for the four scores by a factor of approximately 2. This is precisely what would be predicted from the increased reliability of the averaged scores.

In summary, the internal influence model seems to fit the data. On the average there was 4.7% "significant" error for the test with regular scores and 2.8% "significant" deviation for the test with averaged pretest and average posttest scores, both of which are at the 5% chance level. Thus it seems that the internal influence model with parameter $\beta = .10$ is supported by the data.

Test of the External Message Models

This section is divided into five parts. In the first four parts the message impact models are tested in the order in which they were presented. In the fifth part a comparison of the adequacy of the models is presented.

For the BUR group, the mean change in *BU* following the message was from 16.90 to 20.93 on a scale from 4 to 28, an increase of 4.03, which was highly significant ($z = 7.65$, $p = 0$). For the ICC group, the change in *IC* was from 19.28 to 13.02, or a decrease of 6.26 ($z = -7.45$, $p = 0$). Thus both messages were highly effective.

Mean change during the control periods was random in direction but greater in magnitude than had been expected. This probably reflects the existence of greater individual differences in the extent of thought about the hierarchy outside the experiment than would be optimal. To obtain the most stable basis possible for testing models of message effect, the two premessage means (times 1 and 2) were averaged for each attitude to use for the pretest mean; the two postmessage means (times 3 and 4) were averaged for each attitude to use for the posttest mean. The one subtlety introduced by this operation is that the difference between times 1.5 and 3.5 is two units rather than one. Thus, in particular, the parameter for the internal change processes would not be $\beta = .10$ but $\beta = .20$.

The averaged pretest and posttest means for each attitude are presented in Table 15.5.

TABLE 15.5

MEANS FOR AVERAGE PRETEST AND AVERAGE POSTTEST AND CHANGE FROM PRETEST TO POSTTEST
FOR BOTH GROUPS

	BUR *Group*			ICC *Group*		
Hierarchy attitude	*Time 1.5[a]*	*Time 3.5[b]*	Δx	*Time 1.5[a]*	*Time 3.5[b]*	Δx
BU	15.93	20.10	+4.17	15.54	15.42	−.12
RC	18.90	20.01	+1.11	18.47	17.69	−.88
FC	20.54	20.94	+.40	20.14	19.15	−.99
IC	19.24	19.72	+.48	19.05	14.59	−4.46
JD	21.78	21.76	−.02	21.12	20.35	−.77
DE	19.91	20.38	+.47	20.06	19.63	−.43
BP	17.35	18.71	+1.36	17.59	17.62	+.03

[a] Time 1.5 = $(X_1 + X_2)/2$.
[b] Time 3.5 = $(X_3 + X_4)/2$.

The effective time interval for the internal processes of the hierarchical model is not the amount of metric time that passes but rather the average number of times the subjects think about the concepts in the hierarchy. This number of transitions cannot be specified in advance. So, for each of the models below, the number of internal process transitions was taken to be the number that gives the best fit for that model.

Test of the Simultaneous Change Hierarchy Model

The first model set forth in Chapter 14 assumes that external and internal attitude change processes happen simultaneously in response to a message. It also assumes that *BU* is not subject to a superordinate concept. The parameters used in Table 15.6 are $\beta = .2$ and $\alpha = .5$ for the first transition (the message impact) and $\beta = .2$ for succeeding internal process transitions. This table shows the predicted means and the deviations of predicted from actual means. For the ICC group the fit is fairly good after the first transition and gets worse after the second. For the BUR group there are large deviations from the actual values for both transitions. After one transition the hierarchical model for message effect results in fairly good prediction for the ICC group (.32 average squared deviation), but there are large deviations from the observed scores for the BUR group (.76 average squared deviation). A second transition does not improve the fit in either case.

Because this message model did not result in very good fit, several alternative models were built that embodied changes in the assumptions of the hierarchical message model. These models are those tested next.

TABLE 15.6

PREDICTED MEAN VALUES FOR THE SIMULTANEOUS CHANGE HIERARCHY MODEL AND DEVIATIONS OF PREDICTED FROM OBSERVED MEANS[a]

Hierarchy attitude	BUR Group				ICC Group			
	First transition	Deviation	Second transition	Deviation	First transition	Deviation	Second transition	Deviation
BU	20.08	.02	20.08	.02	15.54	−.12	15.54	−.12
RC	18.31	1.70	18.66	1.35	17.88	−.19	17.41	−.27
FC	20.21	.73	19.83	1.11	19.81	−.66	19.41	.26
IC	19.17	.55	19.00	.72	13.71	.88	15.37	−.78
JD	20.61	1.16	20.50	1.26	20.00	.35	19.11	1.24
DE	20.28	.10	20.35	.03	20.27	−.64	20.18	−.55
BP	18.24	.47	18.71	.00	18.31	−.67	18.63	−1.01
Σ dev^2	5.30		5.16		2.24		3.62	
Ave. dev^2	.76		.74		.50		.60	

[a] For this table, $\alpha = .5$; $\beta = .2$.

Test of the Delayed Change Hierarchy Model

The delayed change hierarchy model separates the external message effect and internal influence process into two successive phases. In phase 1 the external message is integrated into the hierarchy of attitudes. This phase is a transition in which the only change is that produced by the external message. In phase 2 the internal attitude influence occurs. The predicted means and their deviations from the observed means are reported in Table 15.7. Note that there is only one message (phase 1) transition, because no more messages are received after the experimental message.

Prediction after one internal process transition is very good for ICC (.21 average squared deviation) and gets worse with a second internal process transition (.29 average squared deviation). Prediction of the value of IC is notably improved for the ICC group over the original hierarchy model. With

TABLE 15.7

PREDICTED MEAN VALUES FOR THE DELAYED-CHANGE HIERARCHY MODEL AND
DEVIATIONS OF PREDICTED FROM OBSERVED MEANS.[a]

Group	Hierarchy attitude	Message transition	First transition	Deviation	Second transition	Deviation
BUR	BU	20.08	20.08	.02	20.08	.02
	RC	18.90	19.14	.87	19.33	.68
	FC	20.54	20.21	.73	20.00	.94
	IC	19.24	19.17	.55	19.16	.56
	JD	21.78	21.44	.33	21.17	.59
	DE	19.91	20.28	.10	20.51	−.13
	BP	17.35	18.24	.47	18.88	−.17
Σ dev^2				1.93		2.05
Ave. dev^2				.28		.29
ICC	BU	15.54	15.54	−.12	15.54	−.12
	RC	18.47	17.88	−.19	17.41	.27
	FC	20.14	19.80	−.65	19.41	−.26
	IC	13.83	14.75	−.16	15.37	−.88
	JD	21.12	20.00	+.35	19.11	1.24
	DE	20.06	20.27	−.64	20.18	−.55
	BP	17.55	18.29	−.67	18.63	−1.01
Σ dev^2				1.48		3.79
Ave. dev^2				.21		.54

[a] For this table, $\alpha = .5$, $\beta = 0$ during message, $\beta = .2$ thereafter. The model is taken through one message and two internal transitions.

respect to the BUR group, prediction of observed means after one transition over the hierarchy model (.28 average squared deviation) was greatly improved. A second transition did not improve the fit of the model for the BUR group.

In summary, the delayed change hierarchy model improves the fit for both groups over the fit obtained with the simultaneous change hierarchy model.

Test of the Pullback Model

The pullback model is identical to the delayed change hierarchy model except that it assumes that BU has a superordinate attitude. Thus, in phase 2 of the transition, the actual message effect on BU would be expected to decay somewhat. Fitting this model to the data requires a much stronger parameter for BUR message, $\alpha = .75$, rather than $\alpha = .50$. The ICC message retains the same message parameter $\alpha = .50$. The predicted means and their derivations from the observed means are reported in Table 15.8.

TABLE 15.8

PREDICTED MEAN VALUES FOR THE PULLBACK MODEL AND DEVIATIONS OF PREDICTED FROM OBSERVED MEANS[a]

Group	Hierarchy attitude	Message transition	First transition	Deviation	Second transition	Deviation
BUR	BU	22.00	20.80	−.70	19.83	.27
	RC	18.90	19.52	.49	19.78	.23
	FC	20.54	20.21	.73	20.07	.87
	IC	19.24	19.17	.55	19.24	.48
	JD	21.78	21.82	−.06	21.62	.14
	DE	19.91	20.28	.10	20.59	−.21
	BP	17.35	18.24	.47	18.96	−.25
Σdev^2				1.80		1.24
Ave. dev^2				.26		.18
ICC	BU	15.54	15.54	−.12	15.54	−.12
	RC	18.47	17.88	−.19	17.41	−.27
	FC	20.14	19.80	−.65	19.41	.26
	IC	13.83	14.75	−.16	15.37	.88
	JD	21.12	20.00	+.35	19.11	1.24
	DE	20.06	20.27	−.64	20.18	−.55
	BP	17.55	18.29	−.67	18.63	−1.01
Σdev^2				1.48		3.79
Ave. dev^2				.21		.54

[a] For this table, $\alpha = .50$, $\beta = 0$ during message, $\beta = .2$ thereafter. The model is taken through one message and two internal transitions.

For the ICC group the predictions are exactly the same as in the modified hierarchy model. This is because BU starts at the value of the superordinate concept Q and is not predicted to change in the ICC group. Thus both models predict the same result for different reasons.

For the BUR group the prediction after one internal transition is good (.26 average squared deviation) and gets better after the second transition (.18 average squared deviation). The fact that the fit improves for the BUR group after two internal transitions indicates that the subjects' attitude hierarchies actually go through two transitions between pretest 2 and posttest 1.

The assumption of different message coefficients for the two messages is defensible given the nature of the two messages. The BUR message defended the federal government bureaucracy on the grounds of its efficiency, effectiveness, fairness, and democratic nature. Several subjects interviewed said that the message presented them with a new perspective on bureaucracy. The message was unique, salient, and effective in changing receivers' attitudes. On the other hand, the ICC message was an indictment of corruption in a federal government agency. Such a message is common today. Although it may have presented people with new information on the ICC, it did not contain a new perspective. So a difference in message parameters may be justified by the nature of the two messages.

The observed values for the ICC group are in general best predicted after one internal transition, whereas the observed values for the BUR group are predicted more accurately after two transitions. One possible explanation for this lies in the argument that the BUR message is more salient than the ICC message. This salient message may have caused receivers to think more about the hierarchy after receiving the BUR message than they did with the ICC message.

In summary, the pullback model provides better fit for the BUR group after two transitions than either of the previous two models. For the ICC group it provides the same fit as the delayed change hierarchical model and better fit than the original hierarchy model.

Test of the Generalization Model

The generalization model assumes that a certain proportion of the people hearing a message generalize that message to the whole hierarchy.

The message coefficient for the generalization is determined by looking at the graph in Fig. 15.2, which shows the change in each attitude from the pretest average to the posttest average Δa plotted against the initial average value of the attitude a_1. The parameter for the generalized message value is assumed to be the value of the message given, that is, 24.23 for BU and 8.62 for IC. This parameter serves as the intercept along the "a_1" axis. The "best-fit" straight

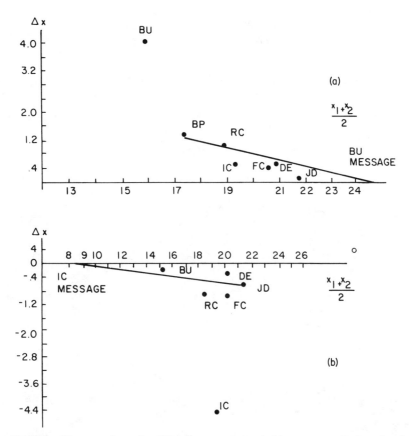

Fig. 15.2. The mean change in attitude from average pretest to average posttest as a function of mean pretest score for (a) BUR groups and (b) ICC groups.

line is determined visually and is the line shown in each graph in Fig. 15.7. The slope of each straight line is then obtained by careful measurement on the line drawn. The generalization coefficient p is .20 for the BUR message and .06 for the IC message. This would imply that 40% of the people in the BUR group generalized the message whereas 12% of the people in the ICC group generalized the message. The generalization model assumes a two-phase attitude change process similar to that of the delayed change hierarchy model. The predicted means and their deviation from the observed means are displayed in Table 15.9, for $\alpha = .50$ and $\beta = .20$.

After one message and one internal transition there is very good fit for both groups, with the exception of the JD attitude in the ICC group (.18 average

TABLE 15.9

PREDICTED MEAN VALUES FOR THE GENERALIZATION MODEL AND DEVIATIONS
OF PREDICTED FROM OBSERVED MEANS

Group	Hierarchy attitude	Message transition	First transition	Deviation	Second transition	Deviation
Bur	BU	20.08	20.08	.02	20.18	.02
	RC	19.97	20.00	.01	20.04	−.03
	FC	21.28	21.02	−.08	20.85	.09
	IC	20.24	20.19	−.47	20.15	−.43
	JD	22.27	21.84	−.08	21.50	.26
	DE	20.77	21.07	−.69	21.22	−1.84
	BP	18.73	19.44	−.73	19.92	−1.21
$\sum$ dev^2				1.24		2.43
Ave. dev^2				.18		.35
ICC	BU	15.12	15.12	.30	15.12	.30
	RC	17.88	17.33	.36	16.88	.81
	FC	19.45	19.14	.01	18.79	.36
	IC	13.83	14.64	−.05	15.18	−.59
	JD	20.37	19.32	1.03	18.48	1.87
	DE	19.37	19.57	.06	19.52	.11
	BP	17.05	17.71	−.09	18.03	−.41
$\sum$ dev^2				1.29		4.91
Ave. dev^2				.18		.70

For this table, $\alpha = .50$, $p = .06$, $\beta = 0$ during message, $\beta = .2$ thereafter. The model is taken through one message and two internal transitions.

squared deviation for the ICC group and .18 average squared deviation for the BUR group). Taking a second internal transition results in worse fit for both groups.

Comparison of the Message Models

Table 15.10 shows the overall average squared error for each of the four models, along with the chance level that would be predicted by the sampling error in the posttest means. The significance level of each average squared error is assessed by a chi-square (χ^2) test and the resulting significance level is shown in the last column of Table 15.10. The error for the simultaneous change hierarchy model is significantly greater than chance level ($p = .001$), but all the other three models are at chance level. The difference in error among the other three models is not significant.

Because there are no significant differences among the delayed change, pullback, or generalization models in terms of fitting the data, we must turn to

TABLE 15.10

THE AVERAGE SQUARED DEVIATION IN THE PREDICTION OF MESSAGE
IMPACT FOR EACH OF THE FOUR MESSAGE EFFECT MODELS[a]

Model	Average squared error	Significance level(p)
Simultaneous change hierarchy	.53	.001
Delayed change hierarchy	.28	.37
Pullback	.20	.70
Generalization	.18	.77

[a] The chance level for the data in this table is .25. A χ^2 test was used to establish significance level. Significance implies lack of fit.

the earlier analysis of the nature of the hierarchy to determine which model is more appropriate. We noted that the pullback model assumed a superordinate attitude Q for BU. On the other hand, the fit of the generalization model and the delayed change hierarchy model depends on the assumption that BU is functionally autonomous, that is, it has no superordinate attitude. The correlational results indicated that BU was indeed influenced by some other attitude. The theory would associate this influence with a superordinate attitude. Additional support for this contention comes from looking at the average means in Table 5.5. There is almost no mean change in the pretest and posttest means for BU in the ICC group. Existence of a superordinate attitude Q with a value of approximately 15.50 would explain this stability. If some other factor (such as upward influence from an attitude further down the hierarchy) were invoked to explain the "nonautoregressive" nature of BU over time, that factor should also produce mean change in average BU for the ICC group. However, as we noted, there is no such mean change. The regression data for BU showed that BU is not autoregressive and hence suggested that a model such as the pullback model should fit the data, and it does. Moreover, the same regression data stand in contradiction to either the delayed change or the generalization model.

In sum, the bulk of the available evidence seems to support the pullback model. This model, as well as the other three, assume an internal transition matrix identical to the B matrix used to test the internal influence model.

OBSERVATIONS

The main objective of this study was to test the hypotheses stated in Chapter 14: (a) that a message impacted at the top of a hierarchy would indirectly create change all through the hierarchy, whereas (b) a message input at the bottom of the hierarchy would have no such filtering process up and would in fact decay over succeeding time periods. This hypothesis was borne out in the present results.

The internal process model with parameter $\beta = .10$ was supported by two path analytic tests. Moreover, three out of four of the message models, all of which used the internal process model with $\beta = .10$ for internal transitions, gave good fit and so also lent support to the internal influence model. Because the difference between the simultaneous and the delayed hierarchical models lay only in the two-phase message impact assumption, the failure in fit for the simultaneous hierarchy model is only an indictment of the message impact equation and has no implication for the internal process model. The support for the internal model indicates that (a) internal influence moves downward only along hierarchical paths, (b) internal change in subordinate attitudes depends on the discrepancy between superior and subordinate attitudes, and (c) the parameter for internal change is fairly small.

The pullback and generalization model fit the data equally well. However, the regression data for BU show it to be nonautoregressive and that supports only the pullback model. The existence of attitude Q superordinate to BU is perfectly plausible in terms of the models developed in Chapter 14. Thus success of the pullback model supports the main assumptions of the original theory. First, the direct effects of messages are present only during the transition immediately after they are heard; during later transitions the message effects filter indirectly through the hierarchy. Second, the size of message effects is a function of the discrepancy between the message and the attitude to which it is addressed. Third, the experiment indicates that the occurrence of transitions does not depend on metric time but rather on the receivers' thinking about the hierarchy. For the same time period after receipt of the message, the ICC group experienced one transition and the BUR group experienced two internal transitions. Apparently the number of transitions depends on some factor other than metric time expired between measurements.

The pullback model does imply one change in the hierarchy model. The simultaneous change model assumes that influences from both external messages and the internal process occur simultaneously in a single transition. The results of the experiment indicate that the message effect occurs in two phases. First, the attitude directly addressed changes in accordance with linear discrepancy theory, and then general effects are produced by a second internal influence transition. The fact that the experimental messages were information-intense stimuli must be taken into account here.

More leisurely written messages in a more leisurely atmosphere might allow the receiver to think about the message while he is reading it, as was assumed by the simultaneous change model. Shorter messages may simply be easier to keep track of and thus present fewer problems of integration to receivers. However, at least for more salient and more information-intense messages, the delayed change model appears to be more appropriate.

CONCLUSION

This study confirmed the information processing model of attitude change toward hierarchically organized concepts. First, the impact of an external message on the attitude addressed by the message is governed by discrepancy theory. Second, change is produced in other attitudes by thinking about the relations between them, that is, there was the predicted internal change during nonmessage intervals and there were the predicted indirect changes in attitudes not discussed in the external message. Third, causal influences between attitudes followed the direction of logical inference: from superordinate to subordinate attitude, or top down in the hierarchy. The specific quantitative form of the model was confirmed in all but one small detail: a strong salient external message has its effects in two phases rather than one. The message first changes the targeted attitude and then sets internal change processes in motion that modify the targeted as well as all other attitudes.

CHAPTER 16

Behaviors and Attitudes in Hierarchical Systems

Contributed by M. Scott Poole and John E. Hunter

PROBLEMS IN MEASURING BEHAVIOR

There has been a great deal of error in the literature on the relationship between attitudes and behavior. Many of these errors stem from poor measurement of behavior. Most studies assess behavior as a single act in a single setting at a single time and treat such an observation as if the behavior were perfectly measured. For studies in which repeated observations were made, behavior was usually found to have a very large random element. Test–retest reliabilities for single acts are rarely greater than .50 and are often near zero. A woman may not purchase her favorite brand on a given day because another brand is on sale, because her favorite brand is not carried, or because it is present only in too large or too small a size, and so on.

Behavior in single settings is also subject to minor instrumental considerations. A man who believes in the advancement of minority people may not give to the United Negro College Fund street drive because he carries no cash, because he does not believe in charity, or because he believes that college

This chapter is an edited version of "Behavior and hierarchies of attitudes: a deterministic model," by M. S. Poole, and J. E. Hunter, in *Message-Attitude-Behavior Relationship*, D. P. Cushman and R. D. McPhee (eds.), New York: Academic Press, 1980.

students should work themselves through school, and so on. However, that same man might mail a substantial check in response to a letter asking for contributions to the defense fund of a black trash collector falsely accused of rape. A bigot might give a quarter to a street collector because she is pretty and reminds him of his daughter.

When behavior has been reliably measured, and when behavior–attitude correlations are transformed from point biserial to biserial correlations, the correlations are usually found to be substantial. However, the literature review presented in this chapter shows that attitude behavior correlations are not always high. We present a theory of the relationship between attitudes and behavior that attempts to explain the variation in correlation by linking behaviors to hierarchies of attitudes. In a nutshell, we assume that behaviors are linked to the bottoms of attitude hierarchies, that is, to specific rather than general attitudes. According to the top down assumption of the information processing model of hierarchical attitudes, the general attitude will only be indirectly linked to the behavior. Path analysis predicts that the correlation between the general attitude and a specific behavior will be reduced by each intermediary attitude. Thus the correlation between an attitude a behavior will be high for the relevant specific attitude that is immediately superordinate to the behavior, will be smaller and smaller with each step upward to superordinate attitudes, and near zero for specific attitudes at the bottom of other branches of the hierarchy. On the other hand, if an index were formed by measuring all the behaviors attached to the bottoms of all the branches of the hierarchy, then that index would have a very high correlation with the general attitude.

This chapter links behavior to a hierarchy of attitudes.

LITERATURE REVIEW

From a number of reviews, it is evident that attitudes, under certain conditions, are related very strongly to behaviors [Ajzen and Fishbein (1977), Schuman and Johnson (1976)]. Various factors other than attitudes or attitudinal properties, including situational constraints and societal expectations or norms, were shown to influence behavior. When these are operating, they can introduce "error" into attitude–behavior relationships by acting counter to or overriding the effect of attitudes. But these are not the only factors that can mask attitude–behavior relations: the complexities of our cognitive organization can foil even the most discerning researchers. For example, if one concept lies between another concept and an individual's conception of a behavior in a logical hierarchy, it will mediate the effect of the attitude toward the second concept on the behavior in question. Even if he is correct in assuming that a person's attitudes influence behavior, the researcher may not be measuring the attitude toward the correct concept or taking intervening attitudes into account. The result of these omissions may be a relatively low attitude–behavior correlation and an incorrect acceptance of the null hypothesis.

Fishbein (1973) noted that attitude toward *general* objects is often a poor predictor when behavior is measured by single acts, but a good predictor when multiple acts are used as the criterion of behavior (Tittle and Hill, 1967). Weigel and Newman (1976) found that, although subjects' general attitudes toward environmental issues exhibited only moderate correlations to single behaviors relating to environmental improvement, their correlations with a set of several such behaviors was .62. Fishbein and Ajzen (1974) found that attitude toward objects (which are general) exhibited a mean correlation of .14 with single behaviors and a mean correlation of .66 with multiple behavioral criteria. On the other hand, Fishbein (1973) presents evidence that attitude toward a *specific* act is a good predictor of intention to act for a single behavior when the situational and normative factors discussed are taken into account. These findings are understandable if we note that a large number of specific behaviors are likely to be associated with general attitudes, whereas for more specific attitudes, there will be fewer associations with specific behaviors. For a question asking the respondent's attitude toward a specific act at a specific time and place, there will probably only be one behavior associated with the attitude. We should expect a higher correlation between attitude and behavior when only one behavior is associated with an attitude than when there are several options and our instruments can only tap one or two. The limitation in our instruments artificially attenuates the attitude–behavior relationship in the latter case (i.e., for general attitudes) because some behaviors associated with the attitude will not be counted by the experimenter.

The more general an attitude is, the more behaviors the investigator must consider to gauge the full impact of the attitude on subjects' behavior. A general attitude will be connected to a large number of behaviors through the strands of the hierarchy leading from it to more specific attitudes and hence to behaviors. The influence of the general attitude on an individual's behavioral choice comes through the effect it has on more specific attitudes that directly pertain to the behavior. Having a favorable general attitude will influence the individual to undertake any of a large set of behaviors. The specific behavior chosen from this set depends not only on specific attitudes as influenced by the general attitude but also on additional situational factors such as norms, others' expectations, or recently received messages that temporarily draw one specific attitude out of line with the others and give a more favorable valence to its associated behavior. However, as important as these other factors are, over the long run the general attitude plays the dominant role in determining behavioral choice. The general attitude sets the stage for the effects of situational factors through its influence on lower-order attitudes. If the general attitude is favorable, subordinate attitudes will also be favorable and the balance toward the behaviors referred is tipped to by the specific attitudes. However, if the general attitude is negative, lower attitudes are also likely to be negative, and the scales are weighted against undertaking the behaviors. The general attitude will also diminish the effects of external messages on specific attitudes. An external message may temporarily change a specific attitude so that it is favorable toward a behavior the individual did not previously favor or vice versa. Over the long run, however, the message effect will decay, as the higher-order attitude draws the specific attitude back into line in the internal-influence process. These temporary changes in specific attitudes can lower the correlation between the general attitude and behavior. Nevertheless, if we consider the long run and look at relatively stable situations, general attitudes will be found to exert an influence on behavior through their effects on specific attitudes. Although a general attitude has a large impact on behavior, a low attitude–behavior correlation may result if (a) only a subset of the total set of behaviors the general attitude effects is measured and (b) short-run changes in lower-order attitudes due to external messages or other sources of error are not considered.

General attitudes also serve another important function in the motivation of behavior. Does an individual actually have a preexisting attitude toward a specific act at a specific time and place (e.g., going to a party at 7:30 on Friday night at Joe's house)? Most people probably have no such attitude in their cognitive organization; instead they construct an attitude on the basis of more general attitudes (i.e., on the basis of their attitudes toward parties and toward Joe). Schwartz (1978) recently made a similar argument. What we have, then, is the mediating constructed attitude "going to a party," between attitude toward "parties" and the intention to go to the party. This specific attitude can be regarded as a downward extension of the attitudinal hierarchy of which "parties" is a member. There might be several other specific attitudes involving parties associated with "parties," which, in turn, might be only one of a number of subordinate attitudes to the next higher concept (e.g., recreation). Let us assume that (a) every specific attitude at the lowest level of the hierarchy has a single behavior associated with it; (b) behaviors are associated only with these lowest-level attitudes; and (c) the other assumptions of the hierarchical model of attitude organization hold. As we move up the hierarchy, we find more and more behaviors associated with each more general attitude (see Fig. 16.1). They would, however, be associated only indirectly. More general attitudes would only exert influence on behaviors through their influence on the specific attitudes associated with the behaviors. Given a high level of consistency (e.g., $r = .70$) among attitudes in the hierarchy, the general attitude toward recreation could best be predicted by considering all behaviors

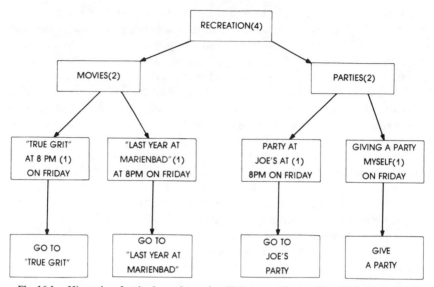

Fig. 16.1.   Hierarchy of attitudes and associated behaviors. The number of behaviors directly or indirectly associated with the attitude is in parentheses. Behaviors are on the bottom line.

associated with the hierarchy because the correlation between recreation and any one specific behavior should be attenuated by the two mediating causal paths.

What evidence is available bearing on the ideas advanced in the preceding paragraphs? Most studies of the attitude–behavior relationships have not attempted to measure attitudes at several levels of generality. The predictions made by the hierarchical model for cases where several levels of attitudes are measured are quite clear. In studies such as those by Ajzen and Fishbein (1969), DeFleur and Westie (1958), and Green (1968), where sizable relationships were found between general attitudes and behaviors, we should also find a fairly large amount of consistency between more and less general attitudes. Moreover, specific attitudes toward the behavior should mediate the effect of the general attitudes on behavioral intention. In studies such as those by LaPiere (1934), Bray (1950), or Berg (1966), where little relation between general attitudes and behaviors is found, we should find no hierarchical relationship between the general attitude and more specific attitudes. Indeed, we should find that the specific attitude toward the behavior is part of a hierarchy entirely different from the one belonging to the general attitude. For example, in the LaPiere (1934) study, the behavior consisted of willingness to serve a specific well-dressed Chinese couple, usually accompanied by LaPiere himself. The attitude measured referred to willingness to serve "members of the Chinese race." Whereas the hierarchy containing "members of the Chinese race" is one that could cover the attitude toward serving LaPiere and the Chinese couple, there are also others, such as "well-dressed and pleasant customers." If our hierarchical formulation is correct, we expect to find that the attitude toward the behavior is subsumed under a different general attitude than the one measured. The studies just discussed are not offered as evidence for our formulations; instead they are mentioned as illustrations of the types of findings we would expect if the data suitable to testing the hierarchical assumption had been collected by these investigators. Luckily, several studies have reported findings that allow a preliminary assessment of the model's viability.

Liska (1974) compared attitude–behavior consistency across five levels of attitudinal generality and two levels of behavioral generality for eight academic "coping behaviors." He found significant correlations between the lowest three levels of attitudes and the more specific behavior. However, where the five attitudinal levels were entered into a multiple regression equation predicting the specific behavior, the partial regression coefficients for the higher level attitudes went to zero, whereas those for the most specific attitude remained significant and about the same as the zero-order correlations. This is consistent with the argument that specific attitudes mediate the relationship between more general attitudes and behaviors. Weigel, Vernon, and Tognacci (1974) measured low, moderate, and high specificity attitudes toward the Sierra Club and environmental issues and correlated these measures with level of participation in the Sierra Club. The most specific attitude had the highest correlation with participation ($r = .60$), middle-level attitudes exhibited moderate correlations ($r = .38$), and the least specific attitude had a low correlation ($r = .16$). Partial correlations between the moderate specificity attitudes and behavior controlling for the most specific attitude are approximately zero, as is the second-order partial correlation between the low specificity attitude and behavior when high and moderate specificity attitudes are controlled. If we assume that low, moderate, and high specificity attitudes make up a three-tiered hierarchy with the low specificity attitude corresponding to the highest level of the hierarchy, these results support the assumptions just discussed, where lower-level attitudes mediate the relationship between higher-level attitudes and behavior. Ajzen and Fishbein (1970) and Heberlein and Black (1976) report findings that also support the hierarchical model, in terms of both the relative sizes of attitude–behavior correlations for general and specific attitudes and the effects of partialling more specific attitudes from the correlation of general attitudes and behavior.

Schwartz and Tessler (1972) and Ajzen and Fishbein (1969) also found that a more general attitude toward the object shows a lower correlation with behavior than specific attitude toward the act. However, separating the more specific attitude toward the act from the correlation of attitude toward the object with behavior does not reduce this correlation to zero, although it is reduced. Part of the reason for this may lie in the fact that measures of specific attitudes were not corrected for unreliability by Schwartz and Tessler or by Ajzen and Fishbein. Separating an unreliable measure of specific attitude from the correlation of the general attitude and the behavior might leave part of the mediating influence of the specific attitude uncontrolled: a significant partial correlation could thus result even if there were no direct influence of the general attitude on the behavior.

For the most part, evidence garnered from past research favors the hierarchical formulation. Several scope conditions and extensions of the basic model suggest themselves. First, the relationships posited will hold only for people who have thought about the attitudes in a given hierarchy in relation to one another. Otherwise, the consistency-producing internal-influence process will not occur, and causal paths for internal influence will not be well defined. Because existence of the hierarchy depends on the amount of thinking people have done, in any given sample we are likely to find some people with relatively undeveloped hierarchies and some with extremely well established hierarchies. Only for those people with well-established hierarchies will the relationships elaborated in this section hold. Schwartz (1978) reports evidence germane to this point. In a study of volunteering behavior, he found that temporal stability of general attitudes was a moderator of attitude–behavior relationships. Only for stable general attitudes, such as would be expected in a well-established hierarchy, were correlations between specific attitudes and behaviors significant.

Second, the behavior must be linked with the attitudinal hierarchy for a particular attitude to influence it. A consideration of the various motives that people give for their behaviors indicates the extremely diverse range of attitude objects with which a given behavior can be associated. A person may go to a party primarily for recreation, to make business contacts, or in search of sexual conquests. People may participate in a demonstration because they enjoy open air events, believe in a political party, seek excitement, hate government, or support the cause behind the demonstration. Hence, one or another of any number of possible attitudes may have the primary role in governing a behavior for different people. For some acts and situations the dominant general attitude will be the same for most people whereas for others, there will be a number of dominant general attitudes in any sample. Insofar as the wrong general attitude (or only one of a number of appropriate general attitudes) is selected, the correlation between general attitude and behavior will be attenuated. Which attitudes a person associates with a behavior will be largely a product of the messages he or she has received about the behavior and the attitude. Depending on experience and the messages received, a person may place different behaviors under different classes of attitude objects. Thus one person may attribute going to church or participating in church activities to his liking for his church, whereas another may relate these activities to his religious attitudes or his love for God or for his family. A pretest eliciting attitudes associated with a given behavior could help resolve this issue. Rather than merely assuming that the behavior corresponds to an attitude object, the experimenter could determine beforehand which attitudes are actually relevant to the behavior. In considering the relationship of attitudes to behavior, the researcher must realize that different subjects may relate the behavior to different general attitudes—that is, for different subjects the specific attitude toward the behavior may be subsumed by different general hierarchies. Thus, depending on what messages people have received in the past, there may be subgroups in any sample for which different superordinate attitudes are relevant.

The preceding discussion assumes that a behavior is attached to only one hierarchy; but this need not be so. Figure 16.2 shows a behavior, "Give to the United Negro College Fund," which is attached to two hierarchies—a hierarchy of ethnic attitudes and a hierarchy of financial attitudes. In such a case, the correlation between the act and either hierarchy would be low, but the multiple correlation using both hierarchies would be substantial.

In summary, we considered the message–attitude–behavior question in light of the hierarchical theory of attitude change. We developed and reviewed evidence relevant to several propositions:

1. Attitudes are hierarchically arranged and internal influence goes down only along hierarchical channels.

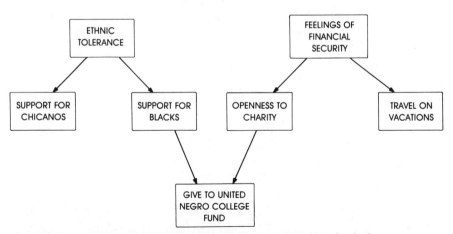

Fig. 16.2. A behavior that is attached to two hierarchies of attitudes.

2. Behaviors are associated only with attitudes at the bottom of the hierarchy.

3. Influence of higher-order attitudes on behaviors is indirect and mediated by more specific attitudes.

4. There are individual differences in the types of hierarchies a given behavior is associated.

IMPLICATIONS OF THE HIERARCHICAL MODEL FOR MESSAGE DESIGN

We have spent a great deal of space on attitude–attitude and attitude–behavior relations and have generally left ideas concerning message–attitude–behavior relations implicit. In this section we attempt to correct this by making this connection explicit.

1. Individual differences in attitudinal structure make predicting the specific effect of a message on an individual at are best difficult and at worst quixotic. Different people will have different hierarchies. Differences in the number and type of superordinate attitudes will result in differences in decay of messages aimed at specific attitudes (Chapters 14 and 15) and in the extent to which message effects on higher-level attitudes filter down to specific attitudes. Differences in the extent to which individual hierarchies are integrated and established will result in differences in the influence general attitudes have over specific attitudes (and thus over behavior). The nature of the concepts in a hierarchy is an important factor in determining predictability across individuals. For concepts that are an important part of a culture, there will probably be a great deal of consistency across individuals, because people have been exposed to many similar messages about these concepts and have had to think about them in relation to one another. At this time, energy issues are probably a good example of the type of cultural commonplaces that would yield a similar hierarchy for many individuals. For concepts that are not regularly dealt with in a culture, such as attitudes toward novels and novelists, there may be great individual differences in hierarchies for most people (although certain subcultures, such as critical schools, may have similar hierarchies).

2. The higher up in a hierarchy a message can strike, the more wide-ranging its effect on behavior will be. Because higher-order attitudes will bring lower-order attitudes into line, they will tend to counter message effects on lower-order attitudes. However, the effect of a message on an attitude at the top of the hierarchy will not decay. Further, though attitude change relatively high or in the middle of a hierarchy will decay, it will also filter downward through the hierarchy and have a relatively long-term delayed effect on more specific attitudes. In addition, attitudes higher in a hierarchy are linked to more behaviors than are less general attitudes, and, as a result, changing general

attitudes will effect a wider range of behaviors than will changing specific attitudes. In general, the higher up a hierarchy an attitude is, the broader the effect of a message directed at that attitude will be. There is, however, a counter-balancing consideration. A person will probably have been exposed to more information about general concepts than about specific ones. As shown in Chapter 12, the impact of a single message on a concept is inversely related to the amount of information associated with the concept. Whereas we may be able to have a more profound effect on people's behavior by addressing messages to general rather than to specific attitudes, single messages are likely to have much less effect on general attitudes than they would on specific ones.

3. A lag will generally occur between reception of a message directed at a general attitude and the indirect impact of the message of behavioral choice, because the filtration of message effects through the hierarchy is gradual. Because thinking about the concepts in a hierarchy triggers the internal influence process, the filtering down of message effects can be hastened if people can be made to review the hierarchy soon after receiving the initial message. A particularly effective stimulus for review can be provided through follow-up messages. If possible, these messages should mention all levels of concepts in the particular strand of the hierarchy to which the behavior belongs to ensure that people do not truncate their reflection on the hierarchy. To the extent that a message can help people organize their thinking about a hierarchy of concepts, it will favor the influence of more general attitudes on behavior.

4. Messages do not necessarily have to change attitudes to influence behavior. They can also rearrange hierarchies of concepts and create linkages between concepts that were previously unrelated or only weakly related. There are at least two ways of doing this. First, as we noted, specific attitudes are often constructed from more general ones. If we knew which of an individual's attitudes were somewhat relevant to a behavior were favorable, we could design a message to encourage the individual to construct an attitude toward the behavior from only favorable attitudes. For example, if we knew that a certain man liked giving to charities, and we wanted him to donate blood, we could provide evidence that blood donation was a charitable activity, thus associating the constructed attitude toward blood donation with the more general attitude toward charitable giving. A second alternative would be to take a concept that presently falls in one hierarchy and attempt to convince people to reclassify it. Once the concept has been logically reclassified, the internal-influence process should change the attitude toward the concept so that it is more in line with its new superordinate attitudes.

The amount of exposure to information about the concepts in a hierarchy will moderate how effective external messages are in rearranging concepts. In areas where subjects have little information about the concepts and the behavior, a potent message is likely to encounter little difficulty in effecting a rearrangement. However, where subjects have a large amount of information about the concepts or the behavior or where hierarchies are well established, messages may run afoul of existing logical structures. A message will be most effective in rearranging a hierarchy if it does not have to compete with past classificatory messages. If a person has received a number of messages about the relationships among a set of concepts, reclassification will be difficult because the new message will have to counteract past information.

CONCLUSION

It is paradoxical that general attitudes, with their wide-ranging effects, often seem to be less important determinants of behavior than specific attitudes. Over the long run, general attitudes exert a much more profound influence over behavioral choice than do specific attitudes. However, because specific attitude toward the act is a more immediate cause than the general attitudes that set the stage for behavioral choice, it usually shows a higher correlation with behavior. If we are interested only in the prediction of behavior, attitude toward the act is as far as we need to go, because it is the most reliable attitudinal indicator of whether a behavior will occur (subject to scope conditions, of course). However, if we want to understand or explain how behavioral choice occurs, we must investigate cognitive processes, and general attitudes and beliefs become more important concerns.

This chapter is an attempt to specify one cognitive process that may mediate the message–behavior relationship. It is immediately apparent that hierarchies may not be the only cognitive structures that enter into behavioral choice. Research on the organization of memory indicates that the logical hierarchy is only one of a number of structural arrangements encountered in mapping memory. It is possible that patterns of internal influence based on different organizational principles could also condition behavioral choice (Chapter 15).

CHAPTER 17

Hierarchical Models from Other Theories

INTRODUCTION

We can construct a hierarchical model from almost any theory developed in Part I. This chapter discusses the major theories. If the effect of an external message is delivered in two phases (a direct effect on the attitude targeted and indirect effects through a second internal process phase), then the only part of the hierarchical model that is new is the model of the internal process. Thus, for simplicity, this chapter considers only the effects of a probe message, such as "What do you think of the war in Iraq?" or an internal probe message that arises from thinking about one of the concepts in the hierarchy. For simplicity, only logical inclusion hierarchies are considered.

Social judgment theory and dissonance theories make attitude change predictions that are identical to those of information processing theory. Because the source of internal messages is the self, balance theory makes attitude change predictions that are identical to those of reinforcement theory without extinction. Because congruity theory predicts that attitude change derives from a source object discrepancy, it is very hard to see how congruity theory would be extended to hierarchically organized attitudes. The "obvious" extension is problematical.

The bulk of this chapter is devoted to reinforcement theory. The basic reinforcement model is easily derived but makes bizarre predictions. The basic model predicts that internal processes will drive lower order attitudes to infinite intensity, even though the attitude at the top of the hierarchy remains constant. The lower the order, the more rapid the intensity grows. Furthermore, this prediction does not depend on the specific mathematical equation used, it follows from the qualitative logic of reinforcement theory without extinction.

If extinction is assumed in the reinforcement model, then probe messages drive all attitudes to extinction. However, the lower order attitudes are still distinguished by the fact that they decay to 0 last. This too follows from the general logic of the reinforcement theory rather than from the specific equations used in the model.

Because balance theory makes the same predictions as reinforcement theory for hierarchically organized concepts, it suffers from the same problems.

The problems of reinforcement and balance theory are triumphs for the formal theory building process. The problems revealed in this chapter are not evident in the domain of isolated attitudes where the theories were originally derived. Moreover, these problems are not obvious on the basis of intuitive reasoning. At least we were caught off guard by the implications that emerged from the mathematical analysis.

SOCIAL JUDGMENT AND DISSONANCE THEORIES

For the internal messages of the hierarchical theory, the source is the self and thus highly credible. When this is true, the basic attitude change equations of social judgment theory and dissonance theory reduce to the linear discrepancy equation of information processing theory. Thus the internal change equations will also be the same as for information processing theory.

Information processing theory predicts no source change (i.e., no change in self esteem) due to just thinking about things. If the self attitude is regarded as perfectly credible, then dissonance theory also predicts no source change. However, social judgment theory predicts that perfect agreement produces an increase in the attitude toward the source. Could a prolonged period of thinking produce a towering ego?

BALANCE THEORY

The attitude change equation for balance theory (Chapter 5) is

$$\Delta a = \alpha sm$$

If the source is the self, then this equation becomes

$$\Delta a = \alpha \sigma m \tag{17.1}$$

where σ is the fixed attitude toward the self. This equation differs from the equation for reinforcement theory only in naming the multiplicative parameter "$\alpha\sigma$" rather than "α." Thus the hierarchical model for balance theory will be the same as the reinforcement model without extinction, that is, the basic reinforcement model (see Chapter 2).

The preceding discussion assumes that there is no change is self esteem. Yet source change is a fundamental assumption in balance theory. Strictly speaking, balance theory will predict attitude change only if there is source change. If there is change in self esteem in the hierarchical situation, then the self esteem of the thinker will change with consideration of every concept in the hierarchy. Self esteem will go up every time the superordinate attitude agrees with the focal attitude in sign and decrease every time there is disagreement. As long as self esteem does not become negative, the change in attitudes proceeds according to the reinforcement model but with speed varying up and down with self esteem. With each round of attitude change, the attitudes become more and more alike in algebraic sign and hence agreement becomes more and more likely. Thus, for most hierarchies most of the time, the attitude change will be predicted to be like that of reinforcement theory and the source change will always be positive.

If internal messages produce no source change, then balance theory makes the same predictions as the reinforcement model without extinction. If there is source change, then balance theory predicts that thinking about hierarchies produces enhancement of self esteem.

CONGRUITY THEORY

The specification of the hierarchical model for congruity theory is problematic. Congruity theory pictures the positive message as setting up a joint conditioning process in which attitudes toward the source and object change in the direction of one another. But the internal messages of the hierarchical model have the self as a source. Would a conditioning theory admit the self as a source?

If self concept is substituted into the attitude change equation for congruity theory, then we have two equations

$$\Delta a = \alpha(\sigma - a) \qquad \text{and} \qquad \Delta a = \alpha(-\sigma - a) \qquad (17.2)$$

depending on whether the superordinate attitude is positive or negative and where σ is the fixed attitude toward the self. These equations are similar to the information processing equation where the message value is $+\sigma$ if the superordinate attitude is positive and $-\sigma$ if the superordinate attitude is negative. In particular, a long series of probe messages will cause all attitudes to converge to the same value: $+\sigma$ if the top attitude was initially positive and $-\sigma$ if the top attitude was initially negative.

The preceding discussion assumed no source change, yet source change is a fundamental assumption in congruity theory. Strictly speaking, there can be no attitude change if there is no source change, because there is no pressure of incongruity (according to one derivation) or there is no simultaneous conditioning (as assumed in the other derivation). If self esteem changes with every internal message, then the theory becomes very complicated.

REINFORCEMENT THEORY: GENERAL CONSIDERATION

There are two fundamental issues for reinforcement theory in respect to hierarchies: should there be a theory of change? If so, then should it make the top down assumption stemming from logic?

Behavioristic reinforcement theory explicitly assumes that thought is an epiphenomenon. If so, then just thinking about something will elicit no change. Thus, for behavioristic reinforcement theory, the internal process either does not exist or has no effect if it does occur. This theory is disconfirmed by the studies done on hierarchies, including those reviewed in Chapter 16.

There can be cognitive reinforcement theories. However, the thought process in reinforcement theory is usually associative rather than logical. For such a theory, the pattern of influence will not be top down. Rather, it will predict that all the attitudes in a hierarchy will affect all the others. This theory is also disconfirmed by the studies done to date.

To fit existing data, reinforcement theory must not only allow cognitive processes but those processes must be logical as well as associative. The next section presents a hierarchical model derived from reinforcement theory using the top down causal hypothesis. However, this model makes dramatically bizarre predictions. Given a series of probe questions, the attitude at the top remains constant but the lower attitudes become infinite. In fact, in the long run the rank order of attitudes is always inversely related to distance from the top and the rate of increase in affect steadily increases.

This result originally lead us to develop the reinforcement with extinction model as a way of "taming" the unanticipated growth of lower order attitudes. The extinction model does tame the growth, but a series of probe messages is then predicted to cause the extinction of all attitudes in the hierarchy.

REINFORCEMENT THEORY: THE BASIC MODEL

If there are no external messages, then the attitude at the top of the hierarchy will remain unchanged, that is,

$$\Delta x = 0 \tag{17.3}$$

The external process generates messages about lower order attitudes in accordance with their immediately superordinate attitudes. Because the equation for attitude change in the basic reinforcement model (Chapter 2) is

$$\Delta a = \alpha m$$

the corresponding impact of the top attitude onto an attitude at the second order is

$$\Delta y = \beta x \qquad (17.4)$$

where the multiplicative parameter is denoted β to distinguish it from the external message parameter α. The impact of attitude y onto an attitude immediately subordinate to it is

$$\Delta z = \beta y \qquad (17.5)$$

Thus, for a hierarchy three levels deep, a probe message will produce change within each strand given by

$$\Delta x = 0$$
$$\Delta y = \beta x \qquad (17.6)$$
$$\Delta z = \beta y$$

If a sequence of n probe messages is given, then the time functions for these attitudes will be

$$x_n = x_0$$
$$y_n = y_0 + \beta x_0 n \qquad (17.7)$$
$$z_n = z_0 + \beta y_0 n + \frac{\beta^2}{2} x_0 n(n-1)$$

The bizarre nature of this prediction is brought out in the example graphed in Fig. 17.1. The value of β is estimated to be $\beta = .1$ in Chapter 15 and this value is used in the example. In the example it is assumed that at the time of the first probe message, the value of the attitude at the top is one and all lower order attitudes start at zero. Each probe message causes the second order attitude to increase due to the impact of the top attitude. Thus attitude y increases with each probe message until it passes the top attitude (after 10 messages). It steadily increases as long as probe messages are generated. Once the second-order attitude y becomes positive, it has impact on the third-order attitude z. As y becomes larger and larger, the impact on z becomes greater and greater and hence z grows faster and faster. The third-order attitude z first passes the top attitude (after 15 messages) and eventually passes the second order attitude (21 messages) as well.

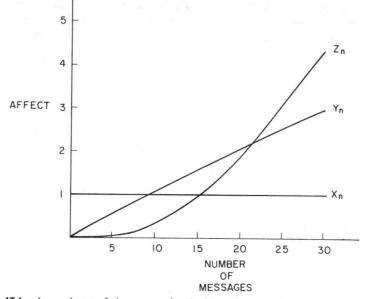

Fig. 17.1. A sample set of time curves for the hierarchical reinforcement model without extinction (x is the top attitude in the hierarchy, y is a second-order attitude, and z is a third-order attitude).

Analysis of the time functions shows this example to be typical of hierarchies in which the top attitude is initially positive. The top attitude drives the second order attitudes linearly to $+\infty$. And so on. If the top attitude is negative, then it drives the second-order attitudes linearly to $-\infty$. As the second-order attitudes become more and more negative, they drive the third-order attitudes quadratically to $-\infty$, and so on.

Careful examination of the logic of the previous paragraph shows that the conclusions do not depend on the specific mathematical equations. A positive attitude at the top of the hierarchy generates a positive message that impacts on the second-order attitude every time the hierarchy is activated. Thus the rise in the second-order attitude until it passes the top attitude is inexorable. Similarly for the other relations between the attitudes. The pattern of low intensity at the top and ever higher intensity at lower attitudes follows from the qualitative assumptions of reinforcement theory and not from the linearity of the basic model.

The predictions just made are not greatly altered by the consideration of external persuasive messages. The crucial thing about a persuasive message is that in addition to the specific change induced, the persuasive message acts as a probe message for the hierarchy. From the point of view of long range effects, it is the probe message effect of persuasive messages that is most important because it induces the explosive growth of lower order attitudes. Only messages directed at the top of the hierarchy have a lasting effect, predictable from the message content.

REINFORCEMENT THEORY WITH EXTINCTION

If the lower order attitudes are not to grow to infinity, then there must be a countervailing force. This suggested an extinction law. The Hullian self punishing response will generate self punishment in proportion to the strength of the response and hence choke the growth off after some level. Thus we introduced the extinction model into Chapter 2, even though the direct evidence from learning experiments and from attitude studies tends to be disconfirming. The attitude change law with extinction (Chapter 2) is

$$\Delta a = \alpha m - \varepsilon a$$

If there are no external messages, then the only force operating on the top attitude is extinction:

$$\Delta x = -\varepsilon x \tag{17.8}$$

The second-order attitudes are influenced by the top attitude and by extinction:

$$\Delta y = \beta x - \varepsilon y \tag{17.9}$$

The second-order attitudes are influenced by the superordinate second-order attitude and by extinction:

$$\Delta z = \beta y - \varepsilon z \tag{17.10}$$

Thus, if there are no external messages, then the internal process generated by a probe message on a three layer hierarchy is described for each strand by

$$\Delta x = -\varepsilon x$$
$$\Delta y = \beta x - \varepsilon y \tag{17.11}$$
$$\Delta z = \beta y - \varepsilon z$$

The time functions for a sequence of probe messages are

$$x_n = x_0(1 - \varepsilon)^n$$
$$y_n = y_0(1 - \varepsilon)^n + \beta x_0(1 - \varepsilon)^{n-1} \tag{17.12}$$
$$z_n = z_0(1 - \varepsilon)^n + \beta y_0(1 - \varepsilon)^{n-1} + \frac{\beta^2}{2} z_0 n(n - 1)(1 - \varepsilon)^{n-2}$$

The predictions of this model are seen in an example in Fig. 17.2. This example again assumes $\beta = .1$, that the initial value of the top attitude is one, and that the lower order initial attitudes are zero. The extinction parameter ε is taken to be as large as the internal influence parameter β, that is, $\varepsilon = .1$.

In Fig. 17.2. the top attitude steadily decays to zero. In the beginning, the impact of the top attitude on the second-order attitude x is stronger than extinction and the second-order attitude grows. Once x has become weak enough, the extinction effect is greater than the impact of the top attitude and the second-order attitude ceases to grow (10 messages) and begins to decay. However, the second-order attitude passes the top attitude after 9 messages and remains larger thereafter. While the second order attitude y is positive, it exerts a positive impact on the third-order attitudes that are subordinate to it. In the beginning, the second order attitude y is strong enough that its influence is greater than extinction and the third-order attitude increases. However, after 19 messages, the impact of the second-order attitude is less than the force of extinction and the third-order attitude z begins to decay. The third-order attitude z passes the second-order attitude after 16 messages and remains higher thereafter.

If the top attitude is negative, then the pattern in Fig. 17.2 is just reversed in algebraic sign.

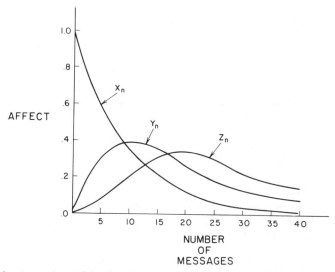

Fig. 17.2.   A sample set of time functions for the reinforcement model with extinction (x is the top attitude, y is a second-order attitude, and z is a third-order attitude).

If the lower order attitudes start out different from zero, then the pattern can be more complicated. However, the general principles are these: a long string of probe messages will extinguish all the attitudes in the hierarchy. As long as an attitude is greater than zero, it will hold its subordinate attitudes above zero. Thus lower order attitudes are usually the last to decay.

Whereas the basic reinforcement model predicted that lower order attitudes grow ever more rapidly to infinity, the extinction model predicts that all attitudes decay to zero. Where the basic reinforcement model predicted that the lower the order, the more rapidly the attitude grows infinitely intense, the extinction model predicts that the lower the order the later the attitude decays to 0.

EXTINCTION AND PERSUASIVE MESSAGES

According to the extinction model, attitudes will be preserved from extinction only if there are external persuasive messages. However, persuasive messages may not preserve the entire hierarchy.

Consider the hierarchy of concepts in Fig. 17.3. Suppose that a series of external persuasive messages are directed at concept *B*. Attitude *b* will be preserved from extinction. So will the immediately subordinate attitudes *d* and *e*. However, the attitude at the top of the hierarchy *a* will decay to zero as will all the attitudes in the other branch, that is, *c*, *f*, and *g*.

REINFORCEMENT THEORY: CONCLUSION

Most learning theorists believe that learning data has shown that extinction does not exist as a separate process. They explain apparent extinction of one response as the counterconditioning of another response. Evidence against extinction from attitude change studies is cited in Chapter 2 under the rubric "mere exposure." There is also evidence against extinction in the hierarchical study of Poole and Hunter reported in Chapter 15. That study had a double pretest in which the first pretest acted as a probe message for the hierarchy. No evidence of decay to 0 was found. The "decay" found in that study was

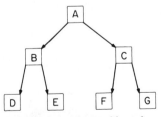

Fig. 17.3. An abstract hierarchy.

not decay to 0 but decay of attitude change back toward a superordinate attitude.

Reinforcement theory appears to be stuck with the prediction of extremely intense lower order attitudes. This is certainly counter to the beliefs of most attitude researchers. Rokeach (1969) for example has argued for years that we hold much more strongly to central beliefs than to peripheral beliefs. He believes that values (which are attitudes towards very abstract concepts) are stronger yet. But we know of no detailed surveys that have proven this point, so maybe the common wisdom is wrong.

Reinforcement theory makes a remarkable prediction about individual differences. According to the basic reinforcement model, only the feeble minded are likely to have any neutral attitudes. Perhaps we are selecting Supreme Court justices by the worst possible criteria.

References

Abelson, R. P. (1959). Modes of resolution of belief dilemmas. *Journal of Conflict Resolution* **3**, 343–352.

Abelson, R. P. (1967). Mathematical models in social psychology. *In* "Advances in Experimental Social Psychology" vol. 3 (Leonard Berkowitz, ed.), pp. 1–54. New York: Academic Press.

Abelson, R. P. (1968a). Comment: uncooperative personality variables. *In* "Theories of Cognitive Consistency" (R. P. Abelson, E. Aronson, W. J. McGuire, T. M. Newcomb, M. J. Rosenberg, and P. H. Tannenbaum, eds.) pp. 648–651. Chicago: Rand McNally.

Abelson, R. P. (1968b). Discussion: minimalist vs. maximalist positions on cognitive structure. *In* "Theories of Cognitive Consistency" (R. P. Abelson, E. Aronson, W. J. McGuire, T. M. Newcomb, M. J. Rosenberg, and P. H. Tanenbaum, eds.) pp. 526–528. Chicago: Rand McNally.

Abelson, R. P., and Rosenberg, M. J. (1958). Symbolic psychologic: a model of attitudinal cognition. *Behavioral Science* **3**, 1–13.

Ajzen, I., and Fishbein, M. (1969). The prediction of behavioral intentions in a choice situation. *Journal of Experimental Social Psychology* **5**, 400–416.

Ajzen, I., and Fishbein, M. (1970). The prediction of behavior from attitudinal and normative variables. *Journal of Experimental Social Psychology* **6**, 466–487.

Ajzen, I., and Fishbein, M. (1977). Attitude–behavior relations: a theoretical analysis and review of empirical research. *Psychological Bulletin* **84**, 888–918.

Albrecht, S. L., Defleur, M. L., and Warner, L. G. (1972). Attitude–behavior relationships: a reexamination of the postulate of contingent consistency. *Pacific Sociological Review* **15**, 149–168.

Aldrich, J. (1975). Candidate support functions in the 1968 election: an empirical application of the spatial model. *Public Choice* **22**, 1–22.

Alford, R. T. (1963). "Party and Society." Chicago: Rand McNally.

Allport, G. W. (1937). "Personality: A Psychological Interpretation." New York: Holt.

313

Anderson, N. H. (1959). Test of a model for opinion change. *Journal of Abnormal and Social Psychology* **59**, 371–381.

Anderson, N. H. (1964). Linear models for responses measured on a continuous scale. *Journal of Mathematical Psychology* **1**, 121–142.

Anderson, N. H. (1965a). Averaging versus adding as a stimulus combination role in impression formation. *Journal of Experimental Psychology* **70**, 394–400.

Anderson, N. H. (1965b). Primacy effects in personality impression formation. *Journal of Personality and Social Psychology* **2**, 1–9.

Anderson, N. H. (1971). Integration theory and attitude change. *Psychological Review* **78**, 171–206.

Anderson, N. H. (1974a). Cognitive algebra. *In* "Advances in Experimental Social Psychology" Vol. 7. (L. L. Berkowitz, ed.). New York: Academic Press.

Anderson, N. H. (1974b). Information integration theory: a brief survey. *In* "Contemporary Developments in Mathematical Psychology" Vol. 2. (D. H. Krantz, R. C. Atkinson, R. D. Luce, and P. Suppes, eds.) pp. 236–305. San Francisco: W. H. Freeman.

Anderson, N. H., and Hovland, C. (1957). The representation of order effects in communication research. *In* "The Order of Presentation in Persuasion" (C. Hovland ed.) pp. 158–169. New Haven: Yale University Press.

Annis, A. D., and Meier, N. C. (1934). The induction of opinion change through suggestion by means of "planted content." *Journal of Social Psychology* **5**, 65–81.

Arbuthnot, J. (1977). The role of attitudinal and personality variables in the prediction of environmental behavior and knowledge. *Environment and Behavior* **9**, 217–232.

Arbuthnot, J., and Lingg, S. (1975). A comparison of French and American environmental behaviors, knowledge, and attitudes. *International Journal of Psychology* **10**, 275–281.

Aronson, E., Turner, J. A., and Carlsmith, J. M. (1963). Communicator credibility and communication discrepancy as determinants of opinion change. *Journal of Abnormal and Social Psychology* **67**, 31–36.

Asch, S. E. (1948). The doctrine of suggestion, prestige, and imitation in social psychology. *Psychological Review* **55**, 250–276.

Ashby, W. R. (1956). "An Introduction to Cybernetics" London: Chapman and Hall.

Ashby, W. R. (1963). "An Introduction to Cybernetics" New York: Wiley.

Atkinson, J. W., and Birch, O. (1970). "The Dynamics of Action" New York: Wiley.

Bandura, A. (1962). Social Learning through imitation. *In* "Nebraska Symposium on Motivation" (M. R. Jones, ed.) pp. 211–269. Lincoln, Nebraska: University of Nebraska Press.

Beer, S. H. (1973). The British political system. *In* "Patterns of Government," 3rd Edition, (S. Beer, A. Ulam, S. Berger, and G. Goldman, eds.) pp. 121–329. New York: Random House.

Berelson, B., Lazarsfeld, P. F., and McPhee, W. N. (1954). "Voting." Chicago: University of Chicago Press.

Berg, K. E. (1966). Ethnic attitudes and agreement with a Negro person. *Journal of Personality and Social Psychology* **4**, 215–220.

Bergin, A. E., (1962). The effect of dissonant persuasive communications on changes in a self-referring attitude. *Journal of Personality* **30**, 423–438.

Bettman, J. R. (1979). "An Information Processing Theory of Consumer Choice." Reading, Massachusetts: Addison-Wesley.

Blalock, H. (1971). "Causal Models in the Social Sciences." Chicago: Aldine.

Bogardus, E. S. (1931). "Fundamentals of Social Psychology." 2nd ed. New York: Century.

Boucher, S., and Insko, C. A. (1966). Communicator discrepancy, source credibility, and opinion change. *Journal of Personality and Social Psychology* **4**, 614–621.

Bray, D. W. (1950). The prediction of behavior from two attitude scales. *Journal of Abnormal and Social Psychology* **45**, 64–84.

Brickman, P., Redfield, Jr., Harrison, A., and Crandall, R. (1972). Drive and predisposition as factors in the attitudinal effects of mere exposure. *Journal of Experimental Social Psychology* **8**, 31–44.

Brock, T. (1967). Communication discrepancy and intent to persuade as determinants of counterargument production. *Journal of Experimental Social Psychology* **3**, 296–309.

Bronfenbrenner, U. (1970). "Two Worlds of Childhood." New York: Russell Sage Foundation.

Brookfield, H. C. (1969). On the environment as perceived. *In* "Progress in Geography: International Reviews of Current Research." Vol. I, pp. 51–80. London: Edward Arnold.

Brown, R. (1962). Models of attitude change. *In* "New Directions in Psychology I." (R. Brown, E. Glanter, E. Hess, and G. Mandler, eds.) pp. 3–85. New York: Holt, Rinehart, and Winston.

Bruvold, W. H. (1973). Belief and behavior as determinants of environmental attitudes. *Environment and Behavior* **5**, 202–218.

Burgess, R., and Sales, S. (1971). Attitudinal effects of "mere exposure": a reevaluation. *Journal of Experimental Social Psychology* **7**, 461–472.

Bush, R. R., and Mosteller, F. (1955). "Stochastic Models for Learning." New York: Wiley.

Butler, D., and Stokes, D. (1969). "Political Change in Britain." New York: St. Martin's Press.

Butler, D., and Stokes, D. (1974). "Political Change in Britain" 2nd ed. New York: St. Martin's Press.

Campbell, A., Converse, P., Miller, W., and Stokes, D. (1960) "The American Voter." New York: John Wiley.

Canter, D. V. (1971). Architectural psychology. Proceedings of the Conference held at Dalandui, University of Strathclyde. London: RIBA Publications.

Cantril, H. (1944). "Gauging Public Opinion." Princeton: Princeton University Press.

Cantril, H. (1946). The intensity of an attitude. *Journal of Abnormal and Social Psychology* **41**, 129–135.

Cappella, J. N., and Folger, J. P. (1980). An information-processing explanation of attitude-behavior inconsistency. *In* "Message-Attitude-Behavior Relationship" (D. P. Cushman and R. D. McPhee, eds.) pp. 149–193. New York: Academic Press.

Cartwright, D., and Harary, F. (1956). Structural balance: A generalization Heider's theory. *Psychological Review* **63**, 277–293.

Cattell, R. B., and Winder, A. E. (1952). Structural rigidity in relation to learning theory and clinical psychology. *Psychological Review* **59**, 23–39.

Cervin, V. B., and Henderson, G. P. (1961). Statistical theory of persuasion. *Psychological Review* **68**, 157–166.

Cohen, A. R. (1957). Need for cognition and order of communication as determinants of opinion change. *In* "The Order of Presentation in Persuasion." (C. Hovland, ed.) pp. 79–97. New Haven: Yale Press.

Cohen, A. R. (1959). Some implications of self-esteem for social influence. *In* "Personality and Persuasibility" (C. I. Hovland and I. L. Janis, eds.) pp. 102–120. New Haven: Yale Press.

Cohen, A. R. (1962). A dissonance analysis of the boomerang effect. *Journal of Personality* **30**, 75–88.

Cohen, A. R. (1964). "Attitude Change and Social Influence." New York: Basic Books.

Cohen, A. R. (1968). Situational structure, self-esteem and threat-oriented reactions to power. *In* "Studies in Social Power." (D. Cartwright, ed.) pp. 35–52. Ann Arbor: University of Michigan Institute for Social Research.

Cohen, S. H. (1971). "Models of attitude change in the passive communication paradigm: information processing, social judgment, dissonance, balance and congruity" Unpublished doctoral dissertation, Michigan State University.

Cohen, S. H., and Hunter, J. E. (April 1970). "Deterministic, continuous-time models of attitude change." Paper presented at Psychometric Society Spring meeting, Palo Alto, California.

Cohen, S. H., and Hunter, J. E. (1972). "A further analysis of attitude change as it relates to source credibility, prior attitude toward the object, and message intensity." Unpublished manuscript.

Cohen, S. H., and Hunter, J. E. (1975). "Source change and attitude change as a function of source credibility, prior attitude toward the object, and message intensity. Unpublished manuscript, West Virginia University.

Coleman, J. (1964). "Introduction to Mathematical Sociology" Glencoe, Illinois: Free Press.

Coleman, J. (1973). The mathematical study of change. In "Methodology in Social Research" (H. M. Blalock, ed.) pp. 428–478. New York: McGraw-Hill.

Collins, A., and Loftus, E. (1975). A spreading activation theory of semantic processing. Psychological Review 82, 407–428.

Collins, A., and Quillian, R. (1972). How to make a language user. In "Organization of Memory" (E. Tulving and W. Donaldson, eds.) pp. 309–351. New York: Academic Press.

Converse, P. E. (1962). Information flow and the stability of Partisan attitudes. Public Opinion Quarterly 26, 578–599.

Converse, P. E. (1964). The nature of belief systems in mass publics. In "Ideology and discontent" (D. E. Apter, ed.) pp. 206–261. New York: Free Press.

Converse, P. E. (1970). Attitudes and non-attitudes: the continuation of a dialogue. In "The quantitative analysis of social problems" (E. R. Tufte, ed.) pp. 168–189. Reading, Mass.: Addison-Wesley.

Craig, F. W. F. (1970). "British General Election Manifestos, 1918–1966." Chichester: Political Reference Publications.

Craig, S. (1971). "Consumer reactions to price changes: an experimental investigation." Unpublished Doctoral Dissertation, Ohio State University.

Crano, W. D., and Cooper R. (May 1972). "A preliminary investigation of a hyperbolic model of attitude change." Presented at the Midwestern Psychological Association meetings, Cleveland.

Crespi, I. (1971). What kinds of attitude measures are predictive of behavior? Public Opinion Quarterly 35, 327–334.

Crewe, I. (1977). "Prospects for party realignment: an Anglo-American comparison." Paper delivered at the Annual Meeting of the American Political Science Association.

Crewe, I., Sarlvik, B., and Alt. J. (1977). Partisan dealignment in Britain 1964–1974. British Journal of Political Science 7, 129–190.

Cronbach, L. J. (1951). Coefficient alpha and the internal structure of tests. Psychometrika 16, 297–334.

Cronbach, L. J., and Furby, L. (1970). How should we measure "change" or should we? Psychological Bulletin 74, 68–80.

Crowne, D. P., and Marlowe, D. (1964). "The Approval Motive: Studies in Evaluative Dependence" New York: Wiley.

Danes, J. E. (1976). "Mathematical Models of Communication and Belief Change: Proportional Change, Belief Certainty, and Accumulated Information." Unpublished Doctoral Dissertation, Michigan State University.

Danes, J. E. (1978). Communication models of the message-belief change process, In "Communication Yearbook II," (B. Rubin, ed.) pp. 110–24. New Brunswick, NJ: Transaction Press.

Danes, J. E., and Hunter, J. E. (1980). Designing persuasive communication campaigns: a multimessage model. Journal of Consumer Research 7, 67–77.

Danes, J. E., and Hunter, J. E. (1982). "Models of Communication and Change in Purchase Intention." Unpublished Manuscript, Department of Marketing, Virginia Polytechnic Institute and State University.

Danes, J. E., and McEwen, W. (1981). Message-market segmentation: a method based on messages that change purchase intention. *In* "Current Issues and Research in Advertising," (C. R. Martin and J. H. Leigh, eds.) pp. 1–16. Ann Arbor: Graduate School of Business Administration, University of Michigan.

Danes, J. E., Upah, G. D., and Kosenko, R. (1982). A hierarchical attitude model for corporate advertising and market segmentation. *In* "Developments in Marketing Science," vol. 5. (Vinay Kothari, ed.) pp. 437–440. Nacodoches, Texas: Academy of Marketing Science.

Davis, J. H., Kerr, N. L., Atkin, N. L., Holt, R. S., and Meek, D. (1975). The decision processes of 5 and 12 person mock juries assigned unanimous and two-third majority rules. *Journal of Personality and Social Psychology* **32,** 1–14.

Deese, J., and Hulse, S. H. (1967). "The Psychology of Learning." New York: McGraw-Hill.

Defleur, M. L., and Westie, F. R, (1958). Verbal attitudes and overt acts: an experiment on the salience of attitudes. *American Sociological Review* **23,** 667–673.

Dillehay, R. C., Insko, C. A., and Smith, M. M. (1966). Logical consistency and attitude change. *Journal of Personality and Social Psychology* **3,** 646–54.

Dion, K. L., Baron, R. S., and Miller, N. (1970). Why do groups make riskier decisions than individuals? *In* "Advances in Experimental Social Psychology" vol. 5. (L. Berkowtiz, ed.) New York: Academic Press.

Dispoto, R. G. (1977). Interrelationship among measures of environmental activity, emotionality, and knowledge. *Educational and Psychological Measurement* **37,** 451–459.

Doob, I W. (1947). The behavior of attitudes. *Psychological Review* **54,** 135–156.

Downs, A. (1957). "An Economic Theory of Democracy." New York: Harper and Row.

Dulaney, D. E. (1961). Hypotheses and habits in verbal "operant conditioning." *Journal of Abnormal and Social Psychology* **3,** 251–263.

Dulaney, D. E. (1968). Awareness, rules, and proposition control: a confrontation with S-R behavior theory. *In* "Verbal Behavior and General Behavior Theory," (D. Horton and T. Dixon, eds.) pp. 340–387. New York: Prentice-Hall.

Duncan, O. D. (1975). "Introduction to Structural Equation Models." New York: Academic Press.

Eagly, A. H. (1974). Comprehensibility of persuasive arguments as a determinant of opinion change. *Journal of Personality and Social Psychology* **29,** 758–773.

Epstein, G. F. (1966). "Machiavellianism, dissonance and the devil's advocate." Unpublished doctoral dissertation, Columbia University.

Feather, N. T. (1966). The prediction of interpersonal attraction. *Human Relations,* **19,** 213–237.

Feather, N. T. (1967). A structural balance approach to the analysis of communication effects. *In* "Advances in Experimental Social Psychology" vol. 3, (L. Berkowitz, ed.) pp. 100–166. New York: Academic Press.

Feldman, S. (1968). What do you think of a cruel, wise man? The integrative response to a stimulus manifold. *In* "Theories of Cognitive Consistency. A sourcebook," (R. P. Abelson, E. Aronson, W. J. McGuire, T. M. Newcomb, M. J. Rosenberg, and P. H. Tannenbaum, eds.) pp. 744–755. Chicago: Rand McNally.

Fenwick, I. (1979). Techniques in market measurement: the jackknife. *Journal of Marketing Research* **16,** 410–414.

Festinger, L. (1957). "A Theory of Cognitive Dissonance." New York: Harper and Row.

Festinger, L., and Aronson, E. (1960). The arousal and reduction of dissonance in social contexts. *In Group Dynamics: Research and Theory.* (D. Cartwright and A. Zander, eds.) pp. 214–231. New York: Harper and Row.

Fishbein, M. (1961). "A theoretical and empirical investigation of the interrelation between beliefs about an object and the attitude toward that object." Unpublished doctoral dissertation, UCLA.

Fishbein, M. (1965). A consideration of beliefs, attitudes, and their relationships. *In* "Current studies in Social Psychology." (I. O. Steiner and M. Fishbein, eds.) pp. 107–120. New York: Holt, Rinehart and Winston.

Fishbein, M. (1967a). A behavior theory approach to the relations between beliefs about an object and the attitude toward the object. *In* "Readings in Attitude Theory and Measurement," (M. Fishbein, ed.) pp. 389–400. New York: Wiley.

Fishbein, M. (1967b). "Readings in Attitude Theory and Measurement." New York: John Wiley and Sons.

Fishbein, M. (1973). The prediction of behaviors from attitudinal variables. *In Advances in Communication Research.* (C. D. Mortensen and K. K. Sereno, eds.) pp. 3–31. New York: Harper and Row.

Fishbein, M., and Ajzen, I. (1974). Attitudes towards objects as predictors of single and multiple behavioral criteria. *Psychological Review* **81,** 50–74.

Fishbein, M., and Ajzen, I. (1975). "Belief, Attitude, Intention, and Behavior." Reading, Mass.: Addison-Wesley.

Fishbein, M., and Coombs, F. S. (1974). Basis for decision: an attitudinal analysis of voting behavior. *Journal of Applied Social Psychology* **4,** 95–124.

Folsom, J. (1931). "Social Psychology." New York: Harper.

Foulkes, D., and Foulkes, S. H. (1965). Self-concept, dogmatism and tolerance of trait inconsistency. *Journal of Personality and Social Psychology* **2,** 104–111.

Freedman, J. L. (1968). How important is cognitive consistency? *In* "Theories of Cognitive Consistency." (R. P. Abelson, E. Aronson, W. J. McGuire, T. M. Newcomb, M. J. Rosenberg, and P. H. Tannenbaum, eds.) pp. 497–503. Chicago: Rand McNally.

French, J. R. P., Jr. (1956). A formal theory of social power. *Psychological Review* **63,** 181–194.

Freud, S. (1909). "The Complete Psychological Works of Sigmund Freud," vol. X, **21,** 107–112.

Furniss, N. (1975). The welfare debate in Great Britain implications for the United States. *Public Administration Review* **35,** 300–309.

Glass, D. C. (1968a). Theories of consistency and the study of personality. *In* "Handbook of Personality Theory and Research." (E. F. Borgatto and W. W. Lambert, eds.) pp. 788–854. Chicago: Rand McNally.

Glass, D. C. (1968b). Individual differences and the resolution of cognitive inconsistencies. *In Theories of cognitive consistency.* (R. P. Abelson, E. Aronson, W. J. McGuire, T. M. Newcomb, M. J. Rosenberg, and P. H. Tannenbaum, eds.) pp. 615–623. Chicago: Rand McNally.

Goldstein, K. (1947). "Human Nature in the Light of Psychopathology," Cambridge: Harvard Press.

Granovetter, M. (1974a). "Getting a Job: A Study of Contacts and Careers." Cambridge, Massachusetts: Harvard University Press.

Granovetter, M, (May 1974b). "The Development of Friendship Structures." Paper presented at the MSSB Mt. Chateau conference on Advances in Social Network Analysis.

Gray, H. L., and Schucany, W. R. (1972). "The Generalized Jackknife Statistic." New York: Marcel Dekker.

Green, J. A. (1968). "Attitudinal and Situational Determinants of Intended Behavior Toward Negroes." Unpublished Doctoral dissertation, University of Colorado.

Guthrie, E. R. (1952). "The Psychology of Learning," New York: Harper and Row.

Harrison, A. (1968). Response competition, frequency, exploratory behavior, and liking. *Journal of Personality and Social Psychology* **9,** 363–368.

Harrison, A., and Crandall, R. (1972). Heterogenity and homogenity of exposure sequence and the attitudinal effects of exposure. *Journal of Personality and Social Psychology* **21,** 234–238.

Harrison, A., and Tutone, R. (1973). "The Effects of Background Variation on Positive Habituation and Tedium." Unpublished manuscript, Department of Psychology, University of California, Davis. NSF grant GS-2791.

Harrison, M. (1966). Television and radio. *In* "The British General Election of 1966," (D. E. Butler and A. King, eds.) pp. 125–148. London: Macmillan.

Harvey, O. J. (1966). System structure flexibility and creativity. *In* "Experience Structure and Adaptibility." (O. J. Harvey, ed.) pp. 39–65. New York: Springer.

Harvey, O. J. (1967). Conceptual systems and attitude change. *In* "Attitude, Ego Involvement and Change." (C. W. Sherif and M. Sherif, eds.) pp. 201–226. New York: Wiley.

Hays, W., and Winkler, R. L. (1971). "Statistics: Probability, Inference, and Decision." New York: Holt, Rinehart & Winston.

Heberlein, A., and Black, J. Attitudinal specificity and the prediction of behavior in a field setting. *Journal of Personality and Social Psychology* 33, 474–479.

Heider, F. (1946). Attitudes and cognitive organization. *Journal of Psychology* 21, 107–112.

Heise, D. R. (1969). Separating reliability and stability in test-retest correlation. *American Sociological Review* 34, 93–101.

Heise, D. R. (1975). "Causal Analysis." New York: Wiley-Interscience.

Hewes, D. (1975). Finite stochastic modeling of communication processes: an introduction and some basic readings. *Human Communication Research* 1, 271–282.

Holt, L. E. (1970). Resistance to persuasion on explicit beliefs as a function of commitment to and desirability of logically related beliefs. *Journal of Personality and Social Psychology* 16, 583–591.

Holt, L. E., and Watts, W. A. (1969). Salience of logical relationships among beliefs as a factor in persuasion. *Journal of Personality and Social Psychology* 11, 193–203.

Hovland, C. I. (1954). The effects of the mass media of communication. *In* "The Handbook of Social Psychology," vol. 2 (G. Lindzey, ed.) pp. 1062–1103. "Special Fields and Applications." Reading, Massachusetts: Addison-Welsey.

Hovland, C. I. (1959). Reconciling conflicting results derived from experimental and survey studies of attitude change. *American Psychologist* 14, 8–17.

Hovland, C. I. (1972). Reconciling conflicting results derived from experimental and survey studies of attitude change. *In* "The Process and Effects of Mass Communication." (W. Schramm and D. F. Roberts, eds.) pp. 495–516. Urbana, The University of Illinois Press.

Hovland, C. I., and Pritzker, H. A. (1957). Extent of opinion change as a function of amount of change advocated. *Journal of Abnormal and Social Psychology*, 54, 257–261.

Hovland, C. I., and Rosenberg, M. J. (1960). Summary and further theoretical issues. *In* "Attitude Organization and Change." (M. J. Rosenberg, et al. eds.) pp. 198–232. New Haven: Yale Press.

Hovland, C. I., and Weiss, W. (1951). The influence of source credibility on communication effectiveness. *Public Opinion Quarterly* 15, 635–650.

Hovland, C. I., Janis, I. L., and Kelley, H. H. (1953). "Communication and Persuasion." New Haven: Yale University Press.

Hovland, C. I., Harvey, O. J., and Sherif, M. (1957). Assimilation and contrast effects in communication and attitude change. *Journal of Abnormal and Social Psychology* 55, 242–252.

Hull, C. L. (1943). "Principles of Behavior." New York: D. Appelton Century.

Hunter, J. E. (1970). "Dynamic Sociometry." Paper presented at the Spring convention of the Psychometric Society.

Hunter, J. E. (1974). "Dynamic Sociometry." Paper presented at the MSSB conference, mathematical techniques in social network analysis. Morgantown, West Virginia.

Hunter, J. E. (1977). Cluster Analysis: Reliability, Construct Validity, and the Multiple Indicators Approach to Measurement." Paper delivered at the U. S. Civil Service Commission Panel on Advanced Statistics, Washington, D. C.

Hunter, J. E. (1979). Toward a general framework for dynamic theories of sentiment in small groups derived from theories of attitude change, *In* "Perspectives on Social Network Research." (P. W. Holland and S. Leinhardt, eds.) pp. 223–238. New York: Academic Press.

Hunter, J. E., and Bell, R. L. (1980). "Asymetric Matrices in Dynamic Balance Theory," American Mathematical Society, Ann Arbor.

Hunter, J. E., and Cohen, S. H. (1969). Package: a system of computer routines for the analysis of correlation data. "Educational and Psychological Measurement," **29**, 697–700.

Hunter, J. E., and Cohen, S. H. (1971). "A reconsideration of Wellens and Thistlethwaite's 'An analysis of two quantitative theories of cognitive balance.'" Unpublished manuscript, Department of Psychology, Michigan State University.

Hunter, J. E., and Cohen, S. H. (1972). "The multidimensionality of attitudes and the temporal course of attitude change." Unpublished proposal, Department of Psychology, Michigan State University.

Hunter, J. E., and Cohen, S. H. (1974). Correcting for unreliability in nonlinear models of attitude change. *Psychometrika* **39**, 445–468.

Hunter, J. E., and Gerbing, D. W. (1982). Undimensional measurement second order factor analysis and causal models. *In* "Research in Organizational Behavior," vol. IV (B. M. Staw and L. L. Cummings, eds.) pp. 267–320. Greenwich, Connecticut: JAI Press, Inc.

Hunter, J. E., and Hunter, R. F. (1977). "PATHPAC: A program for path analysis for recursive systems using either given path coefficients or using calculated OLS path coefficients from given causal influence indicators or using path coefficients calculated from given causal influence indicators by a new Procrustes least squares method." Unpublished Program, Department of Psychology, Michigan State University.

Hunter, J. E., Levine, R. L., and Sayers, S. E. (1976). Attitude change in hierarchical belief systems and its relationships to persuasibility, dogmatism, and rigidity. *Human Communication Research* **3**, 3–28.

Hunter, J. E., Coggin, T., and Gerbing, D. W. (1981). "Random and Specific Error in Panel Data: A Multiple Indicator Measurement Model." Unpublished Manuscript, Department of Psychology, Michigan State University.

Hutchinson, B. (1949). Some problems of measuring the intensiveness of opinion and attitude. *International Journal of Opinion and Attitude Research* **3**, 123–131.

Hyman, H. H. (1943). The Psychology of Status. *Archives of Psychology* **38**, (# 269) 5–94.

Insko, C. A. (1964). Primacy versus recency in persuasion as a function of the timing of arguments and measures. *Journal of Abnormal and Social Psychology* **69**, 381–391.

Insko, C. A. (1967). "Theories of Attitude Change." New York: Appleton-Century-Crofts.

Jaccard, J., and King, G. (1977). The relation between behavioral intentions and beliefs: a probabilistic model. *Human Communication Research* **3**, 326–34.

Janis, I. L. (1967). Effects of fear arousal on attitude change: recent developments in theory and experimental research. *In* "Advances in Experimental Social Psychology." vol. 3. (L. Berkowitz, ed.) pp. 167–225. New York: Academic Press.

Janis, I. L., and Field, P. B. (1959). A behavioral assessment of persuasibility: Consistency of individual differences. *In* "Personality and persuasibility," (I. L. Jones and C. I. Hovland, eds.) pp. 29–54. New Haven: Yale Press.

Janis, I. L., and Hoffman, D. (1970). Facilitating effects of daily contact between partners who make a decision to cut down on smoking. *Journal of Personality and Social Psychology* **17**, 25–35.

Janis, I. L., and Hovland, C. I. (1959). Postscript: theoretical categories for analyzing individual differences. *In* "Personality and Persuasibility." (C. I. Hovland and I. L. Janis, eds.) pp. 255–280. New Haven: Yale Press.

Janisse, M. (1970). Attitudinal effects of mere exposure: a replication and extension. *Psychonomic Science* **19**, 77–78.

Johnston, J. J. (1972). "Econometric Methods" New York: Mc-Graw Hill.

Jones, E. E., and Gerard, H. B. (1967). "Foundations of Social Psychology" New York: Wiley.

Kahan, M. J., Butler, D. E., and Stokes, D. E. (1966). On The Analytical Division of Social Class. *British Journal of Sociology* **17,** 122–132.

Karlson, G. (1958). "Social Mechanisms." Glencoe, Illinois: Free Press.

Katz, D. (1960). The functional approach to the study of attitudes. *Public Opinion Quarterly* **24,** 163–204.

Katz, E., and Lazarsfeld, P. F. (1955). "Personal Influence." New York: Macmillan.

Katz, L. (1950). Punched card technique for the analysis of multiple level sociometric data. *Sociometry* **13,** 108–122.

Kelman, H. (1958). Compliance, identification, and internalization: three processes of attitude change. *Journal of Conflict Resolution* **2,** 51–60.

Kelman, H. C. (1974). Attitudes are alive and well and gainfully employed in the sphere of action. *American Psychologist* **29,** 310–324.

Kelman, H. C., and Baron, R. M. (1968). Determinants of modes of resolving inconsistency dilemmas: a functional analysis. *In* "Theories of Cognitive Consistency," (R. P. Abelson, E. Aronson, W. J. McGuire, T. M. Newcomb, M. J. Rosenberg, and P. H. Tannenbaum, eds.) pp. 670–683. Chicago: Rand McNally.

Kemp, C. G. (1960). "Changes in Patterns of Personal Values in Relation to Open-Closed Belief Systems." Unpublished doctoral dissertation, Michigan State University.

Kiesler, C. A., Collins, B. E., and Miller, N. (1969). "Attitude Change." New York: Wiley.

Klapper, J. T. (1949). "The Effects of Mass Media." New York: Bureau of Applied Social Research, Columbia University.

Klapper, J. T. (1960). "The Effects of Mass Communication." New York: Free Press.

Kothandapani, V. (1971). Validation of feeling, belief, and intention to act as three components of attitude and their contribution to prediction of contraceptive behavior. *Journal of Personality and Social Psychology* **19,** 321–333.

Kounin, J. S. (1941). Experimental studies of rigidity: I. Measurement of rigidity in normal and feebleminded persons. II. Explanatory power of the concept of rigidity as applied to feeblemindedness. *Character and Personality* **9,** 251–272, 273–282.

Krugman, H. E. (1965). The impact of television advertising: learning without involvement. *Public Opinion Quarterly* **29,** 349–356.

Krugman, H. E. (1968). The learning of consumer likes, preferences, and choices. *In* "Applications of the Sciences in Marketing Management," (Frank M. Bass, *et al.*, eds.) pp. 207–225. New York: John Wiley and Sons.

LaPiere, R. T. (1934). Attitudes versus actions. *Social Forces* **13,** 230–237.

Lazarsfeld, P. F., Berelson, B., and Gaudet, H. (1944). "The People's Choice." New York: Columbia University Press.

Lazarsfeld, P. F., Berelson, B., and Gaudet, H. (1948). "The People's Choice." New York: Columbia Press.

Levine, R. L., Hunter, J. E., and Sayers, S. E. (1972). "Hierarchical Structure and Attitude Change: A Multivariate Approach." Research report, Computer Institute for Social Science Research, Michigan State University.

Lewin, K. (1935). "Dynamic Theory of Personality." New York: McGraw-Hill.

Lewin, K. (1936). "Principles of Topological Psychology." New York: McGraw Hill.

Lindsay, P., and Norman, D. (1972). "Human Information Processing: An Introduction to Psychology." New York: Academic Press.

Liska, A. G. (1974). Attitude-behavior consistency as a function of generality equivalence between attitude and behavior objects. *Journal of Psychology* **86,** 217–228.

Ludke, L., Strauss, F., and Gustagson, D. H. (1977). Comparison of five methods for estimating subjective probability distributions. *Organizational Behavior and Human Performance* **19,** 162–79.

Lutz, R. J. (1975). Changing Brand Attitudes Through Modification of Cognitive Structure. *Journal of Consumer Research* **1,** 49–59.

McFarland, S. G., and Thistlethwaite, D. L. (1970). An analysis of a logical consistency model of belief change. *Journal of Personality and Social Psychology* **15,** 133–143.

McGuire, W. J. (1960a). Cognitive consistency and attitude change. *Journal of Abnormal Social Psychology* **60,** 345–353.

McGuire, W. J. (1960b). Direct and indirect persuasive effects of dissonance-producing messages. *Journal of Abnormal Social Psychology* **60,** 354–358.

McGuire, W. J. (1960c). A syllogistic analysis of cognitive relationships. *In* "Attitude Organization and Change." (M. J. Rosenberg, C. I. Hovland, W. J. McGuire, R. P. Abelson, and J. W. Brehm, eds.) New Haven: Yale Press.

McGuire, W. (1964). Inducing resistance to persuasion. *In* "Advances in Experimental Social Psychology." vol. I. (I. Berkowitz, ed.) pp. 191–229. New York: Academic Press.

McGuire, W. J. (1964). Inducing resistance to persuasion: some contemporary approaches. *In* "Advances in Experimental Social Psychology." (L. Berkowitz, ed.) pp. 191–229. New York: Academic Press.

McGuire, W. (1966). Attitudes and opinions. *In* "Annual Review of Psychology," (P. Farnsworth, ed.) **17,** 475–514.

McGuire, W. J. (1968a). Theory of the structure of human thought. *In* "Theories of Cognitive Consistency: A Source Book." (R. P. Abelson, E. Aronson, W. J. McGuire, T. M. Newcomb, M. J. Rosenberg, and P. H. Tannenbaum, eds.) Chicago: Rand McNally.

McGuire, W. J. (1968b). Personality and susceptibility to social influence. *In* "Handbook of Personality Theory and Research." (E. F. Borgatta and W. W. Lambert, eds.) pp. 130–187. Chicago: Rand McNally.

McGuire, W. J. (1968c). Personality and attitude change: An information processing theory. *In* "Psychological Foundations of Attitudes." (A. G. Greenwald, T. C. Brock, and T. M. Ostrom, eds.) pp. 171–196. New York: Academic Press.

McGuire, W. J. (1969). The nature of attitudes and attitude change. *In The Handbook of Social Psychology*, 2nd ed., vol. 3. (G. Lindzey and E. Aronson, eds.) pp. 136–314. Reading, Mass.: Addison-Wesley.

McGuire, W. J. (1976). Some internal psychological factors influencing consumer choice. *Journal of Consumer Research* **2,** 302–319.

McNemar, Q. (1964). Lost: our intelligence? why? *American Psychologist* **19,** 871–882.

Maloney, M. P., and Ward, M. P. (1973). Ecology: let's hear from the people. *American Psychologist* **28,** 583–586.

Manske, A. J. (1937). The reflection of teachers' attitudes in the attitudes of their pupils. *Summarized in* "Experimental Social Psychology," (G. Murphy, L. B. Murphy, and T. M. Newcomb, eds.), p. 950. New York: Harper.

Marlowe, D., and Gergen, K. J. (1969). Personality and social interaction. *In* "The Handbook of Social Psychology." 2nd ed.) (G. Lindzey and E. Aronson, eds.) pp. 590–665. Reading, Massachusetts: Addison Wesley.

Matlin, M. (1970). Response competition as a mediating factor in the frequency-affect relationship. *Journal of Personality and Social Psychology* **16,** 536–552.

Matlin, M. (1971). Response competition, recognition, and affect. *Journal of Personality and Social Psychology* **19,** 295–300.

Meehl, P. E. (1971). The selfish voter paradox and the thrown-away vote argument. *American Political Science Review* **71,** 11–30.

Messemer, D. (1979). Repetition and attitudinal discrepancy effects on the affective response to television advertising. *Journal of Business Research* **7,** 79–93.

Milgram, S. (1977). The small world problem. *Psychology Today* **1,** 61–67.

Miller, G. R., and Rokeach, M. (1968). Individual differences and tolerance for inconsistency. *In*

"Theories of Cognitive Consistency: A Source Book." (R. P. Abelson, E. Aronson, W. J. McGuire, T. M. Newcomb, M. J. Rosenberg, and P. H. Tannenbaum, eds.) pp. 624–632. Chicago: Rand McNally.

Miller, N., and Campbell, D. T. (1959). Recency and primacy in persuasion as a function of the timing of speeches and measurement. *Journal of Abnormal Social Psychology* **59**, 1–9.

Miller, N. E. (1944). Experimental studies of conflict. *In* "Personality and the Behavior Disorders," Vol. I. (J. McV. Hunt, ed.) pp. 431–465. New York: Ronald Press.

Miller, N. E., and Dollard, J. (1941). "Social Learning and Imitation." Hew Haven, Connecticut: Yale University Press.

Nelson, C. E. (1968). Anchoring to accepted values as a technique for immunizing beliefs against persuasion. *Journal of Personality and Social Psychology* **9**, 329–334.

Newcomb, T. M. (1953). An approach to the study of communicative acts. *Psychological Review* **60**, 393–404.

Newcomb, T. M. (1961). "The Acquaintance Process." New York: Holt, Rinehart and Winston.

Newcomb, T. M. (1963). Stabilities underlying changes in interpersonal attraction. *Journal of Abnormal and Social Psychology* **66**, 376–386.

Nunnally, J. C. (1977). "Psychometric Theory," 2nd ed. New York: McGraw-Hill.

Olson, J. C., Toy, D. C., and Dover, P. A. (1978). Mediating effects of cognitive responses to advertising on cognitive structure, *In* "Advances in Consumer Research," vol. 5. (K. Hunt, ed.) pp. 72–78. Ann Arbor, Michigan: Association for Consumer Research.

Osgood, C. E. (1963). Cognitive dynamics in the conduct of human affairs. *In* "Current Perspectives in Social Psychology," (E. P. Hollander and Raymond G. Hunt, eds.) pp. 362–377. New York: Oxford Press.

Osgood, C. E., and Tannenbaum, P. E. (1955). The principle of congruity in the prediction of attitude change. *Psychological Review* **62**, 42–55.

Osgood, C. E., Suci, G. J., and Tannenbaum, P. E. (1957). "The Measurement of Meaning." Urbana: University of Illinois Press.

Pavlov, I. D. (1927). "Conditioned Reflexes" (G. V. Andrep, trans.) London: Oxford Press.

Perlman, D., and Oskamp, S. (1971). The effects of picture content and exposure on evaluations of Negroes and whites. *Journal of Experimental Social Psychology* **7**, 503–514.

Perry, R. W. (1976). Attitudinal variables as estimates of behavior: a theoretical examination of the attitude-action controversy. *European Journal of Social Psychology* **6**, 227–243.

Petty R. E., and Cacioppo, J. T. (1981). "Attitudes and Persuasion: Classic and Contemporary Approaches." Dubuque, Iowa: W. C. Brown.

Phillips, J. L., (1955). A model for cognitive balance. *Psychological Review* **62**, 42–55.

Phillips, J. L. (1967). A model for cognitive balance. *Psychological Review* **47**, 481–495.

Poole, M. S. (1976). "An Experimental Test of Some Mathematical Models of Change in Hierarchies of Attitudes." Unpublished Master's thesis, Michigan State University.

Poole, M. S., and Hunter, J. E. (1976). "Upward Influence in a Hierarchically Organized Set of Attitudes." Department of Psychology, Michigan State University, Unpublished manuscript.

Pulzer, P. G. J. (1967). "Political Representation and Elections." New York: Praeger.

Rachevsky, N. (1957). Contributions to the theory of imitative behavior. *Bulletin of Mathematical Biophysics* **19**, 91–119.

Rainio, K. (1962). A stochastic theory of social contracts. *Transactions of the Westermarck Society* **8**, 1–60.

Rapaport, A. (1963). Mathematical models of social interaction. *In* "Handbook of Mathematical Psychology" vol. 11. (R. Luce, R. Bush, and E. Galanter, eds.) pp. 493–579. New York: Wiley.

Rhine, R. J., and Severance, L. J. (1970). Ego-involvement, discrepancy, source credibility, and attitude change: *Journal of Personality and Social Psychology* **16**, 175–190.

Riland, L. H. (1959). Relationship of guttman components of attitude intensity and personal involvement. *Journal of Applied Psychology* **43**, 279–284.

Roberts, D. (1972). The nature of communication effects. *In* "The Process and Effects of Mass Communication." (W. Schramm and D. F. Roberts, eds.) pp. 349–385. Urbana: University of Illinois Press.

Roberts, D., and Maccoby, N. (1973). Information processing and persuasion: counterarguing behavior. *In* "New Models for Mass Communication Research," (P. Clarke, ed.) pp. 269–307. Beverly Hills, California: Sage Publications.

Robinson, J. P., and Shaver, P. R. (1973). "Measures of Social Psychological Attitudes." Ann Arbor: Survey Research Center, Institute for Social Research.

Rokeach, M. (1960) "The Open and Closed Mind." New York: Basic Books.

Rokeach, M. (1969). "Beliefs, Attitudes, and Values." San Francisco: Jossey-Bass.

Rokeach, M. (1971a). Persuasion that persists. *Psychology Today* **5**, 68–71.

Rokeach, M. (1971b). Long-range experimental modification of values attitudes, and behavior. *In* "Human Behavior and its Control." (W. Hunt. ed.) pp. 93–105. Cambridge, Massachusetts: Schenkman.

Rosen, N. A., and Wyer, R. S. (1972). Some further Evidence for the "Socratic effect" using a subjective probability model of cognitive organization. *Journal of Personality and Social Psychology* **24**, 420–24.

Rosenberg, M. J. (1956). Cognitive structure and attitudinal affect. *Journal of Abnormal and Social Psychology* **53**, 3667–372.

Rosenberg, M. J. (1960). A structural theory of attitude dynamics. *Public Opinion Quarterly* **24**, 319–340.

Rosenberg, S. (1969). Mathematical models of social behavior. *In The Handbook of Social Psychology* (G. Lindzey and E. Aronson, eds.) 179–244. Reading, Massachusetts: Addison-Wesley.

Russell, D. H., and Robertson, I. V. (1947). Influencing attitudes toward minority groups in a junior high school. *School Review* **55**, 205–213.

Saltiel, J., and Woelfel, J. (1975). Inertia in cognitive processes: the role of accumulated information in attitude change. *Human communication research* **1**, 333–344.

Schuman, H., and Johnson, M. P. (1976). Attitudes and behavior. *Annual Review of Sociology* **2**, 161–207.

Schwartz, S. (1978). Temporal instability as a moderator of the attitude-behavior relationship. *Journal of Personality and Social Psychology* **37**, 715–724.

Schwartz, S., and Tessler, R. C. (1972). A test of a model for reducing measured attitude-behavior discrepancies. *Journal of Personality and Social Psychology* **24**, 225–236.

Scott, W. A. (1962). Cognitive complexity and cognitive flexibility. *Sociometry* **25**, 405–414.

Scott, W. A. (1963). Cognitive complexity and cognitive balance. *Sociometry* **26**, 66–74.

Scott, W. A. (1965). Psychological and social correlates of international images. *In* "International Behavior." (H. C. Kelman, ed.) pp. 70–103. New York: Holt, Rinehart and Winston.

Scott, W. A. (1966a). Brief report; measures of cognitive structure. *Multivariate Behavioral Research* **1**, 391–395.

Scott, W. A. (1966b). Flexiblity, rigidity, and adaptation: toward clarification of concepts. *In Experience, structure, and adaptability.* (O. J. Harvey, ed.) pp. 369–400. New York: Springer.

Seagert, S., and Jellison, J. (1970). Effects of initial level or response competition and frequency of exposure on liking and exploratory behavior. *Journal of Personality and Social Psychology* **16**, 553–558.

Sears, D. O. (1968). The paradox of defacto selective exposure without preferences for supportive information. *In* "Theories of Cognitive Consistency." (R. P. Abelson, E. Aronson, W. J. McGuire, T. M. Newcomb, M. J. Rosenberg, and P. H. Tannenbaum, eds.) pp. 777–778. Chicago: Rand McNally.

Sherif, C. W., and Sherif, M. (1967). "Attitude, Ego-Involvement, and Change." New York: Wiley.

Sherif, M. (1936). "The Psychology of Social Norms." New York: Harper and Row.

Sherif, M. (1953). The concept of reference groups in human relations. *In* "Group Relations at the Crossroads," pp. 203–231. (M. Sherif and M. O. Wilson, eds.) New York: Harper and Row.

Sherif, M., and Hovland, C. I. (1961). "Social Judgement." New Haven: Yale Press.

Sherif, M., and Sherif, C. (1967) Attitude as the individual's own categories: the social judgement-involvement approach to attitude and attitude change. *In* "Attitude, Ego-Involvement, and Change." pp. 105–139. (C. W. Sherif, and M. Sherif eds.) New York: Wiley.

Sherif, M., Sherif, C., and Nebergall, R. (1965). "Attitude and Attitude Change." Philadelphia: Saunders.

Shevell, S. K., and Atkinson, R. C. (1974). A theoretical comparison of list-scanning models. *Journal of Mathematical Psychology* **11**, 79–106.

Shibutani, T. (1955). Reference groups as perspectives. *American Journal of Sociology* **60**, 562–570.

Smith, F. T. (1943). "An experiment in modifying attitudes toward the Negro." Teachers College, Columbia University College of Education, No. 887.

Smith, M., Bruner, J., and White, R. (1956). "Opinions and Personality." New York: Wiley.

Spilerman, S. (1972). The analysis of mobility processes by the introduction of independent variables into a Markov chain. *American Sociological Review* **37**, 277–294.

Stang, D. (1974). Intuition as artifact in mere exposure studies. *Journal of Personality and Social Psychology* **30**, 647–653.

Stang, D. (1974). Effects of "mere exposure" on learning and affect. *Personality and Social Psychology* **30**, 647–653.

Steiner, I. D. (1966). Personality and the resolution of interpersonal disagreements. *In* "Progress in Experimental Personality Research" Vol. 3. (B. A. Maher, ed.) pp. 195–239. New York: Academic Press.

Steiner, I. D. (1968). Responses to inconsistency. *In* "Theories of Cognitive Consistency: A Source Book. (R. P. Abelson, E. Aronson, W. J. McGuire, T. M. Newcomb, M. J. Rosenberg, and P. H. Tannenbaum eds.) Chicago: Rand McNally.

Steiner, I. D., and Johnson, H. H. (1963). Authoritarianism and "tolerance of trait inconsistency." *Journal of Abnormal and Social Psychology* **67**, 388–391.

Steiner, I. D., and Vannoy, J. S. (1964). "The Stability of Responses to Interpersonal Disagreement." Unpublished manuscript.

Stotland, E., and Patchen, M. (1961). Identification and changes in prejudice and authoritarianism. *Journal of Abnormal and Social Psychology* **62**, 265–274.

Stotland, E., Katz, D., and Patchen, M. (1959). Reduction of prejudice through the arousal of self insight. *Journal of Personality* **27**, 507–531.

Suedfeld, P., Epstein, Y., Buchannan, E., and Landon, B. (1971). Effects of set on the "effects of mere exposure." *Journal of Personality and Social Psychology* **17**, 121–123.

Tannenbaum, P. H. (1953). "Attitudes Toward Source and Concept as factors in Attitude Change Through Communications." Unpublished doctoral dissertation, University of Illinois.

Tesser, A. (1976). Thought and reality constraints as determinants of attitude polarization. *Journal of Research in Personality* **10**, 183–194.

Tesser, A. (1978). Self-Generated Attitude Change. *In* "Advances in Experimental Social Psychology," vol. 11, pp. 289–338. (L. Berkowitz, ed.) New York: Academic Press.

Tesser, A., and Cowan, C. L. (1975). Some effects of thought and number of cognitions on attitude change. *Social Behavior and Personality* **3**, 165–173.

Tesser, A., and Dannheiser, P. (1978). Anticipated relationship, salience of partner, and attitude change. *Personality and Social Psychology Bulletin* **4**, 35–38.

Tesser, A., and Leone, C. (1977). Cognitive schemas and thought as determinants of attitude change. *Journal of Experimental Social Psychology* **13**, 340–356.

Thurstone, L. L. (1929). Theory of attitude measurement. *Psychological Review* **36**, 222–241.

Thomas, W. I., and Znaniecki, E. (1918). The Polish Peasant in Europe and America" vol. 1. Boston: Badger.

Tittle, C. R., and Hill, R. J. (1967). Attitude measurement and prediction of behavior: an evaluation of conditions and measurement techniques. *Sociometry* **30**, 199–213.

Tosi, H., Hunter, J., Chesser, R., Tarter, J. R., and Carrol S. (1976). How real are changes induced by MBO. *Administrative Science Quarterly* **21**, 276–306.

Tucker, R., and Ware, P. (1970). Persuasion via mere exposure. *Quarterly Journal of Speech* **56**, 437–443.

Tukey. J. W., (1958). Bias and confidence in not-quite large samples. *Annals of Mathematical Statistics* **29**, 614.

Udell, Jon G. (1965). Can attitude measurement predict consumers behavior? *Journal of Marketing* **29**, 46–50.

Vannoy, J. S. (1965). Generality of cognitive complexity-simplicity as a personality construct. *Journal of Personality and Social Psychology* **2**, 385–396.

Veevers, J. E. (1971). Drinking attitudes and drinking behavior: an exploratory study. *Journal of Social Psychology* **85**, 103–109.

Vernon, P. E. (1951). "The Structure of Human Abilities." New York: John Wiley and Sons.

Watts, W. A., and Holt, L. E. (1970). Logical relationships among beliefs and timing as factors in persuasion. *Journal of Personality and Social Psychology* **16**, 571–582.

Watts, W. A., and McGuire, W. J. (1964). Persistence of induced opinion change and retention of the inducing message contents. *Journal of Abnormal Social Psychology* **68**, 233–288.

Weick, K. E. (1968). Processes of ramification among cognitive links. *In Theories of Cognitive Consistency: A Source Book*, (R. P. Abelson, E. Aronson, W. J. McGuire, T. M. Newcomb, M. J. Rosenberg, and P. H. Tannenbaum, eds.) pp. 512–519. Chicago: Rand McNally.

Weigel, R. H., and Newman, L. S. (1976). Increasing attitude-behavior correspondence by broadening the scope of the behavioral measure. *Journal of Personality and Social Psychology* **33**, 793–802.

Weigel, R. H., Vernon, D. T. A., and Tognacci, L. N. (1974). The specificity of the attitude as a determinant of attitude-behavior congruence. *Journal of Personality and Social Psychology* **30**, 724–728.

Weist, W. M. (1965). A quantitative extension of Heider's theory of cognitive balance applied to interpersonal perception and self-esteem. *Psychological Monographs* **79**, (14, Whole volume).

Weksel, W., and Hennes, J. D. (1965). Attitude intensity and the semantic differential. *Journal of Personality and Social Psychology* **2**, 91–94.

Wellens, A. R., and Thistlethwaite, D. L. (1971). An analysis of two quantative theories of cognitive balance. *Psychological Review* **78**, 141–150.

Whittaker, J. O. (1967). Resolution of the communication discrepancy issue in attitude change. *In* "Attitude Ego-Involvement and Change." (C. Sherif and M. Sherif, eds.) pp. 159–177. New York: Wiley.

Wiley, D., and Wiley, J. (1970). The estimation of measurement error in panel data. *American Sociological Review* **35**, 112–117.

Wilke, W. H. (1934). An experimental comparison of the speech, the radio, and the printed page as propaganda devices. *Archives of Psychology* **169**, 35–701.

Williamson, A. C., and Remmers, H. H. (1940). Persistence of attitudes concerning conservation issues. *The Journal of Experimental Education* **8**, 354–361.

Wood, G. (1972). Organization processes and free recall. *In* "The Organization of Memory." (E. Tulring and W. Donaldson, eds.) pp. 49–91. New York: Academic Press.

Wright, J. M., and Harvey, O. J. (1965). Attitude change as a function of authoritarianism and punitiveness. *Journal of Personality and Social Psychology* **1**, 177–181.

Wright, P. (1970). Message-evoked thoughts: persuasion research using thought verbalizations. *Journal of Consumer Research* **7,** 151–175.

Wyer, R. S. (1970). The quantitative prediction of belief and opinion change: a further test of a subjective probability model. *Journal of Personality and Social Psychology* **16,** 559–70.

Wyer, R. S. (1972). Test of a subjective probability model of social evaluation processes. *Journal of Personality and Social Psychology* **22,** 279–286.

Wyer, R. S. (1974). "Cognitive Organization and Change: An Information Processing Approach," Potomac, Maryland: Lawrence Erlbaum.

Wyer, R. S. (1975). Functional measurement methodology applied to a subjective probability model of cognitive functioning. *Journal of Personality and Social Psychology* **31,** 94–100.

Wyer, R. S. (1976). Effects of previously formed beliefs on Syllogistic inference processes. *Journal of Personality and Social Psychology* **33,** 302–16.

Wyer, R. S., and Goldberg, L. A. (1970). Probabilistic analysis of the relationships among beliefs and attitudes. *Psychological Review* **77,** 100–20.

Zajonc, R. B. (1960). The concepts of balance, congruity, and dissonance. *Public Opinion Quarterly* **24,** 280–296.

Zajonc, R. (1968). Attitudinal effects of mere exposure. *Journal of Personality and Social Psychology Monographs Supplement* **9,** 1–27.

Zajonc, R., and Rajecki, D. (1969). Exposure and effect: a field experiment. *Psychonomic Science* **17,** 216–217.

Index

A

Absolute bounds, reinforcement models with, 20–21

Abstract hierarchy, 311, *see also* Hierarchy models

Acceptance, incentives and, 34

Accumulated information, *see also* Information processing models
  belief change and, 204–216
  initial belief versus belief change in model of, 206–207

Active imitation theory, 10

Advertising, purchase intention change and, 218–219

Affective consistency, 4, 69–77, 107

Agreement–disagreement asymmetry, message intensity and, 21–22

American Medical Association, 248

Antecedent event, marginal probability of, 129

Assertion, intensity of, 81

Assertion constant
  in congruity theory, 79, 96–97
  in source-object asymmetry, 94

Asymptotic values, concept hierarchies and, 237–240

Attitude(s)
  behaviors and, 294
  as belief, 132–134
  definitions of, 1–2, 275–276
  interrelations in, 299ff.
  in learning theory, 9
  low-order, in reinforcement theory, 312
  in mass communication, 9
  measurement of, 275–276
  message advocacy and, 35
  in socialization theory, 10

Attitude–behavior consistency, in coping behavior, 297

Attitude change, *see also* Attitude; Hierarchy models
  algebraic sign of, 10–11
  autonomous attitude and, 246
  in balance model, 71–72
  boomerang and, 121, 258–259
  communication and, 1–2
  in concept hierarchies, 231–259
  congruity model for, 74, 85–86, 101–103
  counterargument model of, 46

329

ABX-2991 — v. 1